Central Plains Prehistory

Waldo R. Wedel

Central Plains Prehistory

Holocene Environments and Culture Change

in the Republican River Basin

University of Nebraska Press, Lincoln and London

The paper in this book meets the guidelines for permanence and durability
of the Committee on Production Guidelines
for Book Longevity of the Council on Library Resources

Library of Congress Cataloging in Publication Data
Wedel, Waldo Rudolph, 1908–
  Central Plains prehistory.

  Bibliography: p.
  Includes index.
    1. Indians of North America—Republican River Valley
(Neb. and Kan.)—Antiquities.   2. Republican River Valley
(Neb. and Kan.)—Antiquities.   I. Title.
  E78.R37W43   1986   978.1'201   85-1147
  ISBN 0-8032-4729-X (alk. paper)

For four special people,
Asa T. Hill
William Duncan Strong
Peter J. and Lena Wedel

Contents

Illustrations and Tables

Preface

The North American Great Plains have been known to white men for more than 400 years, more precisely, since 1541. From that first bemused glimpse of the seemingly endless grasslands, the countless numbers of wild cattle they supported, and the picturesque dog-nomads who trailed after the herds, the curiosity of the Euro-American newcomers and those who followed them has lingered. In turn, Spanish, French, English, and American observers learned slowly over the decades that the region was even more vast than they had suspected—some 1,500 miles (2,400 km) north to south by 700 miles (1,100 km) or more east to west. It would be even longer before they realized that the 16th-century dog-nomads they had met there, themselves possibly recent comers from the north, were only the latest in a long succession of native peoples who from time to time inhabited the region; that there were other ways of life that could be successfully pursued here; and that the known record of human experience on the Great Plains would lengthen as spectacularly as its boundaries expanded with growing knowledge and understanding.

Situated in the heart of the Great Plains is the Republican River basin. It centers on the 100th meridian west and on 40° north latitude and includes approximately 26,000 square miles (67,340 sq km), perhaps 3 percent of the total Great Plains area. Nearly 400 miles (640 km) east to west, the basin presents a geographic transect from the semiarid High Plains steppe in the west to the subhumid tall-grass prairie in the east. The changing environmental conditions were reflected in the white man's responses as he moved from east to west up the valley, adjusting his economic and social systems and his lifestyle generally to the increasingly austere climate and diminishing water supply.

The archeological record shows clearly that the cultural reactions of the white man's native predecessors likewise varied from east to west, and, of equal significance, from level to level through time. Important, too, is the fact that the known human record in the Republican River basin spans the full period of native man's demonstrable presence in the Great Plains region, from the late Pleistocene to the closing decades of the 19th century. An unusually favorable opportunity is thus at hand for observing and appraising the long-term relationships between humans and nature in a limited geographical area where archeology can supplement and enrich its understanding with appropriate insights derived from history, ethnohistory, ethnography, geology, climatology, and other relevant disciplines.

In this study, the time span is roughly the past 15,000 to 18,000 years, beginning with the waning Pleistocene and continuing upward to the recent

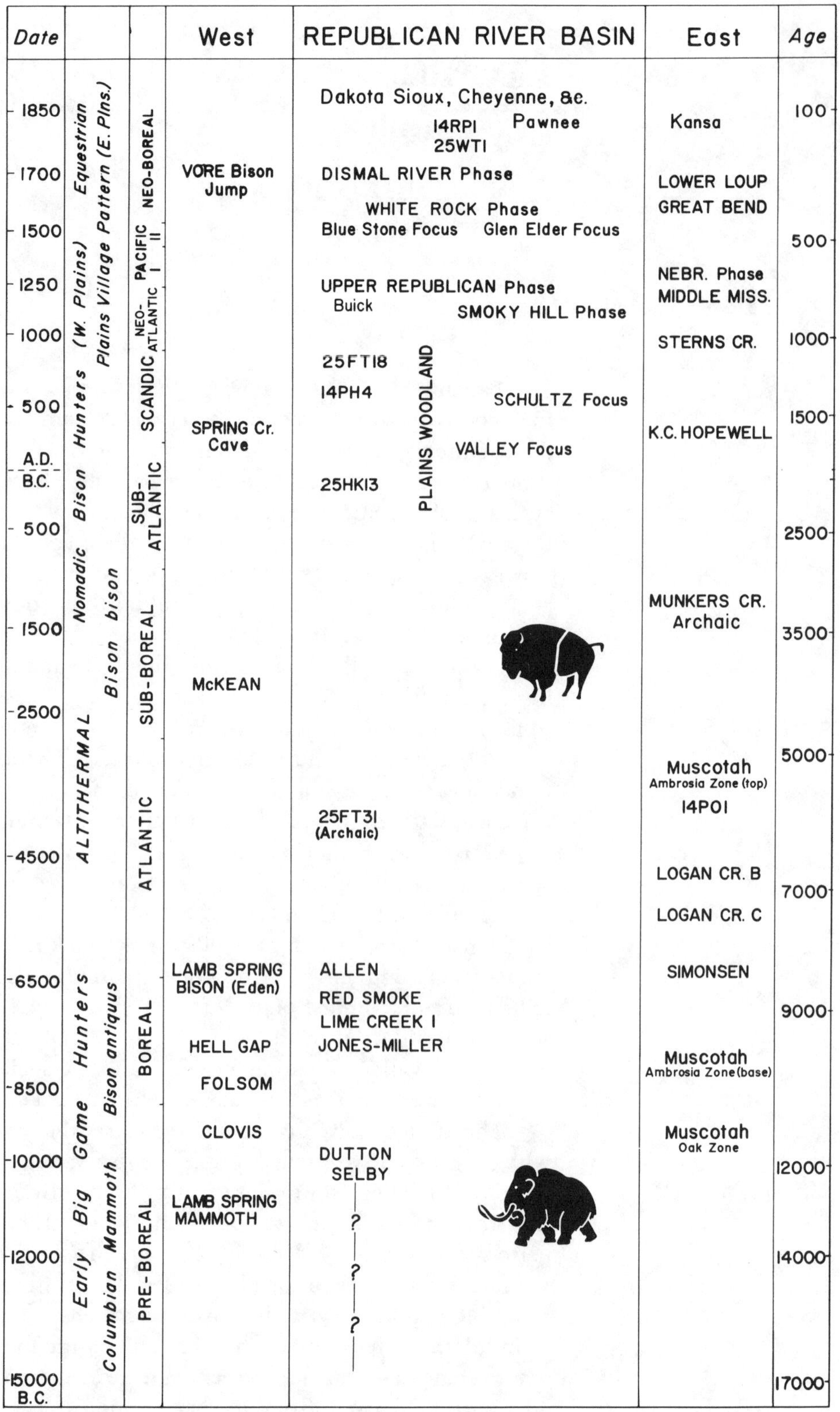

Date			West	REPUBLICAN RIVER BASIN	East	Age
1850		NEO-BOREAL		Dakota Sioux, Cheyenne, &c.	Kansa	100
				14RPI Pawnee		
				25WTI		
1700	Equestrian		VORE Bison Jump	DISMAL RIVER Phase	LOWER LOUP	
	Plains Village Pattern (E. Plns.)	PACIFIC I II		WHITE ROCK Phase	GREAT BEND	
1500				Blue Stone Focus Glen Elder Focus		500
1250	(W. Plains)	NEO-ATLANTIC		UPPER REPUBLICAN Phase	NEBR. Phase MIDDLE MISS.	
	Hunters	SCANDIC		Buick SMOKY HILL Phase		
1000					STERNS CR.	1000
	Bison			25FTI8		
500			SPRING Cr. Cave	14PH4	SCHULTZ Focus	1500
	Nomadic	SUB-ATLANTIC			K.C. HOPEWELL	
A.D. / B.C.				VALLEY Focus		
500				25HKI3		2500
	ALTITHERMAL			PLAINS WOODLAND		
1500	Bison bison	SUB-BOREAL			MUNKERS CR. Archaic	3500
			McKEAN			
2500						5000
		ATLANTIC			Muscotah Ambrosia Zone (top)	
				25FT3I (Archaic)	14POI	
4500					LOGAN CR. B	7000
					LOGAN CR. C	
6500	Early Big Game Hunters	BOREAL	LAMB SPRING BISON (Eden)	ALLEN	SIMONSEN	9000
	Bison antiquus			RED SMOKE		
				LIME CREEK I		
			HELL GAP	JONES-MILLER	Muscotah Ambrosia Zone (base)	
8500			FOLSOM			
	Columbian Mammoth		CLOVIS		Muscotah Oak Zone	
10000		PRE-BOREAL		DUTTON SELBY		12000
12000			LAMB SPRING MAMMOTH	?		14000
				?		
				?		
15000 B.C.						17000

Fig. 1. Chronological relationships of certain Republican River basin archeological sites and complexes, and contemporary features in adjacent areas.

past that we call the historic present. Within the temporal and spatial limits here recognized, which are subject to transgression when clarity requires, there occurred a series of cultural events whose sequence, duration, and relationship to their contemporary environmental setting have attracted the attention of students of Plains prehistory and culture development for more than three-quarters of a century. In salient outline (fig. 1), these events include a slow progression from heavy dependence by early man on the specialized hunting of large game of species now mostly extinct, through a hunting-gathering or forager stage, to semisedentary maize-growing communities whose most recent representatives were the Indians met by the European and American invaders. The character of these changes through time, and the environmental variations that may have been in differing measure responsible for them, are the subject of this study.

This is in no sense an endorsement of environmental determinism. It is rather a recognition of the fact that the opportunities and limitations of the natural setting have varied significantly—sometimes drastically—from time to time and from place to place; that these variations have provoked differing cultural responses in the survival strategies of the human groups involved; and that, in one way or another, people have coped more or less successfully with the vagaries of nature for a dozen millennia or longer. I am inclined to agree with Barrows (1923:13) that "those relationships between man and the earth which result from his efforts to get a living are in general the most direct and intimate . . . [and] that most other relationships are established through these." At the same time, I hope I have not lost sight of Julian Steward's (1955:31) timely reminder that "man enters the ecological scene . . . not merely as another organism which is related to other organisms in terms of physical characteristics. He introduces the factor of culture."

There is still much that we do not know about the prehistory of the Republican River basin and the surrounding plains. Despite the shadowy corners and dark spots, however, it seems increasingly clear that the human prehistory of the basin is very likely synoptic of the story of native people and their activities throughout a much larger portion of the Great Plains. The basin, that is, provides a cross-sectional sampling of a large region of which it can be seen as the center. It is to be hoped, then, that the review and analysis here undertaken will indicate the direction in which historically oriented archeologists have been moving, how they are seeking deeper understanding of native man's adjustments to his natural surroundings, and what prehistorians have learned and are learning about the human experience here during some thousands of years before and after Euro-Americans came on the scene.

The approach followed reflects my biases as well as my particular interests and background training. The environmental setting is reviewed in considerable detail, since it bears so directly and powerfully on man's activities. I then examine in historical perspective the human adaptations, insofar as archeologists and their co-workers have interpreted them. Subsistence economies or lifeways or traditions are emphasized rather than the taxonomic designations by which specialists in archeology usually categorize their data. By tradition I mean here a distinctive way of life, traceable through a long period of time, varying in details from place to place or from time to time, but maintaining a basic, overall consistency throughout. Between traditions, as between less comprehensive categories or complexes, there are only transitions, not sharp breaks. Radiocarbon, tree-ring, or other "precise" dates, used where available, provide guidance, not absolute time limits.

Other biases should be noted. For one thing, I have undertaken this study without setting up a specific hypothesis to be tested, since I am not convinced that interpretations based on such a proposition are necessarily any more valid or scientific or satisfying than those derived from observations not shackled by such preset procedures. The artifacts that provide the core data herein I view as cultural fossils, to be analyzed, compared, and interpreted in terms of human activity, not as commodities to be run through a computer from which arcane print-outs can be produced in order to meet a contractual deadline. If the understanding I seek, or clues to it, can be found in historical or ethnographic avenues, I welcome that approach as offering a possible solution, not an absolute one. All too often, it has seemed to me, fieldwork and its follow-up in laboratory and library are less concerned with how the makers of those artifacts coped with their environment, natural and cultural, than with looking ahead to bigger and better-financed cultural resource management projects. Contract deadlines are a necessary evil, but they and the considered conclusions of the thoughtful scientist are more often than not at opposite poles in our research. I have chosen herein to pursue what seems to me an appropriately humanistic approach.

I am also acutely aware of the pitfalls awaiting the archeologist who deals with materials that are far removed temporally and spatially from the populations involved in their creation or where there are major cultural barriers to be overcome in the quest for understanding and interpretation. These obstacles are, of course, not unique to this particular study, but they should be borne in mind in evaluating the presentation and its judgments.

In a sense, my preparation for doing this book began in 1930 with my first professionally oriented archeological fieldwork in the Great Plains. In the half century that has elapsed, I have come under a heavy debt of gratitude to many colleagues and co-workers. For far too many, I have, unfortunately, no record of what they told me specifically in discussions and letters, or on what particular points; I have only an awareness that in the field and laboratory, at professional meetings, by letter, and in other ways they have offered guidance, suggestions, and where needed, admonitions, when and as I sought them over the years. Some, I fear, will remain nameless here.

Among those who have been particularly helpful and stimulating, whether we agreed or disagreed, but who are in no instance to be held blameworthy for any misuse I may have made of their counsel, are the following: William Duncan Strong, A. T. Hill, John L. Champe, Marvin F. Kivett, George S. Metcalf, and Dolores and James H. Gunnerson, from my early professional years in the plains and since; A. Wetmore, A. Remington Kellogg, Herbert Friedmann, H. W. Setzer, J. P. E. Morrison, E. P. Henderson, H. A. Rehder, T. D. Stewart, M. T. Newman, J. C. Ewers, D. H. Ubelaker, and B. D. Smith, now or formerly at the National Museum of Natural History, Smithsonian Institution, where I served actively from 1936 to 1976 and have enjoyed emeritus status since.

Photographers, illustrators, and archivists of the museum support staff have likewise been unendingly helpful and cooperative. Janette Saquet, while

John Wesley Powell librarian at the National Museum of Natural History and since, has been helpful in tracking down elusive reference works, in clarifying bibliographic problems, and in translating key terms and passages in 17th- and 18th-century French. For assistance with illustrations, I am deeply indebted to Victor E. Krantz, Photo Laboratory; to James Glenn, Paula Fleming, Nigel Elmore, and Vyrtis Thomas, National Anthropological Archives; and to G. Robert Lewis and Marcia Bakry, scientific illustrators.

Outside the Smithsonian, I have benefited over the years from conversations and correspondence with the following, among others: O. S. (Nick) and Joyce Fent, Salina, Kansas; David M. Gradwohl and Nancy Osborn, Iowa State University; R. L. MacGregor, University of Kansas Herbarium; Paul W. Parmalee, University of Tennessee; Russell W. Graham, Illinois State Museum; T. A. Witty, Jr., Kansas State Historical Society; Larry Banks, United States Army Corps of Engineers, Dallas; Roger T. Grange, Jr., University of South Florida; Carlyle S. Smith and A. E. Johnson, University of Kansas; Peter W. Bleed, University of Nebraska–Lincoln; Holmes Semken and G. Edgar Folk, State University of Iowa; Charles E. Hanson and James A. Hanson, Chadron, Nebraska; Gayle Carlson, Nebraska State Historical Society; Douglas R. Parks and Ray DeMallie, Indiana University; Gary Haynes, Washington, D.C.; Irene Emery, Textile Museum, Washington, D.C.; and A. P. Nasatir, San Diego State University.

On various problems relating to Early Man and to lithic technology, I have been greatly helped by Dennis J. Stanford, Smithsonian Institution; George C. Frison, University of Wyoming; and Bruce Bradley, Crow Canyon Campus, Northwestern University. For advice on climatological and water supply matters, I owe thanks to Reid A. Bryson, University of Wisconsin; Wayne M. Wendland, Illinois Institute of Natural Resources; Glenn R. Scott, United States Geological Survey, Denver; and E. G. Lappala, United States Geological Survey, Lincoln. Entomologists Karl V. Krombein, National Museum of Natural History, and David A. Nickle, United States Department of Agriculture, provided helpful information on wasps, grasshoppers, and other insects. Finally, to the young men and the not-so-young who served as crew men at low pay or indeed gratis in many field parties collecting much of the information here included, though they must remain unnamed here, go my sincere thanks for their patience and industry under often trying circumstances.

I am indebted to the following organizations and persons for providing photographs and other illustrative material and for granting permission to use them here: National Anthropological Archives, Smithsonian Institution, plates 4.1 upper, 4.3 upper, 6.6 upper, middle right, and lower, 6.2 lower left, 6.5, 6.7, 7.1 upper, 7.2 upper and lower, 7.3 upper and lower, 7.4 upper and lower, 7.6 upper, 8.2 upper, 8.3 lower, 9.1 upper, 10.2 upper; Nebraska State Historical Society, plates 2.1 upper, 2.8 lower, 2.10 upper and lower, 5.1, 6.2 upper left, upper right, and lower right, 6.3 upper, 6.4 upper and lower, 6.6 middle left, 7.7 upper right, 8.2 lower, 8.3 upper, 9.1 lower, 9.3, 9.6, 9.7 upper, middle, and lower, 10.1 upper; University of Nebraska, Department of Anthropology, plates 7.6 middle and lower, 7.7 upper left, middle, and lower; University of Nebraska State Museum, plates 4.1 middle and lower, 4.4; University of Kansas Museum of Anthropology, plate 6.1 upper left, upper right, and lower; Milwaukee Public Museum, plate 2.7 upper; *Journal of Heredity*, plate

2.7 lower; National Geographic Society and D. J. Stanford, plate 4.2; Library of Congress, Prints and Photographs Division, plate 4.3 lower (LC-USF 343-1617-ZE); National Museum of Natural History, Smithsonian Institution, plates 2.5 lower, 8.3 middle, 10.2 lower, 10.3; United States Bureau of Reclamation, plate 10.1 lower; Helen Dwight Reid Educational Foundation, figure 3.1; Kansas State Historical Society, figure 9.3. Figure 2.4 has been redrawn from United States Forest Service *Range Plant Handbook* (1937) W157. Specimens in plate 2.6 are courtesy of Mrs. Marion Willey (upper) and O. S. Fent (lower). Other photographs and figures, if not specifically credited otherwise, are mine.

Special thanks go again to my wife, Mildred Mott Wedel, whose patience, counsel, and encouragement have been major contributing factors to whatever success this effort may enjoy as it leaves my hands. We have not always agreed on how some matters should be handled or interpreted, but the discussions they brought on have been highly beneficial, at any rate to me. She has had the fortitude, moreover, to read and criticize the entire manuscript, again to my great benefit.

Other readers to whom I am deeply indebted include Nick Fent (chapters 1–3), Bruce Bradley (chapter 4), N. Osborn (chapter 6), D. Parks (chapter 9), and R. DeMallie (chapter 10). The criticisms and comments by the unnamed individuals who reviewed the full manuscript for the information of the press have also contributed much useful material, which has in most cases been incorporated. The manuscript has benefited from certain suggestions for reorganization from those persons.

There are, finally, some very personal feelings that have figured heavily in my selection of the Republican River basin for this enterprise. When I initially decided on the Great Plains area as the setting for my career in archeology, the Republican valley was among the first localities in which I worked to acquire field experience as a graduate student at the University of Nebraska. There were then no dams to stem the river's flow or that of its numerous clean-running tributaries. Like most of the Great Plains region, the Republican basin was essentially an untilled and little-known archeological field in which each day's digging brought new and often unexpected finds and the thrills of pleasure that accompany such discoveries. The world of plains archeology was still bright and new and wonderful in 1930, and the tree-shaded banks of the Republican, with its clear waters, sandy riffles, and placid pools in sharp contrast to the sun-drenched uplands, were a delightful and rewarding place to camp and relax and reflect. As my first mentor at Nebraska, William Duncan Strong, so aptly phrased it, those were the "gee-whiz" days in plains archeology.

It was in the Republican River basin, too, that self-trained nonprofessional investigators in the 1920s first uncovered and recognized evidence of rectangular house floors associated with pottery, charred maize and beans, bison shoulder-blade hoes, and other features by which they satisfied themselves that prehistoric Indians had, long before the coming of Europeans, practiced a food-producing garden economy 200 miles and more west of the Missouri River. This thought, of course, was contrary to conventional anthropological dogma of the day in which professional anthropologists and archeologists held that only tipi-dwelling bison hunters could survive in those regions. The time-honored and mostly unchallenged concept among eastern intellectuals that the Great Plains were uninhabitable by humans before the horse was introduced by the Spaniards in the 16th century was becoming increasingly unpalatable to the few discerning local individuals who were familiarizing themselves with the archeological resources of the plains.

It was my great good fortune to be associated with one such individual whose pioneering investigations included key localities on the Republican—Asa T. ("AT") Hill of Hastings and Lincoln. An able and successful businessman, AT has not been without his detractors in the academic community. I found, in twenty years of close personal association and frequent correspondence, that his thinking on plains archeology was solidly grounded in historical reading, richly seasoned with homespun insights and critical interpretation, untrammeled by orthodoxy, and generally free of professional cant and the pronouncements of pedagogy. As much cannot be said for some of his professionally trained contemporaries and successors, particularly those who lacked his firsthand experience with the local environment and its vagaries. AT's reflections and judgments, always freely delivered but never rigidly insisted upon, have influenced much of what appears in the following pages.

Systematic archeological investigations at various points in the Republican River basin during the past five decades have amply demonstrated the correctness of the collectors' views that along this stream an interesting and important story of human endeavor unfolded over some millennia of time. It is that story, as seen and interpreted today by one long-time observer, that is here recounted.

A word of explanation about the title of this study with its inclusion of the term *prehistory* may be desirable. In its usual connotation, *prehistory* concerns the period before written history, which in North America would be the long period before the arrival of the white man. A substantial segment of the later chapters of the present work deals with peoples, cultures, and events that post-date the year A.D. 1800. Concerning some of these matters, much of our information has been derived from archeology, illuminated and sometimes clarified by the documentary record in a mutually beneficial reciprocal relationship between archeology and history. To a considerable degree, moreover, the post-1800 happenings involve people, cultures, and influences that were deeply rooted in the past. At least to me, a better understanding of the later years in the region is complementary to much that has gone before. To omit or further abbreviate consideration of these events that occurred after white exploration would have significantly diminished the interest and meaning of the story of the ten millennia or more that preceded the coming of the white man. The title might have been changed to reflect more accurately the content and range of this study. I have chosen to retain the term *prehistory* in a looser and less precise sense because so much of what we have learned about the post-Conquest peoples, cultures, and their settings has been obtained through archeology and is in a sense an extension of the very much longer story of the unwritten past.

The principal collections of archeological materials from the Republican River basin, including specimens, photographs, and related records, are at the following establishments: the Nebraska State Historical Society, Lincoln; the University of Nebraska State Museum and Department of Anthropology, Lincoln; the Kansas State Historical Society, Topeka; the University of Kansas

Museum of Natural History, Lawrence; the University of Colorado Museum, Boulder; the National Museum of Natural History Department of Anthropology and the National Anthropological Archives, Smithsonian Institution, Washington, D.C.

Chapter 1 History of Archeological Research in the Basin

In the Republican River basin, as elsewhere, the data of archeology are extremely fragmentary and one-sided. More—far more—has been lost from the record than remains to us. Prehistory must be reconstructed by the archeologist from scraps of bone, stone, shell, pottery, and other materials; from house structures, cache pits, and skeletons; and from such other leavings of debris as may be found in and on streamside terraces and around upland ponds where they were dropped by people who left no written records. Before 1930, when professional inquiry into the prehistory of the region began, most of what was done must be classed as opportunistic endeavor conducted largely by untrained amateurs and relic collectors, long on enthusiasm and often on industry but short on know-how and technique (Wedel 1981). Here and there, to be sure, was to be found an enlightened individual, motivated as much by a desire to know as by the wish to accumulate Indian relics, making an honest effort to maintain some sort of record of what was found, where, and under what particular circumstances.

Not surprisingly, the first findings of record from the Republican are from the lower valley in Kansas, where white settlement preceded that in Nebraska and Colorado. Settlement along the river here began as early as the 1850s, following the establishment in 1853 of Fort Riley at the junction of the Republican with the Smoky Hill River. In the 1850s, Henry Rowe Schoolcraft, Samuel F. Haven, Lewis Henry Morgan, Joseph Henry, and other eastern scholars, all apparently persuaded of the essential validity of the concept of the Great Plains as the Great American Desert and too ready to add their prestigious voices and pens to the denigration of the plains and mountain West, promoted the thesis that human occupation in the treeless trans-Missouri grasslands was impossible without the horse. The general absence of conspicuous artificial mounds, earthworks, and other highly visible monuments of antiquity like those of the Ohio valley seemed indeed to provide support for these views, which were destined to become deeply embedded in professional thinking in the next several decades.

In the decade following the establishment of Fort Riley, roads were built up both banks of the Republican and settlement got underway. The inconsiderable mounds perched on the bluff tops along the valley margins attracted attention early from the newcomers and were occasionally reported on with brief notices or descriptions (Parker 1887). Spadework soon established that these were built mainly of rocks and earth, and that they were primarily for burial of the dead. Bones were mostly in very fragmentary and partly calcined condition. Artifacts

1

were not infrequent accompaniments of the dead but were seldom numerous or exciting. From the random digging done by farmers, schoolteachers, clergymen, and a wide range of craftsmen and dilettantes, a few specimens found their way into the cabinets of curiosities that eventually developed into museums of natural history, history, and science. Already before 1900, it was in the published record (Brower 1899:103) that prehistoric Indian villages with lodge remains, pottery fragments, and abundant other debris occurred on the lower Republican, as well as on the Smoky Hill and Kansas rivers nearby. For too much of this work, unhappily, little or nothing useful to the present-day scholar survives, and the artifacts collected were mostly scattered and lost without record.

Following the close of the Civil War and the acceleration of westward expansion, interest in the antiquities was reawakened, though it was still incidental to programs in geology, geography, and natural history. Thus, in connection with his geological survey of the Nebraska Territory, Ferdinand V. Hayden in 1867 observed traces of "old dirt lodges and pieces of pottery . . . all along the Missouri, in the valley of the Little Blue, Big Blue, Platte, and Loup Fork," but he made no mention of the Republican valley (Hayden 1868).

In Kansas, the state university (founded in 1866), or more accurately, members of its professional staff in geology, paleontology, and other natural sciences writing papers for the Kansas Academy of Sciences (founded in 1871), led the way. Few of those papers or ones produced by the state university staff members in Nebraska dealt with the Republican valley. Other state agencies would point the way in the area of Indian remains where no direct or immediate economic returns to the states and their citizens could be demonstrated.

The state historical societies of Nebraska and Kansas were active early, though they were severely hampered from the first by limited funds and a chronic shortage of qualified personnel. The Kansas State Historical Society was organized in 1875, the Nebraska State Historical Society in 1883. Both organizations were directed by their constitutions to include the study of prehistoric people and materials in their programs. Their publications, even in the early days, reflected their concern for these matters by brief papers and notices of chance finds—burials, pictographs, and debris-littered camp and village sites. Their museum collections include materials donated in early days, all too often with data so meager that it tantalizes rather than informs the modern-day researcher. The state universities and other educational institutions also acquired donations of such materials, though no special efforts at systematic sampling or study were undertaken.

The Kansas State Historical Society about 1899 was given a historic Pawnee village site in Republic County, then thought to represent the scene of Lt. Zebulon M. Pike's visit to the Republican Pawnees in the summer of 1806. Marked by a granite shaft in 1901 and graced by an excellent museum since 1968, this spectacularly situated bluff-top site escaped systematic investigation until the University of Kansas undertook excavations in 1949. In 1965–1967, further researches were conducted here by the Kansas State Historical Society (Witty 1968; Sanborn 1973).

Farther downstream, mounds in Clay, Riley, and Geary counties were extensively worked by a private collector, Floyd Schultz of Clay Center, Kansas, during the 1930s (Schultz and Spaulding 1948). The artifacts and records from this sustained activity have been deposited in the University of Kansas Museum of Natural History and, like the data from the Republic County Pawnee site, continue to provide base materials for research by students and staff of the university and the society.

In Nebraska, the state historical society staff included an archeologist as early as 1902, when E. E. Blackman was appointed archeologist and museum curator (Diffendal 1978). Surveys of sites began almost immediately, including sections of the Republican River valley, but these were severely limited in scope by shortage of funds and were seldom reported in the detail we would welcome today. His early travels greatly facilitated by a free railroad pass, Blackman (1903, 1905, 1906, 1907) visited sites and collectors in many parts of the state. In 1907, he made a trip to Orleans on the Republican to investigate the circumstances surrounding the finding of a silver cross a mile west of town in association with bones at first thought to be those of the martyred Father Juan de Padilla, who accompanied Francisco Vásquez de Coronado to Quivira in central Kansas in 1541. Blackman reported pottery vessels from a village site five miles north of Orleans, where cache pits were eroding from a creek bank. At another site, a 120-foot circle with a shallow pit at the center aroused his curiosity but left him puzzled about its purpose. West of the town he found a site littered with flint of good quality, "brown to light yellow in color," and closely resembling the material used by the Indians in manufacturing stone artifacts found on the Platte and Elkhorn rivers. This may be one of the earliest references to the use of Graham or Republican River or Smoky Hill jasper by the Indians. In Kansas, three miles south of Hardy, Nebraska, at a place known as Big Springs because of extensive water emissions, Blackman mentioned another village site with jasper litter. At several of the villages visited, lodge sites were, or recently had been, visible. The record does not indicate that follow-up work was undertaken at any of these reported locations.

In the 1920s, the Nebraska State Historical Society became more deeply interested in the archeological materials in the Republican valley. Blackman (1922, 1928, 1930) reported in 1922 that he had studied flint deposits in the valley, but their location is nowhere specified nor are there any known surviving samples that he might have collected at this time. In 1927, he reported another survey of the valley and excavations at several points, including the permanent villages of three bands of Pawnees, which "have been cross-sectioned and studied." Again, there are no archival records of what was found or of the artifacts recovered. In 1927, after examining sites near Franklin, Nebraska, Blackman (1930) reported a wind-laid overburden from 10 to 24 inches (25–60 cm) thick over some locations and speculated on the possibility of prehistoric dust storms that might have buried the ancient locations even as current dust storms were burying fields of the 1920s and 1930s.

Another important development of the 1920s was the involvement of A. T. Hill of Hastings, Nebraska, in archeological matters. A well-traveled businessman with a wide acquaintance in central Nebraska and northern Kansas, for many years a member of the historical society's board of directors, Hill contributed greatly to the advancement of Plains archeology. In large part, his involvement began as an outgrowth of a lively controversy between Nebraska and Kansas over the archeological identity and correct location of the Republican Pawnee village visited in 1806 by Pike (Hill 1927). Nebraska's choice, located in 1923 by Hill and identified now as 14WT1 in Webster County, was purchased by Hill in 1925, and he extensively tested the site on weekends and holidays over the next few years. With volunteer labor, Hill opened and mapped two circular house floors here before 1927, in addition to opening a number of graves and cache pits. A third house floor was cleared in 1929 by the University of Nebraska Archeological Survey under W. D. Strong (Wedel 1936:46). On a much larger scale was the work of the Nebraska State Historical Society in cooperation with the Work Projects Administration in 1941, when additional house floors, numerous cache pits, and a number of burials were opened. A landmark in the study of Pawnee archeology and prehistory, the site has been owned by the Nebraska State Historical Society Foundation since 1979.

The state historical society also supported limited test excavations and surveys on Medicine Creek in 1933 and on the Republican main stem in 1934 (Wedel 1934, 1935). Large-scale excavations were made with the cooperation of the Works Progress Administration at Dismal River Apache sites in Chase and Dundy counties in 1939 (Hill and Metcalf 1942), and with the cooperation of the National Park Service at Massacre Canyon (25HK13) and other sites in Hitchcock County in 1950 (Kivett 1952).

With the establishment of the University of Nebraska Archeological Survey in 1929 by William Duncan Strong, that institution became actively involved in field archeology in the state. In 1929 with modest support from the Smithsonian Cooperative Fund, the survey party investigated the Hill site (14WT1), surveyed several prehistoric sites in Franklin and Harlan counties, and briefly surveyed Medicine Creek (Strong 1935; Wedel 1982a:25ff). In 1948, following further surveys by the Smithsonian River Basin Surveys in connection with the federal water-control program, another university party under J. L. Champe worked Dismal River and other sites in the Harlan County Reservoir area (Champe 1949). Surveys of proposed reservoir sites in the Republican River drainage were carried out by the River Basin Surveys in 1947. Large-scale excavations followed at Medicine Creek in 1948 with funding by the United States Bureau of Reclamation and under the field leadership of M. F. Kivett (Kivett 1949, 1953). Concurrently, the Nebraska State Historical Society had a party working under A. T. Hill at a number of the village sites slated for inundation by the impounded waters. Important sites relating to Early Man were under investigation at the same time by the University of Nebraska State Museum (Schultz and Frankforter 1948; Davis and Schultz 1952). A University of Nebraska party under contract with the National Park Service investigated village sites in the Norton Reservoir area on Prairie Dog Creek in 1962–63.

The Colorado section of the Republican valley has become known largely from its Early Man sites and materials. These began showing up during the drought years of the 1930s, when high winds caused extensive soil movements and revealed an abundance of ancient weapon points and other remains. River Basin Surveys explorations at Wray and Bonny reservoir sites revealed other and later materials. In 1953, the Claypool site in Washington County was partially excavated by a party from the University of Colorado (Dick and Mountain 1960), and further excavations were made by a party from the Smithsonian Institution in 1975. On a much larger scale were the sustained investigations by the Smithsonian Institution and the National Geographic Society at the Jones-Miller bison kill site near Laird in 1972–1975, and at the Selby and Dut-

Plate 1.1. Three students of Republican River basin archeology during the 1930s. *Left to right:* Waldo R. Wedel, United States National Museum; William Duncan Strong, University of Nebraska and Bureau of American Ethnology; Asa T. Hill, Nebraska State Historical Society.

ton sites near Vernon and Idalia, respectively, in 1975–1978. These operations, organized and managed by Dennis Stanford and incorporating interdisciplinary studies along with up-to-date field and laboratory methods, have promised to bring new perspectives on the antiquity of man in this region and on the manner in which people functioned here in the distant past (Stanford 1974, 1975, 1979).

The archeological site designations used in this study are trinomial and include symbols for state, county, and site. The state is indicated by the first number, according to the numerical position of the state name in an alphabetical list of the 48 states as of 1946. Thus, for example, 5 indicates Colorado, 14 indicates Kansas, and 25 indicates Nebraska. Counties are designated by a two-letter abbreviation, for example, YM for Yuma, HN for Harlan, RP for Republic, and so on. The final number refers to the specific site within the indicated state and county, often but not always in the order in which the sites were recorded.

This system is an elaboration of one devised in Nebraska during the Works Progress Administration archeological salvage programs. It was developed in the summer of 1946 by the Missouri basin office of the Smithsonian's River Basin Surveys in Lincoln, Nebraska. There it satisfactorily met the immediate need for an expandable system of site designation that would be applicable interstate and so could be used anywhere in the Missouri basin. The specimens collected by the River Basin Surveys, the field records, and the photographs were marked with the appropriate site numbers, which served also as a guide to the permanent record files when they were deposited in the National Anthropological Archives at the Smithsonian Institution.

The adoption of this system, of course, does not preclude the use of the time-honored custom of naming a site for its discoverer, a property owner, financial backer, or some other person, or from its geographical or other context. It does, however, provide a much-needed specificity for recording and discussing purposes, which is not readily achieved when the same family name comes to be applied to more than a single site. The system, with some variations, has been widely adopted throughout the Great Plains area and beyond (Wedel 1948:5–6).

Chapter 2 The Environmental Setting

The Republican River is a stream of the plains. Unlike the Arkansas, the Platte, and the Missouri, it receives no waters from the Rocky Mountains but gathers them instead from the high, rolling tablelands of northeastern Colorado. The principal headwater tributaries—the Arikaree and the South Fork Republican—both rise in Lincoln County, respectively north and east of Limon. From there they trend generally northeastward in shallow valleys 10 to 20 miles (15–30 km) apart, with occasional springs but few or no tributaries that add significantly to their flow, now mainly intermittent. As they approach the eastern border of Colorado, the valleys deepen and rocky ledges appear on their margins. At Haigler, Nebraska, the Arikaree is joined by the North Fork Republican, whose source is mainly in strong springs 10 or 12 miles (15–18 km) southwest of Wray, Colorado. The combined streams form the Republican River. Less than 30 miles (48 km) to the east, the South Fork Republican enters the Republican at Benkelman, Nebraska. Gathering the waters of Frenchman, Blackwood, Red Willow, Medicine, and numerous lesser creeks from the north, and Beaver, Sappa, Prairie Dog, and other shorter creeks from the south, the river meanders eastward through the loess plains of southern Nebraska to Superior. Here it turns south into Kansas to join the Smoky Hill at Junction City, becoming the Kansas (Kaw) River, which empties into the Missouri at Kansas City (fig. 2.1).

From east to west, the Republican River drainage basin measures approximately 360 miles (575 km), airline. Its greatest width, about 120 miles (190 km), is at the Colorado state line, along the 102d meridian. Below Harlan County, Nebraska, the basin narrows sharply to 30 miles (48 km) in width. Surface ground elevations decrease from 6,000 feet (1,800 m), mean sea level (hereafter msl) at Cedar Point, where the Arikaree heads at longitude 104° west, to 1,050 feet (320 m), msl, at Junction City. Along the main river, distances approximate 150 miles (240 km) in Colorado, 250 miles (400 km) in Nebraska, and less than 200 miles (320 km) in Kansas. Of the 26,000 square miles (67,000 sq km) that compose the watershed, 40 percent of the total is in Nebraska and the remainder is about equally divided between Colorado and Kansas. By the 1970 census, there were 175,000 residents there, an agricultural population mainly occupied with the cultivation of wheat, corn, and other cereal crops; stock-raising; and supporting activities.

Like most other sections of the Great Plains region, the Republican basin exhibits considerable topographical diversity. The undulating tablelands around the headwaters in Colorado give way between the North Fork and the

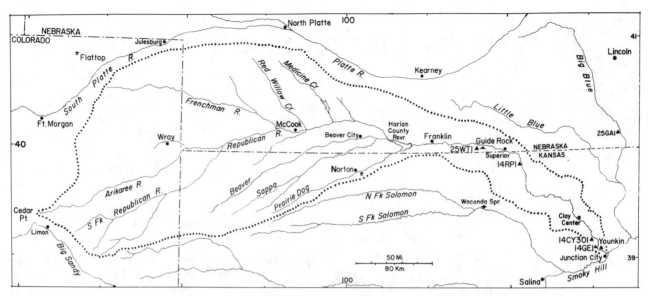

Fig. 2.1. Map of the Republican River basin (dotted line), showing principal streams and location in relation to modern state boundaries and geographical coordinates.

upper Frenchman Creek to a flat, dune-covered area with sandy soils, poorly developed surface drainage, and no through-flowing streams. This topography extends into Dundy and Chase counties, Nebraska. Eastward for another 150 miles (240 km), the river then runs in a flat-floored, bluff-lined valley, 200–400 feet (60–120 m) deep. On the north side of the main valley, the major tributaries and lesser creeks have produced an intricately dissected area of loess tables and steep-sided canyons, where local relief ranges from 100 to nearly 300 feet (35–100 m), and narrow divides are common. A notable feature of many of these canyons, long and short, is their flat, grassy floors, often too limited in size to cultivate and commonly serving now as hay flats or pasture for livestock. In earlier days, bison grazing in these sheltered pockets must have been attractions for native hunters working on foot, singly or in small groups (plates 2.1 to 2.5; figs. 2.2 and 2.3).

South of the river in northwestern Kansas, the long tributaries that flow east have produced prominent upland divides and, by the action of their many short branches, smaller rounded hills and interfluvial ridges. Along the principal streams are deeply dissected zones with narrow, steep-walled canyons that contrast sharply with the flat uplands and their numerous undrained depressions and shallow swales (Frye and Leonard 1949; Walters 1956). East of Harlan County, the Republican has only very short tributaries from the north, beyond which are the broad, fertile loess plains uplands. Once grazed by countless bison and pronghorn antelope, these are now given over almost entirely to grain production. Below the Kansas-Nebraska state line, the river valley, cut through Cretaceous limestone and then sandstones, is characterized by broad alluvial bottoms and prominent divides with frequent rocky ledges. Here the principal tributaries are White Rock and Buffalo creeks, both entering from the west.

The Republican River basin consists of a number of subbasins. These vary greatly, depending upon which stream or portion of the stream is taken as the

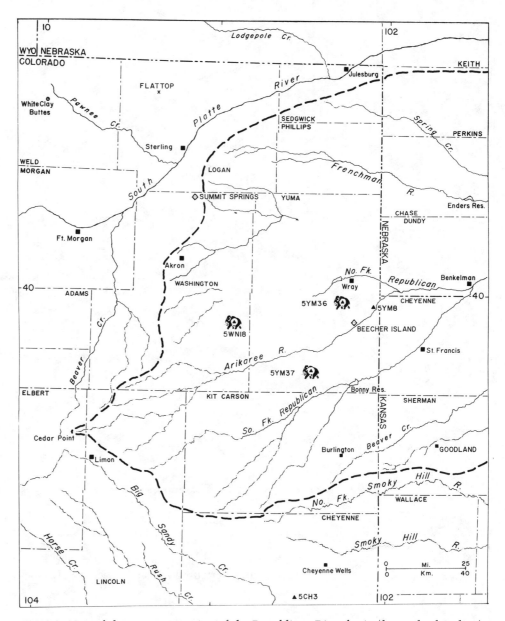

Fig. 2.2. Map of the western portion of the Republican River basin (*heavy broken line*), showing headwaters, counties, towns, and selected archeological sites and features.

control. For present purposes, the principal ones, with the area of each, are as follows:

	Sq Mi	Sq Km
Arikaree River at Haigler, NE	1,460	3,780
Republican River at Benkelman, NE	4,770	12,355
South Fork Republican at Benkelman, NE	2,580	6,655
Frenchman Creek at Culbertson, NE	3,080	7,977
Republican River at McCook, NE	12,560	32,530
Red Willow Creek near Red Willow, NE	710	1,840

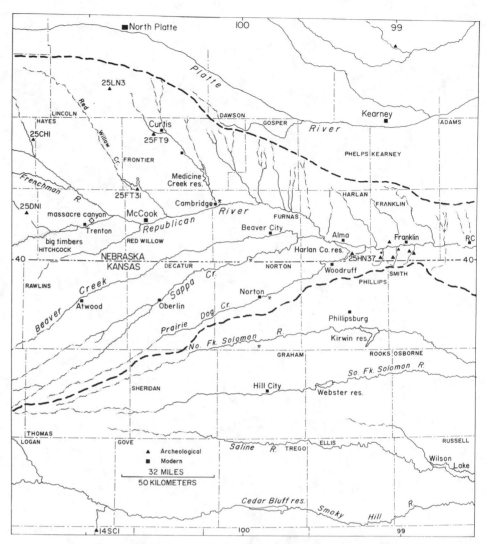

Fig. 2.3. Map of the central portion of the Republican River basin (*heavy broken line*), showing counties, certain towns, and selected archeological sites and features.

	Sq. Mi	Sq Km
Medicine Creek at Cambridge, NE	1,070	2,770
Prairie Dog Creek above Woodruff, KS	1,000	2,590
Republican River near Bloomington, NE	20,000	53,870

Some Aspects of Climate

In the Republican River basin, lying hundreds of miles inland from any ocean, the climate can be regionally denominated as continental (Kincer 1923; Bates 1935; Thornthwaite 1941). It comprises an extremely wide and variable range of local weather conditions whose effects on the biota are often obscured by the averages by which the regional climate is characterized. Several notable aspects of the climate directly affect man's welfare in the area. These include hot summers and cold winters, both usually dry; frequent, unpredictable, and often wide fluctuations, both short- and long-term, in the precipitation and temperature patterns; strong and sustained wind movement that varies widely from cat's-paws to tornadoes; and high evaporation rates. These characteristics

Plate 2.1. Republican valley views in southern Nebraska ca. A.D. 1900 and 1976.
Upper, view north across the Republican valley near Cambridge in the early 1900s.
Note the absence of trees. Courtesy Nebraska State Historical Society. *Lower,*
Republican River near Culbertson in August 1976, looking downstream.

reflect the interaction of three great air masses that meet in the center of the
continent and determine the weather, and over time the climate (Borchert
1950). The movements of these air masses vary widely from time to time, but
their directions are generally toward the continental interior and then eastward. Mild air moving east from the Pacific Ocean has been drained of most of
its moisture in crossing the Great Basin and the Rocky Mountains, in whose

Plate 2.2. Republican River views in Kansas and Nebraska 1976. *Upper*, Republican valley above Scandia, Kansas, looking southwest; *lower*, South Fork Republican River near St. Francis, Kansas, looking downstream.

rain shadow the Great Plains are located. East of the Rockies, the Pacific westerlies meet moist warm air moving north from the Gulf of Mexico and cold dry air flowing south out of Canada. Along the fronts where these masses collide, storms develop. A strong flow of westerly Pacific air, by preventing or deflecting toward the east the meeting of Arctic and tropical air masses, causes the aridity of the Great Plains, which is most pronounced in the west, that is, on the

Plate 2.3. Utilization of natural draws along the Republican River in Nebraska. *Upper*, cattle grazing near the upper end of a flat-floored draw tributary to the Republican near Massacre Canyon; *lower*, small cornfield in a draw near Franklin, Nebraska.

short-grass steppe. When a change in the atmospheric circulation patterns weakens the westerlies, an earlier meeting of the moisture-laden tropical air with cold Canadian air may significantly increase regional precipitation in the plains. If the southerly air originates over the arid southwestern United States and northern Mexico instead of the Gulf of Mexico, its dryness may increase the problems of the crop-grower in the Great Plains. As Bates (1935:93) has

Plate 2.4. Republican valley views in Nebraska and Colorado. *Upper*, Rock Creek valley and whiteface cattle grazing on natural pasture, Dundy County, Nebraska; *lower*, Sandhills north of Republican River in Yuma County, Colorado, along the probable route of Lt. F. T. Bryan's explorations in 1856.

observed with respect to the western plains, "Winds which originate west of the Gulf of Mexico bring nothing but dryness."

Around the Republican River headwaters, the climate is semiarid. Annual precipitation averages approximately 14 inches (350 mm), with violent storms, hail, and tornadoes not uncommon during the summer months. Toward the east, the average precipitation rises about 1 inch (25 mm) in every 20 miles (32

Plate 2.5. Upland scenes in the Great Plains. *Upper,* whiteface cattle at a temporary upland water hole near Limon, Colorado; *lower,* bison herds near Lake Jessie, North Dakota, sketched by John Mix Stanley, Pacific Railroad Surveys, 10 July 1853. A decade earlier, on the uplands between Beaver Creek and the Republican in present northern Kansas, Frémont reported bison "present in great numbers, absolutely covering the face of the country."

km), and at Junction City the annual total averages about 32 inches (800 mm). Temperature maxima of 110°F (43°C) and minima of −25°F (−13°C) have been recorded in every county in the basin. Recorded extremes for the entire basin are 118°F (48°C) and −38°F (−36°C). Sharp changes ranging up to 40 or 50°F may take place within a few hours. The number of days per year without killing frosts ranges from 140 on the northwestern margin to 180 days in the southeast. In four years out of five, these numbers drop to 120 and 140, respectively (United States Department of Agriculture 1936).

Native Vegetation

Generally throughout the Great Plains, the natural vegetation consisted originally of grasses with trees limited to narrow belts of gallery forest along the stream valleys (Kellogg 1905; Weaver 1954, 1968; Weaver and Albertson 1956; Küchler 1964; Costello 1969). In and near the Republican valley, little unspoiled natural grassland remains to demonstrate the truth of Costello's (1969:23) observation that its summer aspect "is one of profusion of species and variegated patterns," constantly changing, where "new forbs blossom with such prodigality that one must visit favorite spots again and again to view the endless parade of color."

Typical of the headwaters steppe in Colorado are short grasses, including the dominant blue grama (*Bouteloua gracilis*) and buffalo (*Buchloë dactyloides*). In the sandy areas north of the Arikaree and east to the Medicine Creek drainage, sand sagebrush (*Artemisia filifolia*) and bluestem (*Andropogon* sp.) are more characteristic. Prickly pear (*Opuntia*) and yucca (*Yucca glauca*) are locally abundant, the former especially so in overgrazed or drought-stricken ground. In dry seasons, prickly pear was one of the very few plants whose fruits could be depended upon by prehistoric man for food. Farther east, in northern Kansas and adjacent to Nebraska, wheatgrass (*Agropyron*), needlegrass (*Stipa*), bluestem (*Andropogon*), and other medium-tall grasses occur in varying proportions, constituting a mixed prairie. In the east, this finally grades into the tall-grass or "true" bluestem prairie lying roughly east of longitude 98°30′ west at the lower end of the Republican River basin.

The western short grasses are low-growing, shallow-rooted, small-leaved, sod-forming types, rich in protein and low in fiber. Highly drought resistant and dormant through the winter, they resume growth quickly with spring moisture. *Bouteloua* and *Buchloë* are warm-season types, northern representatives of grasses widespread in Mexico; western wheatgrass and Junegrass are cool-weather forms much less resistant to drought. All cure, without cutting, into a palatable and nutritious winter forage, which could provide year-long grazing for bison, pronghorn, or range cattle. They adapt to rainfall deficiencies by reducing plant size, stems, and leaf growth; and by curling, folding, or dropping their leaves. Persistent severe drought may eventually damage the root system and reduce or even eliminate much of the stand, with recovery usually requiring several years of favorable weather.

The bluestem prairies lying east of the 20-inch (510 mm) isohyet, which coincides roughly with longitude 101° west, consist of deep-rooted grasses and forbs. They produce abundant growth in average years but start later in spring and provide scant winter forage because they do not cure well when left standing. During the spring and early summer growing season, their carrying capacity in grazing animals per acre is three to five times that of the short grasses. According to Costello (1969:84), "an acre of tall grass, producing up to 3,000 pounds (1,350 kg) of forage per year, could easily support a bison for two months or more." The palatability and high nutritional value of tall grasses make them a favorite of most grazers. They react adversely to severe drought, at which times the prairie grasses give way to shorter grasses on the higher and drier locations, and the prairie-steppe transition zone may shift far to the east, only to move west again when average rainfall returns. Bluestem and other tall grasses are of eastern and southeastern origin.

With reference to the nutritional value of short grasses vis-à-vis tall grasses in midsummer, some observations made by Capt. John Frémont are of interest. In mid-July 1844, returning from his explorations in Oregon and California, Frémont proceeded down the Arkansas River to a point about 20 miles below Bent's Fort and then crossed to the headwaters of the Smoky Hill River. Descending that, he passed through the transitional or mixed prairies. About midway between the Arkansas River departure point and the confluence of the Smoky Hill and the Republican rivers, somewhere in present north central Kansas, Frémont (1845:289) noted that

> the beautiful sward of the buffalo grass, which is regarded as the best and most nutritious found on the prairies, appeared now only in patches, being replaced by a longer and coarser grass, which covered the face of the country luxuriantly. The difference in the character of the grasses became suddenly evident in the weakened condition of our animals, which began sensibly to fail as soon as we quitted the buffalo grass.

Although grasses dominated the plains landscape generally, there was also a great variety of herbaceous flowering plants, some with specialized parts of particular interest to native man. These occurred most plentifully in the eastern sectors, and their availability to people living west of the 100th meridian, for example, may have been restricted. To such groups, trade or seasonal gathering trips at appropriate times would have been possible alternatives to doing without.

In historic times, the most important of the native food plants was the Indian breadroot or prairie turnip (*Psoralea esculenta*). This grew on well-drained hillsides and produced enlarged starchy tubers, one per plant (fig. 2.4), which were dug up in quantities by the Indians in May and June (Wedel 1978a). They could be used fresh or dried and were popular ingredients of soups, stews, and other dishes, with or without meats and other vegetables. For drying, they were peeled and braided into strings (plate 2.6) to be hung up in the lodges for future needs. Commonly, they were pounded into meal or flour for thickening various dishes. Although the prairie turnip was widely used by both the mobile hunter tribes and the sedentary village Indians, and by early white travelers in the plains, there is no evidence so far as I am aware that the American Indians ever attempted the domestication or garden cultivation of the plant.[1]

In the streamside woods of the bottomlands grew the Indian potato or groundnut (*Apios americana*). This was a twining leguminous vine whose long, stringy roots developed farinaceous tubers growing at intervals like beads on a string, hence their French designation *racines des chapelet* or "rosary root" (plate 2.7). Here, too, could be found the ground bean (*Amphicarpa bracteata*), another vine that produced both small aerial and large beanlike underground seeds that were coveted by Indians and rodents alike. The underground seeds were gathered by the rodents into hoards containing up to several quarts of beans, which were then sought out and appropriated by the Indian women. This procedure was also used to gather the hoarded tubers of the groundnut (James 1823:218; F. V. Hayden in Warren 1875:113).

Fig. 2.4. The prairie turnip (*Psoralea esculenta*), showing foliage and florescence, enlarged tuber, and stem scars from previous years' growth. Tubers are usually more globular than indicated here.

The tuberous roots of the Jerusalem artichoke (*Helianthus tuberosus*) were yet another important source of carbohydrates (plate 2.6); they were usually dug up but could sometimes be taken from rodent hoards. The seeds or achenes of the related sunflower (*Helianthus annuus*), which became available in August and September, were ground up and used fresh or dried, or they could be boiled for their high yield of edible oil. Among the semisedentary village Indians after ca A.D. 1000, the sunflower was cultivated along with maize and beans, and its charred achenes have been found repeatedly in archeological contexts.

In the drier western portions of the Republican basin, the huge roots of the bush morning glory (*Ipomoea leptophylla*) were used as an emergency food by the roving hunters and foragers, but they were not generally considered a desirable food item otherwise. The fruits of the prickly pear, with the spines and bristles singed off, were available in dry periods, when the plant usually spread rapidly at the expense of the drought-weakened stands of grass.

In the boggy meadows fed by seep springs at the headwaters of such tributary creeks as the Frenchman, Red Willow, and Medicine, as well as around the headsprings on the North Fork Republican, there were doubtless extensive stands of cattail (*Typha*) and arrowhead (*Sagittaria latifolia*), remnants of which may still be found here and there. The tender young spring shoots of the former, and the starchy tubers of the latter gathered in late summer and early fall for roasting, were popular foods in historic times and undoubtedly long before. It seems likely that their special habitats were more extensive in the days before white settlement, before the falling water table dried up many of the springs and seeps along the valley margins.

The food plants just noted by no means exhaust the list of those that we may suppose were used by the Republican valley natives long before the arrival of white men. The prehorticultural Indians undoubtedly drew far more heavily on grass and weed seeds than did the maize-growing groups, whose representatives in the 19th century had for so long been away from the way of life of the

Plate 2.6. Some wild plant foods of the Plains Indians. *Upper*, peeled and braided tubers of the prairie turnip (*Psoralea esculenta*), prepared by the Dakota Indians for storage. Courtesy Mrs. Marion Willey. *Lower*, tubers of the Jerusalem artichoke (*Helianthus tuberosus*). Courtesy O. S. Fent.

seed-gathering forager that even the common wild food seeds once sought by their ancestors had been largely forgotten or were remembered as horse feed, ritual items, and the like (Gilmore 1913, 1919; Castetter 1935; Vestal and Schultes 1939; Carlson and Jones 1940). Improved recovery techniques of archeology, such as water flotation and others, when applied to charred vegetable refuse from burned-out caches, house ruins, and temporary camp sites, can be expected to increase significantly the list of species drawn upon by the Indians

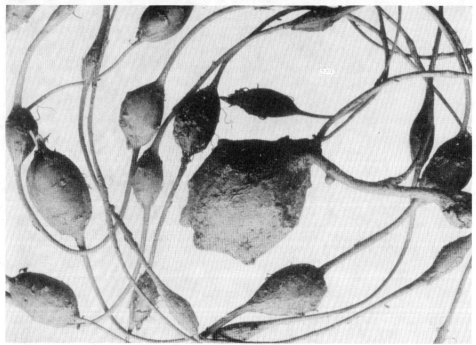

Plate 2.7. Wild plant foods of the Plains Indians. *Upper,* foliage and blooms of the groundnut (*Apios americana*), the pea vine of the early-19th-century American explorers in the eastern Great Plains. Courtesy Milwaukee Public Museum. *Lower,* tubers and connecting roots of the groundnut, the *racines des chapelet* or "rosary roots" of the French explorers and traders. Courtesy *Journal of Heredity,* v. 16, pp. 113–230, 1925; photograph by W. E. Safford.

for medicinal, ritual, and household use. Relevant studies of this nature in the Great Plains, though not specifically concerned with the Republican River basin, include Cutler and Blake (1973), Benn (1974), Johnson (1976), Robinson (1976), and Nickel (1977). Older studies that have lost none of their relevance in ethnobotany include Palmer (1871), Havard (1895), Henkel (1906), and Yanovsky (1936).

Trees

The natural tree growth in the Republican valley is a floodplain woodland that is a westward extension of the eastern oak-hickory-maple deciduous forest (Kellogg 1905; Pool 1966; Küchler 1964; Stephens 1969, 1973; Barkley 1977). It consists almost entirely of broad-leaved species, notably elm (*Ulmus americana; U. rubra*), bur oak (*Quercus macrocarpa*), white ash (*Fraxinus americana*), box elder (*Acer negundo*), hackberry (*Celtis occidentalis*), honey locust (*Gleditsia triacanthos*), black locust (*Robinia pseudoacacia*), catalpa (*Catalpa speciosa*), cottonwood (*Populus deltoides*), and black willow (*Salix nigra*). Basswood (*Tilia americana*) and sycamore (*Platanus occidentalis*) occur along the lower course of the stream. Nut trees are uncommon, but black walnut (*Juglans nigra*) grows west to Harlan County, Nebraska, or slightly beyond. Red cedar (*Juniperus virginiana*) and western yellow pine (*Pinus ponderosa*) once fringed the rocky ledges along the south rim of the main valley in Nebraska, the former occurring at least as far west as the Colorado line. The pines have long since succumbed to the needs of early settlers for firewood and fence posts, but juniper still flourishes from Franklin County westward. Underbrush and vines, including Virginia creeper (*Parthenocissus quinquefolia*), poison ivy (*Rhus radicans*), and wild grapes (*Vitis riparia, V. vulpina*), are often heavy along the stream banks.

Forest growth was heaviest along the lower Republican. Here the rich bottoms before white development were, "for a prairie country, well interspersed with wood," according to Frémont in 1843 (Jackson and Spence 1970:432). Timber presumably covered much of the floodplain and bluffs, but considerable areas were in grass. Ascending the Republican, tree stands became progressively thinner and the trees smaller toward the west. The hardwood forests substantially ended about longitude 101° west except for open scattering clumps of cottonwood and willow that have returned to the Colorado valleys within the past half century, that is, since the great flood of 1935. Beyond 100° west, the floor of the main valley becomes increasingly sandy, with low stream banks that are easily eroded by freshets, and here the cottonwood and willow in open stands decidedly predominate. Photographs of a century ago suggest that trees were restricted to the immediate riverbanks in the main valley. Tributary valleys from both north and south are usually much less sandy, often with heavy soils in which elm, ash, box elder, and other deciduous trees may grow more densely and vigorously than do the trees along the main stem. Thickets of wild plum (*Prunus americana*) and scattered choke cherry (*Prunus viginiana*) trees or shrubs may be found. Plum thickets are not uncommon in many of the dry draws branching off from the perennially watered creek valleys.

Kellogg (1905, map 1) shows no valley forest west of the Colorado line in the Republican drainage, and this appears to coincide with the preagricultural observations by Lt. Francis T. Bryan (1857) during his descent of the Republican

River in 1856. Occasionally, however, "big timbers" developed west of the 100th meridian. These extensive floodplain concentrations of large cottonwoods, good grass, and strong springs in certain localities were areas where mounted bison-hunting Indians retired during hard winters, along with the herd animals upon which they subsisted (Wedel 1963). In the Republican valley, such a winter refuge was available during the mid-19th century in the present district of Dundy and Hitchcock counties, immediately above Swanson Lake reservoir. It was described in 1864 by Capt. Eugene F. Ware (1960:341) as about 14 miles (22 km) long, filling most of the river bottoms, and consisting of cottonwood trees up to and exceeding two feet in diameter. The density was about one tree to every 2,500 square yards (2,100 sq m), approximately 17 trees per acre (42 per hectare), and free of underbrush. Heavy use of this area by both Indians and bison was clearly manifested, according to Ware.

Native Fauna

During the 19th century, the Republican country was widely renowned as a hunting ground for big game. The hunters included both Indians in quest of subsistence and Euro-Americans seeking sport, trophies, and also choice cuts of meat. The game sought then was undoubtedly available, probably in even greater plenty, to the prewhite inhabitants. Of primary importance was the bison (*Bison bison*). Ecologically a dominant species in the short- and mixed-grass country, the bison probably varied in abundance and availability from time to time over the millennia (D. Gunnerson 1972; Dillehay 1974; Reher 1978). The record clearly shows that for some thousands of years the Indians drew heavily on this animal for subsistence: for food, clothing, shelter, fuel, and a wide variety of household tools and utensils made from bone, horn, skin, sinew, and hair. Techniques for drying, freezing, or otherwise preserving the meat for later use were probably developed or introduced very early, and these helped to offset the local shortages when the herds moved to new grazing grounds. Hunted by stalking, by drives on foot and horse, communally by surrounds, and in other ways to be noted later, and yielding up to several hundred pounds of nutritious meat and fat per animal, the bison, despite its often erratic and unpredictable occurrence and behavior, made possible man's settlement and long-time residence on the Great Plains; its disappearance at last foreshadowed the passing of the native lifeway of the Indian as well. As Frémont (Jackson and Spence 1970:185) observed in 1842, "Indians and buffalo make the poetry and life of the prairie."

Less important to the Indian, to judge from the archeological record as well as documentary evidence, was the other common grassland herbivore, the pronghorn (*Antilocapra americana*), which was probably preferred for its skin as much as for the meat. Other plains species taken were the coyote (*Canis latrans*), wolf (*Canis lupus*), badger (*Taxidea taxus*), prairie dog (*Cynomys ludovicianus*), and black-footed ferret (*Mustela nigripes*). These were supplemented by woodland and forest-edge animals whose range extended far into a primarily grassland environment by way of the narrow winding ribbons of forest and brush bordering its streams. Thus were made available the wapiti or elk (*Cervus canadensis*); mule deer (*Odocoileus hemionus*); plains grizzly (*Ursus horribilis*); black bear (*Ursus americanus*); cougar or puma (*Felis concolor*); wildcat or bobcat (*Lynx rufus*); beaver (*Castor canadensis*); river otter (*Lutra canadensis*); raccoon (*Procyon lotor*); mink (*Mustela vison*); muskrat (*Ondatra zibethicus*); and other smaller fur-bearers. The bones of most of these mammals have been identified in prehistoric refuse deposits at Republican River Indian sites, as well as among the worked bone and artifacts. With improving recovery techniques, the remains of smaller animals once overlooked in archeological excavations are coming to light, adding to the faunal inventories and providing data for significant interpretations regarding contemporary environmental conditions, seasonality, and other points with cultural connotations. How these various forms were used, if other than for their pelts and as food, will be made clearer in later sections of this study.

Birds were present in a considerable range of forms, reflecting the transitional nature of the Great Plains region where both eastern and western species intermingle. With some exceptions to be noted presently, birds were of relatively minor importance as food items for the Plains Indians, but they figured variously, and often significantly, in ritual and mythology. Their bones were used for making tools and ornaments, the feathers, skins, skulls, and feet or talons of certain species for ceremonial trappings and personal or household fetishes (Ubelaker and Wedel 1975; Parmalee 1977). "The cormorant," wrote Samuel Allis in 1836, "is a bird one of which the Pawnees will give a horse for," but he gave no reason (Allis 1918:708). The abundance and distribution of the various species today is undoubtedly quite unlike that in prewhite days, owing to drastic modification of the original landscape through large-scale agriculture, the draining of upland ponds and other wetlands, the extensive planting of trees in hedgerows and around farmsteads, and other developments.

The observant traveler following one of the highways along the Republican River in summertime, with occasional side trips on secondary and farm roads, will quickly become familiar by sight or sound, or both, with the western meadowlark (*Sturnella neglecta*), dickcissel (*Spiza americana*), mourning dove (*Zenaidura macroura*), eastern and western kingbirds (*Tyrannus tyrannus, T. verticalis*), red-headed woodpecker (*Melanerpes erythrocephalus*), golden-shafted flicker (*Colaptes auratus*), crow (*Corvus brachyrhynchos*), red-tailed hawk (*Buteo jamaicensis*), marsh hawk (*Circus cyaneus*), kestrel or sparrow hawk (*Falco sparverius*), magpie (*Pica pica*), and turkey vulture (*Cathartes aura*). Less frequent, or less obvious, are the killdeer (*Charadrius vociferus*), horned lark (*Eremophila alpestris*), lark bunting (*Calamospiza melanocorys*), and bobolink (*Dolichonyx oryzivorus*). Still less common except in particular habitats are the burrowing owl (*Speotyto cunicularia*), upland plover (*Bartramia longicauda*) and long-billed curlew (*Numenius americanus*), and on occasion, the sandhill crane (*Grus canadensis*). In swampy spots with cattails and reeds, or around some upland ponds, the red-winged blackbird (*Agelaius phoeniceus*), avocet (*Recurvirostra americana*), cowbird (*Molothrus ater*), yellow-headed blackbird (*Xanthocephalus xanthocephalus*), and long-billed marsh wren (*Telmatodytes palustris*) may be seen, along with coots, sandpipers, rails, and grebes.

A casual drive along bottomland roads or a walk along the stream bank will yield a somewhat different set of bird sightings. These could include the cardinal (*Richmondena cardinalis*), blue jay (*Cyanocitta cristata*), Baltimore and orchard orioles (*Icterus galbula, I. spurius*), robin (*Turdus migratorius*), yellow-billed cuckoo (*Coccyzus americanus*), mockingbird (*Mimus polyglottos*), brown thrasher (*Toxostoma rufum*), catbird (*Dumetella carolinensis*), crested flycatcher (*Myiarchus crinitus*), chickadee (*Parus atricapillus*), wood thrush (*Hylocichla mustelina*), house wren (*Troglodytes aedon*), yellow warbler (*Dendroica petechia*), redstart (*Setophaga ruticilla*), bluebird (*Sialia sialis*), goldfinch (*Spinus tristis*), blue grosbeak (*Guiraca caerulea*), scarlet tanager (*Piranga olivacea*), tree swallow (*Iridoprocne bicolor*), bank swallow (*Riparia riparia*), cliff swallow (*Petrochelidon pyrrhonota*), green heron (*Butorides virescens*), great blue heron (*Ardea herodias*). The rattling call of the belted kingfisher (*Megaceryle alcyon*) is often heard. In the evenings or at night, there are the nighthawk (*Chordeiles minor*) in the west, and the whip-poor-will (*Caprimulgus vociferus*) in the east, along with the great horned owl (*Bubo virginianus*), the barn owl (*Tyto alba*), and the screech owl (*Otus asio*). Many more passerine songbirds, raptors, and shorebirds could be added to the list (Bruner 1896; Rapp et al. 1958; Johnston 1960).

Among game birds, the sharp-tailed grouse (*Pedioecetes phasianellus*) and possibly the prairie chicken (*Tympanuchus cupido*) were found on the uplands in great numbers, where they could be shot or snared by young boys practicing their hunting skills. Here, too, there may have been bobwhite quail (*Colinus virginianus*), whose bones have so far appeared infrequently, if at all, in the archeological record. The eastern turkey (*Meleagris gallopavo*) ranged west as far as trees for roosting and shelter could be found, even when the customary mast had to be given up for grasshoppers and other food items on the plains (Aldrich and Duvall 1955; Schorger 1966). Ponds, upland waterholes, and reedy streams sheltered resident ducks, geese, and other waterfowl. The Canada goose (*Branta canadensis*), mallard (*Anas platyrhynchos*), pintail (*Anas acuta*), shoveler (*Spatula clypeata*), and blue-winged teal (*Anas discors*) are the species most commonly identified in the archeological materials, which can be presumed to include both resident and migrant populations. Residents could have been most effectively harvested from late June to early August, during the flightless moulting period for adults and before the young of the prairie-nesting species developed their flight feathers. The success of this seasonal hunting technique in the capture of incompletely fledged cygnets and goslings, especially with the help of a dog, has been historically documented by Meriwether Lewis during the passage of The Corps of Discovery through the Montana region in the summer of 1805 (Lewis and Clark 1904, vol. 2, p. 255).[2]

Migrating species moving along what are now recognized as the Western and Mid-Plains corridors (Bellrose 1968) southward from the northern plains to the shores of the Gulf of Mexico may have added substantially to the potential supply of ducks, geese, swans, and cranes. The eggs and nestlings of resident species were probably available in abundance, but if they were used, little or no evidence has been detected by archeologists. The almost certain presence of much more surface water at times in the prehistoric period would undoubtedly have attracted a larger resident population of breeding waterfowl. An unknown but perhaps substantial proportion of the migrants from the north may well have wintered in central plains country where open water remained available, as thousands of mallards and Canada geese still do today where water-control projects have provided large reservoirs along the Republican and other streams in lieu of the long-vanished natural upland ponds and lakes that the Indians knew and used.

In a particularly penetrating and comprehensive study of bird bones from

51 archeological sites on the Missouri River in South Dakota, Parmalee (1977) has contributed greatly to our understanding of birds in their relationship to native man in the Great Plains. He found strong preferences for certain groups and apparent disregard for others that were presumably plentiful and are known to have been much used by other peoples outside the plains. Relatively well represented in the South Dakota materials were the Canada and snow geese, eagles, accipitrid hawks, sharp-tailed grouse, sandhill cranes, ravens, and crows. A total of 66 species from 23 families were identified. As food items, the birds in this study must have represented a very small fraction of the animal protein gotten by the native hunters from the mammals taken concurrently, but the uses to which many of the bones were put add significantly to what can be learned from the ethnographic and ethnohistoric record about the use of birds by the Plains Indians.

The human populations on the plains seem to have made even less use of the available fish, reptiles, and amphibians. Among finned fish, catfish and suckers were common in the streams, and the former has been recognized repeatedly in the archeological record. Shellfish seem to have been more commonly used but perhaps as much for their shells as for the edible parts, as I will consider in more detail elsewhere. Among land reptiles, the venomous prairie rattlesnake (*Crotalus viridus*) and the nonvenomous bull snake (*Pituophis melanoleucus sayi*), the hognose (*Heterodon nasicus*), garter (*Thamnophis sirtalus parietalis*), and blue racer (*Coluber constrictor foxi*) were common. Water snakes (*Natrix*) were abundant along the streams. Whether lizards were eaten, or, as may have been the case with an occasional snake, were fortuitously trapped in open cache pits, is uncertain. The box turtle (*Terrapene ornata*) or dry land terrapin was common everywhere, and its shell was at least occasionally used for cups, containers, or in making rattles. The common snapper (*Chelydra serpentina*), the soft shell (*Trionyx*), and the painted turtle (*Chrysemys*) were characteristic forms in the watercourses everywhere.

Food Potential of Insects

The possible role of insects in the subsistence economies of the Plains Indians is impossible to assess with the information now at hand. That some of these creatures were present in impressive numbers seems clear, for example, grasshoppers, ants, and wasps. Outside the Great Plains, as in the basin-plateau country and in northern California, these constituted an important food resource, not necessarily only as a last resort in the face of starvation. According to Steward (1938:34), among the foragers of the Great Basin region, "even insects were sometimes of great importance. In some years grasshoppers and 'Mormon crickets' were extremely abundant and could be taken in quantities that would last for months." Among the Maidu of northern California, Dixon (1905:184) observed that "yellow jacket larvae were, however, eagerly sought as were also angleworms. Grasshoppers, locusts, and crickets were highly esteemed, and in their dried condition were much used in trade." In northern California generally, according to Kroeber (1925:84, 814), the Indians "did not scruple to eat earthworms, grasshoppers, hymenopterous larvae, certain species of caterpillars, and similar invertebrates when they could be gathered in sufficient masses to make their consumption worthwhile."

In the Great Plains, widely stereotyped as the land of the buffalo, the historic Indians since the days of white contact seem to have made little or no

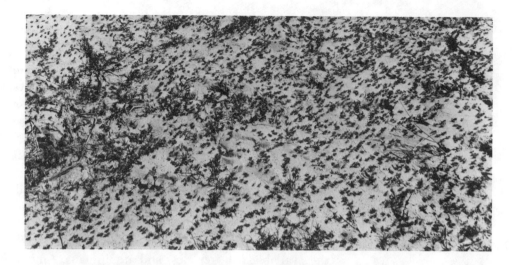

Plate 2.8. Insect depredations in the Republican River basin. *Upper,* the long-winged grasshopper of the plains (*Dissosteira longipennis*) migrating during the heat of midday, western Nebraska. *Lower,* cornfield devastated by grasshoppers, in Marshall County, Kansas. Photographs courtesy Nebraska State Historical Society.

known use of insects as food. One can perhaps imagine their being occasionally driven to such *in extremis,* if and when other more common meat or vegetable foods failed. In earlier days, among the Archaic foragers and even the Early Big Game Hunters, the search for food may have involved a much wider spectrum, and appetites were probably less squeamish than those of most white observers today (Freimuth and LaBerge 1976). Their seasonal abundance is certainly beyond question and would make them a useful food resource (see plate 2.8).

What is becoming increasingly evident is the fact that the potential food value of insects has been ignored much too long by archeologists. Since insects usually leave very few or no bony or chitinous remains for recovery in the field, they are not likely to have been observed in work carried on using older methods preceding the days of "total recovery." The meager but suggestive evidence so far turned up by archeologists on insects and ancient man's quest for food in the plains will be considered in chapter four.

Meanwhile, experimental and analytical work on insects in Mexico, in a search for protein sources to replace the increasingly costly beef, pork, and other common Western protein foods, has produced some interesting results. Concentrating on insects of species currently widely used among the poorer human groups in Mexico, researchers have ascertained that certain insects yield, when dried, far more protein, pound for pound, than either beef or pork. Thus Eerde (1980–1981:8) reports, "Dried grasshoppers are 60% protein, cicada 72%, and wasps 81%," compared to cooked pork at 29.4 percent, and cooked beef at 19.7 percent, the latter roughly equivalent to dried ants at 20.4 percent. All but two of the insect species tested contained more than the required standards of amino acids set by the Food and Agricultural Organization of the United Nations.

Game and Prewhite Hunting

Early Euro-American explorers in many parts of the Great Plains repeatedly testified to the abundance of game and its ready availability to the hunter before white settlement and prior to large-scale agriculture and water-control programs. As early as 1598, Vicente de Zaldivar Mendoza, exploring the bison plains eastward from Pecos, marveled at the numbers of "wild cattle" and at the way "they roamed so close to the tents and the houses"; and in 1601, Juan de Oñate commented that the bison were "so tame that unless chased or frightened, they stood still and did not run away" (Hammond and Rey 1953:401, 749). In 1805, when the Lewis and Clark expedition was ascending the Missouri River in present Montana, observers noted that the bison were so tame and inoffensive that the land party opened its way through the herds by throwing sticks and other missiles at the animals. Lt. John C. Frémont's westbound expedition of 1843, traveling from the upper Republican to the South Platte in present northeastern Colorado, "passed through many thousand buffalo, the whole country being perfectly black with them. They would just open a lane, as it were, for us to pass through, and then immediately close up behind. They are unusually tame, not having been disturbed for some time. On getting wind of us they would run off two or three miles and then stop to feed again" (Talbot 1931:16; plate 2.5).

On the middle Missouri in 1868, Henry Boller (1868:128) complained that hunting the innumerable wild fowl was "like shooting into a flock of barnyard fowl." Six years later, when George A. Custer led the Seventh Cavalry on a reconnaissance of the Black Hills from Fort Abraham Lincoln near Bismarck, North Dakota, the naturalist accompanying the expedition, George Bird Grinnell, noted that ducks and geese were nesting on practically every pond between the Missouri River and the Black Hills; Canada geese were "abundant on the small streams between the Missouri and Little Missouri . . . in families of from 10 to 14 individuals . . . [and mallards were] very numerous in the same localities and under the same conditions" (Ludlow 1875:101; see also Hind 1859:46, 47).

Such abundance of game birds and animals, and their apparent fearlessness before man began to employ firearms and horses in hunting them by brass band tactics, was probably not new on the Great Plains. The procurement of an adequate and balanced meat supply may not always have been attended by the difficulties and uncertainties commonly envisioned by some present-day observers.

Minerals

Mineral resources of varying significance were also conveniently available to the native residents of the Republican River basin. Of first importance among those in the manufacture of chipped stone implements—projectile points, hide scrapers, cutting and chopping tools, and so on—was the distinctive yellowish to brown Graham jasper (Cragin 1896:51). Red, green, and black variants are not uncommon, occurring sometimes as multicolored bands in a lens an inch (25 mm) or so thick, with or without the yellows (Carlson and Peacock 1975). Often referred to as Alma or Republican River or Smoky Hill jasper, this is a silicified chalk peculiar to the upper beds of the Smoky Hill chalk in the Cretaceous Niobrara formation. In the field, it is apparently restricted to those areas of the Smoky Hill chalk where the Tertiary Ogallala directly overlies the Smoky Hill, from which it is normally separated by the Pierre shale. Silicification in the Smoky Hill beds is thought to have come about through leaching and redeposition from silica-laden groundwaters percolating downward from volcanic ash beds in the immediately overlying Ogallala (Frye and Swineford 1946:56–60; Miller et al. 1964:10).

On many of the small creeks tributary to the Republican from Webster County, Nebraska, west as far as McCook, north along the Medicine Creek and its branches, and south into Kansas on the Beaver, Sappa, and Prairie Dog creeks, Graham jasper occurs in thin strata sandwiched between layers of white or yellow chalk or as nodules of widely varying sizes and chipping quality. Although indisputable evidence of aboriginal quarrying operations has not yet been reported in print, the great number of artifacts and working debris of Graham jasper is convincing indication of the ready accessibility of essentially unlimited quantities of the stone throughout much of the area where it is recognizable today in surface exposures or as barely subsurface ledges in commercial quarry pits. The area of known occurrence includes the Smoky Hill River and many of its tributaries in north central Kansas (plates 2.9 and 2.10).

At outcrops four miles (6.5 km) east of Norton, Kansas, now mostly obliterated by road construction, the jasper nodules were associated with a soft, easily worked whitish, pink, or yellowish chalk suitable for carving stone pipes and as a source of pigment. At Norton, on the north side of Prairie Dog Creek valley, the jasper was once extensively quarried for commercial purposes (Logan 1897:220). The abandoned quarries have been filled in long since and obliterated by recent housing developments, but samples taken from the old tailings show much good chippable material. Native workshops and chipping stations have been located near these and other exposures north and south of Norton, suggesting extensive utilization of the outcrops.

Other locations that deserve further scientific investigation for aboriginal quarrying and working operations include southern Norton County, Kansas; Dutch Creek in southern Furnas County, Nebraska, where jasper nodules can be found in abundance in the creek bed or are easily dug out of the alluvial

Plate 2.9. Jasper deposits in the Republican River valley. *Upper,* Graham jasper and pipestone quarry east of Norton, Kansas, on Prairie Dog Creek in 1930. Road construction has obliterated this feature; *lower,* Graham jasper quarry near Norton, Kansas, on Prairie Dog Creek in 1904. Courtesy Nebraska State Historical Society.

Plate 2.10. Jasper and shell debris, Republican River valley, Nebraska. *Upper,* fragmented Graham jasper in the bed of Dutch Creek, Furnas County, Nebraska; *lower,* discarded mussel shells from an Upper Republican cache pit, Medicine Creek reservoir.

banks nearby; the Medicine Creek reservoir (Harry Strunk Lake) district in Frontier County, Nebraska; and the beds of many small tributaries whose chalky bottoms at times of low water could be worked for the thin seams of jasper, one-quarter to an inch (6–25 mm) thick, as reported long ago at Lost Creek in Franklin County, Nebraska (Strong 1935:87).

Much less frequently utilized by the native toolmakers was a green quartzite of Tertiary (Ogallala?) age, which was available at many points in southern Harlan and Franklin counties and west to Furnas and Frontier counties. Varying in color from olive-green to greenish gray and weathering to a dull whitish green, this is a hard, durable stone that was once quarried in large amounts near Woodruff, Kansas, for crushed rock, paving blocks, and riprap (Barbour 1913). More recently, it has been extensively used at Medicine Creek Dam for riprap. To the Indians, it was useful for large scrapers and chopping tools, but it was apparently unsuited for smaller scrapers, projectile points, and knives whose effectiveness depended upon their amenability to fine secondary retouching. The likelihood that this quartzite was quarried on a small scale by Indians at an outcrop east of Cambridge, at the junction of Medicine Creek and the Republican River, remains unverified, and the location of other possible native workings has apparently not been established.

In Republic and Cloud counties, Kansas, where the Republican has carved its valley into Cretaceous formations, there are several saline marshes and creeks that were extensively utilized by 19th-century white settlers to obtain table salt (Fishel 1948:16). Tuthill Marsh, nine miles (14 km) northeast of Concordia, was a principal source of domestic salt more than a century ago. Here, and 20 miles (32 km) to the west, at Salt Marsh Creek northwest of Jamestown, the salinity of the emerging ground waters was calculated early at three times that of ocean water. This was sufficient to prevent growth of vegetation and also to leave on the ground surface a renewable crust of salt that could be easily harvested. From these residues, by simple processes of evaporation, a usable household product was obtained. Tuthill Marsh yielded a bushel (35 l) of salt per 130 gallons (490 l) of brine. These salines, like other salt marshes in the state, were extensively drawn upon by hunters and by pioneers in processing meat (Logan 1897:209; Parker 1911:45; see figure 9.1).

The salt marshes in the lower Republican basin are shown on maps at least as early as the time of Lewis and Clark. On the lost Clark map of 1805, copied by Nicholas King in 1805 and 1806 (Moulton 1983: maps 32*a,b,c,* and p. 9), there is a "Salt Creek" entering the river from the west side, which has two clusters of dots on its lower course that apparently represent salines. On the Clark map of 1810 (Moulton 1983: map 125 and pp. 12, 19), the dotted salt symbols, so designated, are shown on a "Salt Creek" that joins the river from the east. The latter presumably represents the Tuthill locality, the former, the Jamestown salines.

There is no archeological, ethnographical, or historical documentation, so far as I am aware, that the Indians locally made similar use of these salines. With a substantial proportion—perhaps 50 percent or more—of their normal diet consisting of bison meat and other game, the Indians, either semihorticultural or nonhorticultural, may have felt no strong need to add sodium to their usual dietary intake. They could have been drawn to the salines, however, in pursuit of the bison and other large herbivores that must have gathered there from time to time to lick salt (see Tixier, 1839–1840 in McDermott, ed., 1940:224, n. 8, 240, 249–251). The bones of bison, deer, and antelope were reportedly found at various depths in the marsh alluvium by early white users of this important local resource. As appears to be the case at other bone-bearing salt licks, however, carnivore remains have not been reported from the Tuthill or Jamestown salt marshes. From this can perhaps be inferred that the predators, like the Indians, were able to fulfill their physiological requirements for sodium from the herbivores on whose flesh they preyed. (See also Brown 1980.)

Water: Surface and Subsurface

Although itself of secondary importance as a cross-country thoroughfare during the days of westward expansion by Euro-Americans, especially in comparison with the Platte valley to the north or the Smoky Hill–Kansas and Arkansas valleys to the south, the Republican had several notable advantages for residence from the viewpoint of native man. For one thing, throughout much of its course it was exceptionally well supplied with excellent water (Hay 1895; Condra 1907). In Colorado, the main valleys were cut mostly in permeable Tertiary and Quaternary silt, sand, and gravel deposits. In Nebraska and Kansas, they have been deepened through a thick blanket of loess and Tertiary beds to reach the underlying impervious Cretaceous chalk and sandstone formations. Tertiary materials include the Ogallala formation, whose western outcrop limits in Colorado coincide rather well with those of the Republican drainage, except in Kit Carson County.

Long recognized as one of the nation's outstanding aquifers, the Ogallala collects its waters from precipitation in the loess plains and in the sandhills north of the Republican valley. The accumulated groundwaters tend to move east and southeast, with the general slope of the land surface, appearing as springs and seeps wherever the dissected surface intersects the water table. Springs are, or formerly were, abundant and strong all along the north side of the Republican in Nebraska, particularly near the heads of the many tributaries, long and short, that enter the main valley at intervals of a few miles. Other fine springs were scattered along the upper reaches in Colorado, west on the South Fork to the vicinity of Flagler at longitude 103° west, on the Arikaree, and on some of the short ephemeral creeks whose courses disappeared in the poorly drained districts north of the North Fork Republican.

Over much of this westerly region, the surface stream flow diminishes sharply or disappears entirely into the deep sand beds during the heat of midsummer. Here, water could often be found by the knowledgeable wayfarer with a bit of digging in the sand. Alternate dry and running stretches are characteristic of many of these watercourses, and this behavior is enhanced today by the greatly intensified use of pump irrigation. By withdrawing groundwater in marked excess of its recharge rate (Boettcher 1966:119; Lappala 1976), irrigation in the past decade or two has significantly lowered the water table. This depletion of water has reached the point where many springs have dried up or now run at greatly reduced volume and there is only intermittent stream flow even during the nonirrigation season.

Away from the streams and valley margin springs, surface water was obtainable for native man only in the numerous undrained ponds scattered widely over the uplands west of the 100th meridian. Commonly termed *buffalo wallows*, these varied in diameter from a few tens to several thousands of yards, and the larger and deeper ones sometimes formed more or less permanent water holes. In presettlement days, when rainfall patterns possibly differed from today's, these were favorite spots for bison attracted further by the lush grass and for water fowl, whether nesting or gathering for seasonal migrations (Frémont 1845:110; Bryan 1857:469). For prehorse Indians, the spacing of water holes at intervals of one or two days' travel by camp groups on foot greatly expanded the hunting territory available (Wedel 1963), including the now almost dry section between the North Fork Republican and Frenchman Creek.

Rainfall and Its Variability

For the commercially oriented crop-grower and the stockman of today, perhaps the most critical factor in the Great Plains climate is the amount and distribution of precipitation. The cold dry winters leave little stored moisture in the ground, with the result that growing crops and the native vegetation depend heavily on rainfall during the spring and early summer growing season. On balance, this situation is more or less favorable, since about 70 percent or more of the annual precipitation usually falls between April and September. If this came regularly and was evenly distributed, the crop-grower's problems would be minimized. Unfortunately, wide extremes of temperature and precipitation are the rule rather than the exception in this region, as Smith (1925:413) noted: "Averages do not tell the whole story. Averages rarely happen. The freaks of the season decide man's chances." The annual precipitation ranges widely from less than half to twice the long term average or more, often euphemistically called "normal." Below and above average rainfall often occurs more or less simultaneously in areas that may be only a few miles apart within the region. These fluctuations are reflected in runoff and stream flow.

The regional variability in rainfall is well illustrated by the long-term shifts in location of the 20-inch (500 mm) isohyet (Wedel 1953). Normally, this line roughly parallels the 100th meridian, as does the 8-inch (200 mm) summer (June to August) rainfall line, and both bisect the Republican River basin. West of this line, or the north-south zone in which it lies, growing corn without irrigation or other specialized techniques is a high-risk venture. In the very wet year of 1915, the 20-inch isohyet lay in northeastern Colorado along the west end of the Republican basin, most of which enjoyed a rainfall total for the year approaching that ordinarily found in eastern Nebraska and western Iowa. At Fort Morgan, Colorado, the annual total was 26.5 inches (675 mm) compared to an 88-year average of about 14 inches (355 mm). The June to August precipitation that year totalled 9.5 inches (240 mm), approximately that expected at Kearney, Nebraska, or Russell, Kansas, 200 miles (320 km) to the east. Conversely, in the record drought of 1936, the climate usual to eastern Colorado and western Kansas spread into eastern Kansas. Clay Center on the lower Republican experienced precipitation of 17.8 inches (450 mm) versus a long-time average of 30.2 inches (765 mm), a 40 percent shortfall; summer rains produced a scant 3.5 inches (90 mm), nearly 35 percent below that usually received at Fort Morgan, 350 miles (560 km) to the west (fig. 2.5).

Since the average precipitation closely approaches the minimum required for successful corn growing without irrigation or special crop varieties, any marked deviation from the average is likely to be reflected in the productivity of fields and gardens. At longitude 99° to 100° west, a 15 percent deficiency in summer rainfall may reduce the corn yield from unirrigated fields by 30 to 40 percent; a 40 percent deficiency may result in essentially no crop at all. A year or two of subaverage rainfall is thus likely to reduce crop yields drastically; a prolonged drought or a series of droughts like those during the 1930s can be catastrophic for crops and forage production alike over a wide region.

These problems are further complicated by the fact that rainfall deficits are often accompanied by hot dry winds that draw strongly from the south and may persist for days. These sharply increase the evaporation rate, which is high even in so-called normal years. Within a few hours, such conditions may inflict

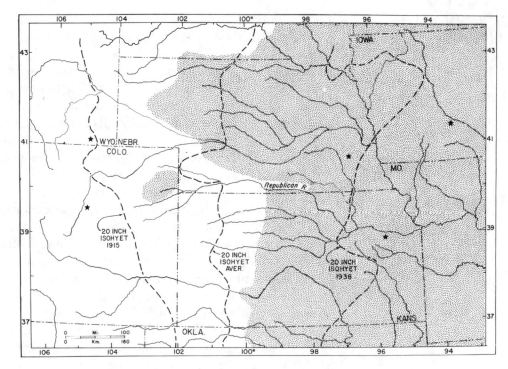

Fig. 2.5. Map of the central plains showing fluctuations in regional rainfall averages and generalized native vegetation areas. *Broken lines* indicate 20-inch (500 mm) annual precipitation in wet (1915), average, and dry (1936) years. *Stippled*, tall-grass prairies; *unstippled*, short-grass steppe. Vegetation after *Atlas of American Agriculture*, 1936; precipitation from *Climatic Summary of the United States*, Weather Bureau, 1930. See United States Department of Agriculture.

irreparable damage to tasseling corn. Nor is the native vegetation immune to these adversities; a lush green grassland can be seared within hours or days by incessant hot winds. As the experience of the 1930s has dramatically shown, this means that stock-growers may experience disastrous losses through sharp reductions in the density and depth of grass cover, lowered carrying capacity, and the resultant need to greatly reduce the number of animals fed per acre or hectare.

Rainfall deficiencies do not affect all portions of the plains simultaneously and to the same degree, nor need they be of regional magnitude to affect man's welfare. The summer rains occur characteristically as thunder storms, commonly of short duration but frequently of great violence. Downpours may exceed in a few hours the average precipitation for the month in which they occur; and, particularly in the Republican headwaters region, they may be accompanied by violent winds, devastating hailstorms, and tornadoes. The storms are mostly local, following short, erratic courses that may leave one small strip drenched while surrounding areas receive little or no effective moisture. In dry years, this pattern can bring about considerable variations in crop yields and forage production among localities that normally share essentially identical climates according to meteorological statistics. Such local rainfall deficits are usually short lived, of one- or two-years duration, and are not uncommonly offset by excess the next year or two. Thus, their impact on peoples or communities depending on cereal crops is far less disastrous than are the major regional droughts and the general crop failures that result from them.

The summer rains commonly appear in the late afternoon or early evening and pursue relatively narrow paths from west to east across the countryside. At their finest, they provide the observer with one of the more awesome spectacles in nature. They are often preceded by oppressively high daytime temperatures, persistent light southerly winds, and a leisurely flow of puffy cumulus clouds beginning in the forenoon. As the day progresses, these mass in the northwest or west, developing eventually into the familiar anvil form—flat, spreading, and white on top, and an ominous, deepening blue-black underneath, all piled to thousands of feet above the earth. From the approaching storm issues the mutter of distant thunder, and jagged streaks of lightning flash from cloud to cloud or from cloud to earth. Night storms are heralded by sheet lightning winking on the western skyline, spreading eventually to cover the northwest quadrant of the heavens. The rain, perhaps preceded by an outrush of wind, begins with large, pelting drops and increases to a heavy downpour, often accompanied or followed by hail. As the storm passes overhead, lightning plays uninterruptedly and the rumble of thunder rises in an ear-splitting crescendo. If the rain persists for several hours, falling perhaps at the rate of an inch or more an hour, disastrous overflows of low-lying areas may be generated and the hail can ruin crops and seriously damage other property. Usually the disturbance passes within an hour, to be followed in daytime by clearing skies, sunshine, a cooled atmosphere, and a refreshed countryside. From the receding storm in the east the murmur of thunder can still be heard, while the towering cloud mass glows pink in the soft light of the setting sun.

Floods and Their Aftermath

Floods, like droughts, are a recurring feature of the central plains region, and their behavior directly and indirectly influences human use of the valley bottomlands. In this respect, too, there is great variation. Dry years usually, but not invariably, mean prolonged low water stages, at which time any remaining stream flow is maintained by abundant springs whose output percolates through the sandy beds. At Superior, Nebraska, past which the Republican funnels the runoff from approximately 22,000 square miles (57,000 sq km), the estimated monthly discharge rate from March through November for the years 1896–1906, prior to dam construction upstream, varied from 2,600 to 352,000 acre-feet, or between 1,300 and 176,000 cubic feet per second (Stevens 1909:198).[3] The mean discharge rate approximated 50,000 acre-feet per month. This is approximately one-twelfth the discharge rate calculated for the Platte River at Columbus, Nebraska, which has a very much larger runoff area.

Floods on the Republican occur mainly during the spring and early summer. At such times, the stream overflows its characteristically low channel banks and expands to cover large sections of the valley floor, causing great damage to property and often threatening the well-being and personal safety of residents. Like the droughts to date, floods come at irregular and unpredictable intervals. Since white settlement began in the 1870s, major floods have been recorded in 1903, 1915, 1923, and 1935. Some were the expected results of unusually heavy and widespread rains, such as those in 1915. Others were the aftermath of more restricted but still inordinately heavy downpours.

Illustrative is the flood of 1935, generally rated the greatest on record for the Republican River. This occurred in the midst of the decade of the most severe drought known for the central plains. It resulted from torrential rains in northeastern Colorado, where the fall was heaviest in localities not served by rain gauges. For example, at Newton, Colorado, the site of which is now covered by Bonny Reservoir on the South Fork Republican, the precipitation was calculated at 24 inches (610 mm) during a 24-hour period. Over a 1,000 square-mile (2,590 sq km) area of the upper river basin, the average rainfall was approximately nine inches (230 mm). At Cambridge, Nebraska, on 31 May through 1 June, these downpours produced a river crest of 380,000 cubic feet per second (Furness 1955:93). On 2 June, the river peaked at Hardy, Nebraska, a few miles below Superior, at 225,000 cfs. Less than 24 hours later, the fast-traveling flood waters crested at Clay Center, Kansas, 103 miles (165 km) downstream (Flora 1948:281). Here the discharge rate was 195,000 cfs on 3 June; only ten months before, on 9–11 August of the very dry year of 1934, the rate was 1 cfs. In Kansas, the floodwaters covered an estimated 125 square miles (325 sq km), and 110 lives were lost in the entire basin.

On a smaller scale, but hardly less spectacular, are the inundations that sometimes occur on the tributaries. Notable overflows occurred on the Frenchman in 1928, on Red Willow Creek in 1909, 1910, 1935, and 1947, on Beaver Creek in 1905, and on Sappa Creek in 1944. A dramatic example is Medicine Creek, which is of direct interest because of its demonstrated record of occupation by semisedentary Indians as well as by hunter-gatherer groups throughout a very long period of time.

On 24 June 1900, the discharge rate for Medicine Creek at Cambridge was reported as 24.5 cfs and that for the Republican River at the same point was 72 cfs (Stevens 1909:212). In June 1947, large sections of the Medicine Creek subbasin, 1,070 square miles (2,270 sq km) in extent, experienced excessively heavy rainfall, again climaxing in localities without adequate gauging stations. At Curtis, the June rainfall total was reported as 9.1 inches (230 mm) compared to a 78-year average of 3.86 inches (98 mm) for that month. Elsewhere in the subbasin, rainfall exceeded 10 inches (255 mm) between 6 P.M. and midnight on June 21. On 22 June, the discharge rate at Cambridge was calculated at 120,000 cfs or 2.75 acre-feet (Furness 1955:92). A wall of water reported as 10 to 12 feet (3.3–3.6 m) high swept down the valley and through the town, destroying bridges, bottomland farm buildings, roads, and crops, uprooting trees (plate 2.11), and covering farmlands with thick layers of silt and sand. Lesser floods occurred simultaneously on Red Willow and other neighboring creeks. The United States Bureau of Reclamation reacted early to the Cambridge disaster by promptly initiating the construction of the Medicine Creek Dam and reservoir (Harry Strunk Lake).

Concerning earlier floods in the Republican River basin, such as the inundation of 1826 said to be remembered in Indian legends, I have found no independent confirmation. It is likely that such events took place in Indian days, as well as later in localities where they went unnoticed by officials and unrecorded by instruments despite grave consequences to local populations (Bowman 1972:3). We can only guess at the Indian reaction. The known historic Indian villages, such as the Hill and Kansas Monument sites, were situated on high ground, well beyond reach of any conceivable flooding. Most Upper Republican village sites are also on terraces or on the nearby bluff tops, and

Plate 2.11. Flood effects in the Republican valley. *Upper,* Medicine Creek below future dam site after flood of 21–22 June 1946, showing channel erosion and damage to trees. Flood crest is indicated by flotsam lodged against tree at extreme right, above the heads of the men. *Lower,* secondary creek in flood, showing silting of overflowed valley bottoms; village terrace in background beyond trees.

their inhabitants would not have been directly affected by high waters. The Village Indians, that is to say, avoided the lowlands for their permanent residence and stayed on the flood-free locations.

On the other hand, bottomland gardens located to take advantage of mellow soils and lingering ground moisture would have been subject to damage or destruction by stream overflows. The nature and extent of such damage would depend in part on the violence and magnitude of the flood. The resulting losses could have been mitigated by replanting if the season was not too far advanced. The silts and organic debris deposited may have helped to maintain or restore the waning fertility of the soil where the flats were not overwhelmed by sand. Trees torn from their streamside moorings and deadwood brought down by the high waters would have contributed much useful firewood to the fuel supply of the Indians, and perhaps some building materials as well.

For less permanent residents of the stream valleys, such as the earlier Woodland and Archaic hunters and gatherers operating on a seasonal basis as various resources became available locally, the inundations might have been more unsettling. Fishing and mussel-gathering stations could have been seriously affected, with the fin fish washed away for a time, the shellfish smothered by silt and sand, and the various habitats generally disrupted. Rodents and other small mammals living along the banks and on the low bottoms, and ground-nesting birds, were potential victims of the flood waters. The disordering of established vegetation patterns and in certain details of the landforms could also have affected the feeding habits and movements of the larger land mammals. Damage to fruit-bearing shrubs and small berry trees would have affected the harvest of fruits and berries for the human groups as well. The briefly occupied seasonal camps on the bottoms and lower terraces, usually safe during the dry summers and winters, were subject to either (a) burial by sediments from the spring floods; (b) stripping of much of their contained cultural leavings, garbage, and the like; or (c) complete removal by erosion. If campsites were buried by sediments or stripped of their contents, especially through repeated episodes, they might become successive stages in a stratigraphic sequence.

Whatever their fate, the discovery of seasonal camps centuries or millennia later by archeologists on survey has been made much more difficult where there has been no bank erosion, gullying, or other scarring of the valley fill to expose the buried soil and occupation levels in a stratigraphic context. This obscuring of evidence from the older and more transitory human occupations, in contrast to the relatively higher visibility of the later Village Indian sites, has quite possibly influenced archeological interpretations of the meager clues that have become available from time to time.

Chapter 3 Climates and Weather of the Past

We do not yet know when man's occupation of the Great Plains began. The accumulating evidence in various disciplines indicates that it was probably well over 10,000 years ago, perhaps twice that figure, or even more. In any event, it appears certain that the landscape viewed by the earliest native Americans here, though perhaps already a grassland or open savanna, was not the same "sea of grass" that greeted the first Euro-American explorers in the mid-16th century, the major characteristics of which have been broadly outlined in the foregoing pages. Plants, animals, and especially the climate that so dramatically influences life in the Great Plains grassland were all in many respects different from the patterns in the recent past with which the white man has become familiar. Since the human adventure in the region clearly involves a time span of some thousands of years, note must be taken here of some of the salient features of the past environmental setting as this is being interpreted and slowly reconstructed from various lines of evidence.

The evidence comes largely from molluscan, mammalian, and other fossil remains of ancient life forms that have been preserved at widely scattered localities in the Kansas–Nebraska–eastern Colorado region and beyond. Many of these are related to living forms. Since the habitat requirements of the living representatives of these animal and plant categories or taxa are known, it is presumably possible to make inferences regarding the probable nature of the environment in which the extinct forms lived. Thus, for example, fossil snail shells from more than 200 sites scattered throughout Kansas reveal the existence of a comparatively rich and varied molluscan fauna throughout most of the Pleistocene, including assemblages of more than 30 species, many of them associated with gallery forest along streams (Frye and Leonard 1967:435).

About 12,000 years ago, a marked change in climatic conditions seems to have taken place, resulting in the deposition of what is known as Brady soil and in a drastic impoverishment of the molluscan fauna in numbers of both species and individuals. The forms that survived—"no more than a half dozen species"—consist largely of species noted for their ability to survive long dry periods and extreme temperatures with wide seasonal contrasts (Taylor 1960). From this and other evidence, it has been inferred that a drying climate has characterized the region since late Pleistocene times (Frye and Leonard 1952:166–180), probably with alternate wet and dry interludes of varying length and intensity. Nothing in the post-Bradyan molluscan fauna indicates a general forest cover comparable to that characterizing the deciduous woodlands east of the Great Plains in historic times. Instead, the late and recent

39

assemblages suggest dry grassy uplands, with belts of trees and shrubs along the watercourses more or less in the pattern of the last half millennium.

Whereas fossil animal remains, including both vertebrates and invertebrates, are relatively abundant, the plant fossils that would provide particularly useful insights into the environments in which they flourished have been found in only a very few localities and are widely scattered, particularly in the central plains. Nevertheless, intensified and expanded pollen studies, correlated with radiometric, geological, and climatological data, have provided further glimpses into the probable nature of the Great Plains landscape during the past 12,000 to 15,000 years and more.

The Pollen Evidence

The usefulness of pollen analysis, or palynology, rests on the fact that many trees and other plants produce and shed pollen that can be microscopically identified as a particular genus and sometimes even species; that the pollen grains are commonly scattered in large quantities by wind; and that they may settle in bog or lake sediments, where they are protected from oxidation and may be preserved for centuries and even millennia. These minute fossils provide important clues to the kinds of plants that were growing in the vicinity at the time of deposition, including upland sites as well as the nearby bog or lakeshore. The varying proportions of different pollens from level to level in a stratified archeological, paleontological, or geological soils column are then interpreted in terms of the changing vegetational assemblages, and from this may be inferred the nature of the climates that brought about those changes. If the vegetational changes can be dated by radiocarbon or other "precise" methods, the approximate time of the vegetational changes can be estimated.

A notable exception to the general dearth of significant pollen profiles in the central plains is the Muscotah spring bog some 80 miles (128 km) east of the Republican River, in Atchison County, Kansas. Lying near the eastern edge of the once-continuous grassland, this is still within the original bluestem tallgrass prairie region and about 25 miles (40 km) west of the Missouri River. The site presents a pollen profile through some 32 feet (9.75 m) of accumulated vegetal material, beginning more than 25,000 radiocarbon years ago. Data have indicated that at that time there was an open boreal spruce forest including some pine, with oak, ash, elm, and other deciduous forms on the uplands, and local stands of willow and alder on the floodplain (Grüger 1973). By 24,500 years B.P. (before the present), the dominant spruce fossils included not only pollen but also needles, twigs, cones, and other debris. Between 16,000 and 12,000 years ago, when the Des Moines lobe of the continental ice sheet still stood at its maximum southward extension in present central Iowa, 150 miles (240 km) from Muscotah, this forest stretched from Iowa and Missouri across northeastern Kansas into Nebraska and the Dakotas (Wright 1970; King 1980). Its southernmost limits remain unspecified, but they may have been not far south of Muscotah. There is no evidence of tundra between the ice front and the spruce forest, though a narrow strip may have been present.

About 12,000 years ago, the spruce forest edge began to withdraw northward, giving way in the Muscotah area to a temperate deciduous upland forest in which oak, elm, ash, hickory, and black walnut were represented. Cattail (*Typha*) and fern pollens are common, indicating marshy conditions. Also present are remains of duckweed (*Lemna*), pondweed (*Potamogeton*), water lily

(*Nymphaea*), arrowhead (*Sagittaria*), bulrush (Scirpus), and sedges (*Cyperaceae*). The decreasing amounts of pollen originating in wetland or moist communities and the increasing incidence of such prairie indicators as sunflower (*Helianthus*), ragweed (*Ambrosia*), pigweed (*Chenopodium*), and others in the higher levels indicate a continuing trend toward a drier climate. If men roamed these primordial forest margins and parklands, there is not yet clear and convincing evidence of that fact from the Kansas-Nebraska region.

Farther west, under a precipitation regime heavier than today's, the present short-grass steppe appears to have been a tree-dotted mid- to tall-grass savanna, sprinkled with lakes and ponds and streaked with timbered watercourses, in late glacial and early postglacial time. In place of the teeming herds of "wild cattle" that greeted the first wandering European invaders ten millennia later, there were mammoth; such ruminants as the camel, native horse, ground sloth, and large bison; along with peccary and other species known to us only by their fossil remains. The accumulating evidence suggests, but does not yet prove, that for a time man may have been associated with these animals at their watering places around the ponds and lakes in what are now the High Plains of eastern Colorado.

By perhaps 10,000 years ago, the upland hardwood forest at Muscotah had been replaced by prairie vegetation, probably with trees along the streams. Floodplain stands included hickory, walnut, oak, elm, ash, and maple. The lower incidence of cattail, fern, and sedge pollens suggests the drying out of the floodplain over large areas. Regionally, the northeastward advance of grasslands at the expense of woodlands continued, taking place 1,000 or 2,000 years later at stations studied north and northeast of Kansas. Chronologically, this marked vegetational change appears to have occurred not far from the time of the major climatic shift thought by some (Frye and Leonard 1952) to have brought on the final stage in the desiccation of the plains and the onset of the "semiarid climate of modern time." The mid- and tall grasses were probably yielding in the west to short grasses as dryness and higher temperatures intensified. In post-Bradyan time, a biologically severe climate set in, "characterized by extremes of aridity and high temperatures in summer, followed by cold, dry winters"—in essence, a climate basically much like that in the region today. The postulated climatic shift between 10,000 and 12,000 years ago appears to have coincided rather well with the archeological transition from Clovis to Folsom occupations in the far western and southwestern plains.

The Muscotah sequence ends with a sharply increased proportion of ragweed and pigweed, a decrease in tree pollens, and an increase in maize pollen. These are taken as indicators of large-scale agriculture, which began here within the last 150 years. As elsewhere, this has brought about drastic vegetational shifts as a direct consequence of Euro-American man's intervention in nature's regime.

To what extent the pollen record at Muscotah and the inferred vegetational and climatic implications can be applied to the Republican River basin remains uncertain. There are no bogs or other known deposits of plant fossils along the Republican in which the nature of the upland and floodplain vegetation has been recorded throughout Holocene time. Insofar as archeological excavations to date have thrown any light on past conditions, they indicate no significant alteration of the plant cover within the past two millennia or thereabouts, other than the changes induced by the white man's clearing and soil-turning activities. For older archeological associations, there are still no systematically developed and trustworthy data from which valid conclusions or inferences may be drawn. That the changes manifested at Muscotah reflect phenomena widespread throughout the central plains seems very probable, and further field researches will undoubtedly be rewarding if properly done.

It has long been recognized that the frequent and sometimes catastrophic climatic oscillations of the documented recent past in the western United States have analogues in the prehistoric past. It is not surprising, then, that computer-assisted statistical studies by climatologists in the Midwest and elsewhere, utilizing quantitative and qualitative pollen analyses and a wealth of radiocarbon dates, have resulted in the partial delineation of a series of late Pleistocene and post-Pleistocene climatic episodes (Baerreis and Bryson 1965; Bryson and Wendland 1967; Bryson et al. 1970; Wendland 1978). With varying success, these have been provisionally correlated with changing biotic assemblages and with cultural events in the northern Great Plains (for example, Lehmer 1970) and on their periphery in northwestern Iowa (Baerreis and Bryson 1967). That the major episodes so identified, provisionally dated, and broadly characterized were nevertheless subject to year-to-year and decade-to-decade variations must be borne in mind as a very strong probability. So, too, should the fact that not all climatologists agree on these paleoclimatological events as reported in the literature. Nevertheless, within the time span that now appears probable for man's presence in the Republican River basin, the postulated climatic episodes and their estimated dates in table 3.1 are of current interest and suggested applicability. They are based on Bryson and Wendland (1967), Wendland and Bryson (1974), Wendland (1978), Bryson and Padoch (1980), and Wendland and Kosobud (n.d.).

Note that the climatic episodes in the table tend to become progressively shorter with recency. This may be in part because better and more detailed records are available, records that have not yet been blurred by the passage of time as have the older episodes. Too, the chronological controls are better in more recent times and make possible a finer-grained interpretation, together with more precise dating through other techniques. A stimulating discussion of problems and prospects can be found in Bryson and Padoch (1980).

Tree Rings and Droughts

One record of great potential usefulness for paleoclimatological determinations comes from the annual growth rings of trees, particularly for the last thousand years. Besides providing a means for measuring the age of a tree, the relative width or thickness of a ring supplies clues to the amount of moisture available when and where the tree was growing. Tree rings have long been used in the southwestern United States not only to determine the time of occupation of a particular structure or camp site but also to reconstruct the climate by the rainfall implied.

The Great Plains are a largely treeless region except along many of the streams and the broken upland margins. Trees along streams and in valley bottoms are usually less dependent on rainfall than upland forest trees, and their rings are usually less variable in width, that is, they are more complacent. In the central plains, tree ring counts extending into the prehistoric past have been developed only for the lower North Platte River district. Running back

Table 3.1
Provisional chronology and some postulated features of Late Pleistocene and
Holocene climates of the Great Plains

Full Glacial	Cooler summers and probably milder winters than at present; boreal forest widespread throughout the northern plains and as far south as Kansas. . . . . to ca. 13,000 B.P.
Late Glacial	Summers probably cooler, winters warmer and less severe than present; retreat of boreal forest to the northeast well underway, while grasslands expand; mean temperatures a few degrees Celsius cooler than now. . . . . to ca. 10,800 B.P. (8850 B.C.)
Pre-Boreal	Continued expansion of grasslands toward the northeast at expense of boreal spruce forest. Beginning of Holocene at ca. 10,870 years B.P. . . . . to ca. 9530 B.P. (7580 B.C.)
Boreal	Abrupt shift in pollen spectra from northern plains at ca. 9,500 B.P. marks replacement of spruce by expanding grassland. Probable change in atmospheric circulation patterns, followed by rapid wasting of continental ice sheet. Ice-free north-south corridor opening along east front of Rocky Mountains. Climate increasingly continental in nature, with warmer summers but colder winters. . . . . to ca. 7900 B.P. (5950 B.C.)
Atlantic	The Altithermal interlude. Stronger westerlies, with drier and/or warmer climate than today; increased frequency of Pacific air results in substantial warming and drying due to Rocky Mountain rain shadow effect; intense desiccation of the plains; mostly a warm episode in central North America, with grasslands well established in the Great Plains. . to ca. 5,000 B.P. (2900–3000 B.C.)
Sub-Boreal	Cooler in the northern plains. Desiccation and increase in grass pollen in western Nebraska. . . . . to ca. 2,900 B.P. (950 B.C.)
Sub-Atlantic	Summers considerably wetter, winters possibly stormier. . . . . to ca. 1,600 B.P. (A.D. 300–400)
Scandic	Return toward Atlantic conditions, warmer and probably drier on northern plains. . . . . to ca. 1225 B.P. (A.D. 700–750)
Neo-Atlantic	Continued warm but also moister; influx of tropical air to the plains, with increased summer rains in central and northern sectors. Prairies spread westward at expense of steppe. Tree pollen increases in western Nebraska at ca. 1,000 B.P. Maximum westward spread of aboriginal maize cultivation west of Missouri River; increasingly droughtlike conditions beginning at ca. A.D. 850 in northeastern plains. . . . . to ca. 800 B.P. (A.D. 1150–1200)
Pacific	Strengthening westerlies around A.D. 1200 bring seasonally dry air into the northern plains, with lower temperatures and decreased precipitation in central and northern parts; steppe conditions spread eastward as prairie retreats. Deteriorating climatic conditions lead to withdrawal of native horticultural peoples from western Nebraska and Kansas. . . . . to 400 B.P. (A.D. 1550)
Neo-Boreal	Colder and moister conditions, with cool summers, cold autumns; glaciers forming again in the Rockies, wetter in New Mexico. The Little Ice Age. . . . . to ca. 100 B.P. (A.D. 1883)
Recent	About 1883, strengthening westerlies resulted in drier and warmer conditions in the plains, ending the Little Ice Age and producing today's climate.

nearly to A.D. 1200, buried tree stumps in the vicinity of North Platte, about 60 miles (100 km) north of the Republican River at McCook and the same distance from the Medicine Creek archeological locality, provided the first solid clues. Further information has come from nonarcheological samples in other sections of western Nebraska. Besides testifying to the probability of tree growth that was once more widespread than has characterized the region since the coming of the white man, these support the notion of recurrent climatic vagaries in the past. Charcoal from Ash Hollow Cave, on the North Platte River some 70 miles (110 km) west of North Platte, has provided a continuous ring sequence to A.D. 1210, with four earlier floating sequences "whose order in time can be determined by the stratigraphy, but which are separated by gaps of unknown length" (Weakly 1946:106).

At North Platte during the 1930s, Weakly (1940, 1943, letter to Wedel, 7 March 1941) studied the growth rings in a number of red cedar (juniper) stumps that had been exposed by the erosion of wind-laid deposits in gullies and canyons. According to Weakly (1940:18):

> The larger trees cut by the early settlers ran from about 175 to over 200 years old. The buried trees predate these by many years, as in some cases they have been found beneath a substantial fill in old gully or canyon floors with the stumps of 200-year old trees in place in the soil many feet above them. At the level of the tops of these old buried trees there is a three to six inch layer of charcoal, and all those observed by the writer or reported to him show evidence of having burned off at the old level of the earth fill about them. . . . The annual rings on the buried wood from these localities indicate a period of over 30 years with deficient moisture. Apparently this drought contributed very largely to the death of these trees.

In his final published statement on the North Platte or Lincoln County situation, Weakly (1943:819) included a table showing the major droughts he had inferred from the tree rings and observed that:

> It is probable that during some of the protracted droughts of the past, the country approached an absolute desert in character, as in 1539–1564, when the heavy filling of canyons by wind-blown soil apparently took place. In all probability the native grass cover of the country was very largely destroyed and great dust storms were doubtless common.

Weakly's table, somewhat amplified and extended in time, is included here as table 3.2. The pre-1539 drought periods I have added, and the remarks, are from a handwritten list sent me by Weakly with his letter of 7 March 1941, and from a later table included by Bark (1978) and attributed to Weakly. Why the 15th-century droughts do not appear in the published paper, I do not know; conceivably, they were recognized after the manuscript had been submitted for publication. In any case, so far as I am aware, Weakly has nowhere repudiated those interpretations nor do I know of any considered challenge that has been made to them.

The dated North Platte droughts (table 3.2) have not been correlated with any of the archeological sites and culture complexes so far recognized in western or southwestern Nebraska. We do not know how widespread any of them were, or whether they or parallel droughts were experienced by native peoples

Table 3.2
Drought periods of 5 years or more, and periods between droughts, ca. A.D. 1200–1957, determined from annual growth rings of trees in western Nebraska

Drought periods of 5 years or more			Periods between droughts	
Dates	Number of years	Remarks	Dates	Number of years
1220–1231	12		1232–1259	27
1260–1272	13		1273–1275	3
1276–1313	38		1314–1382	68
1383–1388	6		1389–1437	48
1438–1455	18	Very dry	1456–1458	3
1459–1468	9	Very dry	1469–1471	3
1472–1477	6	Moderately dry	1478–1486	9
1487–1492	6		1493–1511	19
1512–1529	18		1530–1538	8
1539–1564	26	Very severe	1565–1586	22
1587–1605	18	Very severe except 1594–1596	1606–1625	20
1626–1630	5	Severe	1631–1667	36
1668–1675	8		1676–1687	12
1688–1707	20		1708–1727	20
1728–1732	5	Very severe	1733–1760	28
1761–1773	13		1774–1797	24
1798–1803	6	Extremely dry	1804–1821	18
1822–1832	11	Extremely dry	1833–1857	25
1858–1866	9	Very dry	1867–1879	13
1880–1895	16		1896–1905	10
1906–1912	7		1913–1930	18
1931–1939	9		1939–1952	11
1952–1957	6			

SOURCES: After Weakly (letter) 1941, 1943; Bark 1978.

in the nearby Republican River drainage. If they were as severe in some instances as Weakly suggested, it would be surprising indeed if their effects were not felt on the Republican. The late-13th-century episode, if confirmed by further work, offers a plausible explanation for the abandonment of the Medicine Creek locality by Upper Republican gardening peoples. Otherwise, the inferred dry periods may be too late in time to have directly affected the principal occupations at Medicine Creek, as those have been radiocarbon dated. The 20 dry years at 1688–1707 would have coincided with the Dismal River occupation as it has been dated from tree rings at sites in Chase and Dundy counties, Nebraska (Hill and Metcalf 1942:205). The figures suggest further that shorter or longer periods of deficient rainfall came at sufficiently frequent intervals that few if any generations of resident Indians would have escaped some experience with such phenomena.

The charcoal samples from Ash Hollow Cave on the North Platte, also chiefly red cedar, came from stratified rock shelter deposits. These deposits included seven culture-bearing lenses (A through G) separated by noncultural sand layers to a total depth of some 80 inches (2 m). The charcoal consisted mainly of small branches and twigs, presumably representing firewood. Annual rings in charcoal from the upper three lenses, A, B, and C, have been matched with ring sequences from Lincoln County (North Platte) and a non-archeological sequence from Redington, in Morrill County, Nebraska. Together, these provide a "continuous sequence from the earliest date from Lens C, 1210 A.D., to the present date." Tree-ring dates in Lens C range from A.D. 1210 to 1334, with the major occupation from associated artifacts identified as Upper Republican and dated at ca. A.D. 1300. A gap of unknown length separates Lens C charcoal from the terminal date of the preceding Lens D, which "appears to have ended in a drought period" (Champe 1946:49; Weakly 1946). No other pre-A.D. 1439 droughts are reported from the Ash Hollow charcoal record.

The droughts identified by Weakly before A.D. 1550 would coincide with the later portion of the Pacific episode, according to climatic periods currently estimated by Bryson and his colleagues; thereafter, until the mid-19th century, they would fall in the Neo-Boreal. In any case, they appear to provide further perspective on what is clearly a long-established pattern of precipitation. That pattern features recurrent periods of deficient precipitation of variable duration and intensity, occurring at unpredictable intervals and separated by equally uncertain interludes of average and above-average precipitation. The record of the tree rings, ascertained from trees that actually grew long ago in the western plains, throws additional welcome light on the nature of the environmental setting in which prehistoric man strove to work out his livelihood.

In recent years, scientists in the western United States who study water records as they are revealed in tree rings have worked out a statistical correlation between ring widths and periods of low moisture, that is, a combination of low precipitation and high evapotranspiration rates in the recent past. These correlations have limited value for one- or two-year deficiencies but are more meaningful for droughts longer than two years and less than a century or so. From these correlations, a measure of drought intensity termed the Palmer Drought Severity Index or PDSI has been developed. The western United States has been divided into 40 climatological regions that can then be subjected to analysis in terms of the PDSI. From this in turn results a predictive model whereby Great Plains droughts "have been reconstructed indirectly from patterns of tree growth in surrounding areas" (Stockton and Meko 1975, fig. 3; see also Meko 1982, and Stockton and Meko 1983).

Leaving to the statistically sophisticated and climatologically trained the important question of evaluating these various procedures, I note here that through these mathematical exercises, a model of plains climatic trends since A.D. 1700 has been constructed (fig. 3.1). Indicated here are alternating wet and dry periods, the latter peaking at very roughly 20–25 year intervals but not demonstrably paralleling cycles of sun spot activity. Several long-term droughts are suggested: that of the 1930s, rated the most severe and widespread since A.D. 1700, and a longer but less severe one between A.D. 1729 and the early 1740s. The wettest decade was in the years 1907 to 1916. The years 1757 and 1847 appear as particularly dry individual years. Weakly's North Platte droughts of 1728–1732, 1798–1803, 1822–1832, 1858–1866, and 1880–1895 can be partially matched with droughts of varying magnitude in Stockton and Meko 1975, figure 3.

Like other region-wide constructs that must deal with averages, this one cannot adequately illuminate the often highly localized short-term weather

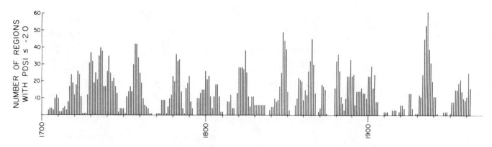

Fig. 3.1. Dry periods in the western United States and the Great Plains as reconstructed indirectly from patterns of the annual growth rings of trees in areas surrounding the Great Plains. Courtesy *Weatherwise*, v. 28, no. 6 (1975), pp. 244–249, a publication of the Helen Dwight Reid Educational Foundation.

events in restricted districts that may well have sharply affected native man's welfare in the small and scattered communities in which he lived. Climatic averages are statistical abstractions devised to introduce a measure of manageability to an almost incredibly varied and intricate mass of weather data. By the same token, they obscure the very details that might help us to understand better the effects of the ever-changing weather on human activities within whatever localities, districts, or regions we are specifically involved.

To illustrate, Stockton and Meko chart 1900–1904 as a dry period, whereas weather records derived from instrument measurements show that during more than half of those years, including 1902–04, summer rainfall was above average at several of the Republican valley stations with which this paper is primarily concerned. On an earlier time level, 1860 was an extraordinarily damaging drought year for many of the Indians in the central and southern plains (Wedel 1941:21), but it is indicated on the PDSI chart as much less severe than a number of years immediately preceding and following. Such local and relatively short-lived fluctuations, while of minor consequence in the regional characterization of climate by scholars on the basis of averages, may well have been crucial to people living in the affected localities and relying in considerable measure on a small-scale, marginal subsistence gardening economy in prehistoric times.

With droughts come dust storms. The soils of the Republican River basin, like those in much of the Great Plains, include a high proportion of fine-grained wind-deposited material that moves easily before the wind when drought, fire, or other agencies destroy the protecting vegetative cover. Still vivid in the memories of an older generation of Great Plains residents are the "black blizzards" of the 1930s dust bowl—blinding clouds of stinging sand and suffocating dust driven by winds that sometimes reached or exceeded 50 miles per hour, and a sudden near-midnight blackness as the sun was blotted out (plate 4.3; Costello 1969:199–203). Miles of weedy fence lines buried by dust and huge drifts around farm buildings and machinery dramatically attested to the awesome transporting power of the wind. In some places, the materials thus blown away lowered the ground surface by as much as two meters; in others, the soil accumulation reached equal or greater depth, sometimes burying orchards, shelterbelts, and other plantings. In the western plains, small streams on which the Indians had once lived were choked with dust and ceased to flow for periods of months or years, as were the springs that fed them.

The fact that such storms and equally massive soil movements have been going on intermittently for thousands of years, long before the white man's plow broke the plains (see, for example, McCoy 1840:408, 409), is abundantly clear from the archeological record and other evidence. Ancient camp sites and hunting stations of multimillennial antiquity buried beneath many meters of wind-laid soil have been investigated in the Medicine Creek reservoir area (plate 4.3; Holder and Wike 1949:260 and figure 66). At other sites in the Republican River basin and elsewhere, human occupation levels of varying ages are separated from one another or from the present ground surface by variable thicknesses of wind-deposited materials (Wedel 1934:148, 152; 1941:18, 19). Since the soils that blanket some sites and constitute terrace fills on many of the streams of the region were carried in from other areas, one suspects that the same winds that thus covered some sites may have uncovered and perhaps destroyed others. One can only wonder, then, how many Paleo-Indian and Archaic sites remain concealed in the terraces of the western Republican River basin, where future erosion or construction activities can be expected to uncover them in time.

To what extent dust storms per se, as distinct from the severe droughts and prolonged water shortages that spawned them, would have discommoded the prehistoric Indians is conjectural. Dust-smothered streams and springs would certainly have discouraged settlement. Gardening difficulties and the problem of finding herds of game animals displaced by dwindling pasturage would have reflected severe water deficiencies rather than the effects of dust storms. Adverse effects on the upland water holes from the blanketing dust can probably be inferred, and this would also have affected the abundance and behavior of the game and fur-bearing animals, and of the Indians who depended upon them.

Chapter 4 The Early Big Game Hunters

The beginnings of human occupancy of the Republican River basin cannot yet be given a firm date, despite increasingly intensive investigations here and on a much wider front. On the Republican, as elsewhere in the Great Plains, the oldest evidence supported by generally accepted radiocarbon and other dates pertains to the Clovis mammoth hunters of ca. 11,500–11,000 years before the present (B.P.). These were followed by the Folsom bison hunters ca. 10,500–10,000 B.P., and these in turn were succeeded by variously designated bison-hunting complexes up to ca. 7000 B.P. Because of their distinctive and distinguishable projectile points, the Clovis and Folsom complexes have sometimes been bracketed together as Fluted Blade cultures, in contrast to the later hunters with their unfluted lanceolate weapon points. In some classifications, all of these groups are subsumed under the rubric of Paleo-Indian. In others, the term Paleo-Indian is applied to Clovis and Folsom, whereas the later groups are classed as Archaic. Here, as previously (Wedel 1961), all are considered Early Big Game Hunters because, so far as archeology has provided evidence, an important and particularly visible part of their basic subsistence economy appears to have been the killing of large game animals, sometimes in considerable numbers. For the Clovis and Folsom hunters, the principal quarry in each case involved species that are now extinct (*Bison antiquus* and *B. occidentalis*) and have been so for some thousands of years. This in no way denies the strong probability, indeed the virtual certainty, that the subsistence strategies also included the utilization of small game, of a wide variety of native vegetable products, and perhaps of other items that have not yet been recognized in the archeological record. The adjective *early* distinguishes these ancient native Americans from the post-Altithermal bison hunters of later times, including of course the pedestrian dog-nomads and the horse-riding peoples who followed them.

The Mammoth Hunters

Mammoth remains are not uncommon in the fossil faunas of the Republican River drainage, but evidence for their direct association with contemporary humans is still very scanty. To the 19th-century Pawnees, who occasionally came across large fossilized bones on their hunting excursions, these were the relics of the ancient giants who first inhabited the region—mythical beings reputedly of such stature and strength that one could walk off with a bison under each arm and four could consume an entire bison at one sitting (Dunbar 1882:743; Platt 1892:130). For the much earlier plainsmen of late Pleistocene and early Holocene times who encountered these giants as living flesh-and-blood animals on four legs, associations have been established or suggested at three locations to date—the Dutton, Selby, and Claypool sites, all in north-eastern Colorado (fig. 2.2), respectively 5YM36, 5YM37, and 5WN18.

Like most mammoth hunter finds to date, these sites are all associated with former water holes. The Dutton and Selby sites (Stanford 1979) lie south of Wray, some 23 miles (37 km) apart. At each, there is a succession of bone-bearing beds situated at the edge of a Pleistocene pond represented now by a depression in the Peorian loess upland plain. These are two of the innumerable playas or so-called buffalo wallows that characteristically dot the upland surface between the stream valleys. From the wind-deposited loess that underlies the depressions, excavations have produced bones of a wide range of mammals, including both living and extinct forms (Graham 1979:64; 1981). Twenty or more species are represented of which four are extinct. They include the rabbit (*Sylvilagus* sp.), ground squirrel (*Spermophilus richardsonii; S.* sp.), prairie dog (*Cynomys ludovicianus*), pocket gopher (*Thomomys talpoides, Geomys bursarius*), grasshopper mouse (*Onychomys leucogaster*), prairie vole (*Microtus ochrogaster*), meadow vole (*M. pennsylvanicus*), vole (*M.* sp.), badger (*Taxidea taxus*), ground sloth (*Glossotherium harlani*), peccary (*Platygonus compressus*), camel (*Camelops hesternus*), and native horse (*Equus* sp.), but not mammoth. Human involvement is uncertain; if present, it is reflected in possibly man-made modifications and markings on some of the bones. The last four species named above are extinct.

Within the playas, immediately overlying the loess, is a lacustrine or lake bed level consisting of fine silts, sands, and clays, probably reflecting a time of increased precipitation. This, too, contains the remains of large game animals, among them mammoth (*Mammuthus columbi*), horse, camel, bison (*Bison* cf. *antiquus*), peccary, deer (*Odocoileus* sp.), pronghorn (*Antilocapra* sp.), ground sloth, a few carnivore bones (*Felis* cf. *atrox; F.* sp.), and fox (*Urocyon* sp.). There were also a number of "probable bone tools and flaked bones" (Stanford 1979:105). The lacustrine level was overlain by a gleysol (bog soil) that was formed under alternate wet and dry episodes with poor drainage. Mammoth bone collagen from this formation has been radiocarbon-dated at 11,710 ± 150 B.P. (SI-2877) and again at 7880 ± 150 B.P. (SI-3541) (D. J. Stanford, personal communication, no date).

Overlying the gleysol at Dutton was a paleosol or old soil layer containing cultural debris: two plano-convex scrapers, a chert core-chopper, flakes, and a few bone fragments, all of which were assigned to a Clovis occupation. On the spoil dirt resulting from the modification of the pond were retrieved a Clovis point, a horse tooth, and a chert flake, all still coated with dirt identified as from the artifact-bearing paleosol. This circumstance, and the fact that "flakes found in the spoils dirt fit onto the core, makes it probable that the Clovis point was also from this level" (Stanford 1979:116). Topping the sequence of soil formations at both sites were Holocene soils from which no bones or artifacts were taken (plate 4.1).

Pollen has not been recovered from either the Dutton or the Selby site, and it is difficult to characterize the nature of the vegetation associated with the various beds. However, the meticulous interdisciplinary studies at these sites have led to revised views of the nature of late Paleo-Indian environments in the region. None of the rodent species indicate wooded habitats, and the larger

Plate 4.1. Weapon points from Early Big Game Hunter sites in the Republican country. *Upper*, weapon points *left to right:* Clovis, Folsom, Agate Basin, Hell Gap, and Eden types; *middle*, projectile points from the Lime Creek site, Zone 3. Courtesy University of Nebraska State Museum. *Lower*, projectile points from the Lime Creek site, Zone 1. Specimen at left shows stem edge different from that illustrated in Davis 1962, figure 10. Courtesy University of Nebraska State Museum.

herbivores represent grazers characteristic of an open grassland. Essentially, the bones indicate a mammalian assemblage such as might be expected in a plains or prairie grassland, "perhaps with sagebrush and short or tall grasses," or a combination of some or all of these forms (Stanford 1979:108; Graham 1981:51ff.). The species composition of this grassland is, in other words, uncertain, though it may well have been quite unlike that of modern times. Desiccation features throughout the various sediments suggest periods of aridity. Absence of mammoth remains from the Peorian loess and their appearance in subsequent horizons may, but does not necessarily, reflect a climatic change from drier windy conditions and eolian deposition to a moister regime that resulted in the formation and maintenance of the permanent water holes required by a population of mammoths. After analysis of the mammalian fauna from Selby and Dutton, and a critical review of the relevant archeological literature, Graham (1981:51) has suggested that prairie vegetation was characteristic of the central and southern plains in pre-Clovis and Clovis times, with a cooler and moister climate not marked by accentuated extremes but with insufficient precipitation to allow major forestation of the southwestern (and central?) plains. Increased moisture between 11,000 and 8000 years B.P. appears to have produced heavier forestation of portions of the plains, including northeastern Colorado, during Folsom and Hell Gap times. This "may have disrupted migratory patterns of the large mammals and caused changes in human adaptation and hunting strategies."

Whether, or to what extent, this inferred afforestation of the western plains during the Pre-Boreal climatic episode (chapter 3) described by Bryson and his co-workers involves the Republican River basin is not clear from any inherent evidence. It remains uncertain whether a generally timbered landscape, including wooded uplands or parklands, or a more limited valley forest, somewhat like the yellow pine (*Ponderosa*) stand that once grew along the rimrock on the south side of the Republican valley, is visualized.

Thirty miles (50 km) west of Dutton and Selby is the Claypool site, 19 miles (30 km) north and two miles (3 km) west of Cope, in Washington County. It is situated in a blowout or deflation basin near the western edge of an extensive treeless sandhills area that runs eastward into Yuma County. Discovered during the dry years of the 1930s by amateur collectors, it was partially excavated in 1953 by the University of Colorado Museum (Dick and Mountain 1960; Malde 1960) and again in 1975 by a party under the leadership of Dennis Stanford of the Smithsonian Institution (Stanford and Albanese 1975).

Two separate cultural manifestations are represented there, in stratigraphically distinct geological beds. The upper, younger level is a massive sandy deposit believed to have been laid down by wind action some 7,000 to 10,000 years ago. The upper portion of this bed shows some soil development, which may have taken place during a cool, dry period. Overlying this are dune sands, now mostly stabilized, thought to have accumulated during the long dry period known as the Altithermal (see table 3.1). Much burned and fragmentary bone, abundant chert flakes from artifact manufacture, and a rather diverse array of stone tools were present. The site has been identified as a camping station of some permanence rather than a game kill, and it was presumably associated with a one-time water hole to which thirsty game animals were attracted and came under attack by hunters.

Identifiable bone included bison, but the species is not known. Chipped stone artifacts consist of a wide range of projectile points, including Folsom, Hell Gap, Eden, Scottsbluff, and later types, and other tools (plate 4.1). There were obliquely edged Cody knives, snub-nosed scrapers, flakes with fine graver points, drill points with flared or expanding bases, and side scrapers. They were made from a wide variety of raw materials, including basalt, petrified wood, yellow and red Graham jasper, and moss agate, all noted as available in gravel deposits near Akron, Colorado, some 25 miles (40 km) northwest of the site. Present also were felsite from New Mexico, Flat Top chert, and Phosphoria jasper from the Big Horn Mountains of Wyoming. In the later excavations, Madero chert from northeastern New Mexico has been provisionally identified. There were also several fragments of longitudinally grooved rubbing stones or shaft smoothers of sandstone.

No hearths or other structural features have been reported. The later investigators attributed the positions of the artifacts they found to redeposition by deflation and erosion, that is, they represent items left behind when the enclosing sand was removed by wind action and thus were no longer in their original position and soil matrix as of the time when the site was abandoned. The cultural materials from this level are ascribed for the most part to the Cody complex ca. 6500–6000 B.C.

The sandy bed in which the Cody complex materials were found was underlain unconformably by an older marl deposit from which were taken the teeth and bones of a young mammoth. Some of these bones had been gnawed by rodents. There were no artifacts in direct association. From the surface of the marl nearby, however, were taken a chalcedony flake with graver tip and a Clovis projectile point. Neither of these artifacts was accepted as in association with the mammoth because of an inferred wide discrepancy in age between the bones and the artifacts. The apparent discrepancy lay in the fact that snail shells collected from the marl, comprising both fresh water and land forms, included four species which had not previously been identified with late Pleistocene deposits. These were *Gyraulus labiatus* Leonard, *Physa elliptica* Lea, *Stagnicola palustris* (Say), and *Lymnaea bulimoides* Lea, the first of which became extinct at the close of Sappa time (Malde 1960:237). From the 1953 fieldwork and the molluscan evidence the marl was correlated with the Sappa formation (early Yarmouth) and estimated to be probably "several hundred thousand years old" (Dick and Mountain 1960:225), far too old to have any human associations.

Extensive backhoe trenching in 1975 suggested that the marl was a relatively limited and localized feature, possibly of late Pleistocene age and therefore much more recent in deposition than was originally supposed. Under those circumstances, the possibility has been advanced that the mammoth bones may have been directly associated with the nearby Clovis artifacts (Stanford and Albanese 1975:26, 28). How fossil snail shells regarded as early to middle Pleistocene came to be associated with a relatively late artifact-bearing formation is not clear.

At both the Dutton and Selby sites, the case for a pre-Clovis human occupancy has been argued as a result of the recent investigations. This argument is based on the belief that many of the large mammal bones from the lacustrine levels show evidence of modification by man and specifically, "human butchering and the processing of animals" (Stanford 1979:108). In the absence to date of demonstrably worked stone, stone debris, hearths, or other convincing evidence of human involvement, the case for pre-Clovis man at these sites rests heavily on the correct interpretation of marks on the bones and bone fragments thought to represent butchering or tool-making activities. These include "expediency" tools made of bone (spirally fractured bones in which the sharp edges of the break presumably served in butchering or hide-working activities); intentionally flaked bone fragments; and bones split or otherwise modified for the extraction of marrow.

Expediency tools were fashioned variously from horse and bison tibiae, camel metapodials, a bison radius, mammoth rib pieces, and innominate and scapula fragments. They could be made quickly at the butchering site from the bones of the animal being processed, and they could be discarded when worn out or on completion of the operation for which they were prepared. They are judged to have functioned as chopping and scraping tools. Bone flakes are thought to have been produced like chert flakes and are regarded as debris of manufacture rather than as implements. Limb bones of mammoth, bison, horse, and camel believed to have been purposely split carry impact depressions with cones of percussion and intersecting radial fractures. These interpretations rest on the thesis that bone can be flaked much like stone (Stanford, Bonnichsen, and Morlan 1981). Unfortunately, too little is yet known about bone-working technology to permit positive identification or interpretation of these presumed bone artifacts. This is even more regrettable because similar features have been recognized on mammoth and other bones of possible pre-Clovis age at the Lamb Spring site near Littleton, Colorado (Stanford, Wedel, and Scott 1981).

As of this writing, the case for pre-Clovis human occupation of the Republican River basin—and indeed of the Great Plains generally—remains unproved. At no site for which a pre-Clovis age has been suggested or is supported by multiple radiocarbon or other "precise" dates, or by convincing geological evidence, is there clear and incontrovertible indication of human activity. Stone artifacts are either absent from pre-Clovis age sites in this region or their association with that time and cultural level is questionable. Presumed evidence of human workmanship or purposeful modification of animal bones is doubtful or unproved. The spiral fracturing of long bones, reflecting breakage while the bones were still green and here presumed to have been for marrow extraction or tool making, is known in the fossil record at geological time levels antedating any possible human involvement. Impact depressions produced in the splitting of long bones, as well as flake scars that suggest human retouching, have been detected in the bone debris left by large carnivores such as bears, wolves, and wolverines. According to G. Haynes (1980):

> Spiral fracturing of long bones showing depressed "points of impact" need not be exclusively associated with human activity. High energy trampling by herd animals can break long bones from bison-sized animals; gnawing by predators and scavengers can also break bones. Low energy trampling by rodents can put polish on the edges of fractured bones; sediment mixing and churning due to animal traffic in wet sediments such as bog or pond mucks can also abrade fractured bone edges and produce in some cases very localized polish.

There is, in short, still no generally accepted evidence of a prelithic bone technology or of prelithic and/or pre-Clovis camp or kill sites in the study area here under review. One might go even further and suggest that no solid proof of such cultural occupancy, prelithic and pre-Clovis, has yet been convincingly demonstrated elsewhere in or near the Great Plains, despite radiocarbon dates and other clues that at times strongly suggest manifestations far older than the established and accepted Clovis dates now at hand. The advocate of pre-Clovis human presence in the region (see Humphrey and Stanford 1979) notes correctly that expediency tools of bone are accepted without question as artifacts at the Jones-Miller and other bison kill sites where they are associated with flaked stone tools but are rejected at other sites as evidence of man's involvement because they are not associated with stone tools. On the other hand, it has not yet been conclusively demonstrated that the "worked" bone in pre-lithic fossil and putatively archeological contexts was actually modified or manufactured by human agency rather than by some nonhuman cause. The evidence bearing on this intriguing and important point, it must be emphasized, is by no means all in hand as yet (see also Conybeare and Haynes 1984; Guthrie 1984; Haynes 1984).

From other sites, outside the Republican River basin, the Paleo-Indian complexes are much more adequately represented and better known. The mammoth hunters have been studied at the Dent and Lamb Spring sites in the South Platte River drainage in Colorado (Wormington 1957; Stanford et al. 1981b), at Blackwater No. 1 (Hester 1972) and elsewhere in New Mexico, at Domebo in Oklahoma (Leonhardy and Anderson 1966), at Naco and Lehner sites in Arizona (Haury et al. 1953, 1959), and most recently at a number of sites in Wyoming (Frison 1978). The search for these early plainsmen and their possible forerunners has, in fact, become one of the most exciting developments of the past two decades in the archeology of the High Plains and other sections of the western United States. It is from these locations that the bulk of our information to date has been developed, and it is against these sites that the more meager data from the Republican basin need to be further considered (see C. Haynes 1964, 1969, 1980, 1982; Jennings 1978; Stanford 1982; and Rutter and Schweger 1980 for recent overviews).

We still know relatively little concerning the lifeways of the late Pleistocene and early Holocene mammoth hunters of the Great Plains, either Clovis or posited pre-Clovis. The finds consist mostly of skeletal remains of one to a dozen or so animals, usually found in proximity to water, i.e., springs, streams, lake margins, or upland ponds, many of which are now dry. Where more than one animal is represented, the investigators tend to think in terms of repeated kills of single animal units (cf. Saunders 1977, 1980). There is no archeological information on the kinds of shelters, hearths, or other structures used, although simple unlined fireplaces have been found at the few camp sites situated near some of the kills. In addition to fluted bifaces, the artifacts recovered include various cutting and scraping tools of flint, gravers, knives, and burins. There are also bone points and foreshafts, awls or punches, and some pigments of red ocher. The tools suggest mainly a hunting, butchering, and skin-working range of activities, along with bone- and wood-working.

There are no skeletal remains from which the stature, the physical appearance of the people, or their somatological relationships might be estimated. We suspect a sparse and scattered population, probably based on roving family units, with seasonal or otherwise recurrent gathering into larger groups for social functions, communal hunts, mate-getting, or other purposes (Hester and Grady 1977). We can infer a climatic setting generally wetter and cooler than the present but with many variations in temperature, precipitation, and other particulars from time to time. The contemporary landscape also differed in many details of topography, native vegetational communities, and animal life from that known to the white man eleven millennia later (Graham 1981).

Elephants: Behavior and Hunting

Neither can we be certain of the habits, social behavior, and psychology of the great beasts with whom the ancient elephant hunters are usually linked in our thinking, and whose procurement by foot hunters without metal or firearms poses perplexing problems to present-day inquirers. The only surviving elephants today inhabit the Old World in Africa and in Asia, where they have lived for centuries in ever more intense competition with growing numbers of humans and where they have been hunted since Paleolithic times. The elephants have been compelled to adapt to shrinking natural ranges, to severe overpopulation with resulting degradation of habitat, and to heavy and expanding exploitation for their meat, ivory, hides, and other trophy parts. Inside and outside the zoos and natural parks, they have been living and evolving for a long time under much more restrictive constraints than did the American mammoths and their human predators of 11,000 years ago. Through time, as their environments changed and their behavior adapted, procurement strategies undoubtedly changed and adapted accordingly.

Much relevant information on elephant behavior has been gathered in recent studies in connection with game control and wildlife management in Africa (Sikes 1971; Laws et al. 1975; Olivier 1982). Also useful and often highly thought-provoking are the reports and observations of early explorers and hunters of a century or more ago. Though academically untrained in animal biology, some of these individuals have left informative insights for our consideration and evaluation. To what degree and in what particulars the behavior of the long-vanished mammoths can be assumed to parallel or approach that of the modern elephants is, and will always remain, conjectural. We can do little more than speculate on the intelligence, resourcefulness, adaptability, and community organizational capacities of the ancient proboscideans in their relations to contemporary man. Still, there is no other analogue from which we can even hope to derive some possible insights regarding the giant beasts on which these early peoples partly subsisted and to whose habits and other characteristics they therefore needed to adapt.

The American mammoth most commonly identified with early man is *Mammuthus columbi*, the Columbian mammoth, whose closest Old World taxonomic relationships are with the Asian elephant (*Elephas major*). The African species (*Loxodonta africanus*) is perhaps better known. Behavior patterns in these living species appear to be generally pretty much alike, thus providing some basis for assumptions about mammoth ecology and behavior. Taxonomic niceties aside, it is likely that the Columbian mammoth was roughly comparable to the modern African elephant in height and bulk—up to 12 feet (3.6 m) in height and perhaps five to eight tons (4,500–7,200 kg) in weight for large bulls (Martin and Guilday 1967; Sikes 1971; Maglio 1973; Laws et al. 1975). Their molar teeth were similarly adapted to grazing as well as browsing, and both sexes were provided with tusks, those of the mammoths being much larger and having a distinctive spiral form. The adult African elephant requires daily from

200 to 400 pounds (90–180 kg) or more of grass and browse, 30 to 50 gallons (115–190 l) of water, and will travel long distances to satisfy these needs. The modern elephants consume primarily grasses with lesser amounts of browse, and they have adapted to a wide range of habitats, including mountains and plains, forests and grasslands, and dry to subhumid climates. They are adversely affected by long exposure to the direct rays of the midday summer sun, from which they seek the protection of tree cover. The mammoths seem to have been adapted primarily to colder prairie or savanna habitats.

African elephants are social creatures, with strongly developed community life. They travel characteristically in family units numbering three to 30 individuals. These highly mobile groups are headed by a large, sagacious old female and may include several other females, adolescents, calves, and young bulls. The matriarch who leads the group is usually the mother, aunt, or sister of the other adult cows. The senior herd bull travels behind the family group; other mature bulls live apart. Several to many family units may gather at times into large herds aggregating many hundreds of individuals, notably when drought or food shortages compel a general migration to distant, more favorable ranges. Regular access to permanent water in adequate amounts is indispensible to the welfare of the elephants. Before their restriction to game parks, seasonal movements from savanna to forest were customary as hot, dry weather approached. They migrated back to the savanna with the return of the rains. Such round trips ranged from 300 to 700 miles (500–1,100 km).

Adult elephants have few serious enemies among predators other than man, but the calves are highly vulnerable to large carnivores and must be protected by their elders. When flight from a perceived threat is not possible, the family group gathers into a tight cluster, "bunching" around the matriarch with the older animals facing the menace behind and at the side of the matriarch while the smaller animals seek protection under and next to them. Against predators not equipped with firearms, such bunching, with its front of large tusks, waving trunks, and pillarlike forelegs, must have had high protective value, much like the circling of musk oxen against wolves and other predators in the Arctic.

Professional hunters in quest of ivory and other trophies have taken advantage of this defensive group behavior, shooting the matriarch first and then, as the leaderless survivors clustered around her body, picking them off one by one. In herds composed of two or more family units, it was imperative that all matriarchs be destroyed quickly, since if one survived to flee, all members followed her as their new leader. It is noteworthy, too, that modern elephant control hunters in Africa, seeking to counter overpopulation in the dwindling ranges available, have been able to destroy groups averaging 15 animals in 45 to 90 seconds with high-powered rifles (Laws et al. 1975:121). In contrast to the bunching behavior of the family groups, the "normal male reaction on being disturbed was flight, each individual for himself, in various directions" (Laws et al. 1975:162).

Whether a herd of elephants at bay, especially if it included several adults, would have been attacked by men armed only with bone- or stone-tipped spears is uncertain, but such action would seem to have entailed a high risk of serious injury or death to one or more of the hunters. That elephants were killed, in the Old World as well as in the New, by hunters without heavy repeating rifles is abundantly clear, as are some of the wide range of techniques employed to achieve this end.

Against the African elephant, several methods for killing that did not involve firearms have been described (Gusinde 1948; Schweinfurth 1969; Sikes 1971:302; Johnson et al. 1980). These included camouflaged pits, sometimes with sharpened upright stakes set into the floor and dug in frequently used trails; foot snares of various kinds, usually anchored to a heavy drag; weighted spears suspended over the trails; the use of fire, either to drive the animals into a trap or to burn them to blindness or death; and poisoned arrows and spears. Hamstringing to immobilize the animal, which could then be dispatched with metal-tipped spears and knives with reduced risk to the hunter, whether afoot or on horseback, was a highly effective technique historically, but it might have been extremely difficult or impractical without razor-sharp cutting edges such as can be easily developed on a metal blade. Spear thrusts into the belly of a passing elephant, usually the last animal in a line, by hunters concealed beside a forest trail, with speedy departure by the assailants into the woods immediately following the attack, have been reported as one of several techniques used by the Pygmies (Gusinde 1948:32). The elephant's foot is a particularly sensitive and vulnerable part of its anatomy. A well-aimed or lucky hit between the toes or into the backward-facing sole of a passing animal's uplifted foot, could effectively hamper or destroy its mobility and consequent capacity for defensive maneuverability, thus placing it at the mercy of its attackers. A basic procedure in most cases seems to have involved the isolation of one animal upon whose immobilization and dispatch a group of hunters then concentrated their energies.

Assuming that the American mammoths also traveled in family units and that their response to danger included bunching, the task of the Paleo-Indian hunters would seem to have involved first separating an animal from the herd, without provoking the others into a defensive group posture if possible. This might have been accomplished by singling out a young animal, perhaps one lagging for a choice morsel of food or another draft of water or lingering for other reasons in a gully or arroyo in whose sinuous course the members of the group might lose sight of one another in a short distance. Once cut off from the herd and set upon by a group of hunters, the animal could then presumably have been dispatched by repeated spear thrusts, its attempts to charge one assailant thwarted by another spear from the rear, thus diverting its intentions repeatedly and eventually wearing it down. Probably, as was sometimes the case among the Pygmies, there were times when the victim broke away and, dying slowly from its wounds, had to be followed and harassed until death came.

Sharply differing views on mammoth procurement tactics have been advanced to explain archeological findings. They range from the scavenging of enfeebled animals at water holes to various kinds of group confrontations (Saunders 1980). At the Naco site in Arizona, eight Clovis points were found between the skull base and forepart of the rib cage of a mammoth, with one point lying directly at the base of the skull where the spinal cord would have been most vulnerable (Haury et al. 1953:7). At the Lehner site, where remains of at least nine mammoths were recovered from an ancient gravel bar, Haury et al. (1959) opted for temporally spaced kills of single animals, chiefly calves or young adults, at intervals of unknown length. Here, following reexamination and aging of the remains, Saunders (1977, 1980) has argued that the teeth and bones are consistent with the view that a family group, including young and adult animals, is represented, and furthermore, that since the well-documented family solidarity of the proboscideans would have militated against the successful isolation of a single animal, a mass kill is indicated. By this interpretation, the uninjured members of the group, in the fashion of the African elephants, would have closed protectively around the fallen animals until the survivors in turn were brought down, one after another.

That this technique, practiced today with deadly efficiency by teams of African game control officials using heavy rifles at 10 to 15 meters, would have been feasible for stone age spearmen with bone- or stone-tipped weapons, is an inference of debatable validity. For one thing, one wonders about the penetration that might be achieved by a thrown spear, considering the probable thickness of skin and subcutaneous tissues of the victim. An exception may be the rib cage area immediately behind the forelegs. Again, while the African elephant walks at five to eight miles per hour, it can charge 50 yards at 25 miles per hour—about the speed of a sprinter running the 60-meter dash in the Olympic championship time of seven seconds. We do not know the comparable capabilities of the American mammoth in this respect, but if they were roughly equivalent to those of the elephant, a confrontation by unmounted spear-wielding hunters with several able-bodied and aroused animals would seem to have posed unacceptable risks for the former unless they were present in considerable numbers.

It can be argued on valid grounds that elephant hunting by the forest-dwelling Pygmies of the tropical Ituri would have involved different problems and therefore other techniques than those effectively pursued in the putatively sub-boreal prairie or savanna environments of the late Pleistocene and early Holocene Great Plains. There is, as we might expect, no archeological evidence of pitfalls, foot snares, or weighted spear drops. Fire would have been feasible in dry seasons and under suitable vegetational conditions, as it was against the African elephant in the grasslands. Its use has been argued for years (Sauer 1944) but remains undemonstrated.

The use of poisons in connection with thrown darts or spears might be further considered. Appropriately processed materials of animal origin provided such aids to hunting and warfare among the historic American Indians, and might have been developed, or obtained through trade, by the ancient hunters as well. Or, there may have been native plants like the water hemlock (*Cicuta*), prairie larkspur (*Delphinium*), monkshood (*Aconitum*), nightshade (*Solanum*), and pokeberry (*Phytolacca*) of today that would have provided parts for preparing extracts that could be made lethal or debilitating to large animals. Such poisons could have been procurable within the technological capabilities of the people and would have left no traces for the archeologists to find or for their colleagues to detect (Hough 1910; Kingsbury 1964; Bare 1979; Stephens 1980).

The deadly efficacy of native poisons in East Africa, when administered by powerful bows and composite arrows with detachable heads against elephants, rhinoceroses, and other large game, has been vividly described by Holman

(1967). The Early Big Game Hunters in the North American Great Plains are believed to have lacked the bow and arrow, but results similar to those of the recent African bowmen might well have been achieved with throwing or thrusting spears against a disadvantageously positioned animal.

The basic problem for Paleo-Indian mammoth hunters would no doubt have remained essentially two-fold. First, they would have needed to learn thoroughly and from close observation the habits and characteristics of the mammoth—its daily and seasonal movements, its defensive strategy singly and collectively, and the points at which it was anatomically most vulnerable, for example, immediately behind the forelegs where the skin was comparatively thin and the vital organs relatively accessible. They also would have had to recognize that all of these factors could vary from case to case. Beyond that, unless the hunters were in sufficient numbers to risk confrontation with a family group, they would have had the problem of cutting out a suitable animal and gang-harassing it until it succumbed (cf. Vereshchagin 1967:380), or else they could catch the victim alone and at a considerable disadvantage because of the terrain, ground conditions and footing, and cover. It is likely that young animals could be more safely attacked and were better eating. The growing number of kill sites coming to light indicates that man's techniques of attack, whatever the details, were often successful—often enough, at least, to persuade some observers to argue that human predation was a prime cause of mammoth extinction.

From the presently known Republican basin sites, little is to be learned regarding processing of the slain beasts by the Paleo-Indian mammoth hunters. In Wyoming, Frison (1978:102; 1982;199) has called attention to the apparent stacking of mammoth bones in a manner suggesting food caches. Large postcranial bones were inferentially piled over the butchered meat as a protection against theft by animal predators and scavengers. The skulls were then placed on top, either to fulfill some ritual requirement or perhaps to facilitate relocation of the cache in deep snow. The meat from late-fall and winter kills would have been protected against spoilage by freezing; at other times, drying or smoking meat, which has been practiced by the recent African natives, would have served, but here again there is no evidence.

Among the Pygmies and other native African elephant hunters, once the animal falls (Sikes 1971:308):

> It is covered by men, women, and children with razor-sharp knives, systematically cutting off the meat in strips. . . . When every minute scrap of flesh has been removed . . . pits are dug in the ground and fires lit in them. Low platforms of thin branches are built and the strips of meat laid across them. . . . The fires are tended constantly and the meat turned carefully and methodically on the smoky platform. If properly built in the old-fashioned style, the entire platform is constantly in the smoke and flies never settle. . . . The drying if thorough and carried out in deep forest, may take a week to complete. . . . The meat will now keep indefinitely and only needs reconstituting by soaking in water prior to cooking when required. Basically, the pattern of butchering and treating the carcass after death is similar throughout tropical Africa. Little or no edible meat is wasted, and usually nothing but the hide, skeleton, and intestinal contents are left to

the scavengers. Not only are the specially favored portions utilized immediately (eaten raw or else barbecued or braised) for a village banquet at which everyone gorges himself to the full, but all the other parts are carefully dried and stored for future use.

Of the elephant-hunting specialists of East Africa, Holman (1967:33ff.) has written:

> The Lingula are the true elephant people of Africa. The elephant supplies all their needs, and hunting it was once their entire life. Originally the pattern of this life would have been extremely simple. The males of a family would kill an elephant, and a group would camp near the carcass until they had eaten the meat or dried it out into biltong. They would then kill another and camp near that one. The name of the tribe is derived from a Giriama word, *ariangulu*, meaning eaters of meat. When the Liangula hunted solely for food, the ivory would have been of little value to them, and they would have preferred the younger, more tender animals, and the big males would have been left to develop into tremendous tuskers.

The way of life here briefly described reminds one of the early Spanish descriptions of the Apachean dog-nomads in the southern plains in the mid-16th century, reportedly supplying all their needs from a single species, the bison. In both instances, one wishes for more particulars about the lifeway represented, now vanished without hope of recovery.

Late Pleistocene Faunal Extinctions

In late Pleistocene times, extinction descended upon several large herbivores, including notably the mammoth, camel, native horse, and ground sloth. Extinction of megafauna took place also in Eurasia and at roughly the same time, with the Siberian mammoth radiocarbon-dated most recently at ca. 11,400 years B.P. Geological history records many extinctions, but this late episode in the New World differs in that man was demonstrably present in America at the time (Martin and Wright 1967). Widely varying explanations have been advanced, usually with environmental change invoked as the principal cause. In the well-known "overkill" hypothesis of Martin (1967), more recently dubbed "blitzkrieg" (Martin 1982), man was the primary agent in the extinction of the New World mammoths. Beginning around 12,000 years B.P., according to this view, man spread swiftly southward across the Bering Strait in a wavelike pattern, annihilating the big game as he advanced. The megafauna, inhabiting a land previously without men and therefore unacquainted with the deadly efficient hunting skills of this newly arrived predator from the Old World, was exterminated before it could develop effective counterstrategies for survival (Mosiman and Martin 1975).

An alternative view, persuasively argued by Guilday (1967), Jelinek (1967), and Graham (1979) among others, sees environmental change as a more likely cause, with man perhaps a contributing factor. Grayson (1977) has pointed out that several genera of North American birds also became extinct about this same time, that these were in no way interdependent on the vanishing megafauna, and that their extermination by man would not be expected from a subsistence economy based predominantly on big game hunting.

With particular reference to the mammoth, Saunders (1980) has argued that the bones from several group kills show no stress-related symptoms and indicate animals in good condition. Thus, Clovis man's efficiency and profligacy in systematically cropping whole family units was "a probable factor in the elimination of *Mammuthus columbi* from the Pleistocene megafauna." Countering this is Haynes's (C. Haynes 1980:118; 1982:391) suggestion that the Clovis hunters would probably have selected their victims on the basis of behavior rather than age, and because "some behavior is independent of age, an accumulation of individual mammoth kills could take on the apparent age distribution of a family unit."

If the presence of pre-Clovis man in America can be established by ongoing field programs (Humphrey and Stanford 1979), that raises the presumption that the New World megafauna was probably subject to human predation for a much longer period than the overkill hypothesis allows, and that the animals were neither so stupid nor so complacent that they were quickly annihilated by the newly arrived Clovis hunters. Meanwhile, the likelihood still seems good that some sort of environmental degradation, perhaps in part climatically triggered, offers a more palatable explanation, with man applying the finishing touches to an impoverished megafauna that included the mammoth, horse, and *camelops.* For the moment, the point must remain moot (Olivier 1982:305; Martin and Klein 1984).

A possible scenario for the Great Plains of North America would involve an environmental change at perhaps 11,000 to 12,000 years ago, correlating with the onset of a generally warmer and drier climate. With this, the mid- and tall-grass prairies or savannas on which mammoths, horses, and some ruminants largely subsisted may have been replaced gradually by the warm-weather short grasses from the south and southwest. The bison, "short-grass specialists using, in addition, tall and mid-level grass new growth, or re-growth after grazing by other ungulates" (Guthrie 1982:314), could then have displaced the other forms and become much more abundant. A late Pleistocene fauna specialized to a tall-grass, prairie savanna flora in a cooler, wetter climate may thus have been unable to adjust to a different vegetational setting and may have become a weakened and less populous fauna by the time man arrived to finish it off. For extended and stimulating recent overviews of Late Pleistocene— Early Holocene megafaunas and their environments and interactions, the papers by Olivier and Guthrie already cited, along with others in Hopkins et al. (1982), are strongly recommended.

The Early Bison Hunters

With the disappearance of the mammoth, whatever the correct explanation and the particulars under which the changes took place, it is clear that man had to turn to other species beginning soon after 11,000 years B.P. These included bison of species now extinct, for example, *Bison antiquus* in the south and *Bison occidentalis* in the north (Wilson 1974). Both of these were larger animals than the modern *Bison bison.* Their habits, disposition, and behavior patterns, like those of the mammoth before them, are conjectural. Presumably, as with modern bison, the earlier animals could have been taken singly or in small groups by stalking, ambush, or other methods. Solitary hunters or small parties could have worked along game trails, around water holes, from blinds, with fires in dry seasons, disguised in the skins of wolves or other predators to whose presence in their vicinity the herds were accustomed, or in deep snow where suitable conditions existed or could be contrived. Upland ponds and lakes, and the well-grassed flats nearby, probably attracted bison in Paleo-Indian days as they did in the 19th century. To Indians without horses and guns, several hunting techniques were productive, as the Spaniards learned when they first observed the early historic pedestrian peoples of the southern plains. This was long after the time when the Paleo-Indians hunted *Bison antiquus* and *B. occidentalis*, to be sure, but the methods reported are strongly suggestive of what was feasible and rewarding. We must never underestimate man's adaptive capacities in devising appropriate strategies for procuring food, once he found himself in the presence of a food resource such as the bison.

From the 16th- and early 17th-century expeditions of Vásquez de Coronado and Juan de Oñate, both of which traveled from the upper Rio Grande to the middle Arkansas River in present Kansas, eyewitnesses reported the use of bone- and stone-tipped spears and of large bows, apparently used from brush blinds at the watering places. Baltasár de Obregón (1928), a compiler of historical information developed by others with firsthand experience, reported that hunters smeared mud over their bodies, then concealed themselves beside the game trails and shot down the bison on their way to water. This is reminiscent of a somewhat similar technique reported from the Pygmies, whose elephant hunters sometimes covered themselves with forest duff and elephant litter to offset the human body odor as they lay in wait for their quarry beside the forest trails (Cureau 1915:221). Stalking by single or paired hunters disguised under wolf hides or the pelts of other predators with whose behavior the bison were familiar was probably a common strategem, then as later among the Plains Indians.

What the 16th-century Spanish explorers in the southern plains never saw were the highly productive, indeed often prodigal, mass procurement strategies that the Indians of the northwestern plains had developed over a time span of thousands of years. These succeeded, sometimes spectacularly, because they exploited the strongly gregarious behavior of the bison and their proclivity for headlong flight en masse when they considered themselves endangered. By the proper exploitation of these traits, the hunters achieved the mass killing of dozens to hundreds of animals by cooperative efforts. The specific techniques for bringing in the buffalo varied widely in their details, depending upon the particular circumstances, the numbers of animals and hunters available, the nature of the terrain, the weather, the season, and so on. To be successful, the element of chance had to be supplemented by careful planning, good organization, coordinated execution, and good luck insured by appropriate ritual sanction.

In the past 20 years, a number of excellent studies on native bison hunting have been produced in the western and northern plains, and a voluminous literature has become available (see, for example, Forbis 1962; Malouf and Connor 1962; Kehoe 1967, 1973; Dibble and Lorrain 1968; Frison 1971, 1972, 1974, 1977, 1978, 1982; Wheat 1972, 1978; Davis and Wilson 1978). As these and other studies indicate, communal hunting of bison was practiced in the western and northwestern plains as long as 10,000 years ago by Folsom man, and with notable changes through time, it continued into the 19th century, long after the adoption of the horse by the Indians. For the southern plains, beyond a few Paleo-Indian and late Archaic drive sites in Texas, there is apparently no incontrovertible evidence of mass kills on the scale indicated for the northern plains.

For the northern plains, the bison procurement methods of the historic Indians have been reviewed in much detail by Arthur (1975) and others. By the time white men arrived there to observe what was going on, the horse was supplementing or largely replacing the dog. The winter's meat supply was more or less regularly obtained by cooperative drives that involved construction of a corral or pound of logs and brush. Into these, bison numbering up to 200 or more were urged or driven through converging lines of piles ("deadmen") of sod, brush, or bison chips whose distant ends began one or two miles or more apart far out on the flats where the herd was gathered for the final drive. Behind some of the deadmen were concealed Indians who at appropriate moments rose briefly with waving blankets to keep the herd moving between the lines. At the corral gate a crosswise log and ditch over which the stampeding animals jumped prevented their return and escape from the pound. In prehorse days, when the range of gathering operations was more limited, the bison were frequently stampeded over a cliff, cut bank, or "jump," perhaps with a holding pen below where animals not disabled by the fall could be dispatched with spear, dart, or arrow. We have, so far as I know, no eyewitness acount of a jump operation, though the basic strategy is not difficult for the practiced observer to reconstruct from the remaining evidence.

There is at least one vivid description of the death scene at the pound. This is by Henry Youle Hind, leader of the Assiniboine and Saskatchewan exploring expedition in southern Canada in 1858. A few miles southeast of the "elbow" of the South Saskatchewan River, Hind came upon a camp of Cree and visited a nearby pound (Hind 1859:55–56):

I accompanied the guide to a little valley between sand hills, through a lane of branches of trees, which are called "dead men," to the gate or trap of the pound. A sight most horrible and disgusting broke upon us as we ascended a sand dune overhanging the little dell in which the pound was built. Within a circular fence 120 feet broad, constructed of the trunks of trees, laced with withes together, and braced by outside supports, lay tossed in every conceivable position over two hundred dead buffalo. From old bulls to calves of three months old, animals of every age were huddled together in all the forced attitudes of violent death. Some lay on their backs, with eyes starting from their heads, and tongue thrust out through clotted gore. Others were impaled on the horns of the old and strong bulls. Others again which had been tossed were lying with broken backs two and three deep. One little calf hung suspended on the horns of a bull which had impaled it in the wild race round and round the pound. . . .

. . . ten days before our arrival, the Indians had driven about 200 buffalo into the enclosure, and were still urging on the remainder of the herd, when one wary old bull, espying a narrow crevice which had not been closed by the robes of those on the outside, whose duty it was to conceal every orifice, made a dash and broke through the fence, the whole body then ran helter skelter through the gap, and dispersing among the sand dunes, escaped, with the exception of eight who were speared or shot with arrows as they passed in their mad career. In all, 240 animals had been killed in the pound.

We are told further that the befouling of the trap with rotting carcasses that could not be dressed out before they became putrid and flyblown after 10 days under the July sun had become so offensive that the "reckless and wasteful savages" found it necessary to construct a new pound in a cleaner and less malodorous location. No further comment on the conservation ethic of the Plains Indian bison hunters is needed.

The Jones-Miller Site
In the Republican River basin, the most carefully studied bison kill is the Jones-Miller site, 10 miles (16 km) south of Laird, Colorado, situated on the left bluff line of the Arikaree River (Stanford 1974, 1975). Here were uncovered the broken and disarticulated bones of some 300 animals identified as *Bison antiquus* (see plate 4.2). Most were the bones of cows and young animals believed to represent several different fall-through-winter mass kills. The precise methods used are unclear; if a corral was involved, no definite traces have been detected. The adjacent terrain is such that a drive into a snow-choked arroyo

Plate 4.2. Bone bed at the Jones-Miller site, 5YM8, on the Arikaree River bluffs in Yuma County, Colorado. The bones are the remains of nearly 300 bison butchered after several mass kills during the Hell Gap period ca. 8000 B.C. Weapon points and other artifacts were found among the bones. Copyright National Geographic Society; courtesy Dennis Stanford.

would have been feasible. Of particular note was the discovery of the mold of a large post located centrally in the bone bed and associated directly with an antler flute (?), a tiny Hell Gap projectile point, and butchered canid (dog?) remains. This was perhaps analogous to the medicine post reported as a feature of the bison pounds among some historic northern plains tribes. Among the bones were numerous projectile points; cutting, scraping, and chopping tools of chipped stone; and bone implements, including expediency tools. These materials are assigned to the Hell Gap culture complex of some 10,000 years ago (Stanford 1974, fig. 1; Wedel 1983a:202).

The kills here represented involved nursery herds consisting of cows, calves, and yearlings, with very few bulls. Disarticulation was total. At an estimated 50 to 100 animals per kill, with an average yield of 300 to 500 pounds (135–225 kg) of meat per animal, there would have been the problem of disposing of as much as 15,000 to 50,000 pounds (6,750–22,500 kg) of meat and other animal products. Also represented in the bone bed were a few canids of dog size, as well as meadow voles, fox squirrels, small lizards, snakes, frogs, and small shore- and songbirds. The contemporary climate is believed to have been cooler and moister than the present, presumably with snowy winters and dry summer-to-fall seasons. The microfauna suggests a partially wooded river valley with well-grassed uplands.

Stone used in the manufacture of tools included Spanish Diggings quartzite from eastern Wyoming, Graham (Republican River) jasper from farther east in the Republican or Smoky Hill drainages, grayish purple Flat Top cherts from a large quarry site 18 miles north of Sterling, Colorado, Bijou Basin petrified wood from central Colorado, and Alibates dolomite from the Texas Panhandle. Whether use of these diverse materials reflects widespread trading patterns, the travels of a single peripatetic band on its yearly round, the congregation of several normally widely scattered bands at a central kill or ceremonial site, or some other adaptive mechanism is not now clear.

No traces of an associated camp site, of possible habitations, or of hearths or storage facilities have been found at Jones-Miller. It has been postulated that there may have been brush shelters or perhaps skin-covered lodges scattered over the floor of the Arikaree River valley near the bone bed, where trees and brush would have provided some protection from the weather. From these could have been drawn the manpower needed for the kills and processing of the harvest when circumstances were appropriate. The implications of fall and winter mass kills for the subsistence strategies of the early Plains bison hunters have been discussed recently by Frison (1982:193–199).

The Lime Creek Sites An important but still incompletely described cluster of deeply buried Early Big Game Hunter sites is located in stream-terrace fills about 100 miles (160 km) to the east in the Medicine Creek reservoir (Harry Strunk Lake) in Frontier County, Nebraska. They include the Lime Creek (25FT41), Red Smoke (25FT42), and Allen (25FT50) sites. All lie within three miles of Medicine Creek Dam, on and just below Lime Creek, and they may be considered collectively the Lime Creek sites. At normal pool level, they are submerged by the reservoir water. They were discovered in 1946–1947 when archeological and paleontological surveys of the Medicine Creek drainage were intensified in connection with water-control construction by the Bureau of Reclamation, and

Plate 4.3. An Early Big Game Hunter site in the Republican River valley, and plains dust storm. *Upper,* beginning of excavations by the University of Nebraska State Museum at 25FT41, a deeply buried camp site (lower right) on Lime Creek in southwestern Nebraska. Courtesy National Anthropological Archives, Smithsonian Institution. *Lower,* approaching dust storm, the dreaded "black roller" of the Great Plains dust bowl days and a recurrent feature of the regional droughts. Courtesy Library of Congress, Prints and Photographs Division.

Plate 4.4. Stone artifacts from the Lime Creek site. Preforms and other chipped pieces from the Lime Creek site. Courtesy University of Nebraska State Museum.

they were investigated by the University of Nebraska State Museum in 1947–1950. The principal available literature includes Schultz and Frankforter (1948), Holder and Wike (1949), Davis and Schultz (1952), and Davis (1953) on the Allen site, and Davis (1962) on the Lime Creek site.

At the Lime Creek site, the most fully reported of the group, two main occupation levels were identified as Zones I and II. Most of the archeological remains were in Zone I, 47 feet (14 m) below the present ground surface (plate 4.3) and in association with a dark carbonaceous clay and silt layer thought to represent an old beaver meadow. Three feet (1 m) above was Zone II, from which came too little material to permit interpretation. Zone III was 4.5 feet (1.4 m) above Zone II. Chipped stone artifacts included straight-based, parallel-sided projectile point preforms originally designated the Lime Creek knife, unifacially flaked end and side scrapers, bifacial knife-choppers, core-choppers, cores, blanks, hammerstones, and large quantities of flakes and spalls. (See plate 4.4.) In ground stone, there were fragments of longitudinally grooved sandstone abraders, an ungrooved abrader, and hammerstones. There were also a few pieces of cut and worked bone and antler. Among eight projectile points or classifiable portions, the Scottsbluff, Milnesand, and Plainview types were identified. Much of the chipped stonework was in locally available Graham jasper, whose ready accessibility at several outcroppings conveniently close by may have been a major attraction for early man's visits to the spot.

Animal bone was plentiful in Zone I, less so in the higher and later levels. Small game was represented primarily in Zone I—beaver (*Castor*) most abundantly, with lesser amounts of pronghorn (*Antilocapra*), deer (*Odocoileus*), wapiti (*Cervus*), prairie dog (*Cynomys*), pocket gopher (*Thomomys*), jackrabbit (*Lepus*), raccoon (*Procyon*), and coyote or dog. The bison was very scantily represented but was the only species found in Zones II and III. The bison bones are reported to be "different from those of modern species, *Bison bison*, . . . [and] most like those of *B. antiquus*" (Davis 1962:29). The detailed paleontological analysis of these faunal remains, including bison classification, was reported to be "nearly complete" (Davis 1962:29). To date, however, neither this long-awaited report nor the detailed analysis of the geology and geomorphology of the Lime Creek sites (Davis 1962:20) have appeared.

There was no evidence of house structures, storage facilities, or long-used hearths. Brief but probably repeated occupancies by small groups of people, primarily in quest of jasper for tool-making and subsisting on the locally available game animals, are inferred. Climatic factors have been invoked to explain the apparent shifts in the kinds of animals utilized through time. The sediments in Zone I suggest swampy conditions, with an abundance of small game in the well-watered creek valley. By the time represented in Zone III, the climate was becoming colder and drier, the swampy meadow bottomlands were being smothered by wind-blown loess, and only the upland grazers—bison, pronghorn, and elk—were readily available for food. How much time was involved in this process is unknown, as is the date of any of the deeply covered occupations. The only radiocarbon date available—9524 ± 450 B.P. or 7575 B.C. (Sample C-471, Libby 1955:107)—is from charred log fragments gathered from a bluish clay a foot or more below Zone I and its included cultural materials.

The Red Smoke site, as described in preliminary and interim reports, consisted of seven or more successive cultural strata that contained evidence of human activity. Most of the artifacts came from a middle level designated Zone 88. Hearths and bone scrap occurred at all levels. Zone 88 yielded large quantities of flint chips, bifacial cutting and chopping tools, projectile point preforms, end scrapers, and projectile points of the Plainview type. Grinding tools, yellow and red ocher, and a stemmed point came from an upper level. It is inferred that, as at the Lime Creek site, the primary activity at Red Smoke was the processing of stone from the nearby jasper outcrops into tools and blanks. Food-getting was centered around the bison, and considerable skin-working activities were also carried on. Stays were probably short but repeated frequently. There are two published radiocarbon dates. One is from an upper cultural level, Zone 92 (VIII), with a determination of 8862 ± 230 years B.P. or about 6900 B.C. (Sample C-824, Libby 1955:110). The other is from Zone 90(VI) at 7970 ± 210 years B.P. or 6020 B.C. (Sample TX-333, Valastro et al. 1967:451).

At the Allen site cultural materials and campsite remains were found in a stratum about three feet (1 m) thick beneath some 20 feet (6 m) of terrace fill. Two strata of concentrated refuse and dark-stained soil including 20 hearths were separated by a lighter-colored intermediate zone in which there was much less occupation debris. Most of the artifacts and nine of the hearths were in the lowest level, designated Occupational Level I. Animal bones were abundant, including those of bison, antelope, deer, coyote, rabbit, mice, rats, prairie dogs, and very rarely beaver, along with occasional reptiles, amphibians, birds, and fish. At least two varieties of mussels were noted. Many of the bones were in long windrows scattered over the contemporary land surface, with campfires situated principally between the windrows. Commonly, the larger bones had been cut or broken up, probably in search of marrow.

Associated artifacts included leaf-shaped, concave-based projectile points reminiscent of the Angostura type; trapezoidal scrapers, some with gougelike bits; lanceolate and ovoid blades; drills; grinding and abrading tools; a flattened stone spheroid with encircling groove (bola stone?); eyeletted bone needles; crude bone awls; a bipointed bone object, perhaps a gorge fishhook; and various cut and otherwise worked bone fragments. The designation Frontier Complex has been assigned to the assemblage of items and traits found here.

The hearths were simple affairs, without lining, sills, or other special features, built on the contemporary ground surface, not let down into it. Some, to judge by the degree of reddening of the underlying soil, were evidently maintained or used repeatedly over a considerable period of time. No traces of possible lodges or shelters, or of storage or baking pits, were reported. A relatively permanent hunting base camp, perhaps recurrently occupied during the late spring to early fall months, is suggested. Occupation Level II is thought to have been "an attenuation and fainter reflection of the original, more successful, Occupation Level I" (Holder and Wike 1949:265). Whether climatic change and environmental degradation were responsible for the inferred cultural impoverishment is not clear.

An interesting indication of the season of occupancy at the Allen site is the finding of burned nests of the mud-dauber wasp (*Sceliphron caementarium*), which the authors (Holder and Wike 1949:261) stated "were found throughout; although characteristically broken open, several were recovered in an unbroken state and there was at least one unfired nest." Since the mud-dauber wasp nests from May to September, a summer camp or at least standing structures during the summer period, may be inferred, but this does not foreclose the possibility of human residence here at other seasons. That the nests were collected to be thrown into the fire so as to forestall attacks by the insects on the residents of the lodges (Freimuth and LaBerge 1976) is also possible, but that seems to me a much less likely option than to view them as one facet of the unending quest for human nourishment. I suspect that the nests were broken open by humans to get at the protein-rich wasp larvae inside, as hymenopterous insects have been utilized in Mexico, California, and other regions (Eerde 1980–81; Dixon 1905; Kroeber 1925:408, 814; see also chapter 2) where meat was scarce, over-priced, or for other reasons beyond the reach of many people.

Three radiocarbon dates for charcoal from the Allen site are used to determine time of occupancy. Two are from the lower occupation zone:

8274 ± 500 B.P. = 6324 B.C. (C-108a; Libby 1955:107)

10,493 ± 1,500 B.P. = 8543 B.C. (C-470; Libby 1955:107)

The third is for a mixed sample of charcoal collected from both occupational levels and is much more recent:

5256 B.P. = 3306 B.C. (C-65; Libby 1955:106)

So far as I am aware, no explanation for these chronological inconsistencies has been provided. In effect, the site and its several occupancies remain undated.

Whereas the Lime Creek and Red Smoke sites have been considered manifestations of culturally related groups, no close relationships between those two and the Allen site have been recognized (Davis 1953).

If mass kills of bison were customary among inhabitants of the Lime Creek sites, no evidence of that fact has been reported. It appears more probable that the animals were ambushed singly or in small groups as they came for water to the pools and springs along Lime and Medicine creeks, or perhaps they were stalked by hunters disguised in wolf skins as they grazed afterward in the meadows and grassy streamside flats. The killing of bison and the mass processing of the flesh, fat, and other parts for current and future consumption seem not to have been primary objectives of the human groups who left the remains here, as they were at the Jones-Miller kill.

It is highly probable that additional manifestations of the Early Big Game Hunters remain to be discovered or recognized in the Republican River basin. Some may already have been submerged, undiscovered, by the Medicine Creek, Harlan County, Red Willow, and other major reservoir projects that have flooded miles of the river valley and its potentially highly significant tributary canyons and terrace fills. Others may turn up in course of time as deeply buried stations, as at Lime Creek, or as relatively shallowly buried kill and butchering sites like Jones-Miller. The upland water holes, now dry but some with standing water as recently as the turn of this century, hold great promise for further discoveries bearing on these ancient pre-Archaic bison hunters. Here the wide boggy margins surrounding the shrinking ponds could have become death traps for bison and other large animals miring down in a last desperate try for water in times of drought. And this could have taken place many times since the close of the Pleistocene and before. Because of our as yet very limited predictive capabilities and the great cost of exploration, chance finds by earth-moving and agricultural activities may be our best hope for future discoveries.

Chapter 5 Archaic Foragers and the Altithermal

In the Republican River basin, and widely throughout the Great Plains, the archeological record appears to be largely lacking in sites dating between ca. 5000–6000 and 2000–3000 B.C. Regionally, an interval of limited or highly transitory occupancy by man has been widely but not universally inferred. In contrast to the Early Big Game Hunter sites, with their skillfully crafted fluted and unfluted lanceolate weapon points and indications of specialization in the taking of large game of species now extinct, the succeeding cultural manifestations are believed to reflect hunting and gathering subsistence economies with a broad and diversified range of interests in food collecting. Use appears to have been extensive of a wide variety of large and small mammals, and seeds and other vegetal products, as well as fish, reptiles, amphibians, and probably insects—almost anything, in short, that walked, crawled, flew, or swam, and could be gathered in sufficient quantities to justify the effort. Still-extant species mainly are represented. For man, intermittent and short-term occupations, probably seasonal, at sites where certain edible items became available at more or less predictable intervals, seem to have been customary—a lifestyle that has been variously characterized as cyclical nomadism (Mulloy 1954) or as scheduling (Flannery 1968). In many respects a continuation and modification of the Early Big Game Hunter lifeway as seen at Lime Creek, for example, this tradition has come to be known as the Plains Archaic. It endured until mound building and pottery making heralded the Woodland tradition around the beginning of the Christian Era.

The earlier portion of the Archaic occupation of the Republican basin, visualized here as roughly 5500–2500 B.C., coincided with the climatic episode long known as the Altithermal and more recently as the Atlantic. Its very existence questioned by some, it has been variously dated, and its effects on the contemporary fauna and flora, including man, have been much debated (Krieger 1950:121; Mulloy 1958:208; Davis 1962:11; Stephenson 1965:692; Hurt 1966; Wedel 1961:254 and 1978b:201; Reeves 1973; Frison 1975; Buchner 1980). By its believers, it has been characterized broadly as a period of higher aridity and warmer temperatures, and probably the warmest of all Holocene time (Wendland 1978). Over large portions of the Great Plains, climatic change may have significantly diminished the grass cover and perhaps expanded the western short-grass steppe at the expense of the mid- and tall prairie grasses. The resulting reduced carrying capacity of the grasslands may in turn have cut deeply into the populations of large herbivores or else displaced their range to areas not as severely affected by the inferred climatic adversities. Just how these developments would have affected the human populations is not well known, but a greater dependence on foraging rather than big game hunting has been postulated. Increasingly penetrating studies by paleoclimatologists, paleontologists, geologists, and archeologists, among others, seem to be dispelling some of the uncertainty that still surrounds the problems of human adaptation and the environmental vagaries that compelled adjustments from time to time (Bryson and Wendland 1967; Bryson, Baerreis, and Wendland 1970).

Projectile points and other artifacts thought to have been left by the Archaic hunters and gatherers during the Altithermal have been collected on the surface in various sections of the Republican River country, but few sites have been seriously investigated. One of these is the Spring Creek site, 25FT31, situated in a terrace fill at the junction of the Spring and Red Willow creeks in Frontier County, Nebraska (Grange 1980). The site has been inundated by Hugh Butler Lake, impounded by Red Willow Dam. The Archaic component here was a thin occupational zone beneath eight to 12 feet (2.6–4 m) of terrace deposits and was exposed by the removal of earth fill for the dam. The overlying deposits included later cultural materials attributable to the Dismal River (ca. A.D. 1700 ±) and Upper Republican (ca. A.D. 1100–1300) archeological complexes, most of which were destroyed by the borrow pit operations (plate 5.1).

Mechanical stripping by power machinery of large portions of the terrace disclosed hearths scattered over some 17 acres (7 hectares) or more. Stained soil with inclusions of charcoal, red pigment, broken animal bone, chipped stone artifacts and debris of manufacture, and bone tools formed an occupational horizon up to six inches (15 cm) thick. No postmolds or other evidence of house structures were detected, but one irregular pit partially filled with bison bone is thought to have been intended for storage. An irregular basin-shaped fireplace contained indurated ash, blackened stones, and animal bones; others were destroyed with few recorded details by borrow pit activities.

Plate 5.1. The Spring Creek Archaic site, 25FT31, in Red Willow Reservoir, Frontier County, Nebraska. Site is on the terrace at the center of view. Courtesy Nebraska State Historical Society.

Animal bone refuse consisted mostly of bison, evidently of the modern species, *Bison bison*. Also identified were remains of deer (*Odocoileus* sp.), antelope (*A. americana*), wolf or dog (*Canis* sp.), swift fox (*Vulpes velox*), beaver (*Castor canadensis*), cottontail rabbit (*Sylvilagus* sp.), pocket gopher (*Geomys* sp.), prairie dog (*Cynomys ludovicianus*), vole (*Microtus* sp.), Canada (?) goose, pintail duck (*Anas* cf. *acuta*), common crow (*Corvus brachyrhynchos*), and some passerines. In addition to the abundant splintered bison bone, there were several concentrations of larger fragments associated with charred stones, flakes, and artifacts.

Chipped stone tools from the site included plano-convex end scrapers, bi-facially worked knives, and unifacially chipped side scrapers. Much of the chipped stone is identified as "local" (Graham?) jasper. Among the bone tools were bison ulna picks, a flaking tool and shaft wrench of rib, a metapodial fleshing tool, splinter awls, and a tubular bone bead. Ground stone included a fragmentary sandstone grinding slab and a cache of sandstone manos, some of which were stained with red pigment.

The projectile points were triangular-bladed, side-notched, and had indented bases with ground edges. They are strongly reminiscent of some of the points from the older Logan Creek Archaic site (4674 B.C.) in Burt County, eastern Nebraska (Kivett 1958, 1959). As at Logan Creek, lanceolate points also occurred at Spring Creek, but unfortunately only as broken and incomplete specimens. Lacking at Spring Creek were the side-notched scrapers characteristic of Logan Creek.

Spring Creek is of particular interest because of the manifestly heavy reliance on bison, which is reflected in the bone refuse, and a radiocarbon date of 5680 ± 160 years B.P. (3730 B.C.; No. M-1364). The date falls well within the range of time commonly allotted to the Altithermal and thus suggests that in the upper Republican River drainage, at least, bison were probably available in sufficient numbers to provide meat in quantity and so to attract hunters.

Undoubtedly, many more occupational sites of the Archaic foragers remain to be discovered or recognized in the Republican River drainage. Deeply buried terrace levels on Bonny Creek below Bonny Reservoir in Yuma County, Colorado, appear to be typologically of Archaic affiliation (D. Stanford, personal communication), but they have not been dated or described in print, or adequately studied in the field. In the lower reaches of the valley they can also be expected (Witty 1963). Here their probable nature and content can perhaps be inferred from the investigations at the Coffey site on the Big Blue River a few miles east of the lower Republican River, and elsewhere on the prairie-plains border (Johnson 1980).

The Coffey site, 14PO1, lies on the left bank of the Big Blue, 26 miles (42 km) north of Manhattan, Kansas, just south of the Marshall County line and about 30 miles (48 km) east of the lower Republican River basin (Schmits 1978, 1980). It consists of a succession of cultural levels separated by thin strata of nonartifactiferous alluvium, buried 8 to 10 feet (2.4–3 m) beneath the ground surface in the floodplain of the river. From the nature of the fill in which the remains occur, it is inferred that the inhabitants of the site lived intermittently and seasonally on the margins of an oxbow lake. Radiocarbon dates place the occupancy at approximately 3250 B.C., or ca. 5200 B.P.

The most productive levels, designated III-5, III-7, and III-8, were littered with refuse animal bone, stone-working debris, charcoal, burned earth, and broken tools. Features included shallow basins containing charcoal, ashes, burned earth, and charred seeds, which were interpreted as hearths. No evidence of lodges or other structures was reported, but a single identified posthole was located near a hearth. Artifacts recovered included milling slabs and manos of quartzite; river cobbles with battered edges, used as hammerstones; a grooved stone fragment; chipped axes and gouges; bifacially chipped knives in various forms; drill points with expanded bases; stemmed and corner-notched projectile points; and occasional lanceolate points. Chipped artifacts were made mainly of locally available Flint Hills chert. Bone artifacts included awls, punches, tubes, and antler-tine flakers (?). One fired clay tube possibly intended for personal adornment was recovered, as well as small quantities of red and yellow ocher pigment.

Refuse animal bone occurred in considerable quantity and variety. Identifications included the bison (*Bison bison*), deer (*Odocoileus* sp.), raccoon (*Procyon lotor*), dog or coyote (*Canis*), striped skunk (*Mephitis mephitis*), squirrel (*Sciurus*), pocket gopher (*Geomys bursarius*), woodrat (*Neotoma floridana*), mole (*Scalopus aquaticus*), and cottontail rabbit (*Sylvilagus floridanus*), among the mammals; teal (*Anas* sp.) and mallard (*A. platyrhynchos*) ducks, white-fronted (*Anser albifrons*) and Canada (*Branta canadensis*) geese among birds; box (*Terrapene*) and soft-shelled (*Trionyx* sp.) turtles; bull snake; toad (*Bufo* sp.) and leopard frog (*Rana pipiens*); and large numbers of catfish bones, representing both bullhead and channel cat (*Ictalurus punctatus*). Less common were flathead catfish (*Pylodictis olivaris*), drum (*Aplodinota*) and a gar (*Lepeso*).

The utilization of flotation recovery techniques produced charred seeds of chenopods (goosefoot) in abundance and lesser quantities of smartweed (*Polygonum*), hackberry (*Celtis*), Solomon's seal (*Polygonatum*), bulrush (*Scirpus*), and grape (*Vitis*). Conspicuously absent from the published lists are such plants as the choke cherry, plum, walnut, hickory, and sunflower.

The aboriginal occupation at the Coffey site is interpreted as a series of seasonal episodes featuring the hunting of large and small animals, the taking of waterfowl, fish, reptiles, and amphibians, and the gathering of wild plant products. There is no evidence of mass game kills in the locality, and both bison and smaller animals were presumably taken by individual hunters or by small groups as opportunity offered. Hunting, trapping, and snaring, both on the upland and bottomland prairies and in the streamside woodlands, may be inferred. There are no indications of fishing devices, such as bone hooks or harpoon heads, or of nets. The fish, mainly catfish, were of various sizes. The likelihood seems good that they represent the sort of harvest that could have been taken in late summer, when the ponds created by spring overflows were drying up and the aquatic life they harbored was being concentrated into progressively smaller areas where it could be easily scooped out by children and adults at their leisure. This technique, familiar a half century ago and more to small boys on seasonal creeks in Kansas and Nebraska in summer time, usually produced a highly varied assortment of fish, mussels, amphibians, reptiles, and insects. From this harvest, the fish, turtles, crayfish, and frogs considered large enough to be dressed and eaten were taken while the small fry, snakes, and the like were abandoned to such predators and scavengers as raccoons and water birds, or to their inevitable death as oxygen in the water gave out and the

water itself finally disappeared. To an earlier native human population endur-
ing an austere subsistence and with less fastidious food tastes, such catches
would have provided nutritious and welcome fare for a time. The use of plant
poisons to stun fish and other aquatic forms may also have been practiced but
can be neither proved nor disproved.

The charred seeds identified from Coffey are all species that would have
been available on drying pond margins and creek banks, probably in large quantities and easily harvested from August through September. Their recovery and
interpretation are a notable contribution to our knowledge of the plant harvesting practices of the early Plains Indians, but our insights still remain much
too limited.

Among the faunal and floral remains from Coffey, some interesting absences of species relatively common in later Plains Indian cultures may be
noted. In addition to the lack of plum and choke cherry pits, there were no
bones of gallinaceous birds such as quail, grouse, prairie chicken, or turkey, or
of such smaller passerines as doves. That these were locally unavailable seems
unlikely, but it is not clear whether cultural preferences, sampling deficiencies, seasonal factors, or other considerations are reflected in the archeology.
Perhaps the main purpose of the human visits to the locality was the gathering
of certain wild plant foods, particularly seeds and tubers, with other edible
items utilized as opportunity offered or immediate necessity dictated. That a
similar subsistence strategy would be effective and adequate today, or would
have been a century or two ago under aboriginal conditions, is not unlikely.

The archeological data from Coffey have been interpreted as reflecting an
environmental setting more arid than the present one, probably similar to that
of the "present-day mixed or short grass areas farther to the west" (Schmits
1978:149). The radiocarbon dates make possible a tentative correlation with
pollen studies and paleoclimatological interpretations at Muscotah spring bog
in Atchison County, Kansas, 65 miles (104 km) to the east (Grüger 1973), in an
environmental setting today much like that on the lower Republican. Here,
about the time of human occupancy of horizons III-5 to III-8 at Coffey, a transition was underway from prairie conditions with few trees to a beginning or a
reexpanding deciduous forest. Streamside woods and treeless upland prairies
are inferred, with a climatic setting probably drier than today's. None of the
plant and animal remains identified from Coffey are out of line with what
would be expected to be native to the locality during the past century or two
prior to the major ecological disturbances resulting from Euro-American intervention in the course of events. To the extent that the Coffey materials fairly
represent a sampling of the resources available on drying pond margins and
stream banks of the Blue River in late summer, they suggest no great dissimilarities from what was available to the later native peoples of the area.

A comparison of the identified Coffey site plant materials with those recognized by botanically trained observers and others as living in the region today is inevitably of great interest. Not unexpectedly, the archeologically recovered materials represent only a small fraction of what was inferentially
available to the contemporary human population. Unfortunately for the archeologist, seeds inadequately indicate the range of wild plants utilized by the
ancients, who drew also upon the roots, tubers, young shoots, fleshy fruits, and
other parts for which there were no hard fractions to resist decomposition or

disintegration. Thus, despite their absence from the list of plant species represented at Coffey, the sunflower, Jerusalem artichoke, and giant ragweed were probably important constituents of the Archaic vegetation along the Big Blue and Republican rivers. Such legumes as the prairie turnip (*Psoralea*), hog peanut (*Amphicarpa*), and Indian potato or groundnut (*Apios*) were likely to be present as well and were probably available in season.

The botanical studies by Barker (1969) in the Kansas Flint Hills and by Morley (1964) in Republic County, Kansas, appropriately drawn upon for insights into the environmental setting at Coffey, include highly relevant caveats that should be borne in mind in any comparison of present-day floras with those inferred for the prewhite past. Morley indicates, for example, that at the time of his observations there were "no unchanged high prairies" in Republic County, that nearly two-thirds of the cultivated land showed "moderate to extreme erosion," that even the rougher untilled lands were mowed annually for hay, and that the vegetation was consequently much changed from its original, that is, prewhite condition. As for the Flint Hills generally, Barker (1969:533) observed that the original vegetation has been more or less continuously disturbed since the 1840s. Although the extent of the resulting degradation is not discussed in detail, some of the principal agents mentioned include year-round grazing pressures from seasonal cattle feeding, the continuous support of herds of cows, and burning to control the spread of undesirable brush. The more recent application of chemical herbicides to control brush invasion has tended to "kill many dicotyledonous forms, especially the leguminous plants, which are important prairie components." The sunflower, Jerusalem artichoke, and giant ragweed are all listed by Barker as common today in appropriate habitats in the Flint Hills.

Barker's comment regarding the deleterious effects of herbicides on leguminous plants should be especially noted in view of the demonstrable importance to later native peoples of the prairie legumes. The historical record suggests that they were prominent components of portions of the Kansas grasslands in preagricultural times. Thus, Lt. W. H. Emory in 1843, traveling from Fort Leavenworth to Bent's Fort, noted that the prairie turnip (*Psoralea esculenta*) was common on the prairie uplands as far west as the 99th meridian, beyond the great bend of the Arkansas (Emory 1848:11). A few years later, when Lt. L. C. Easton (Easton 1953) descended the Republican River in 1849, he recorded a great abundance of pea vines, probably *Apios americana*, from the Smoky Hill–Republican junction east to the Missouri. These documents do not prove that these and other historically important wild food plants, legumes and others, were necessarily abundant in Archaic times, but they raise a presumption that such may have been the case, and that, as Morley and Barker point out, present-day floral lists must be used circumspectly in evaluating the plant resources that might have been available in ancient landscapes.

Still unclear in the archeological record is the extent to which grass seeds and other perishable plant parts were used by the Plains Indians as food. Only rarely, as when charring takes place, are conditions conducive to their preservation. The historical record, unfortunately, is likewise of limited comparative value since most available ethnobotanical studies in the region (Gilmore 1919; Vestal and Schultes 1939; Carlson and Jones 1940) were derived mainly from more recent reservation Indians, to whom grasses seem to have been important largely as horse feed or, less commonly, as sources of medicinal or ritual items. One suspects that information from such latter-day gathering groups as the Mescalero Apache of New Mexico might provide more promising clues (see, for example, Castetter 1935) to the sort of materials the archeologist should be looking for in phytolith studies or by whatever other advanced analytical techniques may become available.

The Spring Creek and Coffey sites provide fleeting but intriguing glimpses into the probable nature of the Archaic lifeway in the central plains, even though the latter site is at some distance from the heart of the Great Plains proper. Regionally, considering the inferred length of time and the great extent of territory involved, the nature of the Altithermal climate and weather in the Great Plains must have varied widely in detail from section to section and from time to time. It follows that generalizations are likely to be oversimplified, perhaps grossly so. Until we have additional firsthand data on Archaic settlement patterns in the present mixed- and short-grass districts beyond the 99th meridian, it will be hazardous and perhaps even foolhardy to attempt to characterize the environmental settings to which native peoples had to adjust in early Archaic times. Almost certainly, though, significantly increased aridity would have diminished the grass cover and its carrying capacity, and thereby would have affected the incidence, abundance, and seasonal movements of herd animals such as the bison.

If, as I have here, we accept as a working hypothesis the judgment of paleoclimatologists that Atlantic time was the warmest of all the Holocene period and that severe desiccation was a notable feature of that climate, particularly on the plains (Wendland 1978; Wendland and Kosobud, n.d.), then we may learn from some of the observations made in the Great Plains during the dry years of the 1930s. By Atlantic or Altithermal times, the flora and fauna of the Great Plains grassland were essentially like those of historic times. So far as I am aware, there is no analogue in recorded history for centuries-long droughts comparable to the conditions postulated for the Altithermal. The record-breaking drought of 1933–1939 on the Great Plains, and the longer but less severe one postulated for the western United States from 1729 to the 1740s (Stockton and Meko 1975), were little more than fleeting blips on the screen of Holocene time. This has been nevertheless the most serious drought for the plains region since it became the seat of a major livestock industry, and its effects have been widely studied (Ellison and Woolfolk 1937; Albertson and Weaver 1945; Weaver and Albertson 1956; Albertson et al. 1957; Coupland 1958). Native grasses responded to drought with reduced plant size and scantier foliage. As desiccation and high transpiration persisted and intensified, root damage and finally death of the plants resulted. The depleted grass cover led to substantial decrease in forage production, in some instances amounting to 80 or 90 percent or even more; and the amount of range land needed for continued maintenance of grazing cattle rose from 10–12 to 50–90 acres (5–36 hectares) per animal. At the end of the drought, with return of "normal" precipitation, several years were usually required to restore forage production and carrying capacity to their previous levels. In some instances, two years of heavy rainfall resulted in a tenfold increase in forage over the amount available at the height of the drought.

Warming and desiccation, in Altithermal times as in the historically documented droughts, would presumably have affected the uplands first, bringing about significantly reduced grass cover on the areas between streams and the disappearance of ponds and water holes as the water table dropped. It is possible that the boundaries of the short-grass steppe region expanded; but the heartland of the steppe, as it was in pre-Altithermal times, must surely have reflected the deteriorating amount of precipitation and rising temperatures also. The resulting environmental stresses would have substantially reduced or redistributed the bison populations and other game available and would thereby have minimized man's utilization of the upland areas and the consequent evidences of his former presence in the area.

In the stream valleys, the effects of the changed climatic conditions may have been less disastrous. The Republican River, as we have already noted, derives its permanent flow very largely from the Ogallala beds, which in pre-agricultural days supported numerous strong and unfailing springs in its upper reaches. The Ogallala, in turn, was replenished almost entirely by regional and local precipitation, since its western margins were completely separated from mountain runoff and snow melt from the Rockies. The region underlain by the Ogallala beds has notoriously low annual precipitation, but this circumstance is partially offset by the unconsolidated nature of much of the overlying material—open-textured sands and gravels that readily absorb rain and snow, and transmit much of this to the Ogallala. There is no evidence, so far as I am aware, that the perennial flow of the Republican has been cut off in Holocene time or that it has ever diminished sufficiently to permit invasion of the valley and blocking of the river channel by dune sands from the north or northwest. The dune fields between Wray and Holyoke, Colorado, and those in southwestern Nebraska all terminate north of the Republican valley and seem never to have extended south beyond or across that stream.

If radiocarbon dates are indicative and reasonably accurate, Spring Creek and Coffey provide important insights into the contemporary environmental setting. At both sites, bison were clearly obtainable, intermittently or seasonally if not year-round. With the few exceptions noted, the additional food resources that may have been available in these districts and probably throughout the Republican basin are only now becoming clearer from the archeological record. Here, as elsewhere throughout the Great Plains, the native peoples undoubtedly settled in proximity to water supplies. In Archaic times, they were inferentially prevailingly seasonal residents who supplemented game animals with plant foods harvested on the floodplains, in streamside timber belts, valley breaks, and upland margins, and probably from wet meadows around the headsprings and seeps.

It seems reasonable, then, that even if warmer and drier climatic episodes during the Altithermal diminished the upland grass cover and reduced the number of gregarious herbivores it could support, the Republican River probably remained a spring-fed stream with grassy bottomlands, some trees, and an assemblage of plants and animals similar to that of the past century or two. Trees were presumably restricted to the immediate stream banks and to tributary creeks as in historic times, and the bottomland grasses, adapting to a diminished stream flow, may have been less luxuriant or more restricted in area than were the stands in the historic period under a heavier precipitation regimen. Instead of a near-desert setting, the Republican valley may have been more like an oasis strip capable of supporting a limited human population even during what has been regarded by some, including this observer, as a habitat poorly suited to residence by man during several millennia in prehistory.

In this light, the apparent scarcity of archeological sites between ca. 6000 and 2000 B. C. may reflect in part the fact that we have searched for them in the wrong topographic locations, or that, if they have not long since been destroyed by erosion, they remain still deeply buried by eolian or alluvial deposits laid down after their abandonment by the Indians. In short, a redistribution of human population, with hunting and gathering camps established in proximity to the reduced surface-water supplies, rather than total abandonment of or general exodus from the Republican basin, was probably the response of the Indians to the environmental stresses of the Altithermal episode. Post-Altithermal Archaic sites may then be expected to reflect changed conditions and presumably increased human populations, but for this the local evidence is still inadequate to permit valid judgments.

Chapter 6 The Plains Woodland Hunters and Gatherers

Around the time of Christ, notable changes in the material culture inventory and lifeways of the Central Plains peoples began to appear. As one result, the number of habitation and burial sites from which archeologists can make their interpretations is significantly larger than those from earlier time and cultural levels, and so is their yield in artifacts, in campsite refuse, and in skeletal remains of the people themselves. There are marked similarities to better-known materials widely spread throughout the eastern woodlands of the United States, where they are assigned to the Woodland cultural tradition. From this circumstance, the westerly materials in the Great Plains have been recognized as a Woodland manifestation since Strong's time in the 1930s and are classed as the Plains Woodland tradition, which equates in time with the Middle and early Late Woodland of the eastern United States.

Like the previous Archaic groups, the Woodland peoples in the trans–Missouri River region still drew their principal sustenance from an economy primarily based on hunting and gathering, which required frequent seasonal or otherwise cyclical shifts in residence. Beyond that, however, the Woodland tradition was responsible for the introduction of at least three major innovations into the Plains region: (1) the burial of the dead in or under purposefully built mounds, (2) the manufacture of pottery, and (3) the cultivation of maize and beans. Insufficient trustworthy data are yet in hand to determine whether the Plains Woodland people were themselves immigrants from the eastern forest margins or, alternatively, whether they were in large measure lineal descendants from the earlier Archaic food collectors of the eastern grasslands who acquired through their eastern connections the characteristics we think of as indicating Woodland culture.

Of the several kinds, or variants, of Plains Woodland culture now recognized by archeologists in the central plains (Kivett 1953:130; Wedel 1959:542), two are particularly well represented in the Republican River basin. In the lower valley, below the Nebraska-Kansas state line, numerous burial mounds have yielded materials that show relationships to a western Hopewellian tradition whose nearest cultural center between the first and sixth centuries of our era was in the Kansas City locality, around the junction of the Missouri and Kansas rivers (Wedel 1943; Johnson 1976, 1981). The Republican valley mounds are at or very near the westernmost limits of the aboriginal burial mounds in the central plains. Farther upstream, in Nebraska and Kansas, other camp and burial sites without mounds and with a somewhat more limited material culture inventory, have been assigned (Kivett 1952) to the Keith focus or phase.

81

Still other sites remain in limbo for want of sufficient evidence to place them firmly in an established classification or to justify a new taxonomic unit.

The mounds along the Republican River, together with those once found on the bluffs of the Kansas River and its tributaries downstream from Junction City, have been objects of human interest for more than a hundred years. Well before the turn of this century, investigators had reported (Parker 1887) on mounds northwest of Junction City; and soon thereafter, Brower (1899) illustrated tumuli from the Blue and Kansas river valleys, and artifacts taken from them, in his privately printed reports on surveys in Kansas. By the early 1900s, probably the larger part of these structures had been destroyed or so badly mutilated by amateur collectors and relic hunters that little remained for observation by professionals when they finally appeared on the scene.

The mounds along the lower Republican River from which have come the best records are, or were, mostly on the east, or left, bluff line between Clay Center and Junction City. These records originated in the field activities of Floyd Schultz, a resident of Clay Center, whose collections and notes from more than 20 years of digging were eventually deposited in the Museum of Natural History at the University of Kansas. These materials have been analyzed and described as the Schultz focus by Charles E. Eyman, in a master's thesis at the University of Calgary (Eyman 1966). That the cultural entity so named by Eyman actually existed, I strongly question, but the included data bearing on the Republican River mounds and their artifact and skeletal content are of direct interest here. I use them with the author's permission.

The mounds were typically situated atop the bluffs and headlands that border the valley. They varied in size from 20 to 50 feet (6–15 m) in diameter and in height from a few inches to nearly six feet (2 m). Some were simple earth-fill structures over a circular or oval basin excavated into the prairie sod. In others, the fill consisted of earth and stones, which were sometimes present as a layer under or over the human remains. The stones varied from an almost complete pavement or blanket to a few scattered slabs, all of which had been carried to the mound site from limestone ledges outcropping along the bluff rim. A few included slab walls somewhat reminiscent of the more elaborate rectangular dry-masonry-chambered mounds erected by the Kansas City Hopewellian people for their dead (Wedel 1943:105, 150). Under some mounds there were small pits that, like the basins in others, contained the disarticulated bones of one or more individuals. In addition to their extremely fragmentary condition, most bones show evidence of partial burning or scorching, presumably from cremation rites carried out somewhere other than in or under the burial mound complex. There is evidence that later peoples, including historic Indians who possessed glass beads and metal objects obtained from white men, sometimes interred their dead in mounds originally erected centuries earlier by the Woodland people.

Associated with the human bones and fragments, and scattered in like fashion haphazardly through the mound fill, were artifacts in various categories. Especially common were disk beads made of freshwater mussel shell, and tubular beads of bird or small mammal bone, which were often incised in spiral or annular patterns. Chipped stone projectile points included large corner-notched dart or spear heads and small stemmed or corner-notched arrowpoints of a form assigned by archeologists in the southern plains to a Scallorn-like type. Some chipped knives and scrapers occurred. From imported marine shell, there were thick cylindrical to barrel-shaped beads made from the columella of the conch, as well as occasional spire-lopped *Marginella* and *Olivella* beads. Many mounds yielded no artifacts, perhaps because the mortuary offerings if any were made of perishable materials such as furs, leather, basketry, wood, or possibly woven textiles.

One of the larger, more productive, and best-reported tumuli in this locality is the James Younkin mound, 14GE6, about six miles (9.6 km) northwest of Junction City (Schultz and Spaulding 1948). Some 50 feet (15 m) in diameter and a little over four feet (1.2 m) high, it was underlain by a shallow basin 23 feet (7 m) across. This was floored with rough slabs, and the overlying fill contained fragmentary human bones, an extended human skeleton, animal bones, and artifacts. The mound fill consisted of angular fieldstones and a little soil. Scorched and calcined human bone fragments indicate the use of fire but not *in situ* burning. A small pottery vessel with dentate stamping, large sherds with cord-roughened exterior surfaces, and other fragments with rocker-stamping and cross-hatched rim incising indicate cultural influences from Hopewellian and perhaps other western Middle Woodland traditions. Whether these people possessed woven textiles, as did Hopewellian groups in the Midwest, is not known from any direct evidence. Other artifacts included stemmed and corner-notched projectile points, an ovoid chipped knife, a platform pipe of limestone, abundant disk beads and a few pendants of shell, long bone pins with expanded and decorated heads, columella beads of marine shell, and several hundred tubular bone beads both undecorated and annularly or spirally incised (plate 6.1). Fifteen distally perforated and proximally truncated deer toe bones, more or less conical in shape, suggest parts of ring-and-pin game sets (Culin 1907:527), or they could have functioned as costume parts or other items for personal adornment. The human bones and teeth recovered are estimated to represent a minimum of 20 individuals, ranging from infants to adults over 40 years old (Phenice 1969:35).

In the mound fill were unworked animal bones identified as mole, ground squirrel, grasshopper mouse, pocket gopher, cottontail rabbit, wood rat; the teeth of carnivores, deer, and bison; woodpecker wing parts; an eagle (?) claw; and fish remains. Some of the evidence suggests campsite debris; how it came to be included in burial mound fill, either accidentally or purposefully, is nowhere stated in the record nor is there mention of a habitation site in the immediate vicinity of the tumulus.

Despite its usually fragmentary condition and poor preservation, the human bone from the Republican River burial mounds has been analyzed in much detail (Phenice 1969), with some interesting results. The material originated in primary burials of extended and flexed skeletons interred in the flesh, in bundle burials made after removal of the softer body tissues and separation of the bones, and in fragments deposited here and there in pockets or scattered loosely through the mound fill. Cutting marks indicate that dismemberment sometimes involved the severing of major muscles and ligaments. The minimum number of individuals represented per mound varied from one to 29 and included remains of both sexes as well as subadults. Cremation was not universal, but when indicated, it appears to have involved individuals of all ages and both sexes.

Plate 6.1. Artifacts from James Younkin mound, 14GE6, Geary County, Kansas. Courtesy University of Kansas Museum of Anthropology. *Upper, left*, bone hairpins (?) with expanded heads; *right*, miniature pottery vessel with dentate stamp surface treatment; *lower*, platform pipe of limestone.

The bones indicate also some of the afflictions suffered by the native populations. They included chronic and acute inflammation of the bone (osteitis) through disease or accident; pitting from malnutrition; chronic and rheumatoid arthritis among older individuals; cuts, fractures, and dislocations; and abscessed and carious teeth. Very tentatively, the people appear to have been more closely related somatologically to the Kansas City Hopewellian racial stock than to the even more scantily represented Archaic physical types of the general region. A small-statured (average 5 feet 5 inches, or 165 cm, for males), gracile folk, possibly with long narrow crania and some occipital (and lateral frontal?) head deformation, has been suggested.

Farther upstream, Woodland remains on the Republican are of different character. Much of the material was also found in burial grounds, but there is also more information from the sites of villages or camps in which people lived (Hill and Kivett 1941; Kivett 1949:282; 1952:3, 59; 1970). The camp sites are usually small and inconspicuous, and they occur in a wide range of locations. Low terraces and flat-topped erosion remnants rising a few feet above the river or creek bottoms were frequently utilized, as were the sloping summits of the bluffs that bordered the valley and terraces on secondary streams. Here, small shallow basins may have been associated with lightly built shelters of poles, presumably covered with rush mats, thatch, hides, or other perishables, such basins seldom numbering more than a half dozen per site. Other small pits may have been for the storage of vegetable or animal foods, or of personal belongings. Occasional burned spots suggest fireplaces, and scattered postmolds are usually present. Animal remains include bones of bison, deer, antelope, and smaller mammals, as well as those of birds, fish, and shellfish. Bison bones seem to be more common than on eastern Plains Woodland sites, but there is no indication that the animals were taken in quantities by mass kills or drives, or by any methods other than such as might be used by a single hunter or two in pursuit of an elk or a deer.

There are no refuse heaps as such, but campsite debris, artifacts, and other material occur in the general mantle of dark soil that usually covers the sites and fills the dug features. Artifacts include work in pottery, stone, bone, and shell. The pottery is a thick utility ware, tempered with calcite, and bearing allover impressions of a cord-wrapped instrument. The usual vessel form appears to be a large jar with a more or less conical or round-pointed base (plate 6.2). Sherd counts suggest that pottery was not abundant, some of the Woodland camp sites yielding a total of fewer vessels than came from a single house site in later Village Indian cultural horizons. Weapon points include both large and small, stemmed and corner-notched forms. There are cutting, scraping, and chopping tools; small ovoid chipped celts are a characteristic type. Small grinding stones may have been used for crushing seeds, berries, dried roots, or other vegetable items, or for dried meat. Perforated deer leg bones probably served as arrow or dart shaft wrenches, and these were sometimes decorated with incising. Most of the tools appear to be those that might have been used in hunting, butchering, and skin dressing. The bison-scapula hoe blade, hallmark of the later Plains maize-growing cultures, is absent, and there is no clear evidence of any other tools that might have been used for crop cultivation. Of the wild berries, tubers, seeds, nuts, and other plant items that must have been gathered and processed to provide some nutritional balance to the otherwise

Plate 6.2. Restored pottery vessels from various cultures in the Republican River basin. *Upper left,* historic Pawnee, ca. A.D. 1800. Courtesy Nebraska State Historical Society. *Upper right,* Dismal River culture, ca. A.D. 1700. Courtesy Nebraska State Historical Society. *Lower left,* Upper Republican, ca. A.D. 1200. Courtesy National Anthropological Archives, Smithsonian Institution. *Lower right,* Keith focus Woodland, ca. A.D. 650. Courtesy Nebraska State Historical Society.

predominantly meat diet suggested by the bone refuse at the campsites, there is no evidence, partly because of generally unfavorable conditions for preservation and partly because of the collecting methods commonly employed to date.

Woodland period burial sites in the Nebraska section of the Republican River valley share a number of details with those of the lower valley, but the mortuary complex differs in one notable feature, the absence of mounds. Instead, from Webster County west to Harlan County, Nebraska, and on the lower Prairie Dog Creek in Phillips County, Kansas, there are ossuaries consisting of a large shallow basin or a group of small pits, or both, which contain the

Plate 6.3. Woodland culture sites in the Republican valley, Nebraska. *Upper,* Woodland culture habitation site, 25HK13, Hitchcock County, Nebraska. Site is on hillside between Massacre Canyon Monument and eroded slope. Courtesy Nebraska State Historical Society. *Lower,* Marshall ossuary (25HK1) under excavation on Republican River bluff, Harlan County, Nebraska.

disarticulated, fragmentary, and often partially burned bones of several or many individuals (Wedel 1935:174; Kivett 1953). These sites occur on the bluffs and valley terraces but not usually on the floodplains. The small pits may contain the incomplete remains of two to a dozen individuals, the larger basins those of as many as 60. At still other locations, for example, at the Massacre Canyon Woodland campsite, 25HK13 (plate 6.3), single flexed burials made in the flesh each occupied its own individual grave pit in or adjacent to the living area, accompanied by bone and shell beads, chipped flints, pigments, and other materials (Kivett 1952:12). The multiple interments of fragmentary bones from several or many individuals, often fire marked, suggest that these ossuaries may have been the final resting places of the deceased from a number of habitations scattered over the nearby stream valleys, or that they represent periodic interments of several years' accumulation of corpses (plate 6.4).

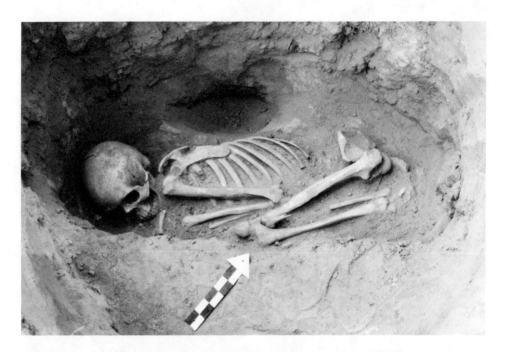

Plate 6.4. Woodland culture burial sites, Nebraska and Kansas. *Upper*, flexed primary burial of an adult male at site 25HK13 Nebraska. Courtesy Nebraska State Historical Society. *Lower*, disarticulated secondary burials at site 25FR9, Franklin County, Nebraska. Courtesy Nebraska State Historical Society.

The lamentable preservation conditions in which most Woodland skeletal remains have been found preclude satisfactory interpretation of the physical appearance and wider relationships of the populations. At the Woodruff ossuary, not fewer than 61 individuals are believed to have been represented, judging from the mandibles and mandible fragments recovered. Children aged 12 and under composed nearly half or 45 percent; adults 25 to 55 constituted 39 percent, about equally divided between the two sexes. Computed from the long bones present, stature appears to have averaged about 65 inches (165.2 cm) for

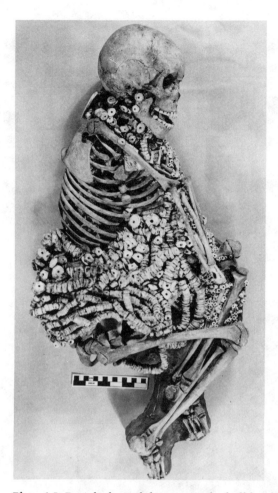

Plate 6.5. Burial of an adolescent with shell beads and other artifacts, Woodruff ossuary, Phillips County, Kansas, dated ca. A.D. 600. Courtesy National Anthropological Archives, Smithsonian Institution.

males and 62 inches (157.7 cm) for females. Dental caries were found in 43 percent of the mandibles; abscesses occurred in 36 percent, inferentially owing to extreme tooth wear, "which was noticeable in early adulthood." There were three cases of fused vertebrae indicating arthritic conditions, as well as lipping of lumbar vertebrae in several instances. The one reasonably complete skull, apparently a male and somewhat asymmetrical, had a cranial index of 83.34 percent and a length-height index of 83.64. The population represented is judged "to have been moderate in size and lack, in general, the robust characteristics of the historic Sioux and Pawnee" (R. B. Cumming in Kivett 1953:137).

A particularly striking feature of the Keith phase Woodland ossuaries is the abundance of disk beads made of freshwater shell, both finished and in unfinished or "blank" form. At most sites these are present by the hundreds; in the larger sites they number in the thousands. At Woodruff ossuary, 14PH4, on Prairie Dog Creek at the Kansas-Nebraska line, radiocarbon dated at ca. A.D. 600 ± 240 (Sample C-928), the complete skeleton of an adolescent reposing alone in a deep pit within a larger bone-strewn basin had been draped at burial with strings of such beads (plate 6.5); the skeleton was also accompanied by several triangular marine-shell pendants and a tool made from a perforated deer

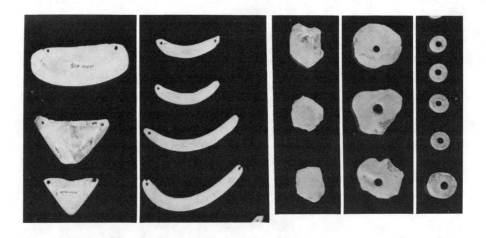

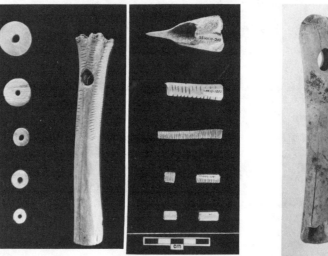

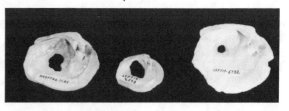

Plate 6.6. Shell, bone, and stone artifacts from Republican River prehistoric cultures. *Upper*, shell pendants, disk beads, and bead blanks from the Woodruff ossuary, Keith focus Woodland. Courtesy National Anthropological Archives, Smithsonian Institution. *Middle left*, shell disk beads, annularly incised bone beads, and shaft smoother from the Massacre Canyon Woodland site. Courtesy Nebraska State Historical Society. *Middle right*, bone shaft-straightener and projectile points from the Woodruff ossuary. Courtesy National Anthropological Archives, Smithsonian Institution. *Lower*, mussel-shell scrapers. Courtesy National Anthropological Archives, Smithsonian Institution.

leg bone. Pendants made of freshwater shell in triangular, oblong, crescentic, and narrow curved shapes also occurred. Marine shell from the Gulf coast was represented by thick, barrel-shaped beads from the columella of the conch, and by gastropods like *Olivella* and *Marginella*. Awls of bone, decorated deer leg-bone shaft wrenches, and plain and incised tubular bone beads also went into the burial deposits. Large corner-notched and small stemmed points, the latter with finely serrate blade edges, as well as chipped knives, scrapers, and other tools were present. There were also a few sherds of Harlan Cord-Roughened pottery, similar to the fragments found in the occupational sites in the same locality. We have no indication of whether perishable materials such as furs, leather, wood, basketry, or possibly textiles were included with the dead. Neither can we judge whether the bead-rich adolescent at Woodruff reflected some sense of rank in the local society or, alternatively, came to its death shortly before a communal burial involving otherwise mostly disarticulated dead from several communities over some years of time (plate 6.6).

Of much interest are two burials discovered during road building south of Indianola, in Red Willow County, Nebraska. Not yet described in detail or identified culturally, these burials were accompanied by artifacts of sheet mica, native copper, shell beads, red ocher, and chipped stone, including a Hopewell-like projectile point. A marine shell gorget resembling the "sandal-sole" gorgets of midwestern Archaic complexes was also present. Shell objects of this sort, and those of sheet mica and native copper, are not common in Nebraska and Kansas prehistoric sites. Whether the cultural affiliations here are with Hopewell or with an Archaic horizon is not yet clear (information from M. F. Kivett and G. F. Carlson, Nebraska State Historical Society, April 1983).

The Woodland lifeway in the plains has long been categorized as one of food-collecting, perhaps much like that of the Paleo-Indian and Archaic peoples previously, with an emphasis on hunting, some fishing, and the inferred gathering of wild vegetal products. At excavated sites, the debris of occupation is commonly scattered through a dark gray or "black" soil zone that may equal or exceed in thickness the detrital mantle associated with village sites of the later semisedentary Indians. Continuous residence over a long period of time seems less likely than repeated short-term occupations, perhaps featuring more or less regular seasonal stops in a cyclical pattern adjusted to the waxing or waning of various wild food crops. Such putative habitations as have been detected or suspected may well have been rebuilt annually when a family or small band returned to its campsite of a year or two before. The frequency of burial sites on the lower Republican and the seeming clustering of ossuaries in the vicinity of present Harlan County Reservoir suggest unusual population concentrations, but whether they were year-round or intermittent is still unclear.

The archeological evidence of foodstuffs consists largely of animal bone, some bird and fish remains, and mussel shells. The field methods used to date on Woodland sites, omitting water flotation, fine mesh screening, and other "total recovery" techniques, have very likely underplayed the true importance of the plant harvests, whose products normally involve recovery of few or no perishable parts such as charred fruit pits, nut shell fragments, and the like.

The bison, once thought to have been of possibly minor economic importance to the Plains Woodland people, now appears to have provided a greater share of the animal protein than the meager archeological remains from the eastern margin of the plains suggested to earlier field-workers. The decided scarcity of bison bones compared to deer bones at the Renner Hopewellian site near Kansas City (Wedel 1943:27) may have been an abnormal situation, or a reflection of butchering practices or of differing availability of local species. The changing viewpoint assumes, of course, that the animals were present in some numbers in Hopewellian Woodland times, as they apparently were in late prehistoric and early historic days. West of the tree line in pre-white times, here considered to have fluctuated between longitude 101° west and the Colorado line at 102°, Woodland cultural materials appear to be uncommon in the Republican River drainage. However desirable the headwaters steppe may have been in spring, summer, and fall as a range for hunting bison, in winter this essentially treeless terrain would seem to have been a most inhospitable and uninviting land for human occupation. Farther east, beginning perhaps in the vicinity of the historic Big Timbers of the Republican, near Atwood on the Beaver, and in Red Willow and Medicine Creek valleys on the north side of the Republican, belts of hardwood timber below the general level of the windswept uplands may have furnished shelter and a year-round supply of big game, though perhaps with some reduction in the numbers of animals actually available compared to their summertime abundance.

The methods used by the Woodland peoples to procure their bison can only be guessed at. There appears to be no evidence, such as extensive bone beds with butchered remains, to indicate mass kills of the sort well known from earlier periods and farther west in the short-grass plains. The animals could have been ambushed as they grazed in small bands on the bottomland grasses, perhaps on their way to or from watering points along the streams. Historical documents from the beginnings of white contact in the plains region leave one with the strong impression that prehorse hunters often found it possible to approach within easy bow shot of the animals, at which times one or two selected victims could presumably have been disabled or dispatched without panicking other members of the herd. Stalking by hunters disguised in the skins of wolves or other common predators was another possibility. The flat-floored grassy valleys, often with brushy heads and slopes, which are so characteristic of the short tributaries of the Republican in Harlan, Furnas, and Red Willow counties, as well as in the Medicine Creek drainage tributary to and above Medicine Creek reservoir (Harry Strunk Lake), would have been effective game traps for pedestrian hunters at all periods in prehistory.

In the timbered portions of the Republican River drainage other animal forms were drawn upon for their skins, flesh, and bones. Deer and elk supplied proteins, while bear, beaver, raccoon, and muskrat provided edible fats as well as proteins. All of these could have been trapped, snared, or shot by individual hunters. Gallinaceous birds, including especially prairie hens, sharp-tailed grouse, and quail, must have been abundant and easily obtained, and the wild turkey was probably available as far west as timber for roosting grew. Ducks and geese migrating along the central flyway augmented the numerous waterfowl bred locally along the slow-flowing, cattail-lined headwater streams and on the upland ponds. The local birds could have been taken with little difficulty, young or old, during the flightless moulting season in June and July, or as incompletely fledged young-of-the-year. Dogs would have greatly facilitated this operation.

Fish bones and mussels remain largely unidentified. Quantitatively, they constitute a relatively small fraction of the food remains found archeologically. There are no fish hooks, leisters, spears, or other devices obviously designed for taking fish in the known inventory of material culture, nor is there evidence of nets or poisons. The shellfish were presumably gathered by women and children in the clear-running streams beside the camps.

The dietary requirements of the Woodland people for starches, sugars, and other carbohydrates were met, inferentially, largely from the wild plant foods they could collect. The extent to which such foods were available and their identities in terms of species is by no means obvious. Ethnobotanical studies of historic Plains tribes, as I have pointed out elsewhere in this study, are not wholly satisfactory since they reflect in large part the fading knowledge of groups subject for a century or more to reservation life and largely ignorant of the wild seeds, grasses, and other plant products once regularly used by their unconfined forebears for food. Some inferences can be made from reports by early explorers and travelers, and also by extrapolation from other regions nearby, where the uses of certain plants prior to the introduction of the horse were remembered long after the equestrian plainsmen had forgotten the old ways.

In the Republican country, important sources of carbohydrates in prehorticultural days undoubtedly included such starchy roots and tubers as the prairie turnip (*Psoralea*), growing on grassy hillsides and meadows; the groundnut (*Apios*) and ground bean or hog peanut (*Amphicarpa*) in the bottomlands; the poppy mallow (*Callirhoë involucrata*); and in boggy meadows, the *Sagittaria* and cattail. The tender young shoots of cattail and bulrush (*Scirpus*) were available in spring, along with such greens as young pigweed (*Amaranth*), goosefoot (*Chenopodium*), dock (*Rumex*), and doubtless others. In July, riverbank grapes and choke cherries could be gathered, to be followed by sandhill and Chickasaw plums in midsummer and ground cherries (*Physalis*). Scattered on the uplands and more abundantly in streamside stands, the hackberry (*Celtis*) yielded its thin-fleshed, large-seeded, sugary fruits; crushed or ground into a pulp, pits and all, these provided a high calcium content as well as sugar. In late summer or early fall, the berries of the juniper provided another source of sugar. Two kinds of sunflower were available—the Jerusalem artichoke for its roots and the common sunflower for its oil-rich high protein achenes. Many of these items—tubers, roots, berries, and seeds—could be eaten fresh or they could be dried for later consumption, perhaps mixed with dried or fresh meat in stews and other dishes. At a considerable expenditure of time and labor, such grasses as dropseed (*Sporobolus*) and some of the sedges (*Cyperus*) could be harvested for their seeds, and the latter for tubers as well. In the sandy west, the fruits of the prickly pear were sometimes abundant, and the bush morning glory with its huge root helped to fill empty stomachs in times when other more palatable and nourishing foods were unavailable or in short supply.

West of longitude 101° west, the Republican country is beyond the range of most of the principal legumes and other edible plant species usually associated with Indians of the eastern plains; or, if the species occur, they are commonly in numbers too limited to make them a dependable food source for a native human population resident around the year. Moreover, their natural occurrence as seeds, fruits, greens, or other nutritive elements is highly seasonal, a deficiency that could be remedied only in part by drying or other storage techniques available to the prehistoric Indians. In this region, too, the scarcity or absence of trees and driftwood suitable for use as fuel would add another complication to the problem of year-round living, and available supplies of *bois de vache* or buffalo chips might not constitute adequate replacement. Alternatives to the rigors of winter living in this region would be (*a*) an eastward withdrawal to districts in which heavier stands of trees and brush would provide additional shelter and firewood against inclement weather or (*b*) dispersal into family or other small groups who could scatter out into the smaller valleys or even into other nearby drainages and try to survive until the next spring. In short, I believe that a case can be made for probable seasonal abandonment of the Colorado portions of the Republican drainage and a withdrawal eastward by the Indians to lower sections of the main valley or elsewhere.

Some of the considerable problems that could be anticipated in the Republican country in winter have been graphically portrayed in both art and literature. We have, for example, Lt. Eugene F. Ware's (1960:346) account of Gen. R. B. Mitchell's January 1865 campaign against the Indians who had been harassing frontier posts and ranches on the overland trail along the South Platte River. The Indians, principally Cheyennes and Arapahos, had taken refuge in the timbered sections of the Republican and its tributaries, where ample firewood, water, grass and cottonwood bark for the horses, herds of bison, and shelter from the biting winds could all be found in the bottoms. Mitchell's command, more than 600 strong, moved south from Cottonwood Springs (later Fort McPherson, near present North Platte, Nebraska), across the headwaters of the Medicine to the Stinking Water, Red Willow, and Frenchman, on to the Republican, across that into Kansas to the Beaver and Sappa creeks, back to the Republican, down that to the Medicine, and up the Medicine back to Cottonwood Springs.

On 22 January, moving down the main Republican through the Big Timbers, the command experienced a sharp turn for the worse in the already very cold weather. The temperature dropped rapidly and the wind "came down from the northwest with the fury of a cyclone." That night nobody slept. The horses were herded into the most sheltered part of the timber, and the men huddled downwind from fires fed by large heaps of logs. At 3 A.M. on 23 January, the general's thermometer registered −20°. The wind speed is not stated, but this is a region of frequent high winds. At −20°F, the wind-chill factor would have produced the equivalent of −67°F at a relatively modest wind velocity of 20 miles per hour, of −79°F at 30 mph, or of −85°F at 40 mph. At such temperatures, the danger of freezing exposed flesh is great. Despite the blazing log piles, "it seemed almost impossible to keep from being frost-bitten," according to Ware. The river froze solid, and next day the supply train of 100 wagons plus six pieces of artillery and more than 600 cavalrymen crossed on the ice without mishap.

Two years later, another detachment of troops found itself in a similar predicament in the same general region. Here, in the words of Col. Richard I. Dodge (Dodge 1877:40; 1883:504):

> While in command of Fort Sedgwick [near present Julesburg, Colorado, 1864–1871], in 1867, I was required to send a company of the 2nd Cavalry to the Republican River in February. It had been gone but a few days when a most violent storm set in. At the proper time the company returned without the loss of a man, but this result was due entirely to the indomitable

will and pluck of the captain [Capt. John Mix] in command. The company had to march for thirty miles in the teeth of the most terrific gale and blinding snow-storm and in at least 18 inches of snow. The men were made to dismount, and each, leading his horse, to take turns in opening the way through the snow. The cold and suffering were so intense and the toil so great, that some of the men refused to do more, and, throwing themselves into the snow, declared their intention of dying there rather than make another effort. Orders, entreaties, and threats, all proving unavailing, the captain finally fell upon them with the flat of his sabre, belabored them into the ranks, and brought all in safety to the post.

A scene from this episode, which took place on 1–2 March 1867, depicted by J. E. Taylor, an artist for *Frank Leslie's Illustrated Weekly* (1863–1883), appeared in Dodge's later book on the Plains Indians (Dodge 1883, facing p. 504; see also Rodenbough and Haskins 1896:180). The scene is reproduced here as plate 6.7.

Since General Mitchell, in the earlier campaign, never caught up with the elusive Indians he was pursuing, we can only speculate on how they fared during that chilly January night in 1865. They may have been waiting out the storm in tipis snugly tucked into sheltered hollows, away from the wind. Lieutenant Ware observed only that the experience "carried out Bridger's theory of the death of women and children" if pursuit of the Indians could be continued during a winter campaign. We do not know, of course, how often such storms occurred, but the two episodes noted above took place only two years apart.

Plate 6.7. A detachment of the Second U.S. Cavalry experiencing a winter storm in the Republican country. Taking his turn at breaking trail through the snow, the soldier in the lead studies a compass. At right, an officer threatens a fallen laggard with the flat of his saber. From Richard Irving Dodge, *Our Wild Indians*, 1883.

Table 6.1
Radiocarbon dates from Plains Woodland sites in the Republican River basin

Site		Date	Sample no.	Comment
25FT18	A.D.	820 ± 200	M-841	Charcoal; Keith focus
25FT70	A.D.	690 ± 80	SI-197	Charcoal; Woodland component under Upper Republican
14PH4	A.D.	607 ± 240	C-928	Woodruff ossuary; Keith focus
25RW28	A.D.	580 ± 100	UM-466	
25RW28	A.D.	530 ± 45	UM-68	
25FT18	A.D.	370 ± 100	SI-126	Charcoal; Keith focus
25RW28	A.D.	30 ± 70	UM-549	
25RW28	A.D.	20 ± 80	UM-470	
14GE12	A.D.	15 ± 75	UGa-381	Charcoal; Elliot site
25HK13	B.C.	130 ± 250	M-181	Shell; Massacre Canyon, Keith focus
25RW28	B.C.	3000 ± 120	UM-469	Too early; unacceptable

The weather records show that every county in the Republican basin west of Franklin, Nebraska, has experienced winter temperature minima of −25°F to −45°F. With or without high winds, these temperatures would probably have produced acute discomfort and perhaps genuine distress to a human population unable to reach the shelter of bottomland groves and a supply of firewood to supplement the usual Plains fuel of bison chips. According to Dodge (1883:501):

> In winter the Plains Indians, who are very susceptible to cold, remain in their teepees nearly all the time, going out only when forced to do so, and getting back as soon as possible to the pleasant warmth of their homes. Their ponies are wretchedly poor, and unable to bear their masters on any extended scout or hunt. They are in the very best possible condition to be surprised, and even to those who escape bullets, surprise is almost destruction from starvation and cold. . . . A day which would be death on the high Plains may scarcely be uncomfortably cold in a thicket at the bottom of a deep narrow cañon. Indians, plainsmen, and all indigenous animals understand this perfectly, and fly to shelter at the first puff.

Radiocarbon dates on the Republican River Woodland complexes range widely (table 6.1), suggesting a time span of some ten centuries. For the Kansas City Hopewellian sites, charcoal dates have a generally similar range. The early part of this span correlates in time with the later Sub-Atlantic climatic episode of Baerreis and Bryson (1965), when the summers were wetter and the winters stormier than at present. The later portion corresponds to the Scandic episode, when warmer and drier conditions may have returned to the plains. The discovery of charred maize kernels in Kansas City Hopewellian sites and at Loseke Creek, Nebraska, and of charred beans at Kansas City, suggests that conditions not unsuited to maize cultivation may have characterized the later Plains Woodland interval in this area. The evidence of malacology, that is, from the molluscan record, does not indicate any appreciable change in climatic conditions in the region compared to the present. Numerous charred wood fragments from the Woodruff ossuary have been identified (Wedel and Kivett 1956) as *Ulmus rubra*, slippery or red elm; *Fraxinus pennsylvanica subintegerrima*, green ash; and *Populus* sp., cottonwood, all common in the region today and strongly suggesting no significant environmental differences from the climate and vegetation of the present.

Chapter 7 Early Village Indians: The Central Plains Tradition

By the eighth or ninth century after Christ, far-reaching changes were taking place in the lifeways of the Central Plains Indians. The dimly marked and perhaps tentative attempts at plant cultivation by the late Plains Woodland peoples west of the Missouri River trench were being replaced by a small-scale but more deeply committed sort of gardening, with distinctive tools and a notable modification in the lifestyle. Just where, when, and how cultivation first reached the Central Plains Indians is not yet clear. In spite of some lingering professional skepticism, charred maize kernels and beans were found in a trash-filled storage pit at the Renner Hopewellian village site near Kansas City (Wedel 1943:26), radiocarbon dated in the early centuries of the Christian Era. Both the hunting of game on the woodland margin and gathering appear to have been more important subsistence strategies there, however.

On present evidence, crop growing as a major or primary subsistence activity seems to have appeared in the central plains about the time of the Neo-Atlantic climatic episode, which is radiocarbon dated at ca. A.D. 700–1100. At this time, moist tropical air is thought by some climatologists to have pushed northward in the Great Plains, bringing more rain to the central and northern sectors. This, in turn, encouraged the westward expansion of the prairies and a corresponding retreat of the short-grass steppe (Baerreis and Bryson 1965), presumably with some increase in the timber and brush cover along the stream valleys. This change in climatic conditions eventually made possible the addition of maize cultivation to a Plains subsistence economy already well adjusted to the pursuit of hunting and gathering. Whatever the time and circumstances of this development, to the gardening hamlet-dwelling peoples who followed the Woodland hunter-gatherers in the archeological sequence the designation of Central Plains Tradition has been given. With many variations in detail through time and space, this relatively settled way of life overspread considerable portions of the subhumid eastern plains from Texas to the Dakotas. The archeological materials from this time interval are sometimes divided into an Early Village and a Late Village period, with A.D. 1500 as the approximate level of transition. The Early Village Indians in the Republican River country, originally discussed as the prehistoric Pawnees, have been broadly designated since as the Upper Republican culture or phase (Strong 1933, 1935) and probably date within the period A.D. 1000–1400 ± 50 years.

The Upper Republican Culture

In our study area here, the Early Village Indian period is relatively well known from extended reconnaissance and excavations in and around Harlan County

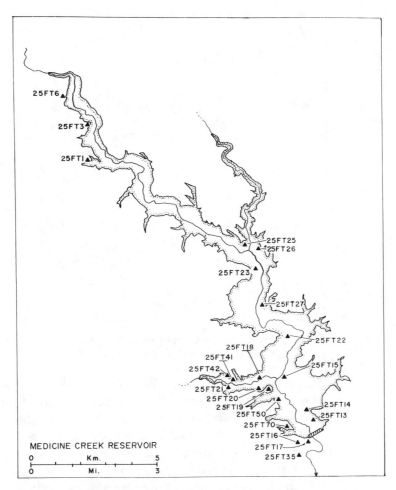

Fig. 7.1. Map of Medicine Creek reservoir (Harry Strunk Lake),
showing selected archeological sites and full pool limits.

and Medicine Creek reservoirs and nearby in Franklin, Harlan, and Frontier
counties (Strong 1935; Kivett 1949; Wedel 1934, 1935, 1959; Wood, ed., 1969).
At Medicine Creek (fig. 7.1), the large-scale mechanized operations in 1947–
1948 by the Smithsonian's River Basin Surveys and the Department of the
Interior's Bureau of Reclamation under the InterAgency Archeological and Paleontological Salvage Program made possible the stripping of overburden from
entire hamlet or small village areas and the examination of community settlement patterns on a scale never before attempted in the central plains. Outside
the Republican basin, a very large and important body of relevant data was
collected in 1939 by the Nebraska State Historical Society and Work Projects
Administration on Davis Creek in the North Loup River drainage. Note must
also be taken of extensive studies at the Glen Elder Reservoir on the Solomon
River in north central Kansas by the University of Nebraska (Krause 1969,
1970; Lippincott 1976, 1978). More limited investigations have taken place at
other widely scattered sites and localities in Nebraska, northern Kansas, and
northeastern Colorado since the 1920s.

The Upper Republican villagers seem to have had a decided preference for
living on the smaller tributaries rather than along the main stem of the Re-

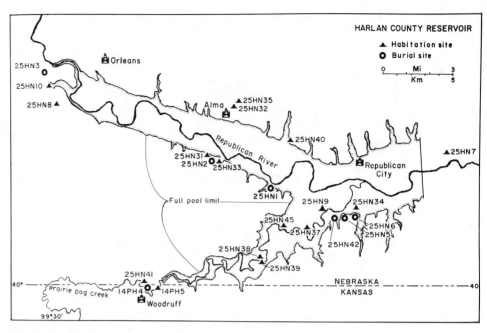

Fig. 7.2. Map of Harlan County Reservoir, showing certain modern towns, selected archeological sites, and full pool limits.

publican. In this area, the Republican valley soils are often sandy and tree growth tends to be limited. The tributaries have firmer soils and many more hardwood trees suitable for use as fuel and building materials. On the tributaries there was also less danger of flooding of habitations by overflow from the nearby streams in times of excessive precipitation. Harlan County Reservoir (fig. 7.2) is in the general area where the Beaver-Sappa and Prairie Dog creeks join the Republican, providing easy and well-watered travel routes toward the west and southwest for hunting, trading, and acquisition of stone for tool making. Here, too, following high water in any or all of the confluent streams, which drain a total area of 20,000 square miles (54,000 sq km), quantities of driftwood probably collected and could be easily salvaged by residents of the adjacent communities: On a much smaller scale, this was true also of the Medicine Creek reservoir locale. In both districts, the hinterlands of small tributary canyons, often flat floored and well grassed in their upper portions, commonly with thickets of wild plum, choke cherry, and buffaloberry, were added attractions to pedestrian horticultural groups with continuing interest in hunting and gathering as supplements to crop growing (plate 7.1).

The Settlement Pattern: Communities and Habitations.

Streamside terraces, gently sloping hillsides, and broad well-drained bluff tops were favored locations for habitations. The sites indicate a small village or hamlet pattern of settlement, with houses scattered singly or in small clusters of three to five or six units at intervals of a few yards to several hundred yards from each other (plates 7.2 and 7.3), within 200 yards of a stream or spring. These loose aggregations of dwellings contrast strikingly with the compactly arranged and generally larger towns occupied by the Pawnees and other historic village tribes of the central plains. The prehistoric Upper Republican communities were apparently never fortified, nor are they situated or arranged to suggest that considerations of defensibility were determinative. Indeed, their

Plate 7.1. Sites and scenes in the Republican country. *Upper*, view north up Medicine Creek (right) at the junction with Lime Creek, Frontier County, Nebraska. A Woodland Culture camp site, 25FT18, is under excavation at center beyond the creek; *lower*, junction of the Republican River (right) and Lost Creek, Franklin County, Nebraska. The Dooley site (25FR3) is at the extreme left on the near side of creek.

Plate 7.2. Upper Republican sites in the Medicine Creek reservoir (Harry Strunk Lake) area, Nebraska. *Upper*, aerial view of a hamlet of three house sites and refuse area at 25FT17, dated ca. A.D. 1150–1220. House floor at left is shown in ground view below; *lower*, house floor with six center posts and two fireplaces, site 25FT17. Courtesy National Anthropological Archives, Smithsonian Institution.

characteristically diffuse layout would have made the construction of effective fortifications nearly impossible with the limited manpower and timber resources inferentially available.

By comparison with the earlier and sparsely evidenced Woodland habitations, those of the Upper Republican people were much more substantially

Plate 7.3. Upper Republican sites in Medicine Creek reservoir (Harry Strunk Lake), Nebraska. *Upper*, aerial view of hamlet of two house sites and refuse area features at 25FT70, dated ca. A.D. 1150–1215; *lower*, house floor with four center postholes and single fireplace at 25FT70. Courtesy National Anthropological Archives, Smithsonian Institution.

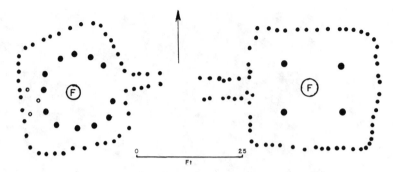

Fig. 7.3. Floor patterns of Upper Republican houses, showing central
fireplace and posthole arrangement. The triangle of postmolds shown
by *open circles* in plan at left, opposite entrance vestibule, suggests
an altar or household shrine. The circular pattern of twelve interior
postmolds is unusual.

built, probably larger, and would certainly have provided better protection in
cold weather. As reconstructed by archeologists from recurrent findings in the
field, houses were typically "square" to subrectangular in floor plan, with
rounded corners (plate 7.3). Size varied greatly: a side averaged around 26 to 28
feet (8–8.5 m), and the floor area ranged between 650 and 800 square feet (58–
75 sq m). Rarely, the floor exceeded 1,000 square feet (92 sq m), the equivalent
of a house 32 feet (10 m) square or about 30 by 35 feet (9 by 10.5 m). A long
covered entrance passage opened away from the prevailing northwesterly
storms and winter winds. The fireplace was a single hole dug in the center of
the floor, usually round and not lined with stones, curbed, or otherwise specially prepared. Very rarely was there more than one such hearth, but signs of
smaller secondary fires have been noted occasionally between the central fireplace and the house wall (fig. 7.3).

Roughly midway between the central fireplace and each corner a large post
was set into the ground; if one or more suitably heavy timbers were not available, their positions were taken by two or three smaller ones, set close together. Other posts, closely spaced and usually of lighter proportions, were
placed around the perimeter of the floor to carry the outer edge of the roof and
the upper edge of the wall, both of which consisted of light poles, grass, and
finally earth or sod. This inferred construction, based in part on fallen roof
and wall sections that were preserved by charring, is much like that observed
in the historic Plains earthlodges, but identical methods cannot be conclusively demonstrated from available evidence. It seems possible that the
walls of some houses, or portions of them, may have consisted of clay plastered
against closely set upright poles in a modified *jacal* construction (Wood, ed.,
1969; cf. Wedel 1970a:229). Although they were once commonly characterized
as pithouses, it now appears more probable that most Upper Republican dwellings were essentially surface structures with floors not more than a few inches
below the contemporary ground surface. Following their abandonment and col-
lapse of the superstructure, the ruins were covered by wind-laid dust and, not
uncommonly, by household trash from still occupied houses nearby. Such ac-
cumulations reached depths of six to 24 inches (15–60 cm) or more and are
sometimes visible today in unbroken ground as low mounds.

There is no way of determining from the house floor plan or the posthole pattern how the sleeping and other domestic conveniences of the erstwhile household were arranged, or the number of persons who may have lived in it. In the larger historic earthlodges of the central plains, about 55 square feet or five square meters of floor space per person has been calculated as a possible ratio (Wedel 1979a). According to this calculation, from three to five individuals could have been accommodated in the generally smaller lodges of prehistoric times. The small lodges, one suspects, were mostly one-family affairs, whereas the larger ones could have sheltered three or four families or a single extended family group, that is, grandparents, parents, and children, for example. As a rough guess, it seems unlikely that many of the still inadequately studied and ill-defined Upper Republican hamlets in the Republican basin had a population much in excess of 50 to 75 persons, and most were almost certainly much smaller. There is no clear evidence of special ceremonial structures or religious centers, unless the larger houses or the occasional ones with six or more center posts or with two or more well-marked fireplaces can be so regarded. Among the Plains Village Indians, we may note further, the number of families living in a house cannot be judged from the number of fireplaces the structure contained.[1]

The life expectancy of these lodges is difficult to estimate. The historic Pawnee earthlodges, constructed of much heavier timbers than those used by most Upper Republican peoples, were said (Weltfish 1965) to have been serviceable for 10 to 12 years; Wilson (1934:372) reported 7 to 10 years for the Hidatsa houses. Excepting the four main center posts, timbers in the prehistoric Upper Republican structures probably seldom exceeded five to seven inches (12–18 cm) in butt diameter, and in many cases they appear to have been little more than half that size. For posts in direct contact with the ground, as these were, red cedar (*Juniperus virginiana*) was by all odds the most durable wood available on the Republican, but trees of suitable size and form were probably limited in quantity and distribution. Bur oak (*Quercus macrocarpa*), which grows today as far west as the Harlan-Frontier county line, is likewise highly resistant to decay. But it is also much harder, tougher, and more difficult to work, and it may therefore have been less popular among Indian house-builders before iron tools became available to them. Osage orange (*Maclura pomifera*) was unavailable. The far more common hardwoods, including cottonwood (*Populus*), willow (*Salix*), ash (*Fraxinus*), elm (*Ulmus*), and perhaps box elder (*Acer negundo*), were the usual construction materials. Of these, only the slippery or red elm (*U. rubra*), which grew naturally as far west as Frontier County (Pool 1966:103), provided much durability, with cottonwood and willow the least satisfactory. Hackberry (*Celtis*), green ash (*F. pennsylvanica subintegerrima*) and American elm (*U. americana*) offered somewhat better potential.

Posts made from most of these common hardwood species may have rotted out at the base after three to five or six years of use, leaving a shaky frame or a leaky roof. If enough of the house timbers were thus failing, the occupants may have found it more satisfactory to relocate in a new structure a few rods up or down the stream; or, if the available timber supply had been used up or was inadequate for other reasons, a move to the next unoccupied creek valley a few miles distant might have been in order. Under such circumstances, a single family or household could have been responsible for four or five house sites or more during a normal adult lifetime. From this, it follows that an abundance of house ruins in a creek valley is perhaps as likely to reflect frequent moves by a small population as a heavy or intensive occupation by a larger one. The limited refuse deposits at most known western Upper Republican sites seems to confirm short-lived occupation and frequent shifts in location of residence.[2]

In nearly every house were to be found one or more subfloor storage or cache pits, and these occasionally occurred outside as well. Not infrequently, a small trash heap was also present just outside the doorway. Abandoned houses were sometimes used as garbage dumps. From the debris associated with these various features and in the mantle of refuse that covers most community sites, we may judge something about the subsistence basis for Upper Republican living and the activities of the inhabitants.

The Subsistence Base

The Early Village Indians of the Republican country relied upon a garden economy based on maize, beans, squash, and sunflowers cultivated by hoe, combined with hunting, some fishing and gathering of mussels, and inferentially the collecting of various wild plant foods in season. The bison-scapula hoe, with the bone blade attached at a right or acute angle to a wooden handle, was the hallmark of the Plains Village Indian period, and the wooden digging stick can be safely inferred. Bison were regularly utilized, their bones usually far outranking in the refuse any other species in terms of the quantity of meat implied and the proportion of animal protein thus supplied. As many as 36 other species of large and small mammals, nine reptiles and amphibians, and at least 20 species of birds have been identified from Medicine Creek Upper Republican sites. All are still present in the regional fauna as witnessed by white men, and they indicate no significant climatic or other environmental differences from the present. From a few cache pits used secondarily for garbage disposal at Medicine Creek were recovered quantities of freshwater mussels, most of them unburned, and many still retained the greenish brown periostracum and had hinges in articulation. They reveal another source of animal protein, but their remains are in very limited amount compared to the land forms and their importance in the Indian diet should not be overemphasized from the seeming abundance of the valves in a few trash pits. Fish bones also occurred, as did curved barbless bone hooks. Of the wild vegetal products that were available and might have been used, and in what proportions, we have virtually no evidence at present. (See appendix B.)

Arts and Industries

Prominent also in the community debris are the broken and discarded products from the arts and crafts practiced by the ancient villagers. These included pottery making and varied other activities in the manufacture of bone, stone, horn, and shell artifacts. A common vessel form in pottery was a full-bodied, round-shouldered, and round-bottomed jar with constricted neck and mouth, and a collared or braced rim (plates 6.2 and 7.4). Bowls and other forms seem to have been uncommon. The exterior vessel surface either was left plain and smoothed or else was roughened with impressions from a cord-wrapped paddle. On the unthickened vertical or outflared rims that constituted a minority, the cord impressions were usually carried up to the vessel lip. The outer panel of the collared rims usually bore incised or trailed decoration, varying from three to six parallel horizontal lines to repeated triangular areas filled with slanted lines or various combinations of horizontal and diagonal lines, and

Plate 7.4. Upper Republican artifacts. Courtesy National Anthropological Archives, Smithsonian Institution. *Upper,* cord-roughened pottery vessels from sites in Medicine Creek reservoir; *lower,* chipped stone knives and chopping tools from Upper Republican and Woodland (lower right) sites in Medicine Creek reservoir.

other motifs. Finger-pinched nodes sometimes embellished the lower edge of the collar. There is some evidence that rim decoration became more elaborate and varied in later times.

The cord markings on Upper Republican pottery are usually finer and often less deeply impressed than those on the earlier Woodland culture vessels. In further contrast to the heavy walls and abundant coarse calcite tempering that characterized the local Woodland pottery, the Upper Republican jars were relatively thin walled and were tempered with sand or moderately fine gravel. They were also much more abundant, a single Upper Republican house ruin commonly producing fragments of more vessels than are taken by the archeologist from an entire Plains Woodland site. Inferentially, some of these vessels may have been used in boiling meat or garden vegetables such as maize and beans, perhaps with wild tubers added, or in combinations of these various ingredients in a thick soup or stew. They would also have been useful for dry storage and perhaps as water containers.

We do not know whether there was craft specialization by certain women, or whether the needed pots and baskets were produced by each family or household for its own use. It is quite possible that a few women produced most or all of the vessels and containers used by the households living within a single or in neighboring creek valley communities. The source or sources of the clay and tempering materials used by the native potters in the Republican basin at this and other periods are still unknown. Their identification in the field and study by a competent ceramist would be a most desirable contribution to knowledge.

Cord impressions on the pottery suggest the presence of textiles, but there is no other evidence from which their presence or their nature can be further argued. Perforated pottery disks found at a few sites, usually fashioned from reworked vessel fragments, may indicate spindle whorls. Locally available sources of vegetal fibers suitable for cordage manufacture included slippery elm (*Ulmus rubra*), nettle (*Urtica gracilis*), and yucca. Cattails may have been used for making baskets and mats. Bison-hair cordage and woven fabrics may have been in use, as they were among the later historic Pawnees. There is no satisfactory evidence of basketry, but here, as with textiles, cordage, and leather products, unfavorable preservation conditions rather than absence of the needed skills or of raw materials are presumably responsible. Well-polished bone awls and needles may be an indirect indication of manufacturing or craft processes whose end products are not otherwise reflected in any evidence surviving for the archeologist to find.

Small triangular projectile points, usually side notched and readily distinguished from the larger corner-notched or stemmed dart and spear points of the Woodland peoples, suggest that the common hunting weapon was the bow and arrow, of which no examples survive. Cutting and chopping tools, including leaf-shaped and ovoid forms as well as diamond-shaped knives with four oppositely beveled blade edges, were fashioned from stone. Snub-nosed or plano-convex end scrapers, presumably set in bone or wooden hafts and used in skin working, and straight-shafted and T-shaped drill points (plate 7.4) were also made of stone.

Bone artifacts, in addition to the ubiquitous bison scapula hoe blades from which the scapular spine had been removed, included split mammal leg bone and splinter awls; eyed needles; bipointed fish gorges and curved fishhooks; edge-slotted knife handles of rib; shaft wrenches of bone or antler; split metapodial gouges or fleshers, not serrated; pierced bison phalanges; bison spine beamers; deer mandibles with polished diastema; oblong game counters (?); and split metapodial beamers for dehairing deer and other small mammal hides (plates 7.5 and 8.3).

Of special interest among the bone artifacts is a worked human calvarium

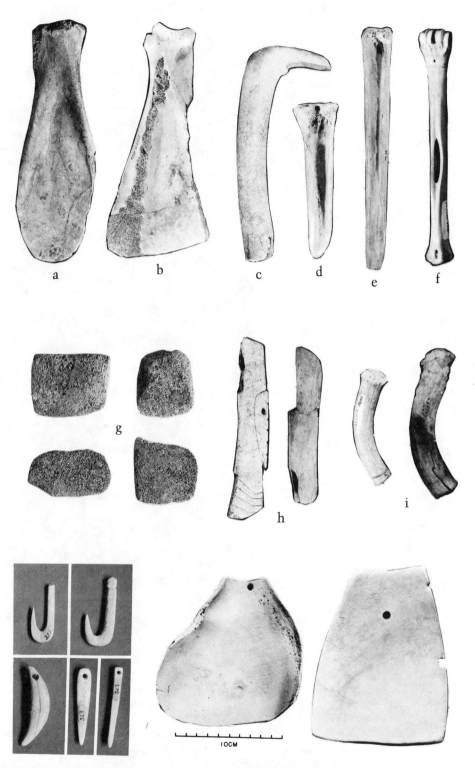

Plate 7.5. Bone, shell, and antler tools from Republican River sites. *a, c, g,* historic Pawnee; others Upper Republican culture. *Upper left,* scapula hoe blades; *upper right,* hide dressing tools; *middle,* cancellous bone paint applicators, edge-slotted knife handles, and flint-knapping tools of antler; *lower,* bone fish hooks, animal tooth and shell pendants, and conch shell gorgets. Bureau of American Ethnology Bulletin 112.

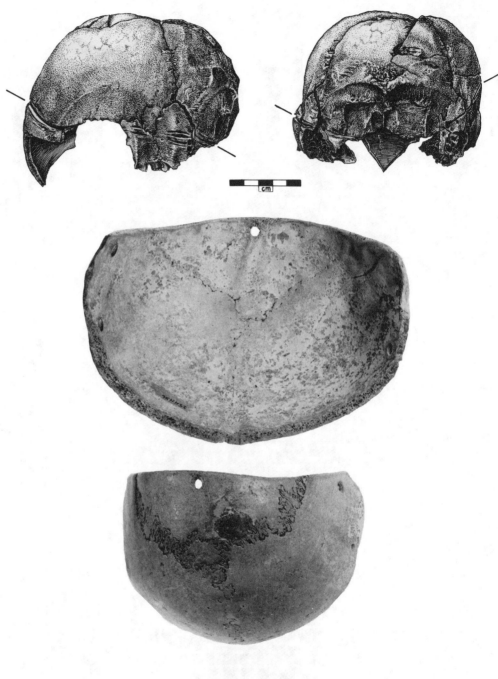

Plate 7.6. Worked human crania from Upper Republican sites. *Upper*, left lateral and rear aspects of incomplete calvarium from site 25FT13 in the Medicine Creek reservoir. Courtesy National Anthropological Archives, Smithsonian Institution. *Middle* and *lower*, cut and drilled calvarium segment from 25HN36, Harlan County Reservoir. Courtesy Department of Anthropology, University of Nebraska–Lincoln.

recovered in pieces from cache-pit fill in a house ruin at site 25FT13 in Medicine Creek reservoir, Nebraska. As reassembled in the laboratory (plate 7.6), it includes most of the occipital and both parietals of an adult. Traces of red hematite are visible on one or two fragments. Shallow cuts begin at the posterior margin of the foramen magnum, pass behind the stumps of the mastoid processes which were forcibly removed, thence curve upward just above the squamous suture, and pass over the vault at or near the bregma. The cuts are deepest on the parietals but nowhere exceed 3 mm. They are much deeper than would have resulted from scalp removal, but they were not deep enough to control the breaking of the bone for what seems to have been planned as a bowl, cup, or container. The bone suggests a seasoned skull rather than a fresh or green specimen and perhaps reflects an attempt to fashion a container from an already damaged and incomplete cranium collected from an ossuary or scaffold burial. The cut marks, with which most of the broken edges do not closely coincide, may then indicate unsuccessful or aborted attempts at the removal of irregularly fractured edges and the achievement of a neatly dressed vessel rim. The piece may have been discarded unfinished because of its intractable nature at the hands of the artisan. It is an unusual piece and its significance is unclear at the moment.[3]

Antler and shell seem to have been used in lesser amounts for artifacts. Antler was used for dressed cylindrical sections with polished ends; thinly scraped incised bracelets or bow guards (plate 7.7); and occasional simple pendants, gorgets, and tubular beads for personal adornment. The scanty shellwork consists of a few disk beads, simple tapered pendants, and mussel shells with serrate edges and unknown function. Most of the shell was of freshwater forms (plates 7.5 and 6.6).

Red and yellow ocher pigments occur in small quantities at many sites. Hammerstones; small anvil stones for crushing berries, bones, and perhaps dried meat and other products; and equal-armed stone pipes are other artifacts in the inventory.

Much of the chipped stonework was fabricated from the locally abundant brown to yellow Graham jasper, which overwhelmingly predominates in the extensive River Basin Surveys Upper Republican collections from Medicine Creek and from the Harlan and Franklin counties districts. Present in much smaller quantities is the reddish to grayish purple Flat Top flint from ancient quarries northwest of Sterling, Colorado, about 175 miles (280 km) from Medicine Creek by way of the Frenchman Creek. Also represented are other chalcedonies, quartzite from the local Tertiary Ogallala and from Spanish Diggings in Wyoming, a scattering of Alibates agatized dolomite from the Texas Panhandle, and other materials.

Imported nonlithic items suggest trade relations with other peoples and areas in several directions. Strong (1935:111–114) has reported artifacts made of Gulf coast conch shell (*Busycon perversum* Linn), freshwater snail shells (*Anculosa praerosa* Say) "common in the Ohio and Wabash Rivers and southward but not known to occur west of Illinois," marine olivellas (*Olivella jaspidea* Gmelin) "from the Gulf or Atlantic coast," and a marginella (*Marginella apicine* Menke) from the Florida or Gulf coast. From a probable early Upper Republican burial location, 14JW207, on White Rock Creek in Jewell County, Kansas, were taken two large pendants of conch identified as *Busycon contrarium* Conrad (Neuman 1963:297).

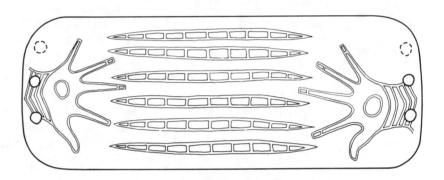

Plate 7.7. Antler and copper artifacts from Upper Republican burial sites. *Upper left,* decorated antler bow guard from the Graham ossuary 25HN5. Courtesy Department of Anthropology, University of Nebraska. *Upper right,* decorated antler bowguard from Christensen ossuary 25HW8 on Davis Creek. Courtesy Nebraska State Historical Society. *Middle,* incised decoration and tie-holes on bowguard from the Graham ossuary. Courtesy Department of Anthropology, University of Nebraska. *Lower,* copper overlays on perforated wooden disks from the Graham ossuary. Courtesy Department of Anthropology, University of Nebraska–Lincoln.

Disposal of the Dead

Treatment of the dead among the Upper Republican people is somewhat reminiscent of earlier Woodland cultural practices. There appear to have been some burials in the flesh and in flexed posture, in dug graves within the village or camp area. Perhaps more common were secondary burials that involved exposure of the corpse until the softer tissues decayed, followed by interment of the disarticulated bones in large communal pits atop the bluffs overlooking the habitation areas (Strong 1935:102; Kivett 1953:130, 135). Associated with these pits is broken ("killed"?) pottery similar in all essentials to that found in the houses and refuse deposits, along with small numbers of shell disk beads, simple shell pendants, and occasional chipped stone artifacts. The shell disk beads are never present in the great numbers usually found in Woodland ossuaries nor do the large triangular shell pendants of the Woodland people occur in Upper Republican ossuaries.

Little detailed information is available on the nature of Upper Republican ossuaries, since numbers of them were severely damaged or destroyed many years ago before systematic work was done or adequate records kept. The Graham ossuary (25HN5) in Harlan County, excavated by Strong in 1930 on Prairie Dog Creek, suggests what properly done investigations might have retrieved in the way of information and artifacts. In addition to pottery, stonework, bone, and shell of local manufacture, there were recovered portions of two thin wooden disks, centrally perforated, about 54 mm in diameter, and covered with thin sheet copper (Strong 1935:114, and plate 9, *2, f, g*). These were presumably obtained from contemporary native people to the east and southeast (plate 7.7).

Further suggesting contacts with alien native groups is a thinly scraped antler bow guard from Graham (Strong 1935:111, and plate 10, *2*), partially described as follows (plate 7.7):

The material appears to be antler, probably elk, split along the grain and then steamed and bent into a circle. Its length, if laid out flat, would be 170 mm, and its width is 55 mm; it has three neatly bored holes in each end for the attachment of thongs to go around the arm. The outer surface is smoothly polished. . . . The incised design consists of an outspread hand at either end reaching along the bracelet, the wrist of each hand is decorated with four angular lines probably representing bracelets, there is a circle on the center of each hand, and the nails of each finger are clearly indicated. Around the greater curve of the object are six double lines, each cross-hatched at 8-mm intervals. Each of these double lines culminates in a point and reaches just within the fingers on both ends. . . . In size, it comfortably fits the forearm of a grown man just above the wrist.

The hand and eye motif, consisting of an extended hand containing a naturalistic or stylized eye in the center of the palm (or on the back of the hand in this instance) is a well-known and common feature in southeastern prehistoric art. It is frequently associated with the Southern Cult or Southeastern Ceremonial Complex of ca. A.D. 1250 (Waring and Holder 1945:4, and fig. I, *VII, a–d*; Fig. III, *u*; Muller 1983:411). Whether the Graham site piece reflects "cult" activities on the Republican it is impossible to say.

**Upper Republican
Maize Horticulture:
Problems and
Prospects**

The evidence of archeology suggests that by combining new or improved food-producing practices with the older Plains food-collecting economy, the Upper Republican people achieved a more complete utilization of the natural resources of the Republican valley than did their nonhorticultural predecessors. It is probably true that they were able to live in larger and more permanent communities whose inhabitants may have enjoyed a more affluent lifeway than that of the preceding groups—affluent, that is, if one measures this quality by the relative abundance of artifacts and other materials left behind.

Unfortunately, we have no way of assessing at the moment the relative effort expended by local groups in exploiting effectively the two diverse subsistence economies now opening to them. It must be recognized, however, that such groups were confronted with new problems and hazards whose aftermath could be a more serious threat to the welfare of a semisedentary society than to hunters and gatherers. Thus, they were more closely tied to the land, or to a particular parcel of it, where their gardens lay. If they left to hunt or for other reasons, they faced the prospect of damage or destruction to unwatched crops by insect pests, the overrunning of maize and bean patches by deer, bison, raccoon, and other predators, and perhaps even theft by persons known or unknown. There was, too, the ever-present question of the weather before and during the growing season, perhaps the most difficult and unpredictable obstacle of all. This merits further discussion here, since these people were the first native Americans we know who attempted crop cultivation in the central plains west of the 100th meridian.

Maize (*Zea mays*) is a warm-weather grass of American origin that requires plentiful moisture and high temperatures for maximum growth and productivity. In the United States, before the days of large-scale irrigation, chemical fertilizers, and high-yield hybrids, little maize was grown west of the eight-inch (200 mm) summer (June–August) rainfall line, roughly at the 100th meridian. Nighttime temperatures below 60°F (16°C) inhibit growth, as do sustained daytime readings in excess of 90°F (33°C), particularly when the latter are accompanied by deficient rainfall and strike during the critical tasseling stage. Nevertheless, through selective breeding by the American Indian over centuries of time, the maize plant has been developed into an extraordinary range of varieties with wide geographical, climatic, and soil tolerances, and wholly dependant on human intervention for survival. Perhaps the last of the world's three major cereals to be domesticated, it has also become the highest in yield. In the ratio of grain harvested to grain planted, production may reach as high as 300 or 500 to one, and more. Measured by the yield per acre or hectare planted, maize again heads the list over wheat and rice. In the Great Plains, the superiority of the strains developed by the Village Indians, including the Pawnees and their ancestors, over the midwestern varieties whose introduction into the central and northern plains was unsuccessfully attempted by the early white settlers, confirmed the magnitude of this native American Indian achievement in plant breeding (Will 1924; Weatherwax 1954; Mangelsdorf 1974; Brown 1978).

Although it is today a major cereal food in many parts of the world and often composes a large proportion of the daily diet for great numbers of people, maize is inferior to other cereals in nutritional value. It is notably deficient in protein, both in quantity and in quality. It is deficient also in niacin in available

Table 7.1
Growing season precipitation and temperature data from selected stations in and around the Republican River basin, 1951–1960

| | Mean monthly precipitation (inches) | | | Mean monthly temperature (F°) | | | No. of days temperature above 90°F | | |
	June	July	August	June	July	August	June	July	August
Genoa, NE	4.55	3.24	3.01	71.0	76.0	75.0	10	17	14
Red Cloud, NE	4.30	3.26	2.67	71.5	78.0	77.0	12	18	18
Franklin, NE	3.97	3.14	2.81	72.0	78.0	77.0	12	18	18
Harlan Co. Dam, NE	4.33	3.12	2.73	—	—	—	9	16	18
Beaver City, NE	3.80	3.38	2.67	72.5	78.0	77.0	15	22	20
Norton, KS	3.72	3.23	2.53	71.5	77.0	76.0	12	18	20
Medicine Creek Dam, NE	3.73	2.91	3.11	—	—	—	10	18	19
Curtis, NE	3.86	2.99	2.58	70.0	76.0	75.0	11	21	18
McCook, NE	3.29	3.06	2.47	71.0	77.0	74.0	13	21	20
Wray, CO	2.90	2.75	2.26	68.0	76.0	74.0	13	20	22

SOURCE: United States Department of Commerce, 1964. Supplement for 1951–1960, nos. 86–12 and 86–21.

form and in the amino acid tryptophan, from which the body can make niacin. Niacin, a B complex vitamin, is essential in the prevention of pellagra, which, except in the United States, is found widely among peoples for whom maize is a principal food. Among the Plains Indians, the regular use of legumes, in both domesticated and wild forms, and the extensive use of bison meat, offset the nutritional deficiencies of maize (United States Department of Agriculture 1959:139–144).

Some characteristics of the Republican River basin growing season that directly affect maize cultivation are summarized in table 7.1 (United States Department of Agriculture 1964). Whether precipitation or temperature is more critical is not important here, nor is it implied that only these two elements are of concern to the maize-grower. As a practical matter, however, the record shows that in the Republican River drainage, the corn farmer today has been able to double, treble, or even quadruple his crop yield by introducing irrigation and thereby assuring a dependable and adequate moisture supply whatever the ambient weather. Table 7.2 shows the relative yields of corn in a recent year from irrigated and nonirrigated fields in the Republican River district. Conversely, it has not been demonstrated just what temperature manipulations would be required to achieve the same increase in yield while holding the moisture supply constant, were that strategy feasible.

Table 7.2
Yields of corn for Republican River counties in Colorado and Nebraska, 1974

	Irrigated yield (bushels per acre)	Nonirrigated yield (bushels per acre)
Nebraska		
Chase	96	24
Dundy	82	18
Franklin	92	23
Frontier	101	25
Furnas	99	28
Harlan	107	24
Hayes	88	23
Hitchcock	110	24
Red Willow	108	31
Webster	91	22
Colorado		
Kit Carson	109	22
Lincoln	84	21
Yuma	108	20

SOURCE: Colorado Department of Agriculture 1976, p. 13, and Nebraska Department of Agriculture 1976, p. 21.

In the central plains of Nebraska and Kansas, the western limits of native Indian maize cultivation by Caddoan-speaking peoples since the coming of Euro-Americans in the 16th century lay near the 10.5-inch (270 mm) summer isohyet. The Pawnees, for example, tilled their garden patches in Nebraska along the Platte and Loup rivers east of St. Paul, on the Republican east of Red Cloud, and on the Blue. In Kansas, the Wichita-related "Quivirans" met by Coronado and other early Spanish explorers did their gardening east of the longitude of Great Bend, again not far from the 10.5-inch summer rainfall line. In both these areas, the expectancy of a subnormal or drought year, with summer rainfall dropping below eight inches (200 mm) and crop shortages or failure in prospect, was about one in four. From the archeological record, we know that maize was being grown in the 12th and 13th centuries as far west as McCook, Nebraska, where summer rainfall today averages between eight and nine inches (200–230 mm), and the likelihood of less than eight inches rises to about one year in two.

Here we direct attention again to the often sharply localized variability that characterizes summer rainfall in this region. The Upper Republican garden plots were presumably scattered up and down the creek valleys, near the houses but in the subirrigated bottoms. Historically, in the Genoa district, the hand-tilled bottomland patches seem to have suffered less from drought and grasshopper infestations than the upland fields planted and cultivated by the government farmers for the Pawnee agency. Even so, when the summer rainfall dropped to an inch or two per month, or less, from June to August, one wonders whether the Indian gardens could still be depended upon to produce the maize needed for consumption, fresh and dried, until the next year's crop. Some figures from the historical records of the white farmer are of interest in this connection.

In table 7.3, the summer rainfall has been indicated for 12 selected years in four separate localities in and around the Republican River drainage. Of the

Table 7.3
Departures in percentages from summer rainfall averages in selected years at certain stations in and around the Republican River basin

	Genoa (Nance)	North Loup (Valley)	Red Cloud (Webster)	Beloit-Cawker (Mitchell)	Franklin (Franklin)	Alma (Harlan)	Beaver City (Furnas)	Cambridge (Furnas)	Curtis (Frontier)	McCook (Red Willow)	Norton (Norton)	Wray (Yuma)
ASP	10.8	10.4	10.2	11.0	9.9	9.7	9.8	9.2	9.5	8.8	9.3	7.9
1894	−37	−31	−57	−10	−52	—	−50	—	−47	−35	−40	−15
1898	−14	−29	−23	−18	−49	−07	−23	—	−21	−28	+19	−18
1900	+39	+28	−52	−57	−45	−49	−48	−39	+21	−22	—(8)	+20
1902	+75(42)	+54	+130(30)	+30	+57(20)	+37	+29(15)	+02	+05(16)	+30(20)	—(5)	+48
1905	−33(35)	+102	+50(41)	—	+63(38)	+62	+155(40)	+53	+90(41)	+92(40)	+16	−10
1908	+33	+53	+118	—	+81	+08	−01	+05	+37	+30	+116	+14
1910	+15(28)	+12	−23(31)	—	−17(37)	−22	−39(14)	−44	−04(10)	−46(6)	−75(5)	−29
1911	−42(15)	+92	+50(21)	−08	+31(24)	+92	+98(10)	+41	+55(5)	−34(5)	+12(2)	−54
1913	+12(22)	−11	−66(1.5)	−58	−74(2.7)	−52	−49(3.4)	−35	+29(5)	−43(1.3)	−42(1)	−41
1915	+22(28)	+88	+120(31)	+58	+145(34)	+147	+52(30)	+48	+120(29)	+81(29)	+85(26)	+41
1917	−29(28)	−51	−76(16)	−32	−62(15)	−21	−34(13)	−56	−52(15)	−45(8)	−49(1)	+01
1924	+108	+100	−35	−22	−36	−31	−17	—	−53	−40	−31	—

SOURCE: Weather data from Climatic Summary of the United States, sections 23, 38, 39, 40, and 41, United States Department of Agriculture, 1930; and supplements for 1931 through 1952, nos. 11–12 and 11–21, United States Department of Commerce, 1952. Crop data from reports of the Nebraska and Kansas state boards of agriculture for the years involved.
NOTE: Figures in parentheses indicate yields of corn (bushels per acre) for the counties in which the stations are located. ASP indicates average summer precipitation in inches for each station.

stations selected, Genoa and North Loup are in the Loup River drainage, 50 miles (80 km) apart and 90 miles (145 km) north of the Republican at Superior. One hundred miles (160 km) to the southwest on the Republican, McCook, Cambridge, and Curtis form a triangle 30 miles (48 km) on a side, with Medicine Creek and a concentration of Upper Republican sites on its northeast leg. Alma, Franklin, and Beaver City fairly well bracket the Harlan County Reservoir 50 miles (80 km) southeast of Medicine Creek, where Upper Republican sites are again numerous and have been studied extensively by archeologists.

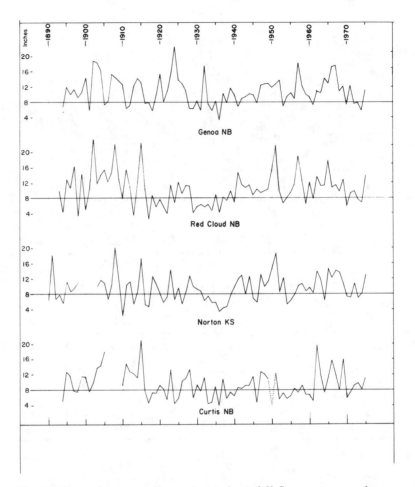

Fig. 7.4. Annual summer (June–August) rainfall fluctuations at three
selected stations in the Republican River basin and at Genoa on the
former Pawnee Indian reservation.

Norton, Kansas, is 20 miles (32 km) to the south, on Prairie Dog Creek. Beloit
and Cawker City, Kansas, are 90 miles (145 km) to the east on the Solomon
River and 40 miles (64 km) south of the Republican at Red Cloud.

With some notable exceptions, the figures suggest that when summer
rains at one of these sites were markedly above or below the long-term average,
they were likely to be so in most other districts. The years 1902 and 1915 were
wet everywhere; 1894 and 1917 were generally dry. The anomalies are of greater interest here. For example, in 1908, one of the wetter years in the region,
Alma, Cambridge, and Beaver City had essentially average rainfall whereas the
other stations enjoyed from 14 to 118 percent above average. In 1913, the Loup
valley stations were 12 percent above (Genoa) and 11 percent below (North
Loup) average. The Republican block was generally below average by 40 to 75
percent and corn production in these counties dropped to one to five bushels
per acre from a 25-to-30 bushel long-term average. For the Medicine Creek
triangle, McCook and Cambridge were seriously short of rain whereas Curtis
was 29 percent above average. In 1915, rainfall at most stations was 50 to 145
percent above average and county corn yields averaged from 26 to 34 bushels
per acre. In 1924, the Loup River stations were 100 percent above average

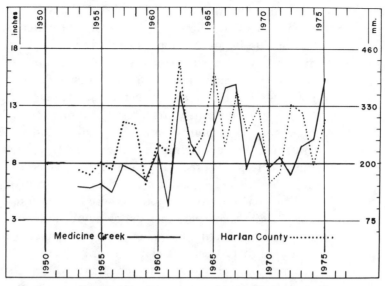

Fig. 7.5. Annual summer (June–August) rainfall fluctuations during a 22-year period (1953–1975) at Medicine Creek and Harlan County dams.

whereas other stations were 17 to 50 percent below. Other summer rainfall comparisons in the region are shown in figures 7.4 and 7.5.

Since, as we shall see presently, a summer rainfall deficit of 15 to 20 percent could result in lowering maize production by 30 to 50 percent or more, these local shortages of rain could have had serious consequences for the maize-growers in their immediate vicinity. On the other hand, such short-term crop declines might have been offset by the higher yields in neighboring communities where more rain fell. Local food shortages, in other words, could sometimes have been made up by sharing local surpluses in other areas. By establishing a system of intercommunity exchanges of foodstuffs, any impending hardships could have been spread out and made easier for all concerned. The existence of such a system among the Indians from at least the 12th century on has been vigorously argued (Blakeslee 1975, 1978).

We have no precise details on the climate of the Republican River basin from the 10th to the 13th century, despite the well-nigh incontrovertible evidence of maize horticulture in the area of the Harlan County and Medicine Creek reservoir districts, and probably on Red Willow Creek as well. Neither are there good leads to the crop yields that might be expected from the Indian gardening practices under climatic conditions like those of the present. On their 19th-century reservation near Genoa, Nebraska, the hoe-using Pawnee gardeners seem seldom to have harvested more than 25 to 30 bushels per acre (2,100–2,600 l per ha) from their family-operated plots. This level of productivity is about the same as that achieved by early white settlers in eastern Nebraska and Kansas, whose average doubtless suffered from the fact that the uplands were being tilled as well as the more productive bottomlands where the Indian gardens would have been located. Interestingly, it is also close to the average documented yield from Republican River cornfields in 1974 without irrigation. These figures perhaps bear out the view that the animal power of the 19th-century white farmer was only slightly more efficient than the hand labor of the Indian women. Assuming that Indian-style maize cultivation, perhaps with specially developed drought-resistant varieties, would have been feasible and productive in the Upper Republican habitat under present-day conditions and that weather conditions were no more adverse in the 11th century than they are today, certain extrapolations may be undertaken in hopes of glimpsing some possibilities in the prehistoric situation.

Early-20th-century crop statistics (Smith 1906:201) for eight leading corn-producing states point to an average yield of about 26 bushels (900 l) per acre under a 10-inch (255 mm) summer rainfall regimen. With each one-inch (25 mm) decrease in precipitation, the yield of corn dropped not less than two bushels (70 l) per acre. But, since the distribution of summer rainfall is no less critical than the total amount, these figures must be used with caution. In 1894, a 40-percent summer deficiency of four inches (100 mm) in Nebraska brought on a decline in maize yield of 70 percent to eight bushels (280 l) per acre; and in 1901, a 1.5-inch (37-mm) or 15-percent drop in summer rainfall lowered the corn yield by 31 percent to 16 bushels (560 l) per acre. These are gross figures and may be extreme figures in the record, but it cannot be safely argued from this that equally disastrous episodes did not occur in prehistoric times. July is perhaps the most critical single summer month in terms of moisture/crop ratios for nonirrigated maize, but again the correlation is not a simple or direct one. Heavy rains in June may partially offset a dry July and conversely an extremely dry June may presage a short crop regardless of the July rainfall. Perhaps especially important to the maize crop is plenty of rainfall during July and August at the time of tasseling and ear formation. Best results may be expected when the summer rainfall is evenly distributed and the occasional hot dry southerly winds do not materialize to wither the tasseling maize.

The yield of 26 bushels (900 l) per acre at 10 inches (250 mm) of summer precipitation parallels the situation in which the 19th-century Pawnees gardened in east-central Nebraska. At McCook, 150 miles (240 km) farther west, two inches (50 mm) less of summer rainfall might be expected to reduce the average maize yield to perhaps 20 bushels (700 l) per acre, with two to three times the likelihood of still further deficiencies, that is, of a drop below eight inches (200 mm) and even greater reduction in the yield of maize from the gardens. Granting the probability that the Upper Republican people may have developed special deep-rooted, early-maturing, or otherwise drought-resistant varieties, and the virtual certainty that they gardened in more favorable spots than did their white successors, it is still reasonable to infer smaller average annual yields than in the Pawnee country to the east in the historic period and the likelihood that recurrent rainfall deficiencies sharply reduced the crop yield from time to time. If climatic conditions in the 10th to 13th centuries were much more favorable than those in the past century or two, we might expect clearcut evidence of successful maize cultivation by Upper Republican peoples much farther west and perhaps even into northeastern Colorado, where to date no such indications have been reported.

Archeology has shown us what crops were grown, or at least the principal ones, but it tells us little about the varieties raised and almost nothing concerning the gardening methods used. Charred maize includes cob fragments with 8, 10, 12, and 14 rows of kernels, apparently representing popcorns,

Northern Flint, and perhaps other races (Kivett 1949; Cutler and Blake 1969). Planting, tillage, and harvesting techniques are essentially unknown except as they can be guessed from analogy with documented Pawnee procedures in historic time. A subsistence or "kitchen" economy was carried on during the spring and summer by women equipped only with scapula-bladed hoes, digging sticks, and perhaps crude wooden or wood and antler rakes, without benefit of draft animals large enough to draw soil-turning devices, and also without known irrigation, fertilizers, or other technological adjuncts of the mechanized modern dry-land farmer with his dominantly commercial orientation.

Around most native communities, such an economy required the modification of only a few acres—perhaps no more than a third to one-half acre of ground per individual or 1.5 to 3 acres for a family of four or five (Will and Hyde 1917). Preferred garden locations were bottomland patches along the creeks, where the ground was mellow and could be easily turned in spring with the primitive tools available and where there was some protection for the growing crops against the hot drying winds of July and August. Situated as these were, often subject to occasional flooding and the renewal of fertility by silting, they were drought resistant if not drought proof. It may be questioned whether such soils would have been exhausted under the gardening systems of the Indians, who are not known to have utilized fertilizers and other stimulants to productivity, who may have spaced their plantings at wider intervals than white farmers, and who presumably were willing to accept 10, 15, or 20 bushels (350–700 l) per acre or whatever the ground might produce under its natural regimen without forcing. Further, considering the scattered nature of the settlements, I doubt that there were often significant shortages of arable ground within easy walking distance of the habitations or that strong social controls were required for the assignment of garden lands to family users. Climatic adversities such as drought, hail, destructive winds, and unseasonal frosts, and perhaps infestations by grasshoppers and other insect pests that left no traces in the archeological record, were doubtless greater hazards to native crop-growers than soil exhaustion.

Food Preparation

For household consumption, the produce from the gardens and products of the hunt were presumably processed much as among the historic Village Indians, that is, mainly by boiling for immediate use and drying for the future. The staples of daily fare were very likely bison meat and maize. Maize and beans, to which could be added fresh or dried bison meat, were cooked up into a thick soup or stew. Green corn could have been roasted in the husk or boiled, cut from the cob with a mussel shell (Gradwohl 1982), then dried on mats or bison hides in the sun and stored underground or in leather cases or bags. This could be cooked later with beans and dried pumpkin, perhaps flavored with bison tallow or bone butter. Prairie turnips, Jerusalem artichokes, groundnuts (*Apios americana*), and other wild plant products could be added to the maize and bison meat staple. Mature corn, boiled with wood ashes, provided hominy. More often, perhaps, maize was ground into meal, then boiled as mush or baked as cakes in the embers. Fresh meat may have been broiled on a bed of coals, or buried in the hot ashes until the interior was sufficiently done to satisfy the consumer. For all of these and various other procedures, there is ethnographic evidence on the later postwhite level among the Village Indians (see, for example, Dunbar 1880a and b). That young field corn, parboiled, cut from the cob, thoroughly sun dried, and stored in a dry vermin-free room could provide tasty eating all through the ensuing fall and winter months I can testify from my own boyhood experiences in central Kansas. My role as a juvenile in this annual summer ritual was to drive away the flies while corn was drying on clean tea towels spread on concrete slab.

Pit Storage and Its Problems

Maize, beans, squash, and other foodstuffs that were not eaten fresh, traded, or given away by the Indians, were dried and stored after harvest in underground pits. These are found today inside and outside the houses, usually between the central four-post square and the house wall when inside, or near the doorway when outside. They vary from bell-shaped to vertical flat-floored cylindrical holes that seldom exceed one meter in depth and floor diameter, and perhaps 25–30 bushels (31–37 cu ft) in capacity. When in use, these were presumably floored and lined with dried grass or woven plant fiber mats to protect the contents from ground moisture and temperature fluctuations. The contents included maize, both shelled and on the cob, beans, and squash cut into strips and woven into mats. Dried berries, roots, seeds, and other wild vegetable foods also went into the pits, and dried meat was sometimes included. The filled pit was covered with more dried grass and then earth, tamped down to provide a tight seal and to conceal the pit. When the contents were used up some months later, the pit might be aired out and then reused for food and artifact storage or, if soured and unfit for this purpose, it was refilled with household trash and garbage. It is in this latter condition that the pits are usually found by the archeologist.

The storage pits, or caches, in Upper Republican houses and hamlets are usually much smaller than those in the early historic Pawnee and Wichita village sites. There, pits two meters or more in depth and in floor diameter, and with capacities of 150–200 bushels (5,000–7,000 l or 5–7 cu m) each were not uncommon. This marked size difference suggests the possibility of scantier crop yields and a much smaller year-to-year carryover among the earlier and marginally horticultural Upper Republican people. Alternatively, it could reflect a less efficient gardening technology, less productive crop strains, a more casual commitment to land tillage, or a preference for garden-fresh vegetables rather than pit-stored dried foods.

Although some modern white farmers, accustomed to storing their corn harvest in well-aired, dry, vermin-proof cribs, seriously question the feasibility of pit storage of maize, there is abundant historic and ethnographic evidence that it was widely and successfully practiced by the Plains Indians for centuries. Moreover, there are detailed descriptions by eye-witness observers of the procedures followed, including some by actual participants in the operation of filling and emptying the caches. Properly dried and carefully stored maize and other crops, sealed off from moisture, temperature changes, and oxygen, which encourage the growth of bacteria and mildew and other fungi, could be preserved in viable, edible, and nutritious condition for months (see also Coles 1973). With outside caches especially, there was always the risk of damage to the underground stores from soaking or protracted rains, of rapid deterioration because of inadequate processing and drying before storage, of contamination by weevils and maggots hatched from eggs deposited on unprotected foods while drying, and from burrowing and other rodents. The woodrat (*Neotoma floridana*) and white-footed mouse (*Peromyscus*) may have been at times commensal residents in the Indian lodges. The grassy patches between the scattered houses may well have harbored pocket gophers (*Geomys*) and 13-lined ground squirrels (*Spermophilus*) whose burrows could have penetrated unguarded food caches from time to time, thus gaining access to the stored grain and breaking the man-made seal that otherwise protected the contents from moisture, adverse temperatures, and other destructive elements.

Carefully controlled and instrumentally monitored experiments in Great Britain have provided interesting insights into the preservative properties and certain shortcomings of the pit storage of foodstuffs (Coles 1973). So far as I am aware, no comparable studies have been attempted anywhere in the North American Great Plains area, and we are still very largely dependent on historical observers for information. Since the Great Plains environment differs in many significant particulars from that in Great Britain, I would like to suggest here that the time is long overdue for equally intensive experiments in this region, using native American crops and testing—in a wide range of soil, topographic, and climatic conditions—the pit storage techniques described historically (e.g., Wilson 1917) and inferred archeologically for the Plains Indians.

Hunting and Animal Foods

It seems likely that hunting may have been as important in the Upper Republican subsistence economy as horticulture, though we have at present no means of evaluating precisely the relative proportion of time and effort devoted to either pursuit. The presence of quantities of bison bone at practically every house, hamlet, and village site where extended excavation has been carried out suggests that the animals were often readily available in the valley bottom meadows and around the upland waterholes in summer, and that they probably wintered in some numbers in the timbered bottoms and in the sheltered valley margin breaks, as they were reported to do in historic times. Documentary evidence is clear that 16th- and 17th-century Indian hunters, without horses, were subsisting on the herds in the southern plains without resorting to mass-killing techniques, that is, surrounds, pounds, or jumps in the style of the northern Plains Indians (Frison 1978); and there is no reason to suppose that the pedestrian hunters in the Republican country in the 10th to 13th centuries could not have done equally well. As a source of animal proteins and fats for human nutrition; of skins for temporary lodge covers, clothing, containers, and other objects; of sinews for sewing and cordage; and of bones for tool making and fetishes, the bison can safely be classed as the animal most important economically to the prehistoric Indians, semisedentary as well as nomadic, as it was also to the historic Plains groups.

The ambushing or stalking of single bison or small groups by Indians on foot would have made possible a fairly steady and dependable supply of meat on a continuing basis. Some butchering of bison outside the hamlet, with the return of the fresh and/or dried meat to the settlements, leaving behind the unwanted bone refuse, is assumed. The biweekly killing of a 900–pound (400 kg) animal in reasonably good condition, with a yield of perhaps 400 pounds (180 kg) of fresh meat, would have provided a household or hamlet of 12 to 15 persons with 1.5–2 pounds (700–900 g) of meat per person per day, with an estimated energy value of 1,500 to 2,000 calories, assuming a rough equivalence to beef (Watt and Merrill 1963:11). A temporary local absence of bison, whether because of their seasonal movements, local shortages of water or grass, adverse climatic or weather conditions, or from other causes, might have been compensated for through foraging and the use of whatever smaller animals, birds, and other forms were still available. It seems unlikely that the thinly scattered and probably briefly occupied hamlets and homesteads of the Upper Republican people would have seriously disrupted the herd movements, except perhaps locally in some small measure. Certainly the quantities of refuse bison bones in most house sites indicate that the animals were often killed and butchered nearby.

This view is at variance with one suggested elsewhere (Wood 1969:104, 108, 110), in which the Upper Republican villagers are regarded as having overstrained and exhausted the limited food resources locally available in their creek valley habitats, as at Medicine Creek. They were thus compelled to leave their settlements periodically or seasonally and make extended excursions west into the short-grass steppe to procure adequate supplies of bison meat. Faunal data recovered at one house site, Mowry Bluff (25FT35), are interpreted as indicating that "Upper Republican lodges were not occupied in the summer." This, of course, is a projection into prehistoric times of the pattern of the historic village tribes of the eastern plains and also of the forest edge Illinois tribes of the 18th century (Liette in Quaife 1947:93–102). In this view, the game procured was processed where it fell, and the meat, hides, and bone wanted for tool making were transported to the Republican River villages via trains of pack dogs.

For the Plains Village Indians, such seasonal community bison hunts are recorded at least as early as 1724, when a large Kansa hunting party, reported to be more than a thousand people from a village of 150 lodges near present Doniphan, Kansas, traveled with Etienne Véniard de Bourgmont west to the general vicinity of present Salina, with more than 300 dogs as beasts of burden (Margry 1886:414). Such a move of 150 to 300 miles (240–480 km) each way involved weeks of absence from the home village. That such enterprises were also customary for prehistoric groups living in much smaller, more open, and more widely scattered settlements 200 miles (320 km) or more west of the Missouri and in the heart of the bison range in prewhite days is still undemonstrated. There is some apparent support for that idea in the documented occurrence of Upper Republican materials, including pottery and stonework, in the Nebraska panhandle, at Signal Butte, in southeastern Wyoming, and in eastern Colorado. For example, at Cedar Point northwest of Limon, Colorado, the westernmost tip of the Republican River basin where the higher peaks of the Colorado Rockies first become visible under favorable conditions to the traveler from the east, structures that do not qualify as earthlodges have yielded materials of this sort (Wood 1971). These materials, notably the pottery, are essentially indistinguishable from wares and products found in the Medicine Creek and Harlan County sites 200–250 miles (320–400 km) downstream. At none of these more western locations have scapula hoe blades or other suggestions of possible crop cultivation been reported. It is entirely possible that they represent hunting camps, but whether or not they therefore symbolize a mass summer migration from, and seasonal abandonment of, the Upper Republican settlements in the loess plains of Nebraska and northern Kansas is a provocative suggestion that is yet to be substantiated. I suspect that the communal Kansa hunting party cited above probably included more people than were living at any one time on Medicine, Red Willow, or Prairie Dog creeks, or in the district now covered by the Harlan County Reservoir, during the Upper Republican occupation.

That bison movements were often erratic and unpredictable is well known from the historic record, but this of course tells us nothing about the behavior and distribution of the herds in prehorse and pregun days. It is arguable, however, that the prewhite human populations of the Republican River basin were so numerous or concentrated, or constituted such a drain on the bison population and other natural resources, that no animals could have been obtained locally, meaning within a few days walking distance of the settlements. The well-watered Republican and its tributaries would seem much more likely to have attracted bison on a year-round basis during favorable years and would have been at least as desirable a rangeland as that farther west where rainfall becomes increasingly uncertain and grazing precarious during dry years or seasons (Wedel 1970a; 1983b:104).

Knotty logistical problems would have been posed for the Upper Republican villagers on these trips. If the postulated dog trains were part of such a system, there would have been the matter of feeding the animals, since, unlike horses, they could not be turned loose to graze at the end of the day's travel. Permitting them to roam freely and hunt their own food, such as rabbits or gophers, was to risk losing their services on anything like a planned schedule. Unless there was a sizable contingent of dogs, carrying or dragging perhaps 35 to 50 pounds (15–22 kg) of meat or camp gear each, a substantial portion of the dried meat processed at Cedar Point, at Signal Butte, or in Wyoming would have been consumed by dogs and humans long before the settlements in southern Nebraska were reached. There, if the hunt had essentially stripped the home villages of personnel, or at least of the able-bodied, the returning hunters would probably have found the unprotected gardens severely damaged and quite possibly destroyed by wild animals and birds. With little or no meat to show from the summer hunt and the garden produce largely consumed by predators, the postulated western junkets must be considered a strategy whose survival value could be seriously questioned. No valid analogy can be drawn between the proposed Upper Republican hunters and the 16th-century dog-nomads of the southern plains, since the latter were fully committed to the bison hunt, had no gardens or fixed villages to which to return, and acquired by trade with the Pueblos such vegetal food staples as they could not obtain from their own efforts as they roamed the grasslands.

Some indication of the kind of short- to medium-range bison hunting trips or sorties that may have been undertaken by the Upper Republican groups is suggested in the Coronado documents from the 16th century in the Arkansas River valley. The first meeting of the Spaniards with the natives of Quivira, whose subsistence economy was divided between bison hunting and maize cultivation, involved hunting parties. Three days after the Spaniards crossed the Arkansas, not far from present Dodge City, Kansas, and marched down its left bank toward the settlements of Quivira, Juan Jaramillo reported that "we met some Indians who were out hunting, killing cattle to take meat to their pueblo, which was about three or four days from us, farther down. . . . Some of them even had their women along." Another account, the Relación del Suceso, relates, "In our march through the valley we met many natives of Quivira who were out hunting" (Hammond and Rey 1940:303, 291). There is no indication that villages three or four days distant, to which the Spaniards came in due course, were abandoned during these hunting activities by members of the communities, or that the hunts were organized and operated on a communal basis, or that the gardens of the Quivirans had been left unguarded and untended while the hunting was being carried on. The archeological sites that mark these 16th-century Quiviran villages consistently yield quantities of bison bone and clearly reflect the same sort of divided subsistence economy that is inferred by archeologists for the Upper Republican communities. No convincing evidence has been adduced to show that similar hunting tactics, on a much more modest scale than the great village or tribal hunts of later horse days, would have been impractical or unproductive in Upper Republican times.

There is no archeological evidence, so far as I am aware, that Upper Republican peoples carried out communal hunts and mass kills of bison like those that were common in the northwestern plains. It may be suggested, therefore, that hunting—like the gathering of plant foods, fishing, and gardening—was probably of such a nature that it could be handled, as seasonally appropriate, by individuals, families, or small groups. In much of the Republican basin, notably from Franklin County westward, around the Harlan County Reservoir district, and in the environs of the Medicine Creek reservoir (Harry Strunk Lake), the deeply dissected valley margins, the flat-floored, well-grassed canyons, and the deep, narrow tributary valleys would have provided near ideal terrain for hunters to stalk bison by foot. With small and scattered communities to support and therefore no need for great quantities of meat to feed towns of many hundreds of people, there would have been no proven necessity for long-range communal bison hunts, and no implied need for the hunt or camp police that were of importance in the historic Plains societies.

Fishing and Shellfish   The consistent occurrence of bone fishhooks in Upper Republican sites is evidence of an established pattern of fish procurement that is generally without parallel among the historic Central Plains tribes. In the usually scant and still poorly studied refuse fish bone, the bullhead and channel cat (*Ictalurus*) are the only species yet identified. Moisture-loving animals other than mammals included in small numbers are the snapping turtle (*Chelydra*) and the land terrapin (*Terrapene*).

At Medicine Creek, as well as at several sites outside the Republican drainage, occasional trash pits containing quantities of freshwater mussel shells suggest still another source of animal protein. No fewer than 17 species and subspecies have been identified and therefore were a potential food resource that was probably harvested only on rare occasions. At none of the sites of record were the valves counted by the field-workers, so the total numbers of individuals utilized can only be estimated. Several pits at Medicine Creek yielded in the aggregate several hundred unburned valves of the maple leaf (*Quadrula quadrula*) with only a very few of other species whose size, if not their abundance locally, might have qualified them as food items (plate 2.9).

The maple leaf (Murray and Leonard 1962:32, 53) in its larval stage is parasitic on the gills of the catfish, by whose movements it is distributed and on whom its early growth takes place. Shifting sands, such as those that characterize the Republican River bed, are lethal to mussels, which prefer muddy, gravelly, or stable bottoms. Such a substrate would have been present in Medicine Creek in preagricultural days. The mussels could have been easily gathered by hand, especially in late summer or early fall when the stream was at its lowest stage. That the gathering was successful on one or more occasions, at least, is indicated by the number of valves recovered archeologically. Since any demonstrated use of the shells as tools or ornaments or in pottery making is all but absent, it may be concluded that the mussels were gathered mainly for food, perhaps to be steamed under a fire or over a bed of coals.

The maple leaf ranges in length up to about five inches (125 mm), with its enclosed soft parts weighing up to 3.5 ounces (100 g) (Parmalee and Klippel 1974:424). Archeological specimens from the Republican drainage were generally smaller, probably averaging about three inches (75 mm) in length and containing 18 grams or less of edible soft parts. On this basis, 25 mussels would have provided about one pound (0.45 kg) of meat, with a food value of approximately 320 calories and a protein yield of 40 grams. This is less than one-third the caloric value and one-half the protein content of beef (Watt and Merrill 1963:11, no. 213), to which bison meat is here considered to be roughly equivalent. To realize from the maple leaf and other mussels at Medicine Creek the food equivalent of 400 pounds (180 kg) of beef or bison—the estimated yield from a medium-sized cow bison—the Indians would have had to gather 8,000 or more bivalves or 40 to 50 bushels (1,400–1,750 l) of the live animals.

From the standpoint of nutrition, shellfish appear to rank fairly high in protein content per unit weight, but one would have to eat enormous quantities to maintain adequate protein/calorie levels. According to Coker (1919:61–62), "The meats, when dried in the sun or by the use of artificial heat, can be ground to make a fine meal, in which condition they appear to keep indefinitely. . . . In dry sunny weather, the meats can be dried in from 30–72 hours to about $\frac{5}{8}$ of their wet-weight." Analysis of the dried mussel meats yields the following figures: protein 44.44 percent, glycogen 9.00 percent, phosphoric acid 9.00 percent, lime 8.00 percent.

In what numbers shellfish may have been available at Medicine Creek in Upper Republican times is uncertain. Possibly, like other potential natural food items in prewhite days, they were abundant and easy to gather. On the other hand, perhaps even an occasional "clambake" would have made heavy inroads on the local population, so that sustained harvesting and the accumulation of sizable shell middens would not have been feasible. Special ceremonial or ritual requirements may have been met by the villagers at Medicine Creek on a one-time basis, or equally, they may have fallen back on shellfish out of physiological necessity resulting from the temporary absence of bison and other food animals locally. Despite their sometimes high visibility and seeming abundance as broken bits of shell on most village sites, and their occasional prevalence in a small proportion of storage or trash pits, the probability seems high that shellfish were a minor food resource and were in no way pivotal to human welfare in the sense or to the degree that bison and other animals were. Even less tenable is the view that reduction in numbers of available shellfish through overuse was a controlling factor in the locating or relocating of aboriginal village and camp communities in the Upper Republican way of life.

Wild Plant Foods

Very little archeological evidence is yet in hand about the gathering of wild vegetal products, but the Upper Republican villagers would presumably have had access to much the same range of roots, tubers, fruits, seeds, greens, and nuts that were available to the historic Indians, for which we have some archeological materials to supplement the documentary records. A strong attraction may well have been the boggy meadows in which Medicine Creek, the Stinking Water, and Frenchman Creek head. Here there are still extensive stands of cattail (*Typha*), arrowhead (*Sagittaria*), and other wetlands plants whose roots and spring shoots would have provided significant amounts of food to be collected seasonally or otherwise under stress of shortages in other categories of edibles. Cattail leaves may have been used in making baskets and mats, *Sagittaria* perhaps for medicine. Family or group collecting trips to gather such comestibles and other materials in quantity may have been mounted by the pre-white Indians. Similar trips to wild plum and berry patches were once customary among white frontier and rural families in our own Great Plains society.

Miscellaneous Comments

In the central plains, the Upper Republican people were, so far as we now know, the earliest maize-growers to attempt cultivation of domestic crops in the Kansas, Nebraska, and Colorado section of the High Plains west of the 100th meridian. The small, dispersed, and probably short-lived communities suggest a society quite different from that in the large historic towns with many hundreds of inhabitants which were encountered by the Euro-American explorers in the eastern plains. Instead of highly organized work or village groups, this seems to have been a loosely structured society, perhaps without influential chiefs or a strong tribal organization, more in the nature of a pioneer or frontier society operating on the margin of a particular ecosystem and in small, dispersed population aggregates.

Another possible but less likely explanation is suggested in certain 18th-century settlement patterns reported among the Red River Caddo groups. Thus, an anonymous draft map in the Bibliothèque Nationale titled "Essai d'une Carte de la Louisiane," dated June 1732 and numbered Ge.C.9905, locates a number of Caddoan tribes in the great bend of the Red. Included are the Kadohadachos, Upper Nasoni, Nadsoos, and others. Curving around the locality is a gloss that may be rendered: "The habitations of these savages are dispersed and they do not form villages." More than a decade earlier, referring to this general locality, Bénard de la Harpe (Bibliothèque Nationale, MSS Fr 8989, folios 13–13 verso) gave as the natives' stated reason for their dispersed settlements "that being separated one from another their enemies will not be able to destroy them all at once, a faulty inference which is the cause of their destruction."

Among the Republican River hamlet and homestead dwellers, group or community enterprises might have included such projects as house building and funerary ceremonies, though even here, as with hunting, gathering, and gardening, family or neighborhood efforts may have sufficed. If there were larger communities that served as ceremonial or trading centers, no convincing evidence has yet been adduced. Whether kinship, descent, and postmarital residence patterns followed the maternal or paternal line I would not attempt to suggest here, though the former has been argued by others (Wood 1969:106).

Neither do I have strong convictions regarding the possible existence of an intertribal trading network of region-wide extent at this time which might have established integrating bonds of mutual interest between geographically remote groups. This, by providing a mechanism for the exchange of a wide variety of foodstuffs and other goods, as well as genes, might have helped to mitigate the adverse effects of local droughts and food shortages (Blakeslee 1975). Against major region-wide climatic adversities and their effects on food production, on the game herds, and on the native wild food plants, or on the exhaustion of timber for house building and fuel, even such a system if it ever existed on a regional or intertribal basis might have collapsed, thus helping to pave the way for a general exodus of the human population and a search for a better home elsewhere.

Dubbed "shifting cultivators" by one observer despite our ignorance of most details of their horticultural procedures, the Upper Republican people have been charged (Krause 1970:109) with not using "many of the techniques within the range of their technical capabilities. Among these were bench terracing, which would allow the use of otherwise unarable tree-covered slopes, and ridging techniques, which would prevent runoff, hinder erosion, and conserve moisture in dry years or in perennially dry fields. Ditching procedures for the reclamation of potentially rich but waterlogged areas and irrigation practices that utilize the potential of perennial springs and small streams . . . [and] heavy annual use of compost enriched with human or collectable animal dung" were other unrealized potentialities. Certain African tribes are cited in contrast, notably the Kofyar in northern Nigeria (Netting 1965).

The Kofyar, it appears, occupy a subhumid wooded savanna 9° north of the equator. Their settlements cluster in an area of some 200 square miles (500 sq km); population averages "close to 300 per square mile and approaches 1,200 in some plains villages". Rainfall is "quite regular" between 40 and 60 inches (1,000–1,500 mm) per year. Subsistence is primarily from cultigens; family plots average 1.2 acres; compost and crops are not far to transport; famine is unknown; and since families reside on their plots, neither theft nor molestation by animals are serious concerns. By contrast, the Upper Republican groups lived in a region that today has 22 inches (550 mm) or less annual rainfall and frequent destructive droughts at unpredictable intervals, but with ready access to nutritious animal protein in the great bison herds. The total Kofyar range is about one-fifth that of the Medicine Creek drainage, whose Upper Republican population at any given time was probably significantly less than that in two or three square miles (6.5 sq km) of Kofyar territory. In the absence of the population pressures to which the Kofyar were regularly subject, and with ample potential garden lands close at hand in the creek bottoms, the Upper Republican cultivators should perhaps not be disparaged for not attempting terrace gardening on "otherwise unarable tree-covered slopes," or undertaking other large energy expenditures for which there was no actual need in their lifeway. Neither the terrain, the climatic setting, nor the inferred demography of the Republican country remotely approach the conditions described for the Kofyar, and one is led to wonder just why the comparison was made.

Upper Republican Radiocarbon Dates

In the Republican valley, the Early Village period as represented by the known Upper Republican settlements seems to have ended soon after ca. A.D. 1250–

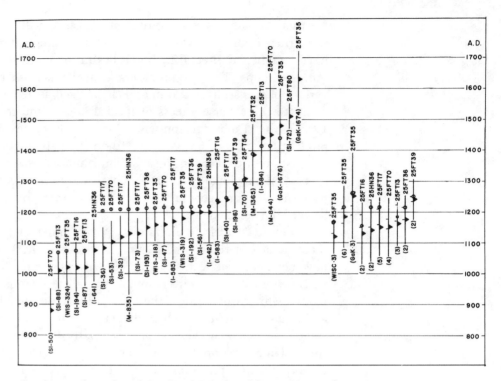

Fig. 7.6. Radiocarbon dates for Upper Republican sites in the
Republican River basin. *Solid triangles* are dates in conventional
radiocarbon years. *Open circles* are adjustments according to Stuiver
and Suess (1966). In the group of averaged site dates at right,
horizontal ticks indicate time range adjusted to bristlecone-pine
calibrations (Suess 1970). (See also table 7.4.)

1275, although there are earlier estimates and scattered radiocarbon dates continue for a century or more thereafter. A local chronology is based on 33 dates
from the Medicine Creek locality, most of which come from seven sites that
are now covered by the reservoir waters. There is also one date from the Harlan
County Reservoir, 80 miles (130 km) down the Republican River (fig. 7.6).

Mean sample dates range from the 5th to the 17th centuries, a most improbable span in light of the archeological evidence generally; but 25 of these,
or 75 percent, fall between A.D. 1000 and 1450. If the mean dates for samples
from each site that is represented by more than one determination are averaged, the span of occupation is narrowed significantly. The eight sites are then
seen to fall within the more limited period of A.D. 1120–1250. The sites can be
further ordered chronologically as in table 7.4, wherein all mean sample dates
preceding A.D. 700 (SI-34, SI-197, GaK-1675) and following A.D. 1600 (SI-195,
GaK-1674) have been deleted. It will be noted that the suggested ordering of
sites changes somewhat when the conventional radiocarbon dates are adjusted
as suggested by Stuiver and Suess (1966) and by Suess (1970); but in no case do
the adjustments or corrections remove any site from the ca. A.D. 1120–1250
time span. On the basis of these site averages, it can be suggested that the
major occupation of that portion of Medicine Creek represented by the available radiocarbon dates need not have endured much longer than a century, that
is, four or five generations, and may indeed have been no longer than two or
three.

Table 7.4
Radiocarbon chronology of certain Upper Republican village sites in the Medicine Creek and Harlan County reservoir areas, Nebraska

Site	No. of samples	Average site dates (A.D.)[a]	Adjusted dates (A.D.)[b]	Bristlecone pine: adjusted dates (A.D.)[c]
25FT39	(2)	1240 ± 65	1240–1260	1235–1250
25FT35	(4)	1210 ± 70	1215	1200–1245
25FT36	(2)	1175 ± 80	1215	1175–1220
25FT13	(3)	1160 ± 70	1185	1170–1220
25FT17	(5)	1150 ± 95	1220	1160–1210
25FT70	(4)	1150 ± 95	1215	1150–1175
25HN36	(2)	1140 ± 100	1215	1150–1235
25FT16	(2)	1130 ± 100	1150	1150–1195
25FT35	(3)	1120 ± 60	1170	1135–1190

[a]Average site dates in conventional radiocarbon years.
[b]Dates adjusted by Stuiver and Suess (1966).
[c]Dates adjusted by Suess (1970).

Certain traits, such as cord-roughening on vessel exteriors, have been seen as possible indicators of relationships to the earlier Woodland culture of the region, and further work may bear this out. At the present, however, the on-going investigations in the Republican basin have yet to produce any real support for the suggestion offered more than a decade ago of a likely direct contact between Upper Republican and Woodland peoples. Wood (1969:103) has suggested that "contacts of some sort, if not trade, are implied by a Woodland vessel on the floor of a house at Red Cloud 3" on Reams Creek southeast of Franklin, Nebraska. At the time of its finding, this large vessel was recognized as atypical of the Upper Republican house site in which it was uncovered (Wedel 1935:188); it has since been identified as Harlan Cord-Roughened ware assignable to the Keith focus Woodland culture of ca. A.D. 600 or earlier (Kivett 1953:132). Keith focus sites are not uncommon in the Republican valley, but in their time of occupancy the people responsible for that complex preceded the Upper Republican groups on the Republican river by perhaps five or six centuries. In light of this wide disparity in time, I would suggest that the Harlan Cord-Roughened jar at Red Cloud 3 (plate 6.2) was probably collected by an Upper Republican householder or occupant somewhere along a nearby creek or riverbank where it may have been exposed by erosion and was carried back as a trophy or curiosity to the village, and there then or later suffered breakage. One need be neither surprised nor disturbed by the occasional finding of earlier and older artifacts in sites of later, sometimes much later, cultures. The foregoing explanation seems to me much more palatable than the suggestion that such a cross-find indicates contemporaneity or direct trade between two widely discrete cultures. Red Cloud 3, incidentally, is today's site 25FR8.

There are other radiocarbon dates that involve chiefly Upper Republican sites outside the Republican River valley. A date of A.D. 1138 ± 200 years (M-835) has been assigned to house-post charcoal from the Coufal site on Davis Creek, Howard County, Nebraska, where 21 lodge sites were excavated in 1939. This, like the seven site datings at Medicine Creek, is intermediate between two occupations postulated by Krause (1970:106) at a Central Plains tradition manifestation at Glen Elder Reservoir in north central Kansas. Krause has proposed, from various lines of evidence and a series of 10 radiocarbon dates, a Solomon River hamlet phase (ca. 9th to 13th centuries) followed by a Classic Republican phase (ca. 11th to 15th centuries), which featured a creek-bank settlement pattern of scattered houses. An unpublished study by Carlson (1971) involving seriation of decorative techniques and motifs on pottery vessel rims appears to lend some support to Krause's thesis of two cultural phases at Glen Elder, one preceding and the other following the dated Medicine Creek Upper Republican sites. Carlson suggests further that this apparent split occupancy may reflect an adjustment by the local population to a 12th-century climatic shift. Unfortunately, the proposed settlement pattern systems and their ordering at Glen Elder have been called into question; and their relations to the dates, instead of becoming clearer with continued and widening discussion, now seem murkier than ever (Krause 1982; Blakeslee et al. 1982).

The Upper Republican peoples, whatever taxonomists eventually decide regarding the status of their nomenclature, did not exist in a vacuum. As visualized here, they were a subregional manifestation of the Central Plains tradition, which includes also the Nebraska culture (or phase) along the Missouri River in eastern Nebraska, southwestern Iowa, northeastern Kansas, and northwestern Missouri; the St. Helena phase of northeastern Nebraska; and perhaps the Smoky Hill phase in north central Kansas (Strong 1935; Hill and Cooper 1938; Cooper 1936, 1940; Gradwohl 1969; Hotopp 1978; Blakeslee and Caldwell 1979). A semisedentary way of life divided between hunting-gathering and horticulture; residence in fixed communities of earth-covered lodges; and a wide range of industries in pottery, stone, bone, horn, and shell characterized all of these cultures. Our current information, much of which is based on incompletely or inadequately analyzed data, does not yet provide the time perspective we need to interpret the beginnings and endings of these several complexes.

The Upper Republican: Whence and Whither?   That the archeological cultures sharing in the Central Plains tradition were in part rooted in the earlier Woodland complexes of the region seems likely. Given the landscape of the Kansas-Nebraska area, with its predominantly eastward-draining streams and ready travel routes from the main-stem Missouri River valley, strong and continuing influences and increments from the east and southeast are to be expected. It has long been evident (Wedel 1935:141) that from the Arkansas River in southern Kansas north to the Niobrara River, the central plains streams can be viewed as the rungs of a ladder up which human populations could travel from south to north with comparative ease. It is thus entirely feasible and likely that a resident late Woodland population could have been melded with a newcomer group or groups from the east, spreading across the plains from the Missouri and/or lower Arkansas river valleys. The little we know concerning the physical types of the region in prehistoric times suggests a mainly mesocephalic Central Plains population in contrast to a mainly long-headed earlier Woodland cranial type, but whether this reflects a new incoming strain or is a result of dietary changes and the greatly increased use of cultigens is not clear.

Uncertain, too, is the ultimate fate of the Central Plains Upper Republican peoples. It has been suggested that the westerly populations, such as those at Medicine Creek, may have been forced out by reduced precipitation and deteriorating climatic conditions and that they perhaps moved south to the Texas-

Oklahoma panhandle district in the Canadian River drainage. Alternatively, an eastward withdrawal and ultimate transformation to the historic Pawnees in eastern Nebraska and to the Coalescent (Arikara) peoples of the Middle Missouri, has also been argued.

The 13th-century termination date proposed above for the Upper Republican occupation at Medicine Creek coincides approximately with the estimated close of the Neo-Atlantic and beginning of the Pacific I climatic episode. At that time, changed atmospheric circulation patterns are suspected by some of having brought cool, dry westerly air into the central and northern plains, resulting in lowered temperatures and decreased rainfall. Under such conditions, maize cultivation may have become increasingly uncertain, so that communities dependent on domestic crops in marginal districts would have found it expedient to leave the region. Since the southern plains in this view are seen as wetter and agriculturally improved, it has been postulated (Baerreis and Bryson 1966; Bryson, Baerreis, and Wendland 1970) that Upper Republican groups in the western Republican valley may have migrated south and settled in the Oklahoma and Texas panhandles. Here a maize-based village complex variously designated as Panhandle aspect, Antelope Creek focus, and so on (Lintz 1978, 1979), appears to have peaked at ca. A.D. 1250–1450, thus following closely on the putative abandonment of the Medicine Creek Upper Republican district. Other observers have questioned this view, preferring to wait for the discovery or definition of a post-Upper Republican complex that can be shown to be intermediate between Upper Republican and the following Lower Loup phase and thus directly ancestral to the historic Pawnees. Such an intermediate stage, which should date between ca. A.D. 1300 and 1550, has in fact been postulated (Ludwickson 1978) but still lacks convincing substantive support. In contrast to the uniformly circular house floors of the Lower Loup phase, Loup River phase houses are prevailingly square to rectangular, and the artifact assemblage generally has a stronger Upper Republican or Central Plains tradition flavor than Lower Loup (Wedel 1978c). Whatever the exact nature of the transition that presumably took place, it evidently transpired elsewhere than in the Republican drainage, very probably in the Loup River drainage nearer the historic habitat of the Pawnees. The region occupied by Ludwickson's proposed Loup River phase seems an eminently plausible one for such a development.

That the general abandonment of the west central plains by semisedentary Village peoples and the withdrawal of horticulturally oriented groups to other and more favorable areas, whether east, northeast, south, or elsewhere, was conditioned by environmental changes seems increasingly likely, as was proposed long ago (Wedel 1941). An alternative explanation that cannot yet be arbitrarily dismissed is the possible arrival of unfriendly alien peoples in the western plains, such as ancestral Apachean or other groups, whose subsistence base presumably centered around hunting and gathering strategies and only secondarily, or belatedly, on the cultivation of domestic crops. The archeological record provides no evidence as yet that the western communities were destroyed by enemy action. Whether such evidence will eventually emerge, or be recognized, as archeological fieldwork goes forward on 14th- and 15th-century sites in the critical localities is, of course, moot.

Chapter 8 Late Village Indians: White Rock and Dismal River

Following the still imprecisely dated disappearance of the Upper Republican culture from the Republican River basin, there is at present a gap in the archeological record of the human occupation of the region. If the change postulated by some climatologists, from the moist Neo-Atlantic to the cool, dry Pacific climate less favorable to maize cultivation around A.D. 1200–1500, is supported by further data, an inferred spread eastward of steppe lands at the expense of mid- and tall grasses may have taken place. This could have reduced much of the basin, especially in the west, to semiarid hunting range with human residence more transient than was characteristic of the Upper Republican hamlet dwellers.

Within this late prehistoric span fall several sites of a little known pottery-making culture termed the White Rock aspect (Rusco 1960; Neuman 1963). These include suggested hunting camps along Prairie Dog Creek in the Harlan County Reservoir area and what are perhaps more permanent village remains on White Rock Creek in Jewell County and on the Solomon River at Glen Elder in Mitchell County, Kansas (figures 2.3 and 9.1). Bison predominates in bone refuse from all sites, with deer, elk, turtle, rabbit, freshwater mussels, and other forms represented in lesser quantities. At the Kansas sites, incomplete posthole patterns centering around simple fireplaces may indicate habitations whose construction details otherwise remain undetermined. Here, too, bison-scapula hoe fragments and bell-shaped storage pits strongly suggest some crop cultivation, presumably including maize and the associated domesticates familiar to the earlier Upper Republican gardeners. Charred maize kernels, "predominantly of the southwestern type," were recovered at one site in Lovewell Reservoir on White Rock Creek (Neuman 1963:292).

Other archeological materials include chipped projectile points, mostly triangular in form but also with stemmed or side-notched examples; plano-convex end scrapers; and various cutting and scraping tools. Both local and imported stone were used, including Graham jasper, blue-gray Flint Hills chert, Sioux quartzite, and catlinite. Grooved mauls, catlinite pipes (at least one of the platform disk type), and a prevalence of small, unnotched triangular arrow points indicate a relatively late time level. So also does the bonework, among which are to be found numerous fragments of worked bison scapula, awls, a serrate-edged bison metatarsal flesher, bison condyle (or epiphyseal) hide scrapers, and scored pottery-working paddles made from the vertebral spines of the bison (plate 9.2).

Pottery seems to have been fairly plentiful, at least on some sites, but the sherds are usually small, and vessel shapes and sizes are uncertain. Sand tempering is characteristic, shell tempering uncommon. Most sherds are plain; a very few have cord-roughened surfaces like the earlier Upper Republican and Woodland wares. When body decoration is present, it consists usually of sets of incised or lightly trailed lines with those in adjacent sets slanted or positioned in divergent directions. These contrast sharply with the earlier Central Plains potterywares, but they conform to a widespread decorative style introduced by Upper and/or Middle Mississippian peoples and taken over whole-heartedly by Caddoan and Siouan Village Indians throughout the eastern plains. In one or another of several variants (Wedel 1947:159; 1959:614; Wood 1962), it has been identified with Pawnees, Arikaras, Poncas, and other historic groups, by or through whom it seems to have been widely disseminated into localities 200 miles (320 cm) or more west of the Missouri River.

In the Republican River basin, neither the time nor the tribal identity of the White Rock people has been established. In archeological taxonomy, the remains just reviewed constitute the White Rock aspect, which is composed of the Glen Elder focus (14JW1, 14JW2, 14JW202, and 14ML1) in the Lovewell and Glen Elder reservoir areas in Kansas, and the Blue Stone focus (25HN39 and 25HN45) in Harlan County Reservoir. They appear to be late prehistoric in time, with no certain evidence of contact with white men. A tubular copper bead and other metal fragments from 14JW202 were found in the upper six inches (15 cm) of soil in a cultivated field and their association with the Indian remains is questionable. On the basis of archeological content, the White Rock materials have been tentatively assigned to a period around A.D. 1500–1600. A wood specimen from 25HN45 has been dated by dendrochronology at A.D. 1614 (Neuman 1963:292). At this time level, a Caddoan or Siouan affiliation seems plausible.

Further investigations into the White Rock archeological complex and its variants in the Nebraska-Kansas area are urgently needed. No quick or easy solutions are likely, for on most sites the remains are sparse and their associations have been sadly disrupted by years of intensive agricultural activity. Deep-lying features that might have escaped the plow, such as house pits and caches, are scarce or absent. By comparison with the larger, more conspicuous, and usually much more productive village sites of the identified historic tribes of the region, or with the earlier hamlets and homesteads of the Upper Republican groups, the less well-marked sites of these temporally intermediate people have been neglected much too long.

The Plains Apaches and the Dismal River Complex

In the mid-16th century, a new element appeared that was destined to have far-reaching consequences for the native peoples of the Great Plains. This was the arrival of the Spaniards, vanguard of an alien race that was to overwhelm the natives eventually and to introduce a wholly new lifeway. It coincided with what some climatologists view as a sharp shift in regional climatic patterns that may be dated at ca. A.D. 1550–1850. Termed the Neo-Boreal or Little Ice Age, it was characterized in the northern plains by a change to a colder and moister climate, with cool summers and cold autumns. In the Rocky Mountain region, glaciers formed again; tree-rings indicate wetter conditions in New Mexico.

Whether or not the Neo-Boreal episode in the Great Plains was a region-wide climatic disaster or even a setback of consequence for either the native hunters or the horticulturists is by no means obvious. Indeed, there is evidence that in some sections this may have been a period of unprecedented abundance of bison (Gunnerson 1972; Reher 1978), perhaps reflecting a greater than usual lushness of steppe and prairie grasses and including extensive eastward expansion of the herds into the trans-Mississippi lands, where in Holocene times they seem to have been rare or absent until this relatively late period in history. There is also archeological evidence suggesting that the 17th and 18th centuries were a time of bountiful maize harvests for the Pawnees in east central Nebraska and the Wichitas in central Kansas, whose village sites of this period include great numbers of large storage pits believed to reflect abundant crop yields and large carryovers. Some of the charred corn samples indicate well-filled ears of excellent maize, in quality and yield probably the equivalent or superior of the white man's corn among the 19th-century plains and midwestern settlers.

The first direct contacts between Europeans and the natives of the Great Plains were made in 1540–1541 (table 8.1). In that biennium, Don Francisco Vásquez de Coronado, governor of the province of New Galicia in New Spain, led an army of Spaniards and Mexican Indians up the west coast of Mexico, through present Arizona and into New Mexico, where they wintered among the Rio Grande pueblos. In the summer of 1541, after some fruitless wandering on the Llano Estacado, a select detail under Coronado moved north "by the needle" to discover the grass-house settlements of Quivira around the great bend of the Arkansas in present central Kansas (Wedel 1970b). Here they spent several weeks, exploring the countryside and visiting outlying villages. There is no evidence that any of these reconnaissance parties reached the Republican River or contacted any of its inhabitants directly. En route from their winter quarters on the Rio Grande at Tiguex near present Bernalillo, New Mexico, however, the Spaniards reported several meetings with roving hunter folk whose lifeway differed sharply from that of any of the people previously encountered by the invaders (Hammond and Rey 1940).

Designated the Querechos, these people had no fixed settlements, did not plant or harvest crops, and made no pottery. Their sustenance came solely from the herds of "wild cattle" that they followed around the grasslands and by whose behavior their own lifeway was regulated. They ate the flesh raw, according to the Spanish chroniclers, or dried it in strips, which could be pounded fine for storage, later to be mixed with fat and eaten; they used bison skins for tent covers, clothing, containers, robes, and other items; they lived in large tents, sometimes painted and always supported by poles tied together at the top and spread at the bottom; they supplied their fuel needs with the dung of the animals, that is, with buffalo chips; and they used large numbers of dogs to transport their camp gear and supplies by means of pack saddles, with the tent poles dragged along behind from camp to camp. They used bows and arrows, with which they were very adept at killing bison at the water holes, chipped flint with their teeth, painted themselves, and were "very skillful in use of signs," that is, they could communicate in sign language.

In winter, these rovers foresook the treeless and inhospitable plains to camp near the pueblos, or else they moved east to be near the more sedentary village tribes whom the Spaniards found in possession of maize and other do-

Table 8.1
Some historical dates in relations between Central Plains Indians and
Euro-Americans

1541	Vásquez de Coronado expedition spends several weeks in Quivira, in central Kansas, and meets chief of Harahey, probably a Pawnee.
1593–1594	Francisco Leyva de Bonilla and Antonio Guatierrez de Humaña expedition annihilated in Quivira, somewhere in Kansas.
1601	Juan de Oñate expedition discovers "gran poblacion" in the southern Kansas–northern Oklahoma region, east of Arkansas River.
1700	Father Gabriel Marest, missionary with the Kaskaskias, reports the Panis carrying on commerce with the Spanish.
1706	Juan de Ulibarri visits El Cuartelejo, finds Apaches growing maize and beans, and learns of a French couple killed by Apaches while with the Pawnees.
1714	Etienne Véniard de Bourgmont ascends the Missouri River by boat to *Rivière des Panis* (Platte River) and reports 10 Panis villages 30 leagues (ca. 100 miles) upstream.
1719	Gov. Antonio Valverde visits El Cuartelejo, confirms Apache crop growing, and notes Paloma Apache difficulties with the French and Pawnees. Bénard de la Harpe visits Wichitas on the middle Arkansas River; hears of the Pawnees and Arikaras to the north.
1720	Pedro de Villazur expedition from Santa Fe destroyed by Indians, probably including Pawnees, somewhere on the Platte River.
1744–1764	Fort de Cavagnial established by the Marquis de Vaudreuil, governor general of French Louisiana, on the Missouri River near present Leavenworth, Kansas.
1751	Jean Chapuis and Luis Feuilli travel from Fort de Cavagnial via Pawnees and Comanches to Santa Fe.
1758	Gov. Louis Billouart de Kerlérec records trade relations between French and the Pani-Mahas, 25 leagues up the Platte River.
1775	Lt. Gov. Pedro Piernas reports trade between Spanish at St. Louis and the *Republic* (Republican Pawnees).
1777	Lt. Gov. Francisco Cruzat inventories presents (and trade goods?) for Indians at St. Louis, including the *Panis* and *La Republica* or *Republiques.*
1790s	Jean-Baptiste Truteau claims to have spent three years with the *panis républicains.*
1795	Pedro Vial travels from Santa Fe to the Pawnee villages "on the bank of Kansas river," there meets French traders from St. Louis.
1806	Pawnees visited by Lt. Facundo Melgares from Mexico via Santa Fe, and Lt. Zebulon Pike, U.S. Army, at their village on the Republican River in present Webster County, Nebraska.

mestic crops. The nomads, commercial as well as subsistence hunters, brought meat, bison fat, and hides to the village dwellers in exchange for maize and, in the case of the Pueblo Indians, for cotton textiles, turquoise, perhaps painted pottery, and other manufactured items. It is not unlikely that, in time, they came also to function as middlemen between the Pueblos and the Village Indians some hundreds of miles to the east and northeast, passing on to the latter some of the glaze-paint decorated pottery, turquoise ornaments, pottery pipes, stone arrowshaft straighteners, and other articles acquired from the former (Wedel 1982b). Bilingual itinerant peddlers traveling with or apart from these wandering hunter bands may also have been active instruments in these intertribal transactions.

There is circumstantial evidence that these dog-nomads, generally regarded as Apachean speaking, may have arrived in the New Mexico region not long before Coronado's entrada, perhaps as recently as ca. A.D. 1525 (Gunnerson 1956). There is no doubt that they were already experienced and well-adjusted plainsmen when the Spaniards first encountered them in 1541. After initially destroying several of the terraced Pueblo towns and trying unsuccessfully to overrun Cicuyé (Pecos), they seem to have settled down to the mutually beneficial symbiotic relationship with the villagers that would be reflected in both cultures or lifeways for several generations to come. We have no hints, unfortunately, about how widely these dog-nomads were distributed over the plains in the 16th century, or whether their representatives or counterparts were then already roaming the Republican country. The short-lived and frequently changed hunting camps, as well as the highly perishable nature of most camp gear carried by these followers of the herds, can be expected to have left little, if anything, to be uncovered by the archeologist three or four centuries later.

Not many details are known about the Apache dog-nomads during the first century after their discovery. We are especially ignorant of the extent to which some of them, in regular or frequent contact during the late 16th and early 17th centuries with their new neighbors and trading partners in the Southwest, may have gradually adopted maize-bean-squash horticulture, crop irrigation, pottery making, and perhaps other material culture traits from their sedentary Pueblo contemporaries. There is evidence that northeast of the Pueblo towns of the Rio Grande and the Galisteo basin, by the mid-17th century some of the Apache groups were practicing horticulture and irrigation and lived in structures more substantial than the skin tents of the 16th-century dog-nomads. In this general region, including northeastern New Mexico, southeastern Colorado, southwestern Kansas, and the western panhandles of Oklahoma and Texas, the low rainfall, high evaporation, and erratic weather patterns made the growing of maize and most other native American Indian domesticates an extremely hazardous enterprise in the absence of irrigation techniques. I shall return to this point in another place.

Sixty years after Coronado, Don Juan de Oñate wrote of the dog-nomads as the "Querechos, or vaqueros," whom he further characterized two years later as the "people of the Apache nation, who are the ones who possess these plains." By 1630, the Apache Vaquero were reported to be inhabiting extensive tracts east of the Rio Grande, ranging "more than 150 leagues along the boundary of New Mexico and extending more than 100 leagues eastward." Around 1639 or 1640, the tensions generated by a century of Spanish oppression drove a group of rebellious Taos Indians far out onto the bison plains, where they "fortified themselves at a place which afterward on this account was called El Cuartelejo" (Thomas 1935:53). From this refuge they appear to have been "rescued" by a Spanish expedition under Juan de Archuleta in 1662, but no details of the Cuartelejo region are provided at this time.

Following the Pueblo Rebellion of 1680, other Puebloans apparently sought refuge among the Cuartelejo Apaches. One of these was a group of Picuris, rounded up in 1706 by Juan de Ulibarri, who described them as apostates that had lived at El Cuartelejo since 1696. The fugitives came out of some little huts to meet the Spanish (Thomas 1935:19, 68). At the end of July, it was reported, the Cuartelejo Apaches had harvested maize, kidney beans, watermelon, and other crops. In addition, they had guns, metal kettles, and other items taken from the French and Pawnees, besides iron hatchets, sword blades, and other items obtained from unidentified white men to the east. Thirteen years later, Gov. Antonio Valverde retraced much of Ulibarri's route in pursuit of Comanche and Ute raiders. He, too, noted evidence of crop growing among the Apaches; and from a wounded Paloma Apache at Cuartelejo, he learned that the man had been shot while he and his people were planting corn "on the most remote borderlands of the Apaches," where they came under attack by combined French, Pawnees, and Jumanos (Wichitas). The Palomas had given up their lands on the Apache frontier under the pressure and were retreating to the Arkansas River. Later, when the Spanish were considering the feasibility of establishing an outpost at El Cuartelejo for defense against the French and their Indian allies, adverse evaluations were offered by members of the Ulibarri and Valverde expeditions because, they maintained, the harvests there were scanty, the winters rigorous, and there was "no supply of firewood for many leagues" (Thomas 1935:132, 157).

In the following year, 1720, in direct response to the French approach from the northeast, Valverde dispatched an expedition of soldiers and Indians under an inexperienced subordinate, Pedro Villazur, to negotiate. This detachment, which included much of the fighting manpower of the Spanish on the Rio Grande, as well as Cuartelejo allies, was effectively wiped out in August, either at the forks of the Platte or near the Platte-Loup junction 250 miles (400 km) downstream. The Villazur expedition may well have crossed the Republican, but most of the journal was destroyed and we cannot profitably guess where such a crossing took place. With this disaster, active Spanish interest in the northeast Apache borderlands and the neighboring Indians and French dwindled and remained low for more than 80 years.

The heart of the old Cuartelejo and Paloma Apache territories has long been regarded as the area lying north of the Rio Napestle or Arkansas River, and as coming to represent a considerable region rather than a single rancheria or locality. Today, it is commonly identified with eastern Colorado, western Kansas, and probably southwestern Nebraska. Not altogether without reason it has been suggested also (Champe 1949:291) that the Paloma settlement where Valverde's informant received his gunshot wound and, along with his compeers, was forced to abandon his incompletely planted corn patches and withdraw to the south may have been located in the Harlan County Reservoir district on the Republican, perhaps indeed at the White Cat village site, 25HN37. This is not more than a hundred miles (160 km) from the early-18th-century habitat of the Pawnees and their resident French traders. More important is the fact that in the Republican valley, the earliest recognized evidence of Indians who were demonstrably in contact with white men involves the materials that archeologists call the Dismal River complex. This dates in time from the 18th-century level in which the Plains Apaches made this a part of their habitat (Hill and Metcalf 1942; Champe 1949; Wedel 1935:180; 1959:422–468,

589–599; Gunnerson 1960, 1968; Gunnerson and Gunnerson 1971; Basso and Opler 1971; D. Gunnerson 1974; Opler 1936, 1971, 1975, 1982; Schlesier 1972).

Dismal River culture sites are widely distributed over the area "between the 100th meridian and the Rocky Mountains from the Black Hills to at least northern New Mexico" (Gunnerson 1969a:169). North of the Arkansas River, the most intensively studied sites, and the ones from which the most complete data are available, all lie east of the 102d meridian in the Kansas-Nebraska region (see Figs. 2.1 and 2.3). Most of these are estimated to fall between ca. A.D. 1675 and 1725 and can be reasonably attributed to Apachean groups who had progressed from 16th-century dog-nomadism to a mixed hunting and semi-horticultural lifeway. We still know far too little about the material culture inventory for Dismal River sites located in the presently dry lands west of the stated meridian, where the feasibility of maize growing without irrigation under climatic conditions no more favorable than the present is highly questionable. In terms of the Plains Apaches recognized by the contemporary Spanish residing on the Rio Grande, these sites probably derive mainly from the Cuartelejo and Paloma bands.

Dismal River sites have been found in a wide variety of topographic locations. The larger sites so far worked have been on open terraces along perennial streams (plate 8.1). Others occur on the shores of lakes and ponds in the sandhill areas of Nebraska and Colorado, in blowouts, in rock shelters, and on butte tops. They vary from small, ill-defined sherd scatters to 60 or 70 acres of bone refuse, flints, small potsherds, and other occupational debris. Visible trash heaps, fortifications, lodge circles or depressions, and other structural features have not been reported from unbroken or unexcavated sites.

House remains, as judged by archeologists from postmold patterns at a few sites, suggest a semipermanent structure, perhaps 20 to 25 feet (6–7.6 m) in diameter. This was erected on a five-post foundation, surrounded by leaners carrying a cover of brush or grass, and built on the ground surface or slightly below it (Champe 1949:286; Gunnerson 1960:146). At the center was an unlined fireplace. Bison long bones were sometimes used to wedge posts firmly upright in their holes. Extra postholes, paired and placed just outside the basic circle of five, may mark the location of the doorway, opening usually (?) toward the east. The finished structures inferred from these configurations are markedly unlike the usual Plains earthlodge or other common house form. Subfloor storage pits, so characteristic of Plains earthlodges, are absent from Dismal River houses. Shallow irregular basins of unknown function occur at most sites (fig. 8.1).

No less distinctive than the houses are roasting or baking pits. They vary considerably in size but are usually two to three feet deep and three to five feet in floor diameter, with constricted mouths and very heavily fired walls and floors that may be almost bricklike in color and hardness (plate 8.1). They usually contain much ash and charcoal, an abundance of fire-reddened or cracked rocks, and they occasionally served secondarily for the deposition of refuse. They have not been recorded from other Plains cultures, but baking pits have been found in post-Spanish levels at Pecos pueblo, in at least one culturally unidentified small site in Angostura Reservoir near the Black Hills, and at Glendo Reservoir in eastern Wyoming (Wedel 1959:591; Gunnerson and Gunnerson 1971:15). Their exact function is unknown, but they were presumably

Plate 8.1. Dismal River culture materials. *Upper,* valley of Stinking Water Creek, the *L'eau qui Peaue* [pue] of the French according to Lt. E. F. Ware. The Lovitt site, 25CH1, is on the hay flat beyond the creek. Archeological excavations are underway at extreme right; *lower,* Dismal River baking pit, ca. A.D. 1700, Scott County, Kansas.

used in the preparation of certain foods by techniques that must have differed markedly from those inferred for other Plains Indian groups. Whether these procedures involved meat or vegetable dishes, or a combination of both, has not been established. In some of these pits, the ground level opening seems so small as to preclude bodily entry by the digger, implying perhaps that the final depth, diameter, and shape were determined by the total reach and tool size of the operator lying on the ground, inserting her arm into the opening, and scraping away to arm's length at the matrix filling the prospective baking pit.

From one such pit at the Scott County site, collectors recovered a male

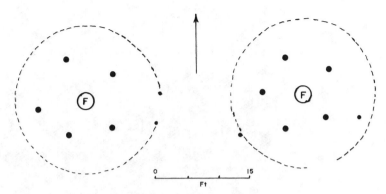

Fig. 8.1. Floor patterns of Dismal River houses, showing central hearth and pentagonal arrangement of main posts. House limits shown by *broken lines* are approximate.

skeleton. Evidently a purposeful burial, the skeleton lay on its right side, flexed, head to the north facing west. There were no artifacts. The deceased was estimated to have been between 22 and 23 years old, 5 feet 7 inches tall, with a cranial index of 77 percent. Whether Apache, Pueblo, or other is unknown (Gunnerson 1969b).

The subsistence economy of the Dismal River people appears to have centered around big game hunting, with horticulture a secondary interest. Bison bones predominate in the debris from occupation sites, with deer, pronghorn, and wapiti (elk) in smaller quantities. There are also remains of prairie dog, domestic dog, coyote, woodrat, and beaver. Fish bones are scarce, as are those of birds, but these absences may reflect recovery techniques rather than actual cultural preferences on the part of the Indians. If these various forms of mammals were taken in any way other than by individual hunters or small parties, we have no evidence of the fact. There are no bone beds or other signs of mass kills, and no jumps, pounds, or drive lines. We have, in short, no indication that bison were killed in numbers by group efforts, as they were by contemporary and also earlier foot hunters in the western and northwestern plains. If bison were present in considerable numbers, as seems likely, the hunting methods observed by the Spanish among the 16th-century dog-nomads may have been entirely adequate as well in Dismal River times. It seems possible, too, that many of the sherd scatters identified as Dismal River stations were short-lived hunting camps occupied by parties of bison hunters wandering about the western plains in contact with the herds, operating in essentially the same fashion as the earlier dog-nomads from whom they were probably descended, at least in part.

The Dismal River people have been characterized as "half-hearted horticulturists" practicing a "perfunctory" or "desultory" gardening economy, compared with the more fully committed semihorticultural natives of the eastern plains, such as the Pawnees and Wichitas. The comparison may not be altogether fair. The Lovitt and Scott County sites, westernmost of those with evidence of horticulture, are very close to the limits of successful maize cultivation in the central plains, given a climatic setting like that of today. Here, low and erratic precipitation, high evaporation rates, and frequent but unpredictable droughts require the application of special techniques not so urgently required farther east, for example, in much of the Upper Republican habitat. One of those special techniques was ditch irrigation, clearly indicated at Scott County and there probably a direct result of Plains Apache contacts with fugitive irrigation-conscious Puebloan people from Taos and/or Picuris. At this site, spring waters were channeled some hundreds of yards through ditches to supply terrace areas of several acres; this technique was repeated successfully by subsequent white homesteaders who cleaned out and reused the Indian canals.

Whether the maize and other crops grown here aboriginally in quantities are of southwestern or Puebloan type and were derived from a marginal Puebloan source is not yet clear, and the same uncertainty holds for the limited quantities of maize, cobs, and husks recovered at the Lovitt site. But whatever the source of the crop varieties and irrigation know-how of the Dismal River people, it is clear that they were using a distinctively Plains type of implement for their cultivation, the bison-scapula hoe. The finding of numbers of these at Scott County and Lovitt sites, along with charred maize samples, supports their identification as gardening tools. They were also found at White Cat Village, where no remains of domesticates were recovered but their former presence seems plausible and where, in any case, the scapula tools would have served as well for other digging and soil-turning functions.

The general absence of storage pits at known Dismal River sites has been noted. Among other Plains horticultural tribes, the underground cache is almost as consistently present as the scapula hoe, and it occurs in practically all Village Indian complexes where maize cultivation is indicated. Its absence in Dismal River sites is therefore of particular interest. Reduced crop yields in the horticulturally marginal districts inhabited by the Dismal River gardeners is one possibility, but the practice of ditch irrigation from strong perennial springs, such as that at Scott County, should have more than offset the environmental handicaps. If the Plains Apache were not "long and deeply addicted" to gardening, as their eastern Plains contemporaries were, they may have preferred storage above ground in containers of skin, basketry, or pottery in their houses, with the surplus beyond immediate needs consumed on the trek to winter quarters at the pueblos or near the eastern villagers. Neither archeology nor history gives us any clues to the crop yields harvested by the Dismal River gardeners.

Still uncertain, too, is the manner in which the harvested crops were further processed. Grinding implements are not common in the archeological record. At Scott County, 14SC1, a mealing bin resembling the Puebloan grinding centers with texture-graded metates (Bartlett 1936) was found in the ruin and doubtless was for use by the erstwhile Pueblo fugitives residing therein. Elsewhere, small grinding slabs (or fragments) and hand stones further suggest Puebloan milling methods, unlike the upright wooden mortar and billet, which were not uncommonly used by the Pawnees. In this respect, we surmise that the Dismal River women were perhaps following procedures learned from their Pueblo neighbors and that resembled those of the early historic metate-using Wichitas of central Kansas rather than those of the Pawnees and other semihorticultural tribes of the eastern plains.

Actually, we have almost no details, either from the archeological record or from documents, on Plains Apache and Dismal River crop tillage methods of the early 1700s. Did the men cultivate, as among the Pueblo Indians, or the women, as among the Plains tribes, or both? How were the gardens laid out and maintained? Was the injured Paloma reported by Valverde shot while carrying a hoe or digging stick, or was he guarding women doing the work? How widespread was irrigation among the Paloma and Cuartelejo settlements north of the Arkansas River, compared to the Lipan communities lying nearer to the pueblos of the upper Rio Grande?

Among the stone and bone tools recovered from Dismal River sites, items presumably associated with hunting, butchering, and skin working appear to dominate. They include chipped cutting tools of various kinds and sizes, hide scrapers, choppers, cigar-shaped or straight drill points, and numbers of small triangular arrowpoints. The exact manner of hafting the knives, scrapers, and other blades is unknown, though antler tips thought to be notched and modified for hafting have been found. Graham jasper was extensively used for chipped tools. Ground and pecked stone tools are much less common. They include sandstone abraders for smoothing arrowshafts or for sharpening awls, needles, and other pointed tools.

There are bone awls and needles for tailoring leather; serrate fleshing tools made from bison leg bones for scraping shreds of flesh and fat from hides in preparation; arrowshaft wrenches of bison rib; wedge-shaped cancellous bone paint "brushes"; hemispheric hide-rubbing tools cut from the rounded joint ends of large bison leg bones; and transversely scored ribs, which have been variously identified as musical rasps, tally bones, or pottery paddles. Conical antler tip projectile points with basal sockets and sturdy bone points with constricted stem are also reported. Most of these tools cannot be readily distinguished from the similar types found in the inventories of contemporary Plains dwellers, such as the Pawnees and Wichitas (plates 8.3 and 9.2).

Pottery of distinctive kinds was also made in some quantity by the Dismal River people. Most common is a thin, hard, dark ware, which in the field is characteristically broken into small bits. Restored and reconstructed vessels (plates 6.2 and 8.2) reveal jars with constricted necks, usually without decoration or handles and apparently intended for utilitarian functions rather than for aesthetic appeal. Much of the pottery contains an abundance of mica particles and resembles the utility wares made at Picuris, Taos, and other eastern frontier pueblos that were in close and continuing contact with the Plains hunters. Surfaces sometimes show corncob striations; at the more easterly sites, notably those nearer to the pottery-making village tribes of the eastern plains, the pieces sometimes show parallel ridges made by impressions from a simple thong-wrapped or carved paddle, very similar to a common pottery-finishing technique used by the Pawnees and other historic eastern Plains tribes (plate 9.2).

A number of items clearly indicate contacts and probable trade with Puebloan people on the Rio Grande. These include occasional finds of turquoise in the form of beads, bead blanks, or pendants; obsidian chips and projectile points; bone flageolets; glaze-paint decorated pottery sherds; finely incised bone tubes of unknown use; arrowshaft polishers of fine-grained New Mexican stone; incised tubular pottery pipes, sometimes with flared or otherwise elaborated bits; and *Olivella* shell beads from the Pacific Ocean via the Pueblo Southwest.

Plate 8.2. Dismal River culture materials. *Upper,* fireplace with iron axhead embedded in the ashes, 25HN37. Courtesy National Anthropological Archives, Smithsonian Institution. *Lower,* restored pottery vessels from the Lovitt site. Courtesy Nebraska State Historical Society.

There is also limited but recurrent evidence of contact between the Dismal River people and white men. At White Cat Village on the Prairie Dog, now covered by Harlan County Reservoir, an iron axhead made from a piece of metal doubled on itself to form the eye and then welded full length, was recovered from the hearth in House VI. Believed to date from the late 17th or early 18th century and to be of French or English origin, it was accompanied by several bits of sheet copper or brass, in addition to scraps of metal from the site surface. Four iron awls and a few other scraps came from the Lovitt site. At Scott County, an iron axhead fragment was found in the pueblo ruin; outside, several pieces of iron were recovered, two of which possibly represent heavily oxidized knife blades. A blue glass bead also came from this site.

Precise identification of these items as to their national origin is probably not possible in their present condition. They may be the tangible evidence of

Plate 8.3. Stone and pottery artifacts from various cultures in the Republican country, Kansas and Nebraska. *Upper*, six stone pipes from the Hill Pawnee site, ca. A.D. 1800. Courtesy Nebraska State Historical Society. *Middle*, three pottery pipes of the Dismal River culture, ca. A.D. 1700. Courtesy National Museum of Natural History. *Lower*, anthropomorphic carving and pipes of limestone, Upper Republican culture, ca. A.D. 1100–1250. Courtesy National Anthropological Archives, Smithsonian Institution.

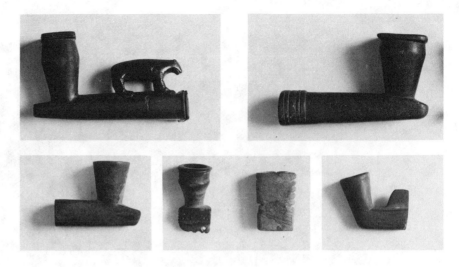

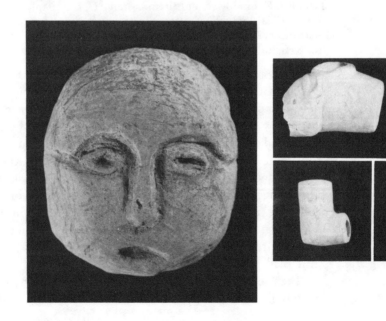

the 18th-century trade carried on by the French from the St. Louis area by way of the Missouri River and the Pawnee villages, to the continuing concern of the Spanish in New Mexico. At none of the sites has any horse gear been recognized nor are horse bones reported in the village refuse, despite the fact that the animal may have been known to and in use by the Kansas Apaches north of the Arkansas River as early as ca. A.D. 1640 (Forbes 1959:200). For none of these Frenchmen or any of the other white men who may have visited the Pawnees, Wichitas, or other Central Plains villagers before Véniard de Bourgmont's time of 1724, or who might have been with raiding parties against the Apaches, have we names or other details that would permit verification of their identities from non-Spanish sources with better and more complete information than the New Mexicans possessed.

As already indicated, the Dismal River sites in which the most detailed research has been accomplished so far are believed to fall within a 50- to 60-year period centering around A.D. 1700. Charred wood samples from three of the Nebraska sites, all located in the Republican River drainage, have been correlated with tree-ring sequences in the North Platte master tree-ring chart, but since the dated specimens originated at some distance from the North Platte collecting district, some uncertainty remains regarding the validity of these determinations (Weakly in Hill and Metcalf 1942:205). In any case, published dates for the outside rings in samples from the sites concerned are as follows:

25CH1	Lovitt site (Chase County)	A.D. 1706
25DN1	Nichols site (Dundy County)	A.D. 1709
25HN37	White Cat site (Harlan County)	A.D. 1723

These dates, if valid, are of particular interest since they place the Dismal River sites in the Republican River basin in the same time span in which the events reported by Ulibarri and Valverde were taking place northeast of the Rio Grande settlements (Thomas 1935). More date determinations are needed, to be sure, but those given are suggestive and of great interest.

More than 100 miles (160 km) to the south, and outside the Republican drainage, the Scott County pueblo ruin 14SC1 and its surrounding Dismal River materials have not been dated by any such "precise" method as dendrochronology. However, a number of distinctively southwestern, i.e., Puebloan artifact types, represented by pieces pretty certainly manufactured in the upper Rio Grande valley and imported into western Kansas, provide helpful clues. The painted pottery, for example, has been identified with New Mexican wares made by Indians in the last decades of the 17th and the first decades of the 18th century. They thus bracket in time the Nebraska tree-ring dates listed above and also the time of at least one recorded 10-year sojourn by Taos fugitives among the Cuartelejo Apaches. That the Scott County pueblo ruin is identifiable with the "El Cuartelejo" of the Spanish documents is perhaps still debatable, but it may nevertheless still have been associated with the Cuartelejo Apaches. Its occupancy by Pueblos around the turn of the 18th century, in what may have been a sizable Plains Apache community, more or less contemporaneous with the dendrochronologically dated Nebraska sites, would not be inconsistent with the historical record or the data of archeology.

The Plains Apaches have been cited frequently as an excellent example of the high degree of cultural adaptability of the Athapascans, of their peculiar ability to adjust their lifeway to whatever pattern functioned best in the local circumstances. Thus, where the pursuit of large game was most successful, they specialized in big game hunting; where a combination of hunting and horticulture was feasible, they turned some of their energies toward gardening. Everywhere, they undoubtedly gathered wild plant products, as some of the New Mexico Apaches still do, or did until recently (Castetter 1935). To the extent that the Dismal River fraction of the Plains Apaches were direct lineal descendants of the 16th-century dog-nomads, their cultural heritage must be recognized as that of fully fledged plainsmen with simple but effective hunting and skin-working tools and techniques such as the ones long and deeply addicted bison hunters in the Great Plains had been using successfully, in some instances, since the days of Early Man in the region. Where and when the distinctive five-post house foundations and the baking pits originated in their history is unclear. Their pottery, horticulture, and irrigation, and perhaps some of the historically recorded house types seem basically of Puebloan derivation. Most of their bone and stone tools fit the regional pattern for the late prehistoric and early historic Plains people, whose subsistence economy included hunting, horticulture, and food gathering. Pottery finishing and other details seem to reflect the influence of their nearest neighbors in the eastern plains. Theirs was a new and different adaptation in the Republican River cultural succession, one that would not reappear once it had run its course and disappeared from the scene.

Among archeologists there is general acceptance of the view that the Dismal River culture is most satisfactorily assigned to a Plains Apache occupation. No other historical Indian group in the region transitional from the western plains to the eastern Puebloan, great basin, and montane areas qualifies as well. Dissenting views have been advanced, most conspicuously and persistently by Morris Opler (1935, 1936, 1971, 1982). In the first of these titles, he notes that the Lipan "have closer cultural ties to the Jicarilla Apache than to any other Apachean tribe and that they probably had little involvement with Dismal River culture." Further, the Dismal River occupation at 1675–1725 "was the period . . . when the Pueblo peoples were fleeing both eastward and westward in an effort to escape Spanish oppression before the revolt of 1680 and Spanish vengeance after that event." If, he concludes, archeologists will adopt the "total anthropology" point of view and pursue this course "faithfully and thoroughly, it is likely that they will eventually conclude, on the basis of the widest range of evidence, that the refugee Pueblo component in the Dismal River aspect is greater than is now accepted and that the Apachean contribution is correspondingly smaller."

In the 1936 paper, Opler argues that the Plains orientation of the Jicarilla culture has been overemphasized, including specifically buffalo hunting and the use of the travois, parfleche, and tipi. Whereas the early historical literature refers to no dwelling other than the tipi, the oldest people in the tribe in the 1930s affirmed that the favorite dwelling was the dome-shaped thatch-covered frame, that hunting expeditions to the Plains were "in the nature of an anxious press forward and a speedy retreat to familiar landmarks," once the kill had been completed. The same informants insisted that the eyeleted bone needle, found in Dismal River complex inventories, was not an element in Jicarilla material culture, and that dogs were never eaten, as has been suggested may have been done by the Dismal River people. And finally, "psychologically, they [the Jicarillas] were anything but a Plains people."

This incomplete litany of discrepancies between Dismal River and late Jicarilla material culture disturbs me less than it does Opler. In the 1930s, when Opler's fieldwork among the Jicarillas was carried out, the oldest people, unnamed and their ages unspecified, must have been born no earlier than the 1830s, more than 100 years or three generations after the time of Ulibarri and Valverde. I am by no means persuaded that the recollections of such twentieth-century Indians concerning details of the lifeway of their forebears of 200 years and more, and five or six generations ago, can be accepted as disproof of the archeologists' interpretations, or as discrediting the observations of the contemporary Spaniards. During those two intervening centuries, I suspect that there were drastic changes in the material culture inventory of the Apacheans. l am likewise unimpressed by the argument that the Jicarillas of the 1930s were "psychologically" not a Plains people. Certainly their presumed ancestors of the early 1700s, as reported to us by Spaniard after Spaniard from eyewitness observations and long-continued contacts, behaved like plainsmen and were evidently participating fully in the well-established and highly functional lifeway revolving around the pursuit of the bison. Such traits as multi-roomed masonry houses and ditch irrigation, as manifested at Scott County pueblo, were quite likely the handiwork of fugitive Pueblo Indians or of acculturated Apaches working with the Pueblos or under their influence. We have no way of being certain, one way or the other, whether we choose to place our faith in archeology, in ethnography, in history, or in a "total anthropology" approach.

If I have not misread or misconstrued Opler's various sorties, he seems to be arguing that the archeologists should accept Dismal River as a manifestation of Pueblo cultural retrenchment or reorientation by fugitives in response to Spanish oppression, rather than as a stage in Apache adaptation. If his supporting criticisms and inferences typify the "total anthropology" point of view, "faithfully and thoroughly" pursued, I remain unpersuaded and unswayed. To me, Dismal River still looks very much like a basically Plains material culture complex, with bison hunting and mobility pivotal to its functioning whereas maize cultivation was supplementary, but with important accretions and perhaps certain deflections in the lifeway resulting from strong contacts and some actual populational accretions from the pueblo area, notably between ca. A.D. 1650 and 1750.

It seems to me quite possible that one reason for the inability of archeologists to locate and identify earlier Dismal River sites to date is the probable absence of some of the traits considered by them to be particularly diagnostic of Dismal River, as currently defined. Can it be assumed, for example, that Dismal River sites scattered through eastern Colorado, in the area where Thomas (1935:16, 19) long ago argued for the location of El Cuartelejo, will disclose five-post houses, baking pits, bison-scapula hoes, maize, and other culture elements similar to those found in and around Scott County Pueblo or at Lovitt or White Cat Village? If the earlier sites for which we search reflect a lesser enthusiasm for the adoption of Puebloan innovations and a stronger addiction to the simpler material accoutrements of the austere dog-nomad lifeway of a hundred years before, are we still dealing with the Dismal River complex or with a differently specialized lifeway to which another designation might more appropriately be applied? As Bowman (1976) has cogently argued in an unpublished paper, scholars dealing with the Dismal River–Plains Apache problems in time and space still face thorny problems of taxonomy, ecology, adaptation, and the harmonization of findings from a wide variety of subdisciplines. I am not at all sure that a more free-wheeling and sweeping synthesis such as Schlesier (1972) offers in reaction to the current "rather static and unimaginative" status of Dismal River studies will materially advance our understanding in the absence of meticulous and widespread analytical archeological fieldwork.

At the heart of our problems, I believe, is the still extremely limited body of information we have concerning the Dismal River archeological complex and its probable variations through time and space. Since the materials so designated existed in part, at least, within the historic period, meticulously done and critically applied correlations between archeology and history or ethnohistory should be productive and enlightening. At the present moment, only three major sites—Scott County Pueblo, Lovitt, and White Cat—have been investigated and reported in some detail. Urgently needed now are comparable samples of materials and data from many other sites well dispersed throughout the known area of occurrence. The sustained program of field, laboratory, library, and archival research, which has been underway for some years by D. A. and J. H. Gunnerson on the archeology and culture history of the Plains Athapascans, seems to me to carry great promise for deeper insights and better understanding when and as the findings and their considered interpretations have been made generally available.

Especially encouraging is the following note (Gunnerson and Gunnerson 1971:7): "With regard to material culture, . . . work in the 1960s on Southern Athapaskan archeology has revealed areal differences, especially in ceramics, and these differences, in turn, are compatible with historical evidence concerning the location of particular Apachean groups and their relations with neighboring non-Apachean tribes." I take this to mean that the Gunnersons have tentatively identified certain archeological variants of Dismal River with historically recognized Apachean groups named by the Spanish and more or less precisely located geographically. How firmly such correlations have been supported by chronological determinations through cross-finds of datable pottery, tree rings, or other time sequences, I am unable to say. Neither is it clear to what extent, if any, they confirm, discredit, or modify Schlesier's comprehensive reconstructions and interpretations of Dismal River archeology and Plains Apachean band distinctions and geography. To the archeological believer, there can be no satisfactory substitute for such direct and personal study of sites over a wide range of territory, and of local collections from those sites. Imagination, however satisfying or plausible its images, if it disregards the details of archeology and the standards of critical scholarship, can lead only to further confusion of the issues we are trying to clarify and understand.

To what extent the Athapascan northerners were responsible for cultural changes in the Plains Indian lifeway as they moved south is still uncertain. Once regarded by some as perhaps responsible for the introduction of hunting techniques characteristic of the caribou area into the bison area, it is now abundantly clear from several decades of systematic archeological research that bison hunting in the plains was well established some thousands of years ago. Organized communal procurement methods were not brought into the region by the late prehistoric Athapascan invaders who were harassing the pueblo towns shortly before the arrival of the Spaniards in 1540. To people of this stock have been attributed the introduction of the bow and arrow, of highly ritualized communal bison procurement, and of the small-point tradition through the Avonlea type in the Canadian plains (Kehoe and Kehoe 1968:30, 35). The validity of this attribution and its applicability, if any, to the central and southern plains, remain to be demonstrated.

Chapter 9 Late Village Indians: The Pawnees

Until 1876 the most populous and influential of the native peoples of Nebraska, the Pawnees were a loose confederacy of four subtribes usually referred to in English as "bands," aggregating perhaps 7,000 to 10,000 persons. During the 19th century, when they became well known to the Americans, they resided mainly in a group of "permanent" but frequently moved earthlodge villages centered around the confluence of the Platte and Loup rivers in east central Nebraska. Their identified town sites begin at Yutan, 15 miles (24 km) below Fremont on the Platte and extend 120 miles (190 km) upstream to Central City and to St. Paul on the Loup. Between Schuyler and Genoa, in the heart of this curving strip for which the designation Pawnee Crescent seems appropriate, was a series of large and prolific archeological sites where, as the *Pani* and *Panimaha* of the French documents, the Pawnees lived from their earliest white contact in the mid-16th century until the latter part of the 18th century. Other Pawnee villages were located at various times on the Blue River near Beatrice and on the Republican near where it crosses the Nebraska-Kansas boundary (figs. 9.1 and 9.2).

The four bands were the Chawi or Grand, the Kitkahahki or Republican, and the Pitahawirata or Tappage, in later times often grouped together as the South Band or Bands; and the Skiri or Loup. They were probably represented in the Indian delegation from "Harahey" (evidently a Spanish corruption of the pan-Caddoan term *Awa:hi* for the Pawnees; see M. M. Wedel 1982) that met Don Francisco Vásquez de Coronado in central Kansas in 1541 (Hammond and Rey 1940:304), and they became well known to the French in the 18th century. During the American period, after ca. 1800, they resided usually in two to five or six principal towns, each estimated to contain 40 to 200 lodges and from 800 to 3,500 inhabitants (plate 9.1). Earlier, there were apparently more numerous and smaller villages or hamlets, dispersed in a more scattered fashion. The Skiris usually lived to the west of the other bands, some or all of which at times occupied a single village.

The villages were governed by head chiefs in what Lt. Zebulon M. Pike called "an hereditary aristocracy," whose authority waxed and waned in accord with family connections, political and administrative ability, and generosity; also governing the villages was a council composed of lesser chiefs and leading men, the "braves." The patrilineally hereditary chiefs and the elected chiefs, the priests, and the braves constituted an upper class, with privileges not shared by the commoners. A well-organized and influential priesthood, which derived its power from sacred bundles, carried on an elaborate series of rituals

152

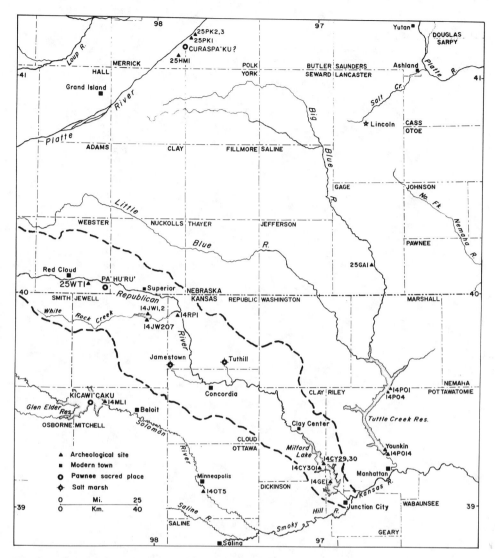

Fig. 9.1. Map of the eastern portion of the Republican River basin (*heavy broken lines*), showing counties, modern cities, and selected archeological sites and features.

and ceremonies, an especially notable feature of which was an extraordinarily well-developed star cult. The villages were endogamous, that is, people married in. Descent was traced through the mother and, after marriage, a man went to live with his wife's family.

During the three centuries or so of demonstrable residence in the Pawnee Crescent, the Pawnee lifeway remained fundamentally much the same but with drastic changes in detail. The earlier village sites, dating ca. A.D. 1550–1750 and known to archeologists as the Lower Loup phase, represent the high-water mark of Pawnee culture. Pottery making and other arts and crafts reached their high point, houses were carefully and uniformly laid out, and ceremonialism probably peaked. After the middle of the 18th century, the material culture declined in quality and also quantitatively, house construction became less formalized, and the earlier standards for doing things seem to have survived chiefly in memory (Wedel 1979a; 1979c:279, 286–290).

From the late 18th century on, we have a relative abundance of contempo-

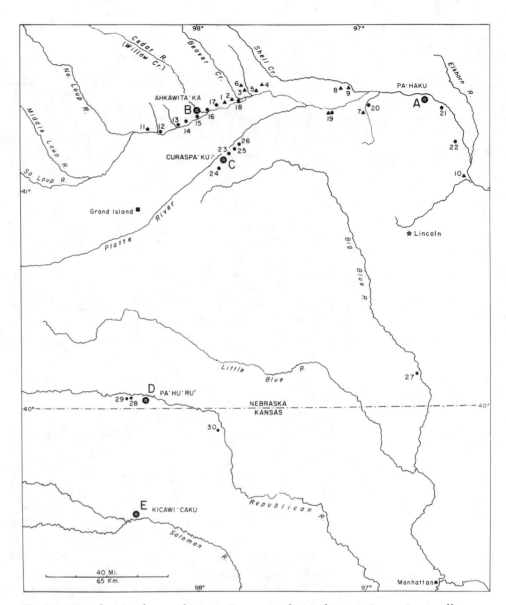

Fig. 9.2. Map showing known historic Pawnee and protohistoric Lower Loup village sites and Pawnee sacred places (A–E) in Nebraska and Kansas.

Lower Loup phase (ca. 1550–1750): 1, Burkett (25NCl); 2, Wright (25NC3); 3, Larsen (25PT1); 4, Monroe (25PT13); 5, Foley (25PT17); 6, Coffin (25NC16); 7, Barcal (25BU4); 8, Wolfe (25CX2); 9, Gray (25CX1); 10, Ashland (25CC1).
Historic Pawnee (ca. 1750–1876): 11, Palmer (25HW1); 12, Cottonwood Creek (25NC5); 13, Horse Creek (25NC2); 14, Vogel (25NC11); 15, Cunningham (25NC10); 16, Fullerton (25NC7); 17, Plum Creek or Burnt Village (25NC14); 18, Genoa (25NC6); 19, Bellwood (25BU2); 20, Linwood (25BU1); 21, McClaine (25SD8); 22, Leshara (25SD2); 23, Clarks (25PK1); 24, Hordville (25HM1); 25, P. Nelson (25PK2), 26, D. Johnson (25PK3); 27, Blue Springs (25GA1); 28, Hill (25WT1); 29, Shipman (25WT7); 30, Kansas Monument (14RP1).
Sacred places indicated: A, Pa·haku ("mound on the water"); B, Ahkawita·ka ("white river bank"); C, Curaspaku (Girl Hill); D, Guide Rock ("hill that points the way"); E, Kicawi·caku ("spring on edge of a bank"-"Waconda or great spirit spring.")

Plate 9.1. Historic Pawnee villages of the 19th century in Nebraska. *Upper*, Pawnee village scene in 1871 as recorded by William H. Jackson near Genoa, Nebraska. Courtesy National Anthropological Archives, Smithsonian Institution. *Lower*, raised rings from collapsed earthlodges mark the site of a Pawnee village (25BU2) of ca. A.D. 1800. These lodges opened toward the southeast, indicated by the extension on each ring to the right. Still in native sod when this photograph was made in 1934, all rings have since been obliterated by farming. Courtesy Nebraska State Historical Society.

rary documentation for the Pawnees as a tribe in the eyewitness reports from explorers, traders, government agents, missionaries, army officers, and other travelers. As with neighboring Plains tribes, the story becomes one of steadily diminishing territory for hunting grounds and residence as white power and thirst for land expanded. Its culmination came with removal of the Pawnees from Nebraska to Indian Territory in 1876, and the transformation of their one-time reservation on the Loup River into Nance County (Wedel 1936, 1938; Dunlevy 1936; Grange 1968, 1979; Champe and Fenenga 1974; Lesser 1978; Wishart 1979; Blaine 1980; Murie 1981).

Republican River Pawnees

Two Late Village Indian sites clearly assignable to the Pawnees have been identified and extensively investigated in the Republican River valley. Both are in the eastern part, one 22 miles (35 km) above and the other eight miles (13 km) below the point where the stream finally leaves Nebraska to enter Kansas. At both sites the principal occupation is believed to date after the mid-18th-century heyday of Pawnee culture, but the precise span of their use has not yet been established. Like nearly all post-Contact Pawnee sites, both are situated on the main stream valley instead of on the secondary creeks, as were most prehistoric Upper Republican hamlets and homesteads.

Farthest upriver, on the south bank in Webster County, Nebraska, is the Hill site, 25WT1, now generally accepted as the location of the Republican Pawnee village where Lt. Zebulon Pike in September 1806 faced down the truculent Pawnees and persuaded their chief to hoist the Stars and Stripes in place of the Spanish flag they had been flying since the visit of Lt. Facundo Melgares and a force of dragoons and militia from Mexico a few weeks before (Pike 1810; Wedel 1936:35; Jackson 1966, vol. 1, p. 325). About 30 miles (48 km) downstream, also on the right side of the valley, in Republic County, Kansas, is the Kansas Monument site, 14RP1, almost certainly the place where Jedediah Smith wintered uncomfortably in 1825–1826 during the temporary absence of the Indians (Morgan 1964:143; Wedel 1936:33; Witty 1968; Sanborn 1973). An earlier occupancy here, perhaps attributable to a mid-18th-century Pawnee group, has been argued from certain archeological evidences (Roberts 1978 MS), but this seems debatable.

There appears to be at least one other Pawnee village site, 14GE1, in the lower Republican valley, eight miles northwest of Junction City. Fortified and including at least three burned house remains (Witty, personal communication; Marshall and Witty 1967), this location on the right bank of the Republican seems to coincide well with the "Panies Republican village" shown on a Lewis and Clark map of 1804 (Jackson 1961), within ten miles (16 km) of the Kansas river on an unnamed tributary that can only be the Republican. The rumored presence of yet other historic Pawnee sites remains unconfirmed.

The identification and correct dating of Pawnee village sites on the Republican are of particular interest, among other reasons, because they mark the appearance in documentary history of the Kitkahahki band of Pawnees, from whom the stream derives its Europeanized name. Linguistically classed as an offshoot of the Chawi, or Grand, these people were identified by the Americans and other early whites as dissidents (Dunbar 1880a:258; Pike in Jackson 1966, vol. 1, p. 327n, vol. 2, p. 5), supposedly with a more "republican" form of government than the parent band. Although the Pawnees seem to have had some contacts with the Spanish by the mid-17th century and with the French by the beginning of the 18th century, their actual location as the *Panis* and *Panimahas* on the Platte and Loup rivers was apparently not well known until after the 1720s.

The Republican River group was reported as the *Republic*, in May 1775 by Lt. Gov. Pedro Piernas, as one of the Missouri River tribes trading at Spanish St.

Louis, their furs having an estimated value of 3,000 *livres,* or about $600 (Kinnaird 1949, part 1, p. 228). Two years later, under the rubric of *La Republica* or *Republique,* they were reported by Piernas's successor, Francisco Cruzat, to be trading and receiving presents at St. Louis, where the traders were predominantly French (Houck 1909, vol. 1, p. 142–145). These Pawnees were said to be located 220 leagues from St. Louis, "about 110 leagues from the Misury river on the shores of Cances [Kansas] river, 40 or 50 leagues from the village of the tribe of that name by land." Via the Kansas and Republican rivers, the Hill site is approximately 312 miles (500 km) from the Missouri River. The exact location of the Kansa village in the 1770s is uncertain; but if it was on the Missouri River near present Leavenworth, and at or near the abandoned Fort Cavagnial (Cavagnolle), by land the given distance of 40 or 50 leagues would correspond to 180–200 miles (300 km).

The Republican Pawnees, according to Cruzat, had 350–400 warriors, whose principal chief he called Escatape. Their major occupation was the hunt, from which came the pelts of beaver, bison, otter, and some deer, to the value of 3,200 *libras* annually. Their trade was in the hands of one man, Don Eugenio Pore (Puree). Cruzat wrote further that the furs from the Republica could not be brought down in 1777 because "the river of the Cansez had no water." In 1793, Pedro Vial designated the Little Nemaha River as "the general disembarkation point for all the traders who have business with the Pawnee nation" (Loomis and Nasatir 1967:398). In 1797, James Mackay reported another route to the Republican Pawnee for boat traffic from the Missouri River, namely that via the Great Nemaha, "navigable some leagues for pirogues," thence overland to the Republican River (Nasatir 1952:488).

The Hill site is on a broad terrace about 25 feet (7.5 m) above the Republican River bottoms, seven miles (11 km) east and two miles (3.2 km) south of Red Cloud, Nebraska. Immediately to the south, the ground rises 125 feet (40 m) to a round-topped hill, where Pike's approaching party was halted for a time in 1806 while the Pawnees ceremonially "smoked the horses" with the Osages in his party, after which the Americans proceeded on their way. Pike reported 44 houses in the village at the foot of the hill, and a population of 1,618. Of these, 508 were warriors, among whom there were 200 guns. There is no mention of sod walls or palisades or other defensive structures. On either side of the village was a smoothed ground on which various forms of the hoop and pole game were played. There were "vast quantities of excellent horses," whose numbers were continually being augmented by careful breeding and by purchase from the Spaniards. Guarded by day, these were brought into the village at night, making it extremely crowded. The chief occupations of the men were said to be buffalo hunting and warfare, while the women raised only enough maize and beans to provide "a little thickening to their soup during the year." Their trade with St. Louis was estimated at 8,000 dollars annually, and included deer, bison, and a few beaver and otter pelts (plate 9.2).

There appears to be no detailed eyewitness description of the village represented by the Kansas Monument site. Jedediah Smith and Robert Campbell stayed in the deserted lodge of the chief, whom they called Ish-ka-ta-pa, and subsisted in part on stored maize dug up from the caches, for which the Pawnees were compensated on their return to the village (Morgan 1964:143). The site is on a commanding bluff-top location on the south or right rim of the

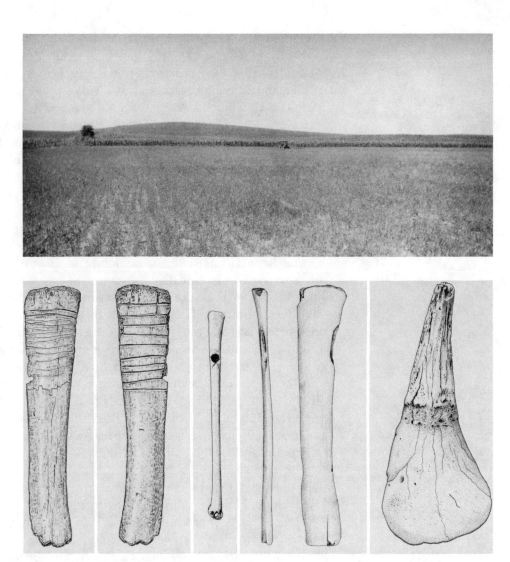

Plate 9.2. Historic Pawnee materials in Nebraska. *Upper,* the Hill site, 25WT1, looking south across the village area toward the main burial hill from which Lt. Zebulon Pike first viewed the Republican Pawnee community in 1806; *lower,* historic bone artifact types from Nebraska; *from left:* pottery-marking paddles, bird-bone whistle, edge-slotted knife handle, digging tool of bison horn core and frontal.

valley, a little more than a mile (1.6 km) below White Rock Creek, a hundred feet (30 m) or more above the valley floor, 1.5 miles (2.4 km) west and one mile (1.6 km) south of Republic, Kansas. Once incorrectly identified as the site of the Republican Pawnee village visited by Pike in 1806, it was donated to the state in 1899 and marked by a 26-foot granite commemorative shaft in 1901.

In a fenced and well-kept six-acre tract comprising perhaps half of the original site, 23 lodge depressions and a number of smaller cache pits have been recognized in native sod that has never been broken by the plow. A segment of defensive wall, presumably built originally of sod, is also preserved. Nine house sites have been opened, wholly or in part—two by the University of Kansas in 1940, the others by the Kansas State Historical Society in 1965–1967. One of the larger floors uncovered has been enclosed by a museum build-

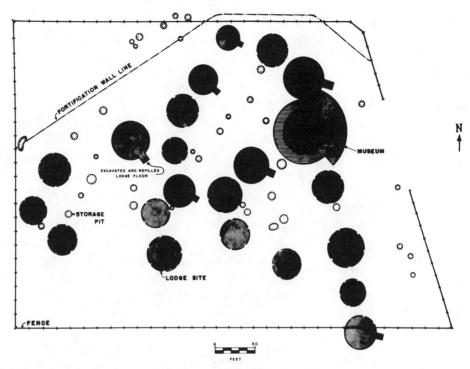

Fig. 9.3. House circles, cache pits, and other features at the Kansas
Monument Pawnee village site, 14RP1, Republic County, Kansas.
Courtesy Kansas State Historical Society.

ing erected in 1967–1968 and operated by the historical society. Few graves
have been opened, at least by persons willing and able to maintain records of
their findings. Artifact collections and records of the investigations here are
preserved at the historical society headquarters in Topeka and at the University of Kansas Museum of Natural History. From the historical society studies,
an occupation date between ca. 1820 and 1831 has been estimated (fig. 9.3).

The Hill site has been under cultivation for more than 100 years, and all
surface features left from the Indian occupation have been obliterated long
since. Its size in number of house ruins can only be estimated. In the early
1920s, about 100 lodge sites were mapped in an area of somewhat less than 25
acres (11 hectares), roughly four houses per acre. Earlier, when the terrace was
first broken out about 1872, it was said that lodge rings, fortification walls,
cache depressions, and other features were readily apparent, and numerous artifacts were reportedly plowed under in the leveling of the house and cache
depressions. The above figures suggest a density in lodge arrangement of about
four houses per acre (9 per ha) for both the Hill and Kansas Monument sites. At
the latter, the total number of houses inferred, about 46, is not far from Pike's
estimate of the number of occupied lodges at the Hill site village in 1806. As
historic documented Pawnee communities go, these were both small villages.
Further, in terms of lodge size, floor plan, post arrangement, density, and construction methods, there were sharp differences between the structures at
these two sites and those in the diffuse prehistoric Upper Republican settlements in the Republican River valley. At this time level, moreover, the findings
of the archeologists at the eight house ruins excavated at the Hill site and the

nine opened at Kansas Monument can be compared with detailed written descriptions left by eyewitnesses of similar structures actually seen in use.

The Pawnee Earthlodge and its Furnishings

In common with the permanent Pawnee houses in the Platte-Loup district, those on the Republican have a circular floor plan and vary in diameter from 25 to 50 feet (8–16 m). To insure a firm and reasonably even floor, the topsoil was usually cleared away to a depth of several inches to a foot or so. The fireplace was a simple unlined basin three to four feet (1 m) in diameter at the center of the floor, where its position is usually marked for the archeologist by six to ten inches (15–25 cm) of fine white ashes underlain by fire-reddened earth. Beside it, there was commonly a crane post or two for suspending cooking utensils over the fire. Between it and the door was an upright wooden mortar, hollowed out by fire and accompanied by a round-ended billet, for grinding maize. Four, or more commonly six, eight, or ten large posts, twelve to eighteen feet (3–4.5 m) high, were set upright midway between fireplace and house wall, and were connected at the top by stringers. A second series of smaller and shorter posts, from eight to twenty in number and similarly connected with stringers, stood three or four feet (1 m) inside the perimeter of the floor, at intervals of six to eight feet (2–2.5 m). Closely spaced poles, their lower ends set either into the floor at the base of the wall or else into the cleared ground surface at the pit edge and their tops resting against the outer set of stringers, provided the foundation for the sloping wall that closed in the house area. Pole rafters running from the top of the wall, with their tips converging around the apical smoke-hole directly over the fireplace, were covered with osiers and grass, after which the whole structure was finished off with a layer of sod or earth. A vestibule entrance passage, similarly sodded over, opened away from the prevailing storms and winter winds, often but not invariably facing toward the east (figs. 9.4 and 9.5; plate 9.1, lower).

Inside these structures, elevated sleeping platforms wide enough to accommodate two to four persons each, occupied the intervals between posts of the outer foundation series, against the house wall. Between these berths and the primary or central roof supports were storage pits in which foodstuffs, household gear, and personal items could be concealed when the house was seasonally deserted during the summer and winter community hunts. Orthodoxy required a small altar platform of earth or wood against the rear wall, opposite

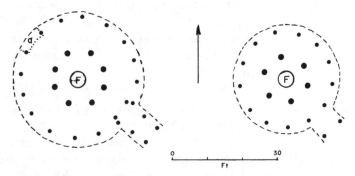

Fig. 9.4. Historic Republican Pawnee house floor patterns from the Hill site, 25WT1. Note altar platform *a* at rear wall of floor on left, opposite entrance vestibule.

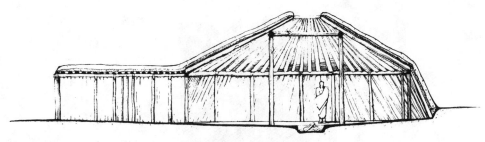

Fig. 9.5. Section through a historic Plains Indian earthlodge to show framework of posts and poles, and covering of willow osiers, dried grass, and earth.

the doorway, and on this might be placed a sacred bison skull and other objects of especial significance to the household. Above the altar was a medicine bundle containing various sacred objects, and stuffed bird or small mammal skins hung on the wall or from the supporting posts or poles as personal fetishes. Traditionally, the altar was at the west side of the house and the door opened to the east, so that the rays of the morning sun could illuminate the shrine. In practice, this ritually prescribed orientation was much less carefully observed by the Pawnees after ca. A.D. 1750 when, to judge from the archeological record, the altar and associated bison skull are not in evidence in most excavated lodge sites. One wonders whether this display of the bison skull was the prerogative of certain qualified individuals or society members, such as Buffalo doctors. Altar platforms, some with a bison skull and other sacred objects, and remains of "medicine birds" have been recovered in archeological contexts (Strong 1935, fig. 3; Wedel 1979a, fig. 1,a,b; Ubelaker and Wedel 1975).

The construction of these lodges was a cooperative endeavor, carried on chiefly by the women, to whom the house belonged. The time required varied. If suitable posts and poles were not available locally, they could be cut or scavenged upstream and floated to the village or nearby, or dragged to the building site by the women. The life expectancy of the lodges probably seldom exceeded 10 to 15 years, depending on the quality of the materials used and the care with which construction was carried out. In these particulars, as in the size, there was much variation. Usable floor diameters in excavated house sites averaged a little more than 30 feet (9 m), providing a total area between 700 and 800 square feet (70 sq m) and accommodating 12 to 18 individuals. Of the larger houses reported historically, up to 60 feet (19 m) in diameter and inhabited by as many as 50 persons, little or no confirmatory evidence has been developed to date from archeological findings. It is difficult to accept Pike's estimate of 1,618 people in 44 lodges at the Hill site village, where the eight excavated house floors average under 35 feet (11 m) in diameter and less than 1,000 square feet (93 sq m) in area (Wedel 1979a).

Household furniture included both native-made pottery vessels and metal containers obtained from white traders. The native wares were strictly utilitarian, much less skillfully made or finished than those of a century or two earlier. Common forms were medium-sized jars for cooking or storage, characteristically with simple stamped body finish and thickened wedgelike rims bearing rectilinear incised designs (plate 6.2). Small undecorated bowls, sometimes provided with a lid, were also common. Metal kettles and cups were in use; many white travelers reported seeing the kettles suspended over the fire

Plate 9.3. Cradleboard from the grave of a child at the Hill site; the lower half has been restored. At the top, a four-pointed morning star combined with a multirayed sun is bordered by a zigzag lightning motif. Brass-headed tacks may be ornamental or perhaps symbolize stars. Courtesy Nebraska State Historical Society.

with meat and vegetable stew bubbling within. Wooden serving bowls in varying sizes and shapes and also platters seem to have been common, although few archeological samples other than fragments remain. Also missing in the archeological record is coiled basketry, common among the historic Pawnees. Rush mats constructed in a simple twined technique were spread on the lodge floor or served for bedding, screens, and coverings. Grooved stone mauls and hammers for driving stakes, smashing marrow bones, pounding up dried meat, berries, and other products, were common, as were iron axes, hoes, knives, and other implements. Freshwater mussel shells served variously as spoons, paint containers, or for scraping boiled green maize from the cob for drying. A wooden cradleboard studded with brass-headed tacks and with a carved morning-star pattern (Munday 1927:192) is unusual, but fragments of other less ornate boards are not uncommon (plate 9.3).

The Pawnee Lifeway For the Pawnees as a whole, if not specifically for the inhabitants of the Republican River villages, frequent contacts with white men and the resulting documents have made their lifeway well known by comparison with what archeology has enabled us to infer about the earlier Upper Republican groups. As with the prehistoric peoples, the lifestyle was based on a combination of hunting, gathering, and the cultivation of maize, beans, cucurbits, and sunflowers. Markedly different adaptive strategies resulted, however, from considerably larger population groups; the intensive use of the horse; and the acquisition of metal tools, containers, and other goods from the Euro-Americans. Along with the greater mobility provided by horses, there were continuing knotty problems that militated against year-round residence in the villages. These included the availability of sufficient fuels for greatly expanded domestic requirements, of pasturage for the herds of horses, and of game in the quantities needed for increased numbers and concentrations of consumers. Public sanitation and waste disposal were other major problems.

In response to the increasing pressures, large-scale community hunts were regularly made to the bison range lying generally to the west, northwest, or southwest of the permanent villages, in whose immediate vicinity the herds and the nongregarious large game animals were soon exhausted or expelled by hunting. During these extended hunts, the Pawnees lived much like the Dakota Sioux, Comanches, and other horse-nomads of the western plains. The portable skin tipi erected on a three-pole foundation; on summer hunts, bowl-shaped shelters called *aka:ririwis* (Murie 1981:7); and other easily moved camp and household gear were then customary. In the permanent earthlodge villages, all east of longitude 98°30' west, the surplus food stores and other unneeded supplies and furniture had been deposited in the subfloor caches, to be retrieved when the group returned again from the weeks-long hunt. The relative importance to the Pawnee system of hunting versus horticulture had undoubtedly changed significantly between ca. A.D. 1600 and 1800, with the chase assuming an increasingly important role. The record clearly indicates, however, that food shortages following either a serious crop failure or an unsuccessful communal hunt meant much discomfort and sometimes acute suffering or even starvation for the community. At such times, and on those occasions when the food caches were discovered and pilfered by unfriendly Indians (Hepner 1856:86), the availability of and successful search for wild roots and tubers could become matters of prime importance for human survival.

Pawnee Horticulture: Crops and Methods

The horticultural fraction of the Pawnee subsistence base in the 19th century rested on the cultivation by women of small family plots. These varied in size up to perhaps an acre but were usually smaller. This system, featuring hoe tillage and unquestionably deeply rooted in some centuries of practice from prehistoric times, continued in use long after government farmers in 1843 began plowing up larger tracts for Indian use. In 1837, for example, at their villages on the Platte their agent at Council Bluffs, Maj. John Dougherty, reported (1838:538) that they planted in maize "about 400 acres of ground, in small patches, scattered about in the ravines from one to ten miles distant from their villages." Again in 1839, J. V. Hamilton, agent, (1840:503) noted that "their method of cultivating the soil . . . is in small patches and by the squaws."

The hoe, consisting of a trimmed and sharpened bison scapula with a wooden handle, was the usual tool, along with the simple digging stick and doubtless a crude but effective antler rake. The bone hoe continued in common use long after iron hoes became available, in fact until the Pawnees finally left Nebraska in 1876. Flour, flint, and popcorn in as many as 13 recognized varieties were cultivated, along with several kinds of beans, squashes, and watermelons. Sacred corn was grown in a separate consecrated field to avoid contamination by common corn, and the best filled ears were set aside for future planting. Sunflowers were raised for their oil-rich seeds, and the stalks were sometimes used for fencing the garden patches. Much of the produce was eaten fresh. The surplus crops were harvested, dried, and stored for winter consumption; if plentiful, surpluses were sometimes shared with neighboring tribes whose gardening efforts had been less productive and who might in consequence be facing food shortages.[1] Storage in underground caches was customary. These were both inside the houses and outside in well-drained locations nearby. George Hepner (1856:86), agent at Council Bluffs, observed in 1855 that "their corn, &c., they cache by digging a hole in the ground in the shape of a tunnell [sic = funnel], little end up, in which they store hundreds of bushels."

In their historic locations east of longitude 99°30' west, whether on the Republican, the Blue, or in the Platte-Loup district, the Pawnees were probably much less drought-prone than their Upper Republican predecessors had been 75 to 100 miles (120–160 km) or more to the west, and their crop expectancy was undoubtedly significantly higher. By the reports of the Indian agents and government farmers after 1837, maize yields estimated at 25 to 30 bushels per acre (2,100 l per ha) were produced even in the years when the Pawnees still grew most of the crop in family plots cultivated by women equipped only with bone hoes. Since the tribe in this period probably did not number more than 6,000 people, the acreage reported under cultivation represented about 1/15th acre (260 sq m) of garden per capita, from which the estimated total yield would have been less than two bushels (70 l) per head. Considering that out of this was taken fresh and dried produce, as well as seed for the next year's planting, one may question the characterization of the Pawnees as primarily a horticultural people at this period. There is, too, the provocative comment in 1847 by Thomas Harvey, superintendent of Indian affairs at St. Louis, that "not a single instance has come to my knowledge where the government has undertaken to farm for Indians in which their supply of corn has not diminished." (Harvey 1848:835).

In good crop years, with abundant harvests, the stored garden produce was perhaps sufficient to carry some surplus over into the following year, provided the bison hunts had been reasonably productive. In severe or prolonged droughts, even the sheltered hand-cultivated plots were subject to damage and reduced productivity, if not total failure. Heavy soaking rains or caching of the harvest before the crops were thoroughly dried could, and sometimes did, result in the souring of the cached stores and rendered them unfit for human consumption. At such times, the next communal hunt might have to be started early to head off the threatened food shortages. Grasshopper infestations were another hazard of record during the later reservation days, though the damage or destruction from this cause could sometimes be offset in some measure by replanting the stricken plots if the season was not too far advanced.

Wild Plant Foods

Essential supplements to the garden produce were the wild vegetables, berries, fruits, seeds, nuts, and tubers that grew in the vicinity of the villages and along the routes traveled on hunting trips. Samuel Allis, a Presbyterian missionary among the Skiris in 1835–1849, wrote (Allis 1918:703) that the Pawnees made very extensive use of roots and other wild plant foods. The starchy tubers of the prairie turnip (*Psoralea esculenta*) and the groundnut (*Apios americana*), as

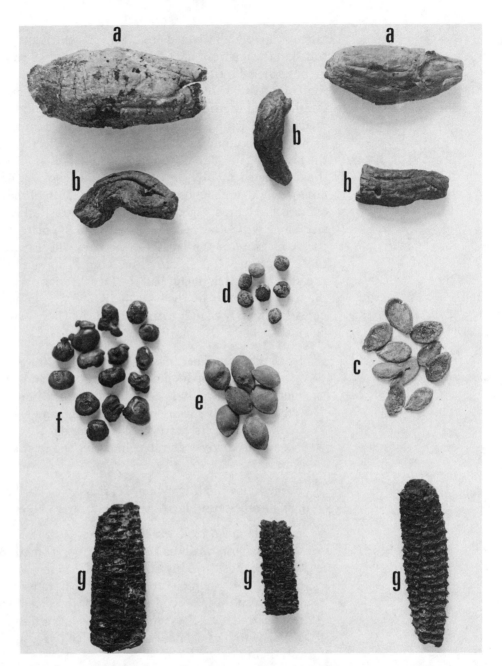

Plate 9.4. Plant food remains from storage pits at the Hill Pawnee site, 25WT1. *a,* tubers of *Apios americana; b,* unidentified roots, possibly *Echinacea; c,* seeds of bush summer squash, *Cucurbita pepo melopepo; d,* pits of choke cherry, *Prunus virginiana; e,* pits of wild plum, *Prunus americana; f,* charred flint corn, *Zea mays; g,* charred corncobs. Bureau of American Ethnology Bulletin 112.

well as roots of the Jerusalem artichoke (*Helianthus tuberosus*) and bigroot morning glory (*Ipomoea*), have been identified ethnographically or archeologically at historic Pawnee sites. Well within reach of the villages were hog peanuts or ground beans (*Amphicarpa bracteata*), wild plums, choke cherries, ground plums (*Astragalus* sp.), currants, and riverbank grapes. Marshy spots along the streams provided spring shoots and fall tubers of cattail, bulrush, *Sagittaria,* and other water- or moisture-loving species. The potential importance of these uncultivated products as an emergency food reserve is well illustrated in the report of the commissioner of Indian affairs for 1844. The government farmers for the Skiri and Republican bands, living in separate villages on the Loup River at the mouth of Cedar Creek and at Council Creek, reported (Mathers and Mathers 1844:149) that on returning to their villages from an unsuccessful winter hunt, "they found a large portion of their corn so badly damaged on account of its having been imperfectly dried before packing away the previous fall, as to be totally unfit for use. . . . For more than two months, they subsisted mainly on [Jerusalem] artichokes and a wild potato [?*Apios americana*] that abounds in this vicinity." Both of these species have been recognized in charred vegetal material from trash-filled storage pits at the Hill site, along with other species (Wedel 1936:59; plate 9.4).[2]

A measure of the labor expended by the Pawnee women in harvesting these emergency foods during the winter shortages has been recorded in the papers of the Rev. John Dunbar, the Presbyterian missionary who accompanied the Chawi Pawnees on their 1834–1835 winter hunt and a co-worker of Samuel Allis. In early March, writing from the Chawi village near present Clarks, Nebraska, Dunbar (1918:611) observed that

> Since the ground has thawed, they have bestowed some hundreds of days of hard labor digging Indian potatoes. A woman does not succeed in digging more than a peck [9 l], working diligently from sunrise till sunset. Soon after light, I have seen droves of women and girls with their hoes or axes on their shoulders, starting off to their day's work. The men do not fail to call up their wives and daughters, as soon as it is light, and set them at work.

In the following July, when Charles Augustus Murray joined the Chawis on their summer hunt, he observed (Murray 1839, vol. 1, p. 187) that they

> had little or no food, except such roots as they were able to pick up. Of these, the principal was an esculent root, something between a potato and a radish, most greedily sought by the Indians when going to the Buffalo country: they are then often reduced to a state approaching starvation; and I have seen these roots dug out, two, three, and even four miles from the regular trail. . . . They are eaten raw . . . are said to be tolerably wholesome, as well as palatable, when boiled or roasted. The French Canadians call them *Pomme blanche*.

The Pawnee Tribal Hunts

Despite the thousands of bushels of maize, potatoes, and other crops grown by the Pawnees in most years on the reservation and their asseveration that maize was their first and foremost food resource, the reports of their agents and farmers make it abundantly clear that the bison hunt was no less important in the native subsistence economy. Unlike gardening, this was considered men's work. The Indian viewpoint was eloquently expressed by Sen. Thomas Hart Benton of Missouri, speaking before the United States Senate on 25 April 1822, during the administration of Pres. James Monroe, in the observation (Benton 1822) that "the Pawnee chief spoke truth to the President when he told him 'that he would never bruise his hands with digging in the ground, while he could find a buffalo to hunt or a horse to steal.' "

Central to the Pawnee hunting system was the bison, taken usually by the tribal hunts staged twice each year. Highly informative eyewitness accounts of this operation are available. The Reverend Dunbar, then newly arrived in the Pawnee country and totally unfamiliar with their language or their culture, traveled with the Chawis during the winter hunt of 1834–1835. His associate, Samuel Allis, followed suit by traveling with the Skiris in the same winter; he, like Dunbar, was totally unfamiliar with the culture and language of their hosts. The English adventurer, Charles A. Murray, was with the combined Chawi and Kitkahahki bands on part of their summer hunt in 1835, in which Dunbar also took part. It seems certain that Dunbar and Murray must have met during the weeks spent on this hunt, but the relationship, to judge from Murray's comments, was less than cordial.

The summer hunt usually began in June or early July, after the second hoeing of the corn, and ended in August or September, when the blazing star (*Liatris*) was beginning to flower and it was time to harvest the ripening garden crops back at the villages. In late October or November, the villages were again deserted for the hunting life, which continued until provisions ran out in March or April, or until corn-planting time in early May was at hand. These dates varied considerably from year to year, but they suggest that at least half the year, and often much more, was spent away from the permanent villages.

On these hunts, the entire village community traveled westward to the bison plains—"Everything is taken with them, big, little, old and young, squaws and all go," wrote George Hepner (1856:85), agent from Council Bluffs, in 1855. Two decades before, of the winter hunt of 1834–1835, Dunbar (1918:602) observed:

> The Pawnees of course travel in Indian file. The procession was, I suppose, when all got under way, about 4 miles long. The women, boys, and girls lead each of them a horse, and walk in the trail before them. The men straggle about anywhere. They sometimes walk beside their wives, and assist them in managing the horses, but this is rare.
> This was much the largest company of horses, mules, asses, men, women, children and dogs, I had ever seen.

During these hunts, abandonment of the villages was essentially complete, with the possible exception of those too decrepit or too ill to undertake the long and difficult trips and so left behind to risk confrontation with unfriendly visitors or raiders. These were called *ka:kusu'*, "Stay Inside" (Weltfish 1965:147, 149, 233, passim).

The Republican country west to Colorado and south to the Smoky Hill and Arkansas rivers was favorite hunting territory for the Grand, Republican, and Tappage bands, often operating together. Traveling six to eight miles (10–13 km) a day, in straggling columns sometimes strung out for several miles, such hunting expeditions covered several hundred miles each season in search of the bison. When the herds were located by scouts, hunt police or "soldiers" directly controlled by the first chief took over to prevent any individuals from hunting without permission, under pain of a severe flogging and probably damage or destruction of personal property, as well.

Bison were usually hunted by the *cerne* or surround, in which a herd was encircled by men on well-trained horses and forced into a milling mass. If the animals broke out or the terrain was too rough, the bison were run down and shot from horseback. The bow and metal-tipped arrows were preferred over the gun, and the lance was often used. Other large game was also taken on these communal hunts, as opportunity offered, including wapiti (elk), pronghorn, deer, and bear. For their skins, as for the heavier bison hides, there were commercial incentives along with domestic needs to fulfil. To the white men, the collecting of peltries was the main occupation suited to the Indian males. There is little information on the methods of hunting beaver and otter, but the Beaver, Sappa, Medicine, Prairie Dog, and other headwater tributaries were reputedly rich in beaver.

A successful hunt could produce thousands of pounds of meat and fat, and it was immediately followed by heavy feasting. What was not consumed was sliced into thin sheets or strips 18–30 inches (0.5—0.75 m) in size, dried in the sun and wind, and then packed away in parfleches or rawhide containers for later consumption. The amount of meat produced by the communal hunts is impossible to estimate except in the most general terms. Dunbar (1918:604) reported the slaughter of 300 bison on the Platte River, somewhere between present Grand Island and Kearney, by the Grand Pawnees with whom he was traveling in the winter of 1834. He estimated the number of Pawnees at 2,000, accompanied by 6,000 horses, mules, asses, and dogs, of which the last-named were not used as beasts of burden.

We know nothing as to composition of the bison herd, condition of the animals, or the thoroughness of the butchering. According to Murray (1839, vol. 1, p. 208), in 15 minutes the Pawnees could dress out a bison so neatly that except the head virtually nothing was left for the dogs and other camp-following scavengers. Dunbar (1910:330) wrote that "in the short space of one hour a band of 200 buffalo are slain, butchered, and their flesh moving toward the dwellings of their destroyers." Assuming conservatively an average of 300 pounds (135 kg) of edible meat from each of the 300 animals slain by Dunbar's hosts, at least half of which may have been consumed immediately in heavy feasting, there could have been as much as 30,000 or 40,000 pounds (13,500–18,000 kg) for drying. At 80 percent reduction, the drying would have produced 6,000 or 8,000 pounds (2,700–3,600 kg) of jerky. For transport, this would have required the services of 30 or 40 pack horses or mules at 200 pounds (90 kg) per animal, or 25 to 30 horses if the individual packs were increased to 250 pounds (112 kg). The meat produced by other kills on the 1834–1835 winter hunt of the Grand Pawnees and their associates is not a matter of record, apparently. Divided among the 2,000 Indians of Dunbar's estimate, the meat from the recorded kill would have provided not much more than two or three weeks' sustenance unless it was substantially augmented with dried maize, beans, prairie turnips, or other vegetable staples.

In a later winter hunt, the Pawnees reported killing a total of 1,600 bison, antelope, elk, and deer (Wheeler 1865). In what proportion the several species were taken is not specified, but it can be estimated that some 300,000 to 400,000 pounds (135,000–180,000 kg), or more, of meat would have been available for consumption. If half of this was dried, there may have been 15 to 20 tons of meat to divide among an estimated 3,000 Pawnees, perhaps three to four weeks of food reserves.[3]

From the seasonal hunts, in addition to meat, came large quantities of hides, as well as sinew for sewing and bones for a wide variety of tools. Unlike the actual chase, this involved the women deeply. Winter hides were preferred for robes, summer ones for tipi covers and clothing. The skinning and butchering were done with metal knives, and the hides pegged out on the ground (plate 10.2) were then processed further with tools common to many other historic Plains Indian bison hunters. The tools included particularly the L-shaped elkhorn fleshing adze set with an iron or chipped-stone blade for removing shreds of fiber and fat, and a sharpened chisel-like, serrate-edged leg bone tool held daggerlike and further secured by a thong or cord around the wrist (plate 10.3). Large oblong quartzite scrapers were used for the preliminary scraping. For punching hides in sewing, and for basket making, bone awls were in common use even after steel needles and machine-made thread were introduced by traders. Wedge-shaped pieces of cancellous bone cut from the joint ends of bison leg bones provided thin edges for fine lines and broad edges for heavier lines in the painting of parfleches, robes, tipi covers, and other heavy leather articles. All of these artifact types have been recovered from house ruins and graves at the permanent village sites, and they were undoubtedly carried on the tribal hunts as well.

Guns obtained from French and other traders, and bows and arrows of native manufacture, were used in killing game and also in raids and warfare. Arrows were sometimes tipped with flint or bone but more commonly with brass or iron cut from hoe blades, hoop iron, kettles, and other suitable items. The shafts were smoothed by drawing them between paired sandstone blocks, boat-shaped and grooved lengthwise. Fragments of these occur in considerable numbers even in postwhite contact sites. Warped shafts were straightened with segments of perforated bison ribs, manipulated like a wrench.

Despite the rigors of the tribal hunts, they were clearly an indispensible part of the subsistence strategy and lifestyle of the historic Pawnees. Around the large permanent villages, with populations running well into the hundreds and even into the thousands, the game was quickly driven away and wild vegetal products were soon exhausted. Wood for fuel and pasturage for the growing herds of horses were likewise soon used up. The frequently moved hunting camps provided access to fresh supplies of fuel, such as bison chips and wood for domestic use, and to new stands of cottonwoods whose bark and branches were the main or sole article of food for the horses in winter. The cold stormy weather frequently encountered on the winter hunts subjected the women and children to extreme hardships and brought about the loss of large numbers of horses and mules through improper care, inadequate food, and exposure. The summer hunts were generally less trying, despite recurrent droughts, high temperatures, and the inevitable rain, hail, and wind storms so characteristic of the Republican country. Water could be a problem for such large village groups and their horse herds in dry summers, but travel-wise Indians who knew the likeliest watering places and followed the ridges could hold dry camps to a minimum. That potable water could often be found by digging in the sandy beds of dry streams was well known to these people as to every experienced western traveler. Whether, when confronted by muddy drinking water, they resorted to the clarifying strategem of "dropping into the vessel containing it pieces of mucilaginous cactus," as Lt. A. W. Whipple (1856:28) reported during his 1853 survey of the Canadian River, is apparently nowhere recorded.

A major hazard, present around the year but most serious in summer, were the roving war parties of hostile Dakota Sioux, Cheyenne, Arapaho, and other enemies, including better armed tribes recently transplanted by the federal government from the eastern United States to lands west of the Mississippi and Missouri rivers.

Male vs. Female: A Missionary's View

The division of labor between sexes among the Pawnees has been succinctly set forth by Dunbar (1918:610–612; cf. Murray 1839, vol. 1, p. 219) as he observed it on the winter hunt of 1834–1835, and later. The women, he commented "are very laborious," meaning industrious; and

> when a Pawnee woman has nothing to do, she seems to be out of her element. They dress the skins for the tent covers, which is done with no small labor, sew them together, and fit them for the tents—make all the robes, which are many, both for their own use and the market—cut and bring all the wood on their backs—make all the fires—do all the cooking of course—dry all the meat—dig the ground—plant—hoe and gather all the corn, of which they raise an abundance, as they also do of beans and pumpkins—cut the timber, and build all their dwellings, both fixed and moveable—set up and take down the portable tents—bridle and unbridle, saddle and unsaddle, pack and unpack all the horses—make all their moccasons [sic], mats, bags, bowls, mortars, etc., etc., and if there be anything else done, besides watering, bringing up and turning out the horses (which the boys do), killing the buffalo, smoking and feasting, the women do it.

Small wonder that the women were made old before their time. As for the men, Dunbar reported that they "are abominably lazy," and insisted that their "proper business is killing the buffalo and war." By treaty with the United States government, the last mentioned business had necessarily been given up and the men "now smoke, talk, feast, sing, and lounge away the time" when they were not sleeping. Dunbar was as yet insensitive to, or unaware of, the fact that much of the male "leisure" time he decried was given over to preparing for and carrying out the many ceremonies and rituals for which the Pawnees were renowned, instructing the boys and young men, storytelling, and other activities regarded as essential to tribal well-being.

Food Preparation

In the preparation of food, the staple of daily fare among the Pawnees was bison meat and maize (Dunbar 1880b:322ff.). When meat could be obtained fresh, it was sometimes broiled over a bed of coals, spitted over the fire, or buried in large pieces under the coals until the interior was sufficiently cooked. More commonly, boiling in pots was the procedure. Dried meat was boiled alone or with maize, beans, and other vegetables, wild or cultivated. Dried maize was cooked alone or with beans, often flavored with bison tallow. Beans and pumpkins, green or dried, were also boiled. The tubers of the prairie turnip and the Jerusalem artichoke were cooked together with groundnuts (Apios) and were often added to meats, stews, and soups. Matured maize was made into hominy, or more commonly, was ground into meal in a mortar, to be boiled as mush or made into cakes and baked in the ashes or on hot stones. The matured kernels were often parched in hot ashes or hot sand, especially when wanted for use as a concentrated high-calorie ration by travelers, war parties, and others on the move. There were no set times for meals, and members of the household, along with visitors present, served themselves or were served as needed from the pot that simmered all day long over the fire.

While many of the details in the immediately preceding pages were observed and reported several decades after the major occupation of the Republican River villages ended, and the Pawnee culture was undergoing rapid changes, there were undoubtedly numerous similarities in the subsistence economies and in material culture inventories between the manifestations from the two periods. Had Dunbar visited either of the two Pawnee villages on the Republican at the beginning of the 19th century, he would very likely have found himself in a cultural setting much like the one he was experiencing 30 years later in the Loup River villages.

Burial Methods and Grave Goods

The slopes and summit of the hill overlooking the Hill village site from the south, where Pike halted for a time in 1806, along with other elevations to the east and west, were extensively utilized for the burial of the dead. Women and children were buried on the lower slopes, men on the higher. From these graves, over a period of many years of digging, have been taken a large number of articles of widely varied kinds (Wedel 1936:91). They clearly indicate, among other things, the degree to which the Republican Pawnees of the time were involved in trade and other contacts with the white man, while still retaining a measure of their old arts and crafts, though often in decadent form.

Burial was by primary interment, that is, in the flesh, with the corpse usually flexed and wrapped in a rush mat, leather robe, or trade blanket. Seated burials were very rare or absent, mortuary offerings common. There is no reported archeological evidence of class distinction or rank, known to have existed. Bits of woven bison-hair cloth and loosely twisted cordlike fragments occur. Blue, white, and red glass beads suggest decorated moccasins, necklaces, or other articles of costume and personal adornment. Metal buttons, knives, gun parts, strike-a-light steels, miscellaneous horse trappings, and the like are not uncommon. Pottery jars and metal containers have been found, the latter including a semicylindrical United States Army canteen of early 19th-century type and possibly a relic of Pike's visit (Wedel 1936, plate 12a; plate 9.5).

Other grave goods include worked wood fragments from boxes, cradleboards, mirror backs, and other items, as well as native-made bowls and platters. Bison-horn spoons have been found. A heavily pigmented wildcat skull with military uniform buttons set into the eye sockets is of particular interest in view of the high esteem in which the Pawnees held that animal (Fletcher 1904:47 and plate XC). Interesting, too, is a large wooden cradleboard with star and sun design (Feder 1978) and an array of brass-headed tacks. Stone tobacco pipes occur in various forms and sizes. Particularly noteworthy is a large high-bowled type with a bearlike animal facing the smoker, carved from catlinite (plate 8.3). This calls to mind Dunbar's (1918:613) allusion, unfortunately without description or other elaboration, to the use of the "big pipe" by his hosts on ceremonial occasions.

Pawnee vs. White Man in Trade

In the judgment of the Rev. John Dunbar, the Pawnees of 1835 had "had less intercourse with the whites than almost any other tribe this side of the [Rocky] mountains" (Dunbar 1918:614). Whether or not this was true, there is archeological and documentary evidence that the tribe by 1806 had been in contact

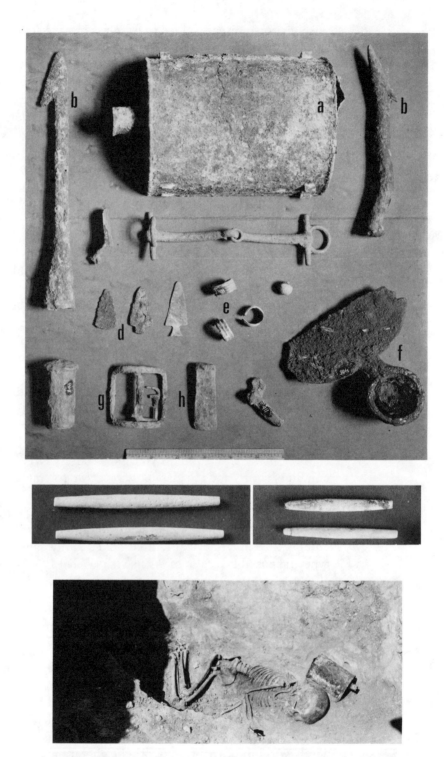

Plate 9.5. Euro-American trade goods from the Hill Pawnee site, Nebraska. *Upper, a,* U.S. Army canteen of early-19th-century type; *b,* beaver spear heads; *c,* bridle bit; *d,* arrowpoints cut from sheet metal; *e,* lead rings; *f,* iron hoe blade; *g,* belt buckle; *h,* iron scraper blade. Bureau of American Ethnology Bulletin 112. *Middle,* shell hair pipes. Bureau of American Ethnology Bulletin 112. *Lower,* burial of a child with U.S. Army canteen beside skull.

with representatives of all of the nationalities who were competing for the friendship and commerce of the Missouri River valley natives. Their villages in the Pawnee Crescent were in an area claimed from early times by the Spanish; but here, some 2,200 miles (3,500 km) from Mexico City, they were in the distant reaches of the *Provincias Internas*, at the far end of a long and arduous 850–mile (1,350 km) overland journey from Santa Fe and more than 1,200 miles (1,900 km) from the provincial capital at Chihuahua. These were trips that few traders and no missionaries of record seem to have attempted. The French, at Kaskaskia on the Mississippi by 1703, were not quite so far away; and from there, the far-ranging *coureurs de bois* and *voyageurs* could move their goods to the Pawnee towns with comparative ease by pirogue or canoe, except during low-water times in the rivers. British traders who came later were sometimes limited in their operations to designated posts that entailed travel by the Indians through the lands of people who were not always friendly. The long-standing Spanish policy of withholding firearms and ammunition from the Indians was in sharp contrast to the more tolerant attitude of the French in this important particular. The archeological record suggests that far more goods came to the Pawnee from the French than from the Spanish, unless the latter were bringing in mainly perishable items such as textiles, which did not survive the passage of the years as did the axes, hoes, knives, guns, and other durable French importations.

Beginnings are seldom possible to identify satisfactorily. Trade between the French and Pawnees may be presumed to have gotten under way even before Etienne Véniard de Bourgmont's explorations of the Missouri River, 1714–1724 (Villiers 1925; Giraud 1958). From the Pawnees, as from other Missouri River tribes known to the French by 1714, "nothing but furs is to be gotten," according to Bourgmont, that is, there were no mines in their country. He noted further that they had "trade relations with the Spanish," but the extent and nature of this is not further set forth (Giraud 1958).

It is relevant to note, however, that when Bourgmont visited the Padoucas (Apaches) in 1724, probably in the Saline or Ellsworth county district of Kansas and a hundred miles (160 km) or so south of the Hill and Kansas Monument Pawnee sites, the chief informed him that the Spanish were only 12 days' march from the Padouca village. Further, he added, "they come every spring to see us, they lead to us horses and bring us some knives and awls and some axes, but they are not like you, who give us a quantity of merchandise such as we have never before seen " (Margry 1886:436–437). This, of course, was 80 years before Pike's time and perhaps even before the Kitkahahki Pawnees had settled on the Republican, but it hints at the probable nature of Spanish trade relations with the Plains tribes remote from Chihuahua and Santa Fe.

All too few details are available regarding this trade between Spanish Santa Fe and the Plains Indians to the north and northeast in the Missouri River drainage. The two- and four-wheeled vehicles that operated over the Camino Real from Mexico City to New Mexico via Zacatecas, Parral, and Chihuahua (fig. 9.6) to supply the missions and the northern settlements after 1600, turned around at Santa Fe (Scholes 1930). Beyond, except for Juan de Oñate's baggage train in 1601 to Quivira on the Arkansas River, there was apparently no wheeled vehicular traffic in the central plains before 1821 when William Becknell brought his wagons over the Santa Fe trail route. Here, as generally throughout

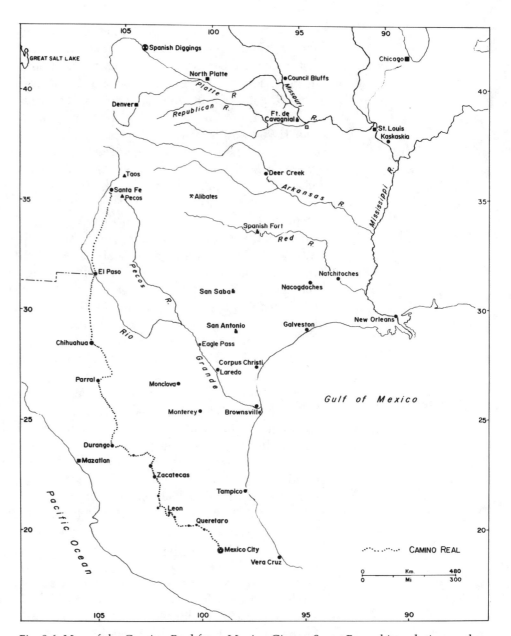

Fig. 9.6. Map of the Camino Real from Mexico City to Santa Fe, and its relation to the Republican River and the Pawnee habitat (lightly shaded area between the Platte and Republican rivers).

the Spanish Southwest, pack trains of mules and horses were much more widely used than wheels (Moorhead 1957; 1958). Mules were preferred, since they throve on the dry, short grass, were more durable than horses or oxen, and could negotiate steeper trails. In the Southwest, as many as 200 animals made up a train, with one muleteer per each 35 to 50 head. On the plains, these animals could carry individual loads of 250–300 pounds (112–135 kg) each and averaged 18-20 miles (30 km) per day. According to Pike (1810, app. to part 3, p. 8), "The journey with loaded mules from Santa Fe to Mexico, and returning to Santa Fe, takes five months." Rest stops for the mule trains were not customary, since the heavily loaded animals, if they lay down, were unable to regain their feet without being unloaded.

By what route the Spanish traders traveled to the Pawnees is not certain. From Santa Fe, the pack trains probably headed north along the mountain front until they struck the South Platte River in the vicinity of present Denver. By descending the South Platte and then the Platte, they could reach the permanent towns around the Platte-Loup junction, some 850 miles (1,350 km) from Santa Fe. To reach the later Republican River villages, traders could leave the South Platte near present Sterling, then proceeding overland to the Frenchman and down that to the Republican, and on to the Hill or Kansas Monument sites, a total distance from Santa Fe of 800–850 miles (1,320 ± km). A somewhat shorter journey was possible via the later Santa Fe Trail route to the great bend of the Arkansas River in central Kansas and then north to the Pawnee settlements. Perhaps six to seven weeks may have been required for this trip, one way.

In 1806, according to Pike (1810, app. to part 2, p. 52), the Republican Pawnees were trading with "St. Louis and Kans," whereas the Grand and Loup bands dealt with St. Louis and "possibly once in three years [with] a few Spaniards." Horses, mules, and "a few coarse blankets" were the items Pike specifically noted as coming from the Spanish. George C. Sibley, factor at Fort Osage on the Missouri, who visited the Pawnees in June 1811 after the Republicans had joined the Grands at Horse Creek on the Loup River, wrote (Brooks 1965:182) concerning their trade with Santa Fe:

> Their trade would be very lucrative if they were settled on a navigable stream. What few goods they get are to be transported more than a hundred miles over land, from the Missouri river. The risk and expense attending this portage deters the traders from visiting them often, and then only with scant supplies. They get no goods from the Spanish settlements, unless they go for them, which they very seldom do. A trading trip to Santa Feè and back would require fully a month.

We can perhaps assume that in addition to the items listed by Pike, knives, axes, scissors, lances, horse gear, and other articles were also involved, though iron goods were relatively scarce and expensive in the Spanish trading territories compared to the French and may have gone chiefly to the Comanches, Apaches, Utes, and other tribes nearer to the Rio Grande settlements (Minge 1979:22). In return, the Spanish received dried meat, tallow, hides, and similar goods from the Plains Indians, essentially the same sorts of trade items that the Plains Apaches of the 16th and 17th centuries had long been exchanging with the Pueblo Indians in the Rio Grande country. Plains Indian bows and arrows for the poorly armed New Mexicans, and dressed buckskin, were also brought in to Santa Fe and the adjacent Pueblo Indian communities.

The Pawnee trade with the French was of a different character. Unlike the all-land routes between the Pawnees and the Spanish bases, the French were able to utilize waterways extensively. During the early 18th century, in and for some decades after Bourgmont's time, French goods presumably came to the Indian villages in the Missouri River country from Kaskaskia, which was supplied in turn from the Great Lakes and Canada. With the founding of St. Louis in 1764, some 60 miles (96 km) upriver from Kaskaskia, supplies for the Indian trade came from New Orleans, approximately 1,200 river miles (1,900 km) distant. From St. Louis, 12 or 15 miles (21 km) below the mouth of the Missouri, the traders and their cargoes traveled chiefly by pirogue up the Missouri to

Table 9.1
Missouri River distances to selected upriver points

| | Missouri River Commission 1895 (miles) | French leagues (at 2.76 miles) | Spanish leagues | |
			common (at 3.45 miles, *legua común*)	statute (at 2.6 miles, *legua legal*)
Missouri River mouth	0	0	0	0
Osage River MO	148	54	43	57
Grand River MO	261	95	76	100
Kansas River KS	392	142	114	102
Little Platte River MO	412	149	119	158
Independence Creek KS	453	164	131	174
Wolf Creek KS	516	187	150	198
Nemaha River NE	529	192	153	203
Little Nemaha NE	570	207	165	219
Weeping Water Creek NE	614	222	178	236
Platte River NE	635	230	184	244
Little Sioux River IA	722	262	210	278
Big Sioux River IA/SD	811	294	235	312
James River SD	888	322	257	342
Niobrara River NE	941	341	273	362
White River SD	1,054	382	306	405

NOTE: Missouri River Commission distances are in miles prior to channel straightening and shortening. The difficult and vexing problem of league values and their variability is discussed at length in Chardon 1980a and 1980b, and in M. Wedel 1978:2. To convert miles to kilometers, multiply by 1.6.

their Indian trading partners. According to United States Army Corps of Engineers figures, the 1890 channel line distances on the Missouri River from its mouth included the following: to Kansas River, 392 miles (630 km); Nemaha River, 535 miles (850 km); Platte River, 637 miles (1,000 km). See table 9.1.[4] Whether or to what extent the traders ventured up these and other lesser tributaries to reach native villages on their banks is not always clear, but low water in dry years or seasons was sometimes a serious hindrance. Via the Kansas and Republican rivers, the Hill and Kansas Monument villages were roughly 300 miles (480 km) from the Missouri River by water; by way of the Nemaha and then overland, these two villages were about 120 miles (190 km) from the Missouri. The principal Pawnee towns around the Platte-Loup junction were from 75–125 miles (120–200 km) from the Missouri by water or about 750–800 miles (1,200–1,300 km) from St. Louis, but the Platte was often a difficult stream to navigate except by bullboat or when in flood. Sometimes, and perhaps characteristically, especially at low water times, pack animals were used for the final stretch from the Missouri River to the individual villages on the Platte-Loup or on the Republican and Blue.

The establishment of a French post, Fort de Cavagnial (Cavagnolle) on the right bank of the Missouri River at a Kansa village near present Fort Leavenworth about 1743–1744 (Nasatir 1952:52; Hoffhaus 1964) must have materially improved the trade situation for the French vis-à-vis the Missouri River tribes. This location cut more than 500 miles (800 km) from the water route between the Pawnees and neighboring tribes and the earlier French base on the Mississippi River, and it may also have introduced a measure of tighter control over the traders in the field. Strange to say, the site of this post remains un-discovered, although it was supposedly functioning for some 20 years. If a sig-nificant volume of trade did pass through its portals, and the Pawnees shared in that traffic, the post may have been one of the major considerations in the "secession" of a substantial segment of the Pawnees from the Platte River communities and their settling as dissidents on the Republican. That their first mention in contemporary documents was in 1775, a dozen years after the abandonment of Fort Cavagnial, still does not answer the question of how much earlier the Republican Pawnees may have established themselves on the stream where Pike visited them in 1806. With the ceding of Louisiana to Spain in 1763, political control of the Missouri River Indian trade passed into the hands of the Spanish, but the traders themselves remained largely French and the sources of their merchandise may have continued much as before, with little or no significant change in their origin (Billon 1971:76; Surrey 1968).

The locating, or relocating, of the Republican Pawnees on the river that came to bear their name, would have offered some distinct advantages over their earlier locations on the Platte. Trade goods from either Fort de Cavagnial or, after 1764, from St. Louis, could be delivered on the Republican River with-out interference from the Otos living below the Pawnees on the lower Platte and thus favorably situated to intercept traders ascending the Platte to reach the Pawnees and other tribes. Via the Kansas and Republican rivers, the Re-publican Pawnee villages could be supplied without trouble from the un-friendly Kansa Indians so long as that tribe resided on the Missouri, either at the Doniphan, Kansas, site or in the vicinity of Fort de Cavagnial. Later, when the Kansa Indians moved their main village to the Kansas-Blue river junction near present Manhattan, Kansas, the Missouri and Nemaha rivers offered an alternative waterway relatively free of obstruction from meddlesome Kansa or Oto raiding parties. The last 100 miles or so of this route, between Republican River villages and the head of pirogue navigation on the Nemaha, wherever that may have been, had the disadvantage of requiring overland travel and pack animal facilities.[5]

That much of the trade material found at the Hill and Kansas Monument sites was of French origin, probably brought in from St. Louis by traders resid-ing seasonally or year-round at the villages, seems certain. Few details are yet available on Frenchmen among the Pawnees for trade, but they were assuredly there—and evidently on something quite different from the triennial schedule reported by Pike for the Spanish visits. In 1794, dropping downriver in search of a safe wintering place after an unsuccessful attempt to establish a trade contact with the Arikaras on the Missouri near the mouth of the Cheyenne, Jean-Bap-tiste Truteau (1794–1796) cached most of his merchandise in a deep pit, claim-ing to be "very expert in these kinds of caches of which I had made frequent use when I was for three consecutive years residing with the nation of the panis republicains." In the early 1790s, this would probably imply residence at the Hill site village. In 1795, under commission from Gov. Fernando Chacon at Santa Fe, Pedro Vial visited "the Pawnee nation (commonly called republic) which has its village on the bank of Kansas River," delivered a medal, and met traders from St. Louis who declined Vial's invitation to accompany him to Santa Fe (Loomis and Nasatir 1967:413). In 1804, Vial visited the Pawnees on the Platte, meeting there "about twenty Frenchmen" who were full of misinformation about the Americans and bringing back "a Spanish captive who was living among them" (Nasatir 1974:117). A small but interesting measure of the French influence among the Pawnees of this period is Pike's observation that at his initial meeting on 25 September 1806 with Characterish or White Wolf, first chief, and his welcoming band of 300 horsemen, the chief "stretched out his hand and cried 'Bon jour'" (Jackson 1966, vol. 2, p. 6).

Before his departure from the Hill village site on 7 October, Pike learned of Meriwether Lewis and William Clark's safe return to St. Louis from two French traders just arrived in the Republican village "to procure horses to transport their goods from the Missouri to the village." One wonders whether these men were from either of the two trading parties passed by the homeward-bound explorers on 16 September below the Kansas River—one in a "large trading perogue bound for the Panias," the other in "a large boat of six ores [sic] and two canoes" under one Robidoux headed for the "Panias Mahaw" (Lewis and Clark 1904–1905, vol. 5, p. 386). By Amos Stoddard's figures (Stoddard 1973:303) of 1812, that one boatman was required for every 3,000 pounds (1,350 kg) of cargo, Robidoux's six-oar boat would have been carrying in the neighborhood of nine tons (8,100 kg) of cargo, equivalent to 80 or 90 pack-animal loads.

Historical sources provide some information on the approximate time involved in travel by boat along the Missouri River between St. Louis and the Pawnee country. Travel times upstream for several 18th- and 19th-century observers who made this run before 1805 are given in table 9.2.

The two entries given for Lewis and Clark represent, of course, the time spent ascending (1804) and descending (1806) the river, the latter requiring less than one-fifth of the time required for the upriver trip. James Mackay, who incidentally estimated the distance to the Nemaha River as 141 leagues, was held up by bad weather and a leaky boat (Nasatir 1931:437, Doc. IV; Abel-Henderson 1924). Jean-Baptiste Truteau was overtaken on the river by Jacques D'Eglise, traveling with a smaller contingent and a lighter, better-protected load (Nasatir 1929:372), but D'Eglise's departure date and the total number of days in transit are not specified. There are, unfortunately, no comparable figures for the traders' journey time between the Pawnee towns and St. Louis, of which Lt. Gov. Zenon Trudeau once reported that "the traders regularly arrived by water in ten days" (Loomis and Nasatir 1967:413). If this time seems im-

Table 9.2

Travel time for some 18th- and early 19th-century boat parties on the lower Missouri

	Bourgmont 1714	Vial 1793	Truteau 1794	Mackay 1794	Lewis & Clark 1804	Lewis & Clark 1806
Leave Missouri River mouth (0 miles)	3/30	6/14	6/07	9/01	5/14	9/12
Kansas River (392 mi)	5/11		7/12		6/26	
Nemaha River (535 mi)		8/24			7/12	
Platte River (637 mi)	6/16		8/06	10/14	7/21	9/09
No. days traveled	76	71	60	44	67	12
Av. miles per day	8.34	7.5	10.6	14.41	9.46	52.8

NOTE: To convert miles to kilometers, multiply by 1.6.

probably short, one may consider Stoddard's (1973:371) observations on Mississippi River travel, where the current is considerably less than on the Missouri. Here, "when the water is low, a boat will float from 45 to 50 miles (70–80 km) in 24 hours; in a middle state from 60 to 70 miles (95–110 km); and in the season of freshes [sic] from 90 to 100 miles (145–160 km) in the same period of time." Wide variations in upstream travel time were certainly to be expected, depending on the size of the boats, their loads, the condition and qualities of the crews and equipment, the state of the river and the weather, and a host of other variables. Upriver travel distances per day may not have averaged significantly higher than the daily performance of overland pack animals, and may often have been considerably less; but the boats did not have to be unloaded at the end of each day and reloaded the next morning, which was routinely the case with mules and horses.

Available at St. Louis to the Missouri River Indians, when the Pawnees were living on the Republican, was a wide range of trade goods. When Lt. Gov. Francisco Cruzat turned over his command at that post to Don Manuel Perez in November 1787, his inventory of presents for the Indians listed 43 items (Houck 1909:268). Twenty-six were hardware or durable goods, including sewing needles, scissors, awls, hawk's bells, thimbles, mirrors, beads, hoes, large and small axes, hatchets, knives, wire, musket flints and balls, muskets, copper kettles, large and small medals, gorgets, and "one hundred ninety useless hoes." Nondurable items included sugarcane brandy in casks, powder, shirts, Limbourg cloth, lace-trimmed garments for chiefs, white plumes, silk ribbons for medals and gorgets, sewing thread, and tobacco. Undoubtedly many of these same items were carried by the traders who traveled from St. Louis to the Indian villages to exchange their goods for peltries.

Excavated house ruins, cache pits, and trash deposits at the Hill and Kansas Monument sites have yielded clear evidence of many of the durable goods listed above, as well as others not on the inventory (Munday 1927; Wedel 1936; Smith 1950; Witty 1968; Roberts 1978). Trash deposits have produced bottles, razors, fire steels, bridle bits, spurs, belt buckles, United States military buttons, an army canteen of early 19th-century type, a single-barbed muskrat or beaver spear, and so on. Some graves have produced traces of milled wood that suggest boxes, chests, or other carpentered containers in which trade goods may have been transported or personal possessions stored by the Indians (plate 9.5).

Not uncommonly, as opportunity offered or necessity dictated, trade items were modified by the Indians. Arrowpoints in various shapes, including stemmed and unstemmed forms, were cut from brass and iron kettles and strap metal pieces. So were conical tinklers with an opening at the apex for attachment to a thong or fringe. Gun barrel fragments with hammered end could have served as tent stakes or picket pins; with one end flattened and finely notched they could be used as hide scrapers. Iron blades often replaced chipped flints in the fleshing adzes. Silver coins, pierced at one edge, and metal thimbles, also pierced, became articles of personal adornment.

The mechanics of the Indian-white trade among the Pawnees are nowhere detailed in the contemporary literature I have seen, but they can be partially inferred from documents pertaining more specifically to neighboring tribes. At the villages, traders undoubtedly dealt largely with chiefs and other prestigious personages to whose households they presumably attached themselves, sometimes by marriage, for protection. The goods they bartered would then have gone first to the chiefs, "braves," elders, and their families, and thereafter in diminishing amounts and quality to commoners. The trade lists and inventories suggest some preference for articles important to males, but metal kettles, hoes, axes, hatchets, knives, and beads would have been equally useful and attractive to women. The persistence of chipped-stone blades and other edged tools, and of bone skin-dressing implements, long after the introduction of iron, may reflect female preference for old-fashioned, native-made tools that perhaps did less damage to peltries or were easier to maintain, besides being more readily available without cost other than the labor of manufacture and maintenance. That males with status had first pick of the incoming goods and took advantage of the opportunity to satisfy their wants is not unexpected, but it is not entirely obvious from the record that females, particularly the wives of chiefs, were necessarily at the end of the distribution line within the community and were therefore short-changed. On this point, note should be taken of Maj. Stephen Long's observation that "the man is the active agent in this barter, but he avails himself of the advice of his squaw, and often submits to her dictation" (James 1823:310).

That the Pawnees on the Republican were probably heavily dependent on the white trade is indicated in the quantities of such goods found archeologically at the sites and in the deteriorating quality and diminishing quantity and variety of the native-made products. An intriguing study for a dedicated and patient scholar would be a thorough comparative analysis of all extant trade materials from both Republican River Pawnee sites in order to further illuminate, among other problems, their respective spans of occupation and perhaps more precisely the sources of the goods, together with the manner in which the various items were worked into the existing native lifeway.

Peace Medals among the Republican Pawnees

An Indian Left his Medal on the shore of the river last evening, while he went in to bathe. It is presumed he had lost it in the sand; but should there be a miscreant so lost to every sense of honor and honesty as to steal it, the good citizens are requested to be on the alert and take up the culprit. Any information on this subject will be thankfully received at the Indian Office.

Missouri Gazette, 28 June, 1817

From the time of earliest white contact, prominent Indians were given presents by visiting Euro-Americans. These usually included vermillion, glass beads, knives, mirrors, cloth, and similar items that could be easily carried with the limited transport facilities available, whether these were pirogues, horses and mules, or backpacks. Of no less interest are the government-issued medals for presentation to chiefs visiting, or visited by, officials or to those participating in treaty negotiations. Increasingly common from the middle 18th century on, the medals were mostly of silver, carried a likeness of the reigning sovereign or incumbent president, and were often dated. Medals of different sizes were designed for recipients of varying rank or status—the more important the personage, the larger the medal given him. They were often accompanied by certificates or commissions and a flag. Grand medals were up to four inches (105 mm) or more in diameter. In awarding these symbols of status,

Plate 9.6. Obverse (left) and reverse of Spanish grand medal of Charles IV, from the grave of a child at the Hill site. Courtesy Nebraska State Historical Society.

the Spanish and British seem to have observed protocol more scrupulously than did the later Americans, who sometimes debased their offerings by the indiscriminate distribution to undeserving individuals (Wilkinson and Sibley in Jackson 1966, vol. 2, pp. 12, 371). For this creation of "made" or improperly qualified "medal" chiefs, the Americans were on occasion chided by the Indians. The medals and flags to be awarded by an official visitor were sometimes withheld until those from an earlier one were surrendered or laid away.[6]

Several medals of diverse national origins have been retrieved from Indian graves at the Hill site. Two are Spanish. Of these, one bears the likeness of Charles, "Carolus III," (1759–1788) and date of 1778 on the obverse. On the reverse are depicted the royal arms and the legend "·HISPAN·ET·IND-·REX·M̊·8R·F·F·" (Spain and Indies, King, M̊ = mint mark for Mexico City, 8R = eight reales, F F = assayer's initials). The medal, actually a Spanish peso minted in Mexico City, had evidently been provided with a short stem or loop at the top for suspension from a ribbon. Its diameter is 39 mm (plate 9.7; cf. Bates 1982:15; Utberg 1970:47; see also *Numismatist*, 39 [1926]:140).

The second Spanish medal appears to have been improvised around another peso. This coin, 39 mm in diameter, bears the likeness of "Carolus IIII" (1788–1808) and date of 1797 on the obverse. It has been set centrally into a large, hand-engraved silver disk 109 mm in diameter, which is decorated front and back with floral and other curvilinear motifs (plate 9.6; see also Prucha 1971:12). With this in the grave were found scraps of textile suggesting a cloth wrapping or container. The age and sex of the skeleton with which this piece was associated is apparently not a matter of record, unfortunately.

A British medal, bearing no date but assigned one of 1762, has a bust of George III (1760–1820) in armor, with the royal arms on the reverse. Its diameter is 60 mm. It closely resembles medals issued in considerable numbers during the American Revolution (1775–1783), when the British were widely courting the good will and aid of the Indians against the rebelling colonists (plate 9.7; see also Jamieson 1936:21—27).

Plate 9.7. Peace medals from Pawnee graves at the Hill site. *Upper,* obverse and reverse of Spanish medal of Charles III; *middle,* obverse and reverse of British medal of George III; *lower,* obverse of two-piece American medal of General Washington. All photographs courtesy Nebraska State Historical Society.

From another grave, which contained the skeleton of a youth, was taken the reverse shell of a two-piece United States peace and friendship medal of the kind that appeared in 1801. This was during the first term of Pres. Thomas Jefferson, whose likeness was on the obverse. On these medals, only the obverse was changed over the next four decades as successive presidents took office. These were struck in three sizes—105, 75, and 55 mm in diameter, or grand, second, and third grades, for the usual selective presentation. Lewis and Clark were supplied with 32 of these in all sizes, and Pike carried at least two when he made his western trip. The Hill site specimen is from an intermediate or second grade size (Munday 1927, facing p. 174).[7]

In 1941, in the course of excavations by the Nebraska State Historical Society in cooperation with the Work Projects Administration, the obverse of a two-piece medal or ornament bearing the likeness and name "GENERAL WASHINGTON" was found in a grave that contained also a cradleboard, bits of rush matting, a bow fragment, and a jack knife. The piece (plate 9.7) is 76 mm in diameter. General Washington is depicted in uniform wearing an epaulet, and he faces to the left. There is no date or other marking. A hole has been somewhat clumsily drilled or punched through the medal between the letters "A" and "S" just below the rim, presumably to permit suspension from a cord of a piece not originally designed for that purpose.[8]

By whose hands these several medals reached the Pawnees buried at the Republican River village there is no way of determining unequivocally. The scanty records that are usually available seldom specify which medals and how many were awarded, to whom they were given, or their ultimate disposition— whether they were buried with the recipient at his death, sold or given away by him, or perhaps exchanged or discarded when political power shifted from the initial donor's nationality to another. However, some intriguing possibilities may be suggested here.

The first American of record to make official contact with the Pawnees at the Hill site village was Lt. Zebulon Pike, who arrived on Thursday, 25 September, and left on Tuesday, 7 October 1806. During his 12-day stay, an "intermediate sized medal" was presented to Iskatappe, the "second great personage of the village" (Jackson 1966, vol. 2, pp. 12–13). A medal of this size and time is consistent with the incomplete peace and friendship medal noted above from the Hill site. To the first chief, Characterish, Pike gave a double-barreled gun, gorget, and other items, but no medal is mentioned (Jackson 1966, vol. 2, p. 151).

On another occasion two days previously, Characterish had worn a "grand Spanish medal" elsewhere described by Gov. Joaquin del Real Alencaster at Santa Fe as "the medal with the Bust of our Sovereign Carlos Quarto" (Jackson 1966, vol. 2, p. 182). One wonders whether this was a standard government-issue piece or a special product, very likely presented to Characterish earlier in the summer of 1806 by Lt. Don Facundo Melgares. Melgares was in command of a force of more than 300 regulars and militia that originated in New Vizcaya (Mexico) and was outfitted in Santa Fe. Among his other assignments, Melgares was to "renew the chains of amity" with several frontier tribes by giving flags, commissions, a grand medal, and four mules to the head chief of each of the following tribes: Tetaus (Comanches), Pawnee Republics, Grand Pawnees, Pawnee Mahaws (Skiris), and Kansa Indians. On Red River, where his orders were to turn back the Freeman-Custis exploring expedition (Account . . . 1806) if that had not already been accomplished by Francisco Viana from Nacogdoches, Melgares met the "grand bands" of the Comanches; the Skiris he encountered later on the Arkansas, but details concerning the perquisites distributed, if any, to these tribes are apparently lacking. At the Republican Pawnee village at the present Hill site, which he reached a few weeks before Pike's arrival, he was met by a delegation from the Grand Pawnees as well and presented to both nations the flags, medals, and other articles "which were destined for them." Whether he anywhere met the Kansa Indians and thus was able to dispose of all the medals as instructed is not clear.

Of particular interest in this connection is a communication of 11 October 1805 from Governor Alencaster in Santa Fe to his superior, Commandant General Nemesio Salcedo at Chihuahua. This related to the preparations for an expedition to the Pawnees that was about to be dispatched from Santa Fe under Pedro Vial but which was aborted shortly after his departure. In this message, Alencaster suggested that Salcedo "ask Mexico for half a dozen seven- or eight-ounce silver medals with the bust of our sovereign . . . and on the other side a border of laurel and some other adornment . . . and two dozen similar medals, also of silver, with the weight of one and one-half ounces and proportionate size " (Loomis and Nasatir 1967:429).

The Spanish sovereign in Alencaster's time was Charles IV, whose bust appears on the centerpiece of the large silver medal from the Hill site; that medal bears floral decoration ("a border of laurel") on both sides; and its weight of 4.31 ounces (122 g) is within the range of sizes recommended by Alencaster. Melgares left Santa Fe in the spring or early summer of 1806, some six or eight months after Alencaster transmitted to Salcedo his recommendations concerning medals for the Indians. Whether that recommendation was forwarded to Mexico City I have been unable to determine. In any case, there would seem to be a good likelihood that the medals carried by Melgares, if all were like the Hill site specimen, originated not in Mexico City but were improvised by silversmiths in Santa Fe when it was decided that smaller medals would compare unfavorably in the Indian mind with those reputedly being distributed by the Americans. I am indebted to Dr. James A. Hanson for pointing out that the centerpiece of the Hill site specimen is a Mexican-made peso of Charles IV (Utberg 1970:51), probably of eight *reales* denomination. This was inset into a large hand-wrought silver placque, which was then embellished on both faces with curvilinear or floral motifs. It would be most interesting to know the nature of the other four medals carried by Melgares, who the silversmith was that produced them, and especially to learn what eventually became of them. Of much interest, too, would be a glimpse of the reverse of the coin set into the Hill site medal.

There is a record of the presentation of at least one other Charles IV medal to the Pawnees. This was by Gov. Fernando Chacon in late 1804 to a party of warriors that escorted Pedro Vial back to Santa Fe from their villages on the Rio Chato (Platte River), where Vial had been sent to insure the continued loyalty of the Indians when word reached the Spanish of Lewis and Clark's passage up the Missouri. From 20 Frenchmen met by Vial among the Pawnee, he learned that these Americans were distributing presents and medals freely to tribes met along their route. Whether the medal given by Governor Chacon was a "grand" medal is not stated (Nasatir 1974:114).

As for the Charles III medal of 1778, one is reminded of Pike's journal entry for 24 September, the day before he reached the Republican Pawnee village. Among several Pawnees who met him a few miles south of the Hill site, one "wore a scarlet coat, with a small medal of general Washington, and a Spanish medal also." Charles III was no longer king of Spain at the time of Pike's visit; but on a smaller medal awarded perhaps to a lesser chief, the inappropriateness of the "white father" depicted may have been of less concern to the wearer than the tangible evidence of his possession of one of the coveted badges of authority. Or, that piece could conceivably be evidence of an earlier contact between the Spanish and the Pawnees. Its date of 1778, and its possible association on a live Pawnee of Pike's time with a medal of General Washington postdating 1775 but predating his presidency (1789–1797), provide a heady draft for historical romanticizing.

Chapter 10 To Clear the Republican Country of Indians

On 3 June 1825, five months before Jedediah Smith led his contingent of the Ashley-Smith fur men out of St. Louis and up the Republican en route to the Great Salt Lake trappers' rendezvous, the Kansa Indians ceded to the United States the lands they claimed on the lower portion of that stream as far west as "the old village of the Pania Republic" (Royce 1899). At the same time, the Pawnees gave up no land but acknowledged the supremacy of the United States and accepted its protection and friendship. Three years after Smith's party wintered at the Kansas Monument village, the Republican band left the stream that bore their name and moved to the vicinity of the Grand Pawnees, who were then at the Clarks site (25PK1) on the south bank of the Platte River. Thus, by 1830, the Pawnees, the last of the Village Indians to inhabit the Republican valley, had to all intents and purposes abandoned the area as their residential habitat. The move northward to the proximity of their more numerous linguistic kindred would, it was hoped, provide a somewhat greater measure of security against their many enemies, old and new. It would also do away with another of the many points of contact and irritation between the resident Indians and the expanding whites pressing westward for furs and homes.

In 1833, by treaty at the Grand Pawnee Village (Clarks site), the combined Pawnee bands ceded to the United States all their lands lying south of the Platte and west to a line curving from present North Platte through Hayes Center and Benkelman, Nebraska, and south along the eastern edge of Cheyenne and Sherman counties, Kansas. Beyond this line were lands claimed by the Cheyennes and Arapahos, and shared by them with various bands of the Sioux, the Kiowas, and other wandering or "wild" tribes. The Pawnees renewed their pledge of fidelity to the United States and their expressed desire for peace with their Indian neighbors, foreswearing punitive action against the latter. In return for their pledge of good behavior, the Pawnees were promised "twenty five guns, with suitable ammunition, [to be placed] in the hands of the farmers of each village, to be used in case of an attack from hostile bands" (Lesser 1978:10–11, n.1).

Between the Pawnees and the lands they ceded south of the Platte, strong ties remained. The Republican was prime bison-hunting country as long as the tribe stayed in Nebraska, and the Pawnees' rights to seek game there and southward into the Smoky Hill and Arkansas River drainages were stubbornly defended.

There were other compelling grounds for their reluctance to give up this land. One of the sacred places of the Pawnees (Grinnell 1889) was situated only

186

Plate 10.1. Pawnee animal lodges or sacred places. *Upper,* Paˈhuˈruʹ, "the hill that points the way," or Guide Rock in Webster County, Nebraska, in 1904. Courtesy Nebraska State Historical Society. *Lower, Kicawiˈcaku,* "spring on the edge of a bank," Waconda Spring, Mitchell County, Kansas, in 1965. Courtesy U.S. Bureau of Reclamation.

five miles downstream from the Hill site and about 30 miles above the Kansas Monument site, on the south bank of the river. It was known as *Pa-hur´,* "the hill that points the way." Now badly defaced by road and canal construction, this landmark has given its name in anglicized form to the town of Guide Rock, Nebraska, across the river about a mile to the north (plate 10.1). Another sacred place, *Kitz-a-witz-uk,* "water on a bank," lay only 35 miles south of the Hill site and about the same distance from the Kansas Monument site, at Waconda Spring on the Solomon River southeast of Cawker City, Kansas. (The modern transcription for these Indian names appears in the caption for plate 10.1) This was a natural artesian spring pool occupying the top of a limestone mound that vaguely resembled an earthlodge. The water level fluctuated and from time to time overflowed the rim. When the pool was cleaned out during its years as a health spa and a source of mineral water, it yielded beads, weapons, moccasins, and other artifacts that had been deposited as offerings by passing bands of Indians (Patrick 1906), including the Pawnees and many others of diverse linguistic affiliations. It is now submerged by the waters of Glen Elder Reservoir (plate 10.1)[1].

The St. Louis treaty that stripped the Kansa and Osage Indians of much of their claimed land set the stage for another far-reaching development. This was the resettlement in Kansas of a number of tribes from the eastern United States whose removal had long been insisted upon, publicly and officially. Within the next decade or two, groups of Iowas, Sacs, Foxes, Kickapoos, Shawnees, Ottawas, Potawatomis, Miamis, Wyandots, and New York Iroquois were settled here, mostly east of a north-south line passing through the mouth of the Republican River. Although essentially farm oriented and classed as "civilized" Indians, many of these became involved in hunting forays into the bison country where, generally equipped with better firearms, they came into conflict with the longer-established "wild" tribes indigenous to the region. The Pawnees in the Pawnee Crescent, still trying to harmonize two divergent subsistence economies, were caught in a squeeze between the newly arrived easterners and the mounted bison hunters to the west. As early as 1832, the Delawares retaliated for the destruction of one of their hunting parties by the Pawnees by burning the Grand Pawnee village where Commissioner Henry Ellsworth negotiated the 1833 peace treaty between the civilized easterners and the "wild" tribes of the Pawnees and Otos. There were other incidents, all of which essentially added new names to an already long list of enemies of the Pawnees.

Further complicating the problems of the resident tribes were the increasingly frequent encounters with the Americans expanding westward. In 1822, the practicality of wheeled vehicular traffic between the Missouri River and the Spaniards at Santa Fe had been demonstrated by Col. William Becknell, and this led to a growing stream of wagon trains moving across the central plains. From the bend of the Missouri at present Kansas City, the road of the emigrants and traders led west by south via Council Grove and Diamond Spring to the northernmost bend of the Arkansas River at the mouth of Walnut Creek, up the Arkansas to one of several crossings between present Dodge City and Lakin, and on past Pecos Ruin to Santa Fe either by way of Bent's (old) Fort (1828–1849) and south across Raton Pass, or via the Cimarron Cutoff. Besides the commercial traffic for Santa Fe, this route carried supplies for traders, trappers, and others who were establishing themselves on the upper Arkansas River and along the adjacent mountain front.

A few miles out of Independence, beginning in the 1830s, the road to Oregon and California branched off near present Gardner, Kansas (Ghent 1929:121ff; Mattes 1969). Crossing the Kaw near Topeka and the Blue near Marysville, Kansas, the route followed the Little Blue River to strike the Platte between Grand Island and Fort Kearny, where it merged with other approaches from various starting points on the western bank of the Missouri. Thence, traffic moved up both banks of the Platte, though the south side was preferred. A few miles beyond the fork, traffic could then cross the South Platte by one of several fords to reach the North Platte at Ash Hollow and proceed on to Fort Laramie, South Pass, and points farther west. Other travelers, notably after the discovery of gold in Colorado, stayed on the South Platte to reach the settlements on Cherry Creek in the area of present Denver. The Blue River portion of this trail roughly paralleled the Republican River trace of the Smith-Ashley contingent of 1825–1826 at a distance of about 30 or 40 miles.

Travelers along the Oregon trail, particularly those from other approaches down the Platte, were a special source of irritation to the Pawnees. The emigrants made heavy inroads on the already limited timber stands upon which the Indians drew for house construction, fuel, and other domestic needs, and on the grazing available for their horse herds. Settlers persistently encroached on lands set aside by treaty for the Indians. Everywhere, the whites were killing bison and driving the herds farther and farther away from the travel routes and from the Pawnee villages. Conversely, the Indians were charged by the westering whites with horse stealing and stock thefts; begging; levying of foods, tobacco, and other items in return for promises of safe passage; and various other forms of harassment. Among the Pawnees, who were by no means the only tribe engaged in these activities, it was the young men who disregarded the treaties made by their elders, and especially those living south of the Platte, who were generally blamed for the difficulties.

The Republican River in Maps

Although not itself a major road for westward expansion, the Republican valley was bracketed between two increasingly busy and heavily traveled routes across the central plains. But, while American traffic along these two routes—the Santa Fe trail in the south along the Arkansas River, and the Oregon-California trail along the Platte—grew ever heavier, the United States government seems to have manifested little official interest in the country lying between them. Various bands of the Sioux, notably the Oglalas and Brules from the Fort Laramie area on the North Platte River, frequently visited the Republican headwaters district in southwestern Nebraska and adjacent Colorado and Kansas, sending war as well as hunting parties into those sections. To them, according to Gilmore (1915:14), the stream was known as *Padani wakpa* (or *Palani wakpa*, D. R. Parks personal communication, 10 April 1982) meaning "Pawnee River." From the south came the Cheyennes and Arapahos, and sometimes the Kiowas and Comanches. By the Cheyennes, the Republican was called the Red Shield River because of a meeting of the Red Shield Society there (Grinnell 1906). Because the Republican River presumably led nowhere of importance and its basin harbored so many unfriendly Indians, whites appear to have ventured only infrequently into its valleys and streamside woodlands so that its geography remained poorly known to the Americans.

Before the Americans, of course, the French in St. Louis had been in contact with the Republican Pawnees at least as early as 1775, and cartographically they had indicated a travel route from the Indian village on the Republican to the Missouri River at the mouth of the Little Nemaha River by 1795 (Diller 1955). The stream on which the Indian village or villages stood was usually depicted on maps or was otherwise reported simply as an unnamed branch of the Kansas River. For example, the Antoine Soulard map of 1795 (Diller 1955) shows the "N[ation] Republiques" on the north bank of an unnamed tributary that joins the "R des Cans" (Kansas) some distance above the "R eau bleue" (Blue River). So far as I am aware, the earliest identification of the Republican by what was to become its proper name was on Perrin du Lac's

1802 map of the Missouri, which shows the "Village des Republiques" on the north bank of the "Fourche des Republiques." The Americans, beginning with the Lewis and Clark map of 1804, anglicized this to "Republican Fork." It is usually so designated thereafter on maps up to the 1860s, that is, until Civil War times, such as on those by Zebulon Pike 1806, William Clark 1810, Matthew Carey 1814, Auguste Chouteau 1816, Stephen H. Long 1819, Isaac McCoy 1830–1836, Josiah Gregg 1844, and J. H. Colton 1860. At least two exceptions may be noted: where "Republican River" appears on the "Lewis" map of 1805, and "Republican Fork or Pawnee River" on G. K. Warren's map of 1857. By the late 1860s, it had become the Republican River and was so indicated on post–Civil War railroad and land promotion maps, on the Philip Sheridan map of 1871, and generally thereafter (Wheat 1957–1963).

There were a few notable exceptions to the apparent lack of official interest in the Republican country on the part of Americans in the first half century following its acquisition as part of the Louisiana Purchase. These were the explorations by Lt. John C. Frémont in 1843, Lt. L. C. Easton in 1849, and Lt. Francis T. Bryan in 1856. Their recorded observations, which include journals, tables of distances, and maps, and their formal recommendations for future operations, are of particular interest here as they reflect the relative unfamiliarity with details of the regional geography and its resources, the slow development of its toponymy, and some of the environmental features that made the area so attractive to the Pawnees and other Indians.

Frémont on the Republican 1843

En route to his explorations of the Oregon country and northern California for the United States Topographical Engineers, Lieutenant Frémont (Frémont 1845; Jackson and Spence 1970) left the town of Kansas at the junction of the Kansas and Missouri rivers on 29 May 1843. His party consisted of about 40 men and included 12 mule-drawn supply carts, a light spring wagon carrying chronometers, barometers, sextants, and other instruments, and a brass 12-pound mountain howitzer. Travel was south of the Kansas River to the junction of the Smoky Hill and Republican forks. After some delay here because of high water, Frémont crossed the Smoky Hill and moved up the west side of the Republican as far as the bend above present Concordia. Here, distressed by its slow progress, Frémont divided the party on June 16. With 15 men, he set out in advance, taking along the instrument wagon and the howitzer. The carts he left in charge of Thomas Fitzpatrick, who, with the rest of the command, was to follow as fast as weather and other circumstances would allow.

Continuing in a general westerly direction, Frémont crossed to the Solomon River drainage and, traveling back from the river so as to minimize the need for bridge building on the numerous tributary creeks and to obtain a smoother road, marched for several days along the Solomon-Republican divide to a point apparently some miles beyond present Phillipsburg, Kansas, on Deer Creek. On 19 June, probably in present Smith County, he crossed the Pawnee trail that led from the villages of that tribe on the Platte and Loup rivers to their hunting grounds on the Arkansas River. On the same day, the party saw its first bison.

On 21 June, Frémont crossed from the Solomon drainage to the Republican, there reaching "a fork, about forty feet wide and one foot deep, flowing with a swift current over a sandy bed, and well-wooded with ash-leaved maple (*negundo fraxinifolium*), elm, cottonwood, and a few white oaks" (Frémont 1845:109; Jackson and Spence 1970:433–434). This stream, which is not named in Frémont's report, was without doubt the Prairie Dog Creek of today, probably crossed by Frémont somewhere in the general vicinity of Norton, Kansas. Camp on 22 June appears to have been on present Sappa Creek, perhaps near Oberlin.

The next day, says Frémont (1845:109),

> at noon on the 23rd, we descended into the valley of a principal fork of the Republican, a beautiful stream with a dense border of wood, consisting principally of varieties of ash, forty feet wide and four feet deep. It was musical with the notes of many birds, which, from the vast expanse of silent prairie around, seem all to have collected here. We continued during the afternoon our route along the river, which was populous with prairie dogs (the bottoms being entirely occupied with their villages) and late in the evening encamped on its banks. The prevailing timber is a blue-foli-aged ash (*fraxinus* near *F. Americana*) and ash-leaved maple [box elder, *Acer negundo*]. With these were *fraxinus Americana*, cottonwood, and long-leaved willow. We gave to this stream the name of Prairie Dog River.

This stream was, without doubt, the Beaver Creek of today, which Frémont probably struck a few miles above the present Nebraska line at or near the Elephant Rock crossing of later times in section 3, township 2 south, range 30 west, Decatur County, 1.5 miles south by west of Traer, Kansas (Volkmar 1869). This creek was followed upstream to a point near or above the present town of Atwood before encamping. The "dense border of wood" noted by Frémont is of particular interest because of a parallel observation made some 62 years later by forester Royal S. Kellogg (1905:24) to the effect that "the best westward extension of timber in Kansas is on Beaver Creek in Rawlins County. The creek is bordered by a thriving growth of green ash [*Fraxinus pennsylvanica*], with a lesser number of other species. The timber reaches to some distance above Atwood, not far from the point where the bed of the stream first carries permanent water."

Frémont's route for the next two days is not easy to retrace. Nothing is said about travel on the 24th, for which the distance is reported as 34 miles. On the 25th, the road lay "over high smooth ridges," with bison present "in great numbers, absolutely covering the face of the country." On 26 June, the party crossed the Republican River, perhaps somewhere near its junction with the South Fork, where the approach from the south was through "bare sand hills" and the scanty vegetation was characterized by a sand-loving flora. Across the river, the dunes presented "almost a mountainous appearance." There were, moreover, few trees in sight at the crossing; these he described as only "one or two distant and detached groves." The river itself was "a large stream . . . whose shallow waters with a depth of only a few inches, were spread out over a bed of yellowish-white sand 600 yards wide" (Jackson and Spence 1970:434).

From this crossing, travel was in a northerly and then westerly direction through a hilly and sandy tract "where there were no running streams," an apt description of the sand dune terrain in Dundy County, southwestern Nebraska, and northern Yuma and Washington counties in northeastern Colorado. A piece of creek shown on Frémont's map north of the Republican may be Indian

Creek or Muddy Creek, not noted in the narrative. Frémont spoke gratefully of the occasional lakes and ponds surrounded by green grass for the horses and around which bison could usually be found for human consumption. His map shows at least two overnight camps beside such water holes. On 30 June, Frémont's party reached the South Platte River near present Atwood, Colorado, having traveled an estimated 456 miles (730 km) in 19 days at an average of 24 miles (38 km) per day. Here the party turned upriver to reach St. Vrain's fort on 4 July.

I have tried, but with indifferent success, to retrace on modern maps the route followed by Frémont between 10 June, when he started up the Republican, and 1 July, when he reached the South Platte. By what method he estimated or calculated the mileage traveled each day is nowhere specified, so far as I can determine. For some days, at least, the figures seem excessive. His estimate of 187 miles (300 km) from the "town of Kansas" near the mouth of Kansas River to the Smoky Hill–Republican junction strikes me as perhaps 30 or 40 miles too high, even allowing for his deviation from a direct line to follow the Oregon and Santa Fe trails at the outset. His calculations of latitude and longitude are often suspect: the 10 June determination for the "encampment on Smoky Hill fork, half a mile from its junction with the Republican" places it 20 miles east of its correct location. Again, on 25 June, his calculated position would put him northwest of present Benkelman, Nebraska, several miles north of the Republican whereas his narrative shows him still some distance south of the river.

Frémont named few streams or other landmarks during this stretch of his travels, and at least one of the names he assigned was eventually transferred to another stream by later mapmakers. On his map, he dotted in those sections of a number of creeks and streams that he did not see and of whose true courses he thus could not be sure. He reported no direct contact with Indians between the Kansas River and the South Platte. His descriptive notes on the vegetation and on other features of the terrain are useful, especially when compared with on-the-ground examination. My wife and I have done this at various times during the summers of 1977 to 1983.

It may not be unfair to suggest that were Frémont to retrace his 1843 route through this section today, he would probably view with some dismay the changes in the valley of the stream he dubbed "Prairie Dog River." In June 1982, his "beautiful stream" was a narrow, weed-grown ditch without water and choked with fallen tree debris. The prairie dogs, of course, are long since gone. In place of the "notes of many birds," he would probably hear the noisy monotone of farm tractors, the occasional snarl of the chain saw eating away at what is left of the "dense border of wood," and the rumble of cattle-haulers and grain trucks on their way to market instead of the thunder of bison hooves. This represents progress, one is assured, but at what cost to the land!

Easton on the Republican, 1849

In the late summer of 1849, Lt. Langdon C. Easton and a party of 26 traveled from Fort Laramie on the North Platte River to Fort Leavenworth, hoping to find a better route to Fort Laramie from the Missouri River along the Republican (Easton 1953). Leaving Fort Laramie on 2 August, Easton proceeded via Lodgepole Creek. Twenty-four miles east of Pine Bluffs, he left the creek and headed southeast for the South Platte River, which he crossed in the vicinity of present Sterling, Colorado, and there encamped. From there he proceeded east southeast and southeast for 86 miles (140 km) to strike the Arikaree Fork about 30 miles (48 km) above its confluence with the North Fork Republican. On this stretch, the first five miles (8 km) after leaving the South Platte crossing are described as "a heavy road over hills of deep sand." After this there was no wood or grass, and after 22 miles (35 km), only a "small pond, with wretched water and bad grass" at which to encamp. Next day, after a 17-mile march over barren plains, they came upon a "very large pond, or lake, of good water," with excellent grazing. West of their camp were other ponds and small lakes, and his French guide, Joseph Hunoit, informed Easton that there were many such between the mouth of Lodgepole Creek and the Republican. From this, Easton concluded that "there are a number of these lakes of good water between the two rivers [South Platte and Republican], and that by winding the road from one to another, an abundance of water can be procured at convenient distances" (Easton 1953:403).

At the valley of the Arikaree, which Easton mistook for the Republican Fork, there was a cluster of trees, a welcome contrast to the preceding four days march "without seeing a stream of water or a stick of timber." This was a few miles above Black Wolf Creek, between present Vernon and Idalia, Colorado. Traveling down the Arikaree, Easton found the countryside below its junction with the North Fork Republican swarming with bison, which had badly trampled the grass in the bottoms. Around the junction itself, trees were noted on the tributaries, and there were large quantities of delicious plums. At the confluence of the Republican with Red Willow Creek, which stream was not identified by name, Easton was told that it led within 45 miles (72 km) of the Platte River, with lakes to be found between its head and that river. Below this point, Easton found an abundance of timber and grass. Below Medicine Creek, also unnamed, a grove of wild plum trees yielded the "finest wild fruit I ever saw." Grouse occurred in great numbers "from this point to the Missouri River." Approaching the present Harlan County Reservoir district, Easton observed that deer, antelope, turkeys, and grouse were plentiful, and that there were "great quantities of fine plums and abundance of summer grapes." In the next few days, plums and grapes were repeatedly noted, the latter particularly occurring "in fine perfection on nearly all creeks we crossed" (Easton 1953:408).

On 1 September, Easton's party crossed a well-worn trail used by the Pawnees in traveling from their villages on the Loup and Platte rivers to the hunting grounds on the Smoky Hill and Arkansas rivers. This was probably near the point where the Republican crosses the Nebraska-Kansas state line into Kansas, between the two now abandoned Republican Pawnee sites, 25WT1, and 14RP1, on its south bank. From this point, wild turkeys were "in great abundance, particularly on all the streams we crossed." On 10 September, when Easton reached the confluence of the Republican and Smoky Hill rivers, he noted an abundance of "Sea [sic] vines," which were greatly enjoyed by the horses. This vine was plentiful on all creeks from this point to Fort Leavenworth, and constituted "a fine food for Horses and Mules." This is evidently a mistranscription or misprint for "pea vines," a reference to the well-known legume that produced the groundnut of the Indians, *Apios americana*.[2]

The route map accompanying Easton's report carries but three stream names for the Republican River system—the Republican Fork, the very short

North Fork, and the South Fork. For the country between the Republican and the Platte, no streams are shown other than a few short tributaries of the former. Such longer tributaries as the Frenchman, Red Willow, and Medicine Creek from the north, and the Beaver, Sappa, and Prairie Dog creeks from the south, are either omitted entirely or else are not indicated in anything even remotely approaching their actual lengths. Between the South Platte and the Republican headwaters, a few ponds are shown. The short tributaries entering the Republican from the north are scarcely hinted at on the map, despite Easton's comment of 22 August (Easton 1953:406) to the effect that

> creeks having now become numerous, and our progress consequently very slow, I was almost induced to leave the River, and take the ridges some 8 or 10 miles from it, in order to head many of the Creeks and cross the others near their sources—But as little was known relative to the Republican Fork, and as it is laid down on existing Maps, merely by an imaginary line, I was anxious to examine it practically and fix its direction."

Bryan on the Republican, 1856

Seven years later, in the summer of 1856, Lt. Francis T. Bryan of the Topographical Engineers led a survey party that was exploring for a wagon road from Fort Riley (Bryan 1857) up the Republican River for 100 miles (160 km), then overland to the Platte and up Lodgepole Creek past the Medicine Bow Mountains to Bridger's Pass. Returning, Bryan descended Cache la Poudre Creek to the South Platte and marched down that to the mouth of Beaver Creek a few miles below present Brush, Colorado. On 13 September, he camped 14 miles below Beaver Creek, on the south bank of the river, probably just below present Prewitt Reservoir. Leaving here on 15 September, he marched southeast to reach an unnamed tributary (probably Chief Creek) of "Rock Creek," the present North Fork Republican River, on the 19th.

The first trees reported were on the South Fork Republican above its junction with the Republican at present Benkelman, Nebraska. Below the confluence, clumps of trees appeared in increasing numbers but still mostly in hollows along the bluffs. On 27–28 September, they scouted what they suspected "might be the Frenchman's fork or the Viho Mappy of the [Cheyenne] Indians," as indeed it was. They found it "larger and deeper than the Republican itself" and treeless near its mouth but with clumps of cottonwoods visible five or six miles up its valley. Bryan reported that "an Indian trail runs along this stream and from its head over to the Platte, touching in the interval at several water holes." The tributaries of the Republican were noted as carrying good water, with trees and fine valleys. On 2 October, a large creek was passed, three feet deep and 20 feet wide, which was said "to be a very long stream, having plenty of timber on its banks. It rises very near to the Platte river." Shown on Bryan's map as Deer Creek, this was probably present Medicine Creek, which name does not appear on his map or in his journal report. Of the Republican valley in general, Bryan noted that it had a wide level bottom, intersected by many creeks, "sometimes every mile or two; sometimes every three or four miles. The banks are generally well wooded with ash, elder, boxelder, etc."

Noteworthy, too, is his further comment (Bryan 1857:475) that

> the bottoms on this river afford subsistence to immense herds of buffaloes and elks. The Cheyennes, Comanches, and Kiowas make it their favorite

hunting ground, and on that account have repeatedly expressed their intention of preventing the making of any road along the river. . . . As compared with the valley of the Platte, this valley is much superior, either for the establishment of posts or settlements. The Platte valley furnishes no wood for fuel or for building, and no cultivable soil. The creeks which run into the Republican are numerous, and the banks of all of them are well timbered with hard woods. The bottom also at many points is of great fertility.

Five or six days march below Deer (Medicine) Creek, Lt. Bryan on 8 October left the main party and crossed over to the Solomon, leaving his topographer, John Lambert, in command of the party, which was continuing down the Republican. Ten miles from the Republican, Bryan crossed "a large creek called by the Delawares Beaver creek." Ten miles farther on, he reached Wolf's creek and encamped, on what is today called Prairie Dog Creek. Lambert, meanwhile, commented only on "the extraordinary number of creeks which flow into it [the Republican] on the north side" below the point where Bryan diverged. Bryan's conclusions were that a road along the Republican and up the Frenchman would be the most direct route west, but he urged further explorations before a final decision was reached. "Until last summer," he observed, "the existence of the French Fork was known only to a few trappers and traders, and no mention has hitherto been made of several large streams emptying into the Republican on its north side." All of that country was almost unknown to whites, and Bryan believed that it might be much better suited to white settlement than was generally realized. There were suitable locations for military posts to keep the Indians under control and to protect the settlers who would respond to the attraction of fertile soils in the valley bottoms.

Americans, Frenchmen, and Republican River Toponymy

These and other explorations of the United States Army, including the Corps of Topographical Engineers, provided our first solid information on the toponymy of the upper Republican River basin. On the lower Republican, white settlement had already begun, following the establishment of Fort Riley in 1853 and the construction of several bridges across the river in the next few years. By 1864 there were roads along both banks, and ferry service was replacing bridges washed out by floods as far upstream as the Nebraska line (Root 1934). Beyond that, the Republican valley was still Indian country when Frémont, Easton, and Bryan undertook their observations, without settlers or transportation routes except as they had been traced out by Indians and a few white adventurers and traders who left no records.

Frémont's 1843 trip across the Republican basin gave us only one name recognizable today—Prairie Dog Creek. That the stream to which he applied it is the same one that carries it today is most improbable. Frémont reports it as the second strong-running creek after he left the Solomon drainage westbound, whereas it is today actually the first—indeed, the first of any consequence entering the Republican from the south above White Rock Creek some 60 miles or more downstream. My growing suspicion that Frémont's "Prairie Dog River" was today's Beaver Creek is confirmed in Bryan's journal entry on 1 October 1856 (Bryan 1857:474), which reads "the creek called Beaver creek by the Delawares, and which is supposed to be identical with the Prairie Dog creek of Colonel Fremont, is also a very long stream."

The journal and map left us by Lieutenant Bryan provide much more substantial information. From the South Platte River, as noted above, Bryan headed southeast to strike an unnamed tributary of "Rock Creek." That tributary
was today's Chief Creek, and "Rock Creek" the North Fork Republican, which
was known to the Cheyenne Indians as Chief River (Grinnell 1906). The
"Arickaree" remains the Arickaree (or Arikaree); but Bryan's "Republican
Fork" that the Arikaree joined is the present South Fork Republican. His
"Frenchman's Fork or Viho Mappy of the [Cheyenne] Indians" is the "White
Man's Fork" or "Wah-Seecha Wocca-Pela" [wašiču wak-pala, D. R. Parks personal communication, 10 April 1982] of the Sioux, as recorded a few years later
by Capt. Eugene Ware (1960:339). The Cheyenne name given by Bryan is interestingly remindful of vèhoemàp (or vè ho-màhpe), meaning "white man's
water" or "whiskey," as rendered by the Mennonite missionary Rodolphe Petter (1915:1,105).

Other tributaries mentioned by Bryan and their probable modern equiv-
alents are "Big Timber" for the Burntwood; "Homa or Beaver Crossing" for
Driftwood; "Deer Creek" for Medicine Creek; "Parsnip Creek" for Deer Creek;
and "Obstinate Creek" for Muddy Creek. There is no mention of Sappa Creek
by Lambert after Bryan's separation, or of the 50 or so smaller creeks recorded
in Bryan's table of distances (Bryan 1857:488). At least some of these latter
were named after members of the party (for example, Larned's, Engelman's and
Wood's creeks) but they include no names that can be correlated with present-
day creek designations in this stretch of the Republican valley.

Lt. G. K. Warren's military map of Nebraska and Dakota, based largely on
his explorations in 1855–1857 for the Topographical Engineers (Warren 1875)
but including also data from Frémont and Bryan, shows a somewhat more re-
fined conceptualization of the Republican country, although there is still some
lingering confusion. Above longitude 99° west, it has the first tributary of the
Republican as Prairie Dog or Wolf's Creek. The second is Sappa Creek and the
third is Beaver Creek. Sappa Creek is shown as forking at ca. latitude 40° north,
with Frémont's trace crossing the east fork and running up the west fork as he
reported his march for an afternoon up the "Prairie Dog River" before encamping. Warren's Beaver Creek is a separate stream from Sappa, shown entering the
Republican perhaps some 50 or 60 miles above the latter, about where present
Driftwood Creek joins the Republican. Frémont's trace on Warren's map
crosses the Republican a few miles below the Arikaree-Republican (= South
Fork Republican) junction. Then, some distance north of this crossing point,
Frémont is shown as crossing an unnamed westerly tributary of the
Frenchman's Fork, for which there is no acceptable counterpart on modern
maps of the locality. A short northerly tributary of the Republican, perhaps
Indian Creek or Muddy Creek, may be involved here.

A decade later, in the 1864 campaign against the Republican valley Indians, Capt. Eugene Ware used stream names freely, and most can be reconciled
with today's designations. Here we take note of Medicine Creek, whose upper
reaches are within 25 or 30 miles (48 km) of the Platte valley at Fort McPherson
and thus provided an easy approach to the upper Republican valley. The creek
was called "Medicine Lake Creek" by Ware, from a lake reported to lie at the
head of its north branch. Of this lake there appears to be no certain historical
record, although a marshy tract near the present town of Curtis in the early

days has been suggested as the probable locus of a one-time lake. Ware's "North Sappa" is today's Beaver Creek, and his "South Sappa" is now Sappa. The Sappa was also known sometimes as "Blackwater" or as "Cut Nose" creek.

Sappa is an anglicized corruption of one of several Dakota words variously meaning "black" or "dirty" or "beaver," depending on the pronunciation of the particular term used. According to the Rev. Stephen R. Riggs (1852:44, 185; see also Cook 1882), *cá-pa* is a noun meaning "beaver," where *c* is the sound *ch* in *chain*. *Sa´-pa* is an adjective meaning "black," where *s* has the soft sound of English *s*. *Śa´-pa* (Riggs 1890:441) is an adjective meaning "dirty, defiled, or blackened."

Since Sappa and Beaver creeks were both known to abound in beaver in the early 19th century, one wonders whether the name "Sappa" here was not originally derived in some way from that animal instead of from the derogatory adjective "dirty or blackened," for which no logical or natural explanation appears.

The Frenchman offers a particularly intriguing problem regarding the origin of its name. Was it intended originally to denote a white man, or more specifically, a Frenchman? It seems highly likely that an early white man in the area, whether trader, trapper, or "squaw man," would have been French. It has been suggested that the Frenchman after whom the stream was named may have been Nicholas (Nick) Janis, Indian trader; or perhaps his older brother Antoine Jannis (variously spelled), an interpreter at the Upper Platte agency near Fort Laramie in 1855 and a trader with the Oglala and Brule Sioux at their villages reportedly at least as early as 1843 (Twiss 1856:82), and perhaps there already in the 1830s. Of French Creole descent and born in Missouri, the brothers were brought to the Fort Laramie area by James Bordeaux; both married Oglala women and reared large families, ending their days at Pine Ridge, Antoine about 1897 and Nick about 1905 (Grinnell [1915]1956:126; Hafen 1961:110).

Another prospect for this distinction is Geminien Beauvais, a trader operating in Colorado as early as 1845 and in the Fort Laramie–Fort Pierre area by 1849–1850. He was also the proprietor of a second post five miles east (west?) of Brule, Nebraska, at the old California or Ash Hollow crossing of the Oregon Trail on the South Platte (Hanson 1969). This post would have been within 30 miles or so of the headwaters of the Frenchman River, which was in turn a logical and much used route for Indians traveling from the South Platte to the Republican country to trap, hunt, or raid other hunting Indians. Another member of the Beauvais family owned a ranch in Frontier County, Nebraska, for a time. Boevau Canyon, which joins the Frenchman eight miles north of Trenton, suggests another French family name, unless it is a misreading or misspelling of Beauvais.

Native Equestrian Hunters and Raiders on the Republican

The Indians of the Republican River country by the mid-19th century included very substantial contingents of the mounted and highly mobile bison hunters and tipi-dwellers of the western plains (plates 10.2 and 10.3). Their lifeway, as represented by the Sioux, Cheyennes, and other 19th century native plainsmen, was noted by many contemporary observers and by later scholars. One was Lt. Gouverneur Kemble Warren of the Topographical Engineers, who was detailed in 1857 to survey portions of the route for a road from Fort Snell-

Plate 10.2. Historic bison hunters and gatherers of the Great Plains. *Upper,* Sioux women scraping bison hides and making jerky in a tipi camp. Courtesy National Anthropological Archives, Smithsonian Institution. *Lower,* women gathering prairie turnips for transport to camp by dog and horse travois. From John Mix Stanley in *Schoolcraft,* 1857, vol. 6, plate 30.

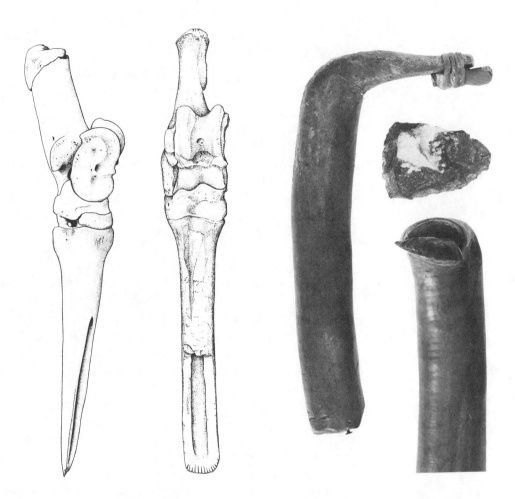

Plate 10.3. Typical hide-dressing tools of the historic Plains Indians used by villagers as well as the hunter-gatherer tribes. *Left*, tooth-edged scraper of bison leg bone; *right*, elkhorn-fleshing adze set with chipped flint blade, often replaced by iron blade.

ing to Fort Laramie by way of the Loup Fork. With characteristic thoroughness and lucidity, Warren included in his report a number of comments on the Indian tribes he met. Of the Sioux, he wrote in part (Warren 1875; cf. Nurge 1975):

> In the summer the Dakotas follow the buffaloes in their range over the prairie, and in the winter fix their lodges in the clusters or fringes of wood along the banks of the lakes and streams. The bark of the cottonwood furnishes food for their horses during the winter snows, and to obtain it many streams have been thinned or entirely stripped of their former beautiful groves. Their horses are obtained by traffic with the Indians farther south, who have stolen them in New Mexico, or caught them wild on the plains toward the Rocky Mountains; considerable numbers are also raised by themselves. The nation is one of the most skillful and war-like, and most numerous in our territory, and could they be made to feel more confidence in their own powers, would be most formidable warriors. In single combat on horseback, they have no superiors, a skill acquired by constant practice with their bows and arrows and lances, with which they succeed in killing their game at full speed. The rapidity with which they shoot

their arrows, and the accuracy of their aim, rivals that of a practiced hand with the revolver.

Although by preference and experience primarily a hunting and gathering people, such 19th-century western plains tribes as the Sioux and Cheyennes, actually relied on a subsistence economy that was a good deal more complicated than Warren's thumbnail sketch implies. The bison hunt was indeed central to their lifeway, but not to the exclusion of all else. Elk, antelope, deer, and other game were extensively hunted, though these forms did not occur in the concentrated quantities provided by the massed herds or in the bulk of individual animals in those herds. Small game was regularly hunted by boys and, when the bison and other large animals failed, by adults as well. Fish and shellfish were occasionally utilized.

Vegetable foods, both wild and domestic, were also important items, particularly when the bison hunt was unsuccessful. Maize was obtained by theft or barter from the Village Indians farther east—the Arikaras, Pawnees, and others. Among native vegetal foods, the prairie turnip, or *tipsina* ranked first. It could be eaten fresh or dried, made into stews and soups along with meat, or stored for use much later. It was also an important article of trade with the village Indians in return for maize and other crops. Less common, but obtainable by trade or seasonal trips, were the groundnut, roots of the *Sagittaria* and other still-water plants, and in hard times, the huge roots of the bush morning glory. Wild fruits and berries were always welcome, especially the choke cherries, wild plums, and buffalo berries, all of which could be eaten fresh or dried and mixed with other items. The Jerusalem artichoke and sunflower seeds were widely used.

Food preparation was neither elaborate nor varied. In camp, the women boiled meat, stews, and similar foods. Men on the hunt broiled meat on live coals or spitted it on a stick over the fire. Birds, rabbits, and other small pieces were covered with live coals and ashes, removed in due course, the skin and feathers stripped off, and the meat eaten. For groups on the move, the morning meal was commonly dispensed with, and the heaviest food intake was in the evening.

To an even greater extent than with the seasonal bison hunters, these nomadic tribes underwent periods of plenty and scarcity, of adequate and inadequate nutrition, of more or less balanced and unbalanced diets. Lacking the food reserves stored underground used among the permanent villages to the east, the hunters had to adjust to even greater extremes in subsistence. The hardships arising from such a routine of living must have exacted a heavy toll in child mortality and among the women during the long hard winters and the rigorous "starving time" of late spring. With the dried meat and stored vegetable reserves dwindling or used up, the game was still lean and scarce from the winter, the grass was not yet greening to feed the herds, and few spring shoots and roots were available for the people to gather to eke out the most meager survival diet.

Gen. R. B. Mitchell's 1864 winter campaign against the Sioux and Cheyennes, extensively reported by Capt. Eugene F. Ware (1960:332–357), provides useful information on how and where the mounted Indians spent their winters. Mitchell's command proceeded south from Camp Cottonwood (later Fort McPherson) on the Platte to Medicine Creek and on to the Red Willow and

Frenchman. On Red Willow Creek, the cottonwood timber was very dense and along the stream were "signs of great Indian camps. We had evidently got right into the country where the Indians lived, and where they had their permanent villages. We could see where they had been cutting down the limbs of the cottonwoods for their ponies to browse on, and the grass was pretty well eaten off around in the neighborhood." Farther south, on the Republican River at the Big Timbers in present Dundy and Hitchcock counties, Nebraska, was "where the buffaloes used to live, and here we found Indian signs everywhere prevalent." Continuing southward, the expedition crossed Beaver and Sappa creeks, then known as the North and South Sappa creeks.

Between 15 and 26 January, Mitchell's expedition marched an estimated 361 miles and saw almost no Indians. Its positive accomplishments, beyond giving the commanding officer's name to the principal tributary of Medicine Creek, were disappointing. Mitchell accordingly decided to burn the Indians out. By telegraph and otherwise, the signal was given on 27 January 1865, that the prairies be set afire simultaneously at every ranch and post between Fort Kearney and Denver. The order, says Ware (1960:355), "was fully carried out. The country was fired for 300 miles. . . . The fire swept the country clean; three days afterward it was burning along the banks of the Arkansas, far to the south, over which it passed in places and ran out down in the Panhandle of Texas." I have been unsuccessful in my search for independent record of this alleged pyrotechnical maneuver or its possible effects on the Indians in the region said to have been burned over.

Lieutenant Warren's 1857 plans to survey the Black Hills brought strenuous objections and threats of hostile reactions from the Tetons with whom he was in conference. Among several arguments advanced by the Indians, and acknowledged as valid by Warren, was the following one (Warren 1875:19), written in early September:

> They were encamped near large herds of buffalo, whose hair not being sufficiently grown to make robes, the Indians were, it may be said, actually herding the animals. No one was permitted to kill any in the large bands for fear of stampeding the others, and only such were killed as straggled away from the main herds. Thus the whole range of the buffalo was stopped so that they could not proceed south, which was the point to which they were traveling. The intention of the Indians was to retain the buffalo in their neighborhood till their skins would answer for robes, then to kill the animals by surrounding one band at a time and completely destroying each member of it. In this way no alarm is communicated to the neighboring bands, which often remain quiet almost in sight of the scene of slaughter.

Beyond this, the Indians argued that treaty concessions gave to whites only the privilege of passage along designated roads, not the license to travel freely elsewhere and frighten away the buffalo "by their careless manner of hunting them." The military usefulness of such data as could be gotten by Warren's surveys away from the established routes of travel was also recognized by the Indians.

The Sioux around the Black Hills with whom Warren was dealing were the Miniconjous, a division of the Tetons, who ranged southward to the Platte.

There they were in touch with the Oglalas around Fort Laramie and the Brules, both of whom shared the same attitudes and views concerning the white man's expansionist moves along the Oregon-California trails. Farther south, the Cheyennes and Arapahos on the upper Arkansas and South Platte rivers, friendly and often allied with the Sioux bands, were reacting in a similar fashion to white travel west through the hunting territory they claimed. William Fitzpatrick, the United States agent in charge of the Upper Platte agency that was responsible for the government's dealings with these Indians, noted in his report of 1853 (Fitzpatrick 1853) that the lands claimed by these tribes had not been owned or occupied by any of them even a half century earlier, and that their claims to ownership were valid only in proportion to their military capabilities and to the extent that they were able to muster the manpower to defend them against any challenges from other Indians or from the whites.

To protect westbound travelers on a main thoroughfare across the central plains, the United States government erected Fort Kearny (Fort Kearney after 1857) on the south bank of the Platte River at the head of the Grand Island in 1848. Increasing depredations by the Indians when army regulars were withdrawn from western garrison and escort duties for Civil War service in the East led to the establishment of more posts along the trail—Fort McPherson (1863–1880) east of the fork of the Platte, and Fort Sedgwick (1864–1871) near Julesburg, Colorado. Farther south, Fort Hays (1865–1889) and Fort Wallace (1865–1882) were erected on the developing Smoky Hill route. Forts McPherson, Hays, and Wallace were destined for lively action in the final days of the Indians in the Republican country.

The Civil War years, and those immediately preceding and following, were not good ones for the Pawnees on the Loup River. The government's failure to provide the promised firearms for self-defense left the villages vulnerable to repeated attacks by the relentless Sioux. In 1862, 1864, and 1865, severe grasshopper infestations heavily damaged early plantings of maize (see plate 2.10). In 1863, their agent (Lushbaugh 1864:252) reported an "immense crop of corn, beans, and other edibles. . . . For the first time in their lives the Pawnees will have not only a full supply for all their wants, but, if properly husbanded, a large surplus to sell." Hunting was becoming increasingly uncertain and of highly variable productivity; but in the summer of 1865, when the Pawnees hunted unmolested on the Arkansas River, they obtained the meat and hides of 1,600 bison, antelope, elk, and deer in an exceptionally rewarding enterprise. A successful winter hunt was reported again in 1866.

In that same year, however, several charges were leveled against the Pawnees for molesting the whites who were crowding in on their Republican River hunting grounds. Maj. Gen. W. F. Cloud of the Kansas State Militia reported (Cloud 1866:222) to Col. E. B. Taylor, superintendent of Indian affairs at St. Louis, the following offenses allegedly committed or participated in by the Pawnees: (a) the murder of a white man by three Indians dressed in U.S. military clothing and carrying sabers and revolvers; (b) the killing of six men on a tributary of the Republican River, 20 miles west of Lake Sibley near Concordia; (c) a Pawnee visit to a white settlement on White Rock Creek in which corn was stolen, people robbed, and a white woman raped; and (d) an invasion by 800 Pawnees and Omahas of cornfields on the Solomon River, threats against the white property owners, and claims that the lands on which the farms were located belonged to the Indians as their hunting grounds. In his reply, Superintendent Taylor promised redress for any wrongdoing, provided proof of tribal identity of the culprits could be established.

Near or at the front of the growing turmoil involving the Republican country—that is, everything between the Arkansas and the Platte rivers—were the Cheyennes, with the Oglala and Brule Sioux from the Fort Laramie vicinity participating as willing allies. The Chivington massacre at Sand Creek in 1864 left deeply smoldering resentments among the Cheyennes; and these were exacerbated in April 1867 by Gen. W. S. Hancock's burning of a Cheyenne and Arapaho tipi camp of 130 lodges on Pawnee Fork 30 miles west of Fort Larned. During much of the summer of that year, in pursuit of elusive Dakota raiders, Lt. Col. George A. Custer led a force of the Seventh Cavalry from Fort Hays north to Fort McPherson, thence up the South Platte to Fort Sedgwick, and back to Fort Wallace. Lt. Lyman S. Kidder and a detail of 10 soldiers from Fort Sedgwick, searching for Custer to deliver dispatches, missed the meeting and were destroyed on Beaver Creek by Indians on 1 July 1867.

As the Civil War wound down and westward expansion resumed along the emigrant roads, the planning and construction of railroads to the Pacific were speeded up. Track laying begun west of the Missouri River by the Union Pacific in 1863 reached Fort Kearney via the Platte in 1866 and was completed across Nebraska by 1869. Farther south, along the Smoky Hill route, the Kansas Pacific reached Salina in April and Hays in October of 1867, Wallace in 1868, and Denver in 1870. Along both lines, the Indians lost few opportunities to harass the surveyors, graders, tie cutters, and other work crews, so that as the work camps moved westward they relied increasingly on the army for protection (Montgomery 1928). The raids seem to have been mostly by parties of Oglala and Brule Sioux and Cheyennes, seeking desperately to protect the hunting lands they claimed against the inroads of more and more whites. Treaties broken, misunderstood, misrepresented, or otherwise disregarded were blamed by both sides. The raiders when pressed generally headed for the Republican valley, where, by splitting into smaller groups and dispersing, they were usually successful in eluding pursuit. In 1867, the Upper Platte agency reported that 170 lodges of Cut Off and smaller bands of the Oglalas, and more than a thousand Brules under Spotted Tail, were wintering or ranging in the Republican valley.

1868–1869: Beecher Island and Summit Springs

By 1868, conditions were approaching a climax for the Indians of the region. In June, a party of Cheyenne Dog Soldiers led by Tall Bull raided the Kaw Indian reservation at Council Grove but was driven off and headed west, committing various outrages against white settlers as they moved along. In August, Black Kettle led another Cheyenne raid on Spillman Creek in Lincoln County and then went on to the Solomon valley, killing a number of settlers and capturing several women, after which the Indians crossed over to the Republican valley and headed west. From the Upper Platte agency, it was reported in 1868 that "nearly all the Brule Sioux, Cheyennes, and Arapahos have gone south to the Republican" to hunt bison (Sheridan 1882; Garfield 1932; Wilson 1904; Cooper 1868:251).

The continuing Indian depredations, followed by increasingly strident complaints from worried settlers, finally prompted stronger measures by the military. In late August, Bvt. Col. George A. Forsyth was directed by Gen. Philip Sheridan, commanding the Military Division of the Missouri, to raise a party of 50 scouts from among the frontiersmen—farmers, traders, trappers, ex-soldiers, and others—to keep an eye on the hostiles in the districts of the Republican headwaters and to punish small parties if they could be brought to bay. Forsyth scouted the Beaver and Prairie Dog creeks, then followed an Indian trail west into the upper Republican country. On 17 September, his command was attacked by a large force of Sioux, Cheyennes, and portions of other tribes (fig. 2.2). Digging in on a sandy, sun-drenched island on the Arikaree Fork, 17 miles (27 km) south of present Wray, Colorado, the scouts fought off repeated attacks until they were relieved on 25 September by black troops from Fort Wallace. Forsyth reported five dead and 17 wounded in his command, and at least 35 hostile Indians killed (Berthrong 1963:310ff). Other estimates of Indian casualties range from an unlikely and undocumented several hundred to an equally preposterous figure of nine by Grinnell (1956:279; Powell 1981, vol. 1, p. 582) on the authority of his Cheyenne informants.

In November, when the Cheyennes and their associates had returned to winter quarters far to the south of the Republican and Arkansas rivers, George A. Custer was sent against them in a winter campaign. Returned hostiles and innocent friendlies, encamped together on the Washita, were attacked and the Indians were severely defeated (Grinnell 1956:298).

In the spring of 1869, a large force of Dog Soldiers under Tall Bull, allied with some Oglalas, headed north again and carried out a series of raids through northern Kansas, terrorizing whites and friendly Indians alike. On the Saline River in Lincoln County, Tall Bull's raiders destroyed a Swedish settlement on 30 May, killing 13 persons and taking two women captives. The Indians then turned west. In June, Gen. E. A. Carr, at the head of eight companies of the Fifth Cavalry and 150 Pawnee scouts under Capt. Luther North, was dispatched from Fort McPherson to the Republican valley, with orders to insure the security of the Nebraska and Kansas settlements, to continue into the Colorado territory, and specifically "to drive the Indians out of the Republican country." (King 1960a, 1960b, 1963; Orders, Bvt. Brig. Gen. G. D. Ruggles to Bvt. Maj. Gen. E. A. Carr, 7 June 1869, National Archives and Records Service, RG 98).

Proceeding down Medicine Creek to the Republican valley, Carr's command spent a month in zigzagging across the upper Republican drainage, skirmishing occasionally with parties of hostile Indians. By July, Carr was in the present Colorado area, touching at Beecher Island on 9 July. Two days later, his command caught up with Tall Bull and his Dog Soldiers encamped at Summit Springs, 13 miles southeast of present Sterling, Colorado, on a small tributary of the South Platte just outside the Republican drainage. High water in the South Platte had delayed the Indians in their crossing, after which they planned to continue northward into friendly Sioux country (fig. 2.2).

On a Sunday afternoon, 11 July, Carr's forces charged the Cheyenne camp in two waves, one to isolate the horse herd and the other concentrating on the tipi camp scattered for a half mile along the creek below the spring. Although the attack may not have been the surprise hoped for, owing to an alert herdboy who aroused the camp, the troops soon won control of the field of battle (Grinnell 1956:310ff.; Berthrong 1963:340ff.; Powell 1981, vol. 2, pp. 728–735). Of the Cheyennes, 52 were reported killed, 18 women and children captured, and several hundred fighting men scattered. General Order No. 48, issued at the headquarters of the Department of the Platte in Omaha on 3 August 1869 listed a "portion of the property captured: 274 horses; 144 mules; 9,300 pounds of dried meat; 84 lodges complete; 56 rifles; 22 revolvers; 40 bows and arrows; 50 pounds of powder; etc., etc." There was also $1,500 in cash, of which $900 was given to the one white female survivor, Mrs. Weichel, injured in an unsuccessful attempt by Tall Bull to kill her when the troops attacked (Grinnell 1973:203). The second captive had been tomahawked when the fighting began. No white soldiers or Pawnee scouts died in the engagement, and only four or five horses were lost. Everything combustible in the Indian camp was burned, one report stating that 160 fires were burning simultaneously in the destruction. The captured horses were divided among the victorious soldiers, and the prisoners were sent to Omaha. Tall Bull was killed. The survivors eventually regrouped and fled northward to join the Sioux.

Summit Springs has been called the "last significant Indian battle on the central plains" (King 1963:118). The Cheyenne Dog Soldiers, depending on one's point of view, were the elite of the tribe's fighting men defending their homeland and hunting grounds, or they were a merciless horde of bloodthirsty killers. In either case, at Summit Springs they ceased to be an effective fighting force, and white control of the Republican country had been substantially advanced. A year later, when General Carr led a 30-man detail on a four-day reconnaissance down Medicine Creek and then west and south along the Republican, he reported no Indians, although his men saw "a few abandoned Teepee frames made of willows which still retained their leaves" (King 1963:123). With his defeat of Tall Bull's warrior band, Carr had essentially fulfilled his charge to clear the Republican country of Indians, although hunting sorties, sporadic raids, and occasional killings took place in the area even after Summit Springs.

After Summit Springs   White settlement of the upper Republican valley began almost immediately in the early 1870s (Olson 1966:171; Riley 1966). First came professional bison hunters and the traders to supply them, and then the homesteaders and ranchers. The Beaver-Sappa junction district was settled in the fall of 1870, Cambridge in 1871, and Culbertson in 1873 as cattlemen's headquarters. Land developers located in Omaha, Nebraska City, and other more easterly cities sent out colonies that settled Riverton in 1870, Alma and Republican City in 1871, and Bloomington in 1872. Farther west, on the Republican headwaters, settlement was initiated by cattlemen, who established their ranches on the spring-fed permanent streams. One of the earliest of these was the Twenty One outfit from Corpus Christi, Texas, which settled in the Wray-Vernon district in 1873. Of its three camps, one was on Chief Creek, then known as Pappoose Creek.

With white settlers came surveyors, and from these came brief but sometimes enlightening reports on the contemporary landscape. In 1873, for example, John A. Lessig (1873:548) noted in his general description of township 3 south, range 43 west, that "there is considerable bottom wood on the Arickaree and also in the ravine in the northeast corner of the township." The ravine is not further identified but must have been a southerly tributary of the Arikaree.

Four years later and a few miles to the north, Adams Fahringer included in his general description of township 2 south, range 43 west, which centers around Beecher Island, the following (Fahringer 1877:569, 598):

> The surface of the township is generally hilly but with very fine grass and well adapted to grazing. There is a large amount of timber along the Arickaree and Black Wolf creeks. On the bottom lands of the creeks are fine meadows, and good homesteads and pre-emptions can be located.
> On a small island in the [Arikaree] creek, I found a revolver and evidence of fortifications thrown up. Also part of the skeleton of a man, and the heads of three horses.
> I think this is where Capt. Forsyth had his Indian fight in 1868 or 1869.

Two miles south of Beecher Island, Fahringer recorded a ravine "containing a fine growth of willow, cottonwood, plum, and grape." Farther north, he reported timber in a ravine that emptied southward into Black Wolf Creek.

On the South Fork Republican, in 1878 Jason Fahringer described township 5 south, range 43 west, in which present Bonny Reservoir is situated (Fahringer 1878:139):

> The surface of this township, except the river bottom, is high roling [sic] prairies. The soil is generally sandy, 2nd rate, with a excelent [sic] growth of Bunch and Buffalo grass that portion of the tp through which the [South Fork]River flows is 1st rate agriculture and hay land, with plenty of water for Iragation [sic] and great portions is taken by settlers There are several stock ranches in this tp with Plenty of water in the River and big timber creek.

In 1948, portions of this township were resurveyed by the Bureau of Land Management for the Bureau of Reclamation in connection with the construction of Bonny dam and reservoir. The surveyor, F. W. Forrest, noted that clumps of young cottonwood and willow stood along the streams, which included the South Fork Republican, Landsman Creek, and Bonny Creek. Of these stands, he observed (Forrest 1948:769) that "these trees have grown mostly since the disastrous flood of 1935 which washed away most of the mature timber."

For the North Republican, there seems to be no mention of timber stands by any of the surveyors whose records I have seen, although the potential of that stream and of Chief Creek for stock raising and the abundance of water that could be used for irrigation were clearly recognized.

The surveyors' records provide an interesting and useful supplement to the earlier and more extended descriptions left us by Easton in 1849 and Bryan in 1856. They suggest that the South Fork Republican as far as Black Wolf Creek and perhaps to the vicinity of Beecher Island supported some stands of hardwood timber. Whether these were continuous along the stream banks or, as seems more likely, were in scattering open clumps poorly suited to use as wintering quarters for the Indians is not made clear. It is of interest to note, however, Grinnell's ([1915] 1956:189 n.6) observation that "the Arickaree Fork of the Republican was sometimes called Timber Creek or Thickwood. The Pawnees called it *Lŭ k ŭ tí kŭ rŭ*—much wood or 'timber is abundant.'" By modern linguists, this is written *ra kis ti kari*', "wood is abundant" (D. R. Parks, personal communication, 10 April 1982). One wonders whether the seeming disappearance or sharp diminution of the streamside timber stands was directly linked with the common and widespread Indian custom in historic times of cutting down cottonwoods in winter to feed their horses as Warren (1875:49) indicated. Major floods may have operated in the same direction against the sandy channel banks.

Summit Springs notwithstanding, the Indians were not yet finished with the Republican country. Even as white settlers moved into the newly cleared district, Indian hunting sorties continued in the upper reaches of the basin, and there were apparently some more or less permanent camps. To insure the safety of the incoming whites and establish a measure of tranquility, Camp Red Willow was established on the Republican at the east side of Red Willow Creek from April to September of 1872. In August, some 2,500 Pawnees made their way through the settlers to hunt above Red Willow Creek. In that summer, too, the Grand Duke Alexis, brother of the Czar of Russia, made a well-publicized bison hunt on Red Willow Creek northwest of present McCook. Coming to the Republican via Fort McPherson and accompanied by Buffalo Bill Cody as guide, the visiting Europeans were treated to an Indian hunting exhibition by a large party of Brules under Spotted Tail. This hunt appears to have been highlighted by the performance of one Two Spears or Two Lances, who reportedly drove an arrow through a bison bull, retrieved the arrow, and presented it to the Duke as a souvenir of the trip. In addition to the Brules, there was a small band of Cut Off Oglalas who had a permanent village near Stockville on Medicine Creek and occasionally moved to Stinking Water Creek farther west during the winter.

Massacre Canyon, 1873

Among the Indians, the old tribal hatreds and animosities remained. Of the intertribal encounters of this period in the Republican country, probably the most notable one occurred on 5 August 1873, near the site of present Trenton, Nebraska, four years after Carr had "cleared" the valley of Indians. Like contemporary versions of the conflicts at Beecher Island and Summit Springs, accounts of this engagement vary considerably in their details (Burgess 1874:194; White 1874; Riley 1973; Blaine and Blaine 1977; see also *Nebraska History Magazine*, vol. 16, no. 3, July–September 1935). The principals here were a Pawnee hunting party of 350 to 400 persons, including 150 women and children, and a war party of 600 to 1,000 Oglala and Brule Sioux. Both parties were in the region by permission and were accompanied by white trail agents authorized to prevent disorders between whites and Indians or between Indians. For the Pawnees, July had been a month of successful hunting on the Beaver and Prairie Dog creeks in Kansas and Nebraska. In early August, claiming a kill of 800 bison and "over 300 horses well laden" with dried meat and hides, they turned north to the Republican main stem and the road back to their reservation at Genoa. Unbeknown to them, apparently, their movements had been under surveillance for several days by Sioux scouts. On the fateful 5th of August, overwhelmingly outnumbered and caught by surprise as they prepared to kill bison once more on a nearby divide, the Pawnees were attacked and lost at least 69 persons, 100 horses, and all the meat and hides from the preceding month's labors. The women, children, and pack animals sought safety by fleeing down the canyon while the mounted Sioux rode along the ridge on either side, firing into the scattered and disorganized fugitives. Among the dead were

Sky Chief and several other prominent chiefs and leaders of the Pawnees. When word of the massacre reached reservation officials at Genoa, some efforts were made to recover at least a part of the lost meat and hides, most of which seem to have fallen into the hands of white settlers rather than to the victorious Sioux. These efforts were only partially successful. Today, the massacre site is memorialized by a 35-foot shaft of Minnesota granite, erected originally in 1930 overlooking the field of slaughter but subsequently removed to a conspicuous spot near U.S. Route 36 (fig. 2.3; plate 6.3).

As one result of this affair, perpetrated while the Pawnees were on a legitimate tribal hunt, the Sioux were forbidden to leave their reservation north of the Platte River for further hunting. For the Pawnees, beleaguered and threatened with extermination by the Brules and Oglalas all through their reservation years, and never provided with the guns and protection promised them by the United States government, Massacre Canyon was another setback, the latest in a long series of costly reversals and disappointments. Sioux raids against the Pawnee villages continued even after Massacre Canyon. White settlers were pressing in closer on the reservation lands, stealing timber on an ever-increasing scale and agitating for the opening of the Indian lands to farmers. Indian attempts to raise their own food were frustrated by drought, grasshoppers, the Colorado potato beetle, and other adversities—natural, social, and political. Barred by the government from tribal bison hunts in the old tradition and still threatened by the Sioux, the Pawnees found it impossible to feed themselves and maintain their tribal integrity (Wishart 1979).

For many years, relations had been more or less harmonious between the Nebraska Pawnees and their southern linguistic kindred, the Wichitas and other Caddoan speakers in the Indian Territory. Group visits had given the Pawnees some familiarity with the lands to the south, and a band of nearly 300 had moved to the vicinity of the Wichitas already in 1873. When the Wichitas, now greatly reduced in numbers, invited the Pawnees to join them, a decision was not long in coming. In 1874, the Nebraska Pawnees in council voted unanimously to move south, despite their agent's objection. By summer 1875, within two years of the massacre on the Republican, the Pawnees gave up their lands and settlements on the Loup River and moved to a new home in the Indian Territory.

Thus ended a tribal stay of several centuries on the prairies of Nebraska and Kansas, and a long record of a Village Indian people who sought, for a time successfully, to establish and maintain an intimate working relationship with the Republican River country. Regrets at leaving the land of their birth and the graves of their fathers would come later.

Indians Leave the Republican Country

Two years after the departure of the Pawnees from their longtime Nebraska homelands, the first railroad—the Burlington—was started up the Republican valley, reaching Wray in 1882. By 1880, the southern tier of Nebraska counties from Webster to Red Willow, and the northernmost Kansas counties from Republic to Decatur, numbered their white populations by the thousands. The Indians had become a decided minority, but as late as 1878 they struck one last blow at the whites by whom they were being supplanted. This happened in late summer, when more than 200 Northern Cheyennes under Dull Knife and Little Wolf fled imprisonment at Fort Reno, Oklahoma, and headed north across

Kansas and Nebraska toward their northern homelands. In Kansas, Rawlins and Decatur counties were hard hit by the Indians; Sappa Creek valley and the town of Oberlin were terrorized; property was stolen or destroyed, women ravished, and some 32 settlers were killed before the fugitive raiders passed on and the reign of terror finally came to an end (Pickering 1906:388).

As I have suggested in an earlier chapter, the prehistoric antecedents of the Pawnees of history are believed to have been among the early Village Indians whose archeological remains are widely scattered through the Republican, Loup, Blue, and other river drainages of the Nebraska-Kansas prairies and plains. The steps by which the prehistoric peoples became the historic Pawnees are still unclear, but the search for clues continues. What is clear, however, is that at some period before the Pawnees came into contact with the 16th- and 17th-century European invaders, the far-flung hamlets and homesteads of antiquity were abandoned, perhaps for climatic reasons, and their former inhabitants moved eastward to an environment climatically better suited to a lifeway resting in considerable part on maize horticulture. The lifeway that had flourished here for some centuries, though not without significant changes, eventually became untenable, reflecting the irreconcilable differences between two radically different lifestyles—the Indian's and the white man's—and the failure of the dominant political system to adjust to the problems of a minority group with sharply dissimilar customs, viewpoints, and values.

Time was running out also for the mounted bison hunters in the Republican country so that they did not long outlast the Pawnees there. White settlement was putting ever more pressure on the dwindling bison herds and reducing the tracts in which the Dakota Sioux and their friends could camp, hunt, and winter in the Republican basin. In 1871, the Oglalas and associated Cheyennes and Arapahos from the Upper Platte agency were placed under the Red Cloud agency, which was moved in 1873 to the White River near Camp Robinson (now Fort Robinson) in northwestern Nebraska; to the Missouri River at the mouth of Medicine Creek in present South Dakota in 1877; and in 1878 to White Clay Creek just north of the Nebraska–South Dakota border, eventually to become the Pine Ridge agency. The Brules and other bands from the North Platte were assigned to the Spotted Tail agency, moved to White River near the Nebraska–South Dakota border in 1874, and to the head of Beaver Creek in northwestern Nebraska in 1875. Eventually, following a brief move to the Missouri River 60 miles above Yankton, this became the Rosebud agency. The Northern Cheyennes, active participants with the western Sioux in the Custer defeat at the Little Bighorn in June 1876, and mainly responsible for the Oberlin raid of 1878, were finally placed on a reservation in Montana, while the Southern Cheyennes went to Oklahoma (Hill 1974).

And so, by 1879, a decade after General Carr received his orders to clear the Republican country of Indians, that clearance was at last consummated.

Chapter 11 Reflections on Republican River Prehistory: Retrospect and Prospects

In assessing the place of the Republican River basin in Plains prehistory, it should be recognized first that the cultural history of this area, like its general environmental setting, can be seen as a microcosm of the Great Plains generally. This, of course, does not mean that the details of its cultural history as we view it are uniform throughout in all particulars or that there were not important differences from locality to locality and from period to period through time. These things varied, often significantly, as did the landscape, its weather, and its plant and animal life. What is implied is that the peoples and cultures or lifeways that occupied the basin or portions of it over the millennia provide a useful and probably fairly representative sampling of what was going on in the larger region of which it forms a part. Incomplete though our studies obviously are, it is already clear that our data sample comprises the major known regional cultural horizons or traditions and that it spans a period of upward of 10,000 years preceding the arrival of Euro-Americans on the scene.

This perspective on the human experience in the Great Plains is in striking contrast with the prevailing dogma as recently as my own arrival on the scene. When I was growing up in central Kansas, the traveler crossing Nebraska, Kansas, and eastern Colorado usually wearied quickly of the monotony along the routes followed westward by the main thoroughfares, whether rail or highway. These were designed to follow the lines of least resistance, to traverse the "empty" spaces as quickly as possible. Few of these transients knew, or cared, what lay beyond their limited field of vision. It was generally seen as a land of little relief, few trees, and scanty rainfall—of sun and wind and grass. Here, so it was said, one could look farther and see less than anywhere else on earth. And when the "dirty thirties" plagued the land with their hot dry winds, recurrent dust storms, and empty thunderheads, many of those hardy souls who had chosen to try living on the land gave up the struggle and moved away in search of a better refuge or a new utopia.

Before the 1930s, when systematic and sustained archeological exploration in the plains can be said to have begun (Wedel 1981, 1982a), the region was generally regarded as unfit for human occupation until the horse was introduced by the Spanish in the 16th and 17th centuries. By some, the rifle and the plow were added as further requirements for successful occupancy. All this was anthropological embellishment for the Great American Desert view of the American West by eastern intellectuals. The argument ran something like this, as put by F. H. Sterns in 1918: successful pursuit of the bison, without which there could be no human occupation of the treeless belt beyond the Mississippi-Missouri, was impossible without the horse; the horse was introduced by the European explorers in or after the 16th century; therefore, the peopling of the plains was necessarily a recent event, probably not long antedating the coming of the white man. This general view was repeated again and again, by Lewis Henry Morgan (White 1959), by Clark Wissler (1907, 1914), and by others, with or without anthropogeographical training, generally with only limited direct contact and no prolonged residential experience in the region, and usually without any regard for what modifications of viewpoint might be necessary if and when archeological investigations replaced ethnographic theorizing.

As recently as 1928, a foremost American anthropologist, Alfred L. Kroeber, was particularly explicit and emphatic about the derivative nature of Plains Indian culture. Thus, he suggested (Kroeber 1928:394–396; 1939:78) that

> the largely negative results of archeology indicate the Plains as only sparsely or intermittently inhabited for a long time. The population was probably in the main a Woodland one along the eastern margin. . . . The western Plains on the whole were still little utilized in this early period . . . , [when the people] probably clung in the main to the foot of the Rockies, where wood, water, and shelter were more abundant, fauna and flora more variegated, a less specialized mechanism sufficient; and from there they made incursions into the Plains to hunt their big game. . . . The Plains traits that have historical depth . . . seem Woodland, and date from the time when such Plains culture as there was constituted a margin at the fringe of a natural area.

Still later, Kroeber expressed the view (1948:823) that "the tepee or conical skin tent dragged on poles; the ordered camp circle of tepees; the bedding, clothing, and even receptacles of skins and rawhide" were of late origin and "had no counterpart in the region even as late as 1600. As a culture area the Plains had a late brilliance, with its war bonnets and ponies; but it had no historical depth." All of this he articulated despite the fact that W. J. McGee and Cyrus Thomas in 1905 had explicitly noted the narratives left by the 16th-century Vásquez de Coronado expedition to the middle Arkansas River in central Kansas and correctly deduced from the Querechos they met that a bison-hunting subsistence economy *was* possible on the plains without the horse. Only the absence of comparable historical records for other regions farther north, they noted, prevented our knowing whether the same dog-nomad lifeway was being practiced there simultaneously and perhaps earlier.

There was archeological evidence even in Kroeber's time to suggest that the older views might be untenable or at least in need of modification. As early as 1895 a chipped projectile point had been found in direct association with a large fossil bison on 12 Mile Creek in Logan County, Kansas (Williston 1902); and much later, there were the Folsom, New Mexico, findings in 1926 (Wormington 1957). These last made it abundantly clear that earlier suspected associations between man and long-extinct animals would have to be taken seriously instead of being dismissed out of hand by doubting anthropologists.

Two major points have emerged with stark clarity from the archeological work since 1930: first, the multimillennial antiquity of human occupation of the region, for most of which time span a relatively sparse and scattered population can be inferred; and second, the profound importance throughout those millennia of the bison as a prime subsistence resource. Archeological fieldwork, augmented by various interdisciplinary researches, has shown beyond question what should have been apparent from the Coronado narratives, namely, that bison could be procured in quantity long before men learned how to ride horses, that in hunting this animal as a major staple a highly mobile lifeway with a minimum amount of portable household and hunting gear was essential, and that methods of food preservation and concentration to reduce bulk and weight were necessary. These things, in effect the quintessence of the Plains Indian lifeway, applied whether humans or dogs functioned as beasts of burden, no less than to the horse when at long last it finally became available thousands of years after humans had moved into the plains and made them their home, seasonally if not year-round. That the bison varied in numbers and in distribution from time to time over the millennia and were not always and everywhere an invariably certain food resource is highly likely. After all, variability—environmental, demographic, and other forms—is a conspicuous characteristic of the plains region and presumably has always been so.

The fact of primary reliance on the bison for human subsistence, perhaps modified from time to time as bison numbers and occurrence varied, and the readily observed effects of this dependence on native peoples whose cultures changed when they entered the region, led to its broad characterization as a distinct culture area when Otis T. Mason in 1896 felt the need for a classification system in the studies of artifacts and of museum collections. Ever since Mason's initial efforts, despite many variations and redefinitions, a key criterion has consistently been that of primary reliance on the bison for food, shelter, and the tools and utensils for daily living. Mason correlated the Plains culture area more or less with the grasslands, and this would seem a sounder scheme than some of those who shift the boundaries widely and freely—for example, east to the Mississippi-Missouri junction or west to include Nevada and Utah, and so on.

It has become fashionable in some quarters to belittle the culture area concept as an imprecise and obsolete device, of no real use to modern studies with anthropogeographic implications. That no hard and fast boundaries can be drawn, nor overall uniformity demonstrated, is true. It seems true also that there need not be insistence on a culture area as an unchanging phenomenon through all time, any more than the vegetational or life zones of the natural historian must remain forever unchanging. To an older generation of archeologists and ethnologists at least, the term *Plains culture area* connotes something rather distinctive, with wide and significant differences from such other areas as the Southwest, the Northeast, or the Northwest Coast. Absolute and everlasting distinctions among the various areas are neither apparent, expected, nor required.

To the two major conclusions noted above—(a) the multimillennial antiquity of humans on the Great Plains and (b) their primary reliance during that time on the bison for subsistence—we may here add a third consideration: the environmental uncertainties, and especially the vagaries of the climate. Some of its possible effects on man and his cultural adaptations through time have been noted in earlier chapters, as have some of the effects on the native flora and fauna. Notwithstanding, the emphasis placed on bison hunting, after the extinction of the mammoth some 11,000 years ago, seems never to have been abandoned so long as there was big game to hunt and political factors permitted. Following the introduction of cultigens—beans, maize, squash, and sunflower—during the first centuries of the Christian Era and the increasingly heavy reliance on them through time by eastern Plains Village peoples, only some rearranging of the scheduling of the bison harvest was necessary on the part of successive peoples and cultures. In effect, the native human history of the Republican River valley in Holocene times, like that throughout the Great Plains generally, is a story of patterned cultural adjustments to a series of environmental changes, some major and some minor, in space and through time. The environmental limitations that once appeared to nonresident latter-day observers so unremittingly hostile have proved, on closer scrutiny by various investigative techniques, to be much less restrictive to human occupation than was realized before systematic archeological investigations were undertaken in depth. Environment has been a potent conditioning factor in the native cultures, but not a determinant. It has undoubtedly been influential in leading to cultural changes and has allowed the exercising of different options as natural circumstances altered through time.

On the historical level, the strong tendency for tribes from outside the plains to modify their material culture complex and their food-getting strategies when they entered the plains region, attracted there by its immense reserves of protein on the hoof and its wide open spaces, has been outlined by Oliver (1962). Often differing in language, and in religious, political, and social systems, they generally adopted the mobile lifeways of the natives they found in the region, already adjusted to its peculiarities. By sign language, they compensated for their linguistic diversity, so that a Shoshonian-speaking Comanche from Texas meeting an Algonkian-speaking Blackfoot from Alberta on the plains of Wyoming could make himself understood.

The Republican headwaters beyond the 100th-101st meridians have been, in historic times, mainly a semiarid landscape with limited surface water, largely without timber, and unsuited to the cultivation of native American food crops without irrigation and perhaps other special techniques. Of the known cultigens, only the native sunflower could have flourished in this section without special attention. As such, the landscape has been used throughout a dozen millennia principally for the hunting of big game, notably bison and pronghorn. As a hunting area, its use by humans is now seen to extend back to the time when the mammoth, camel, ground sloth, and other forms long since extinct roamed the land and flourished in what may have been a savanna or grassy parkland setting unlike that known to us today. That Clovis, Hell Gap, probably Folsom, and other representatives of the western Llano and Folsom-Plano Early Big Game Hunters were in and through the region is virtually certain, though their trails are not easily detected or traced out. It is probably only a matter of time before more kill sites and living places are recognized and explored. Sparse, scattered, and highly mobile populations, not unlike those postulated long ago by Kroeber, and consequent lightly marked, low-profile occupation sites may be anticipated. Since many of these ancient sites were on a terrain and in an environmental setting unlike that of the present, the normal processes of erosion, deposition, and general alteration of the landscape may be expected to have obliterated many, and doubtless has covered many others that still await discovery, by accident or intent.

Following the western-oriented Early Big Game Hunters in the archeological sequence came the succession of groups designated the Plains Archaic. In the Republican River drainage, such sites seem to be rare between ca. 5,000 and 2,000 B.C., perhaps reflecting the adverse climate, hot and dry, inferred for the Altithermal or Atlantic episode by paleoclimatologists. It is possible that various erosional processes have brought about changes in the surface topography that have caused us to search in the wrong places for the archeological evidence. In any event, it appears that bone beds such as those that mark the ancient mass game kills of the preceding hunters are absent. The sites identified as Archaic suggest that the people were now exploiting a much wider range of animals, wild vegetal foods, and particularly small game such as reptiles, amphibians, fish, and probably insects. Judging from their remains here and elsewhere, a pattern of cyclical or seasonal shifts of residence took these groups from one area to another as various edible items became available for harvest, were used up, and had to be replaced by other items more easily gathered elsewhere. Bison were apparently still utilized when they were present; they were perhaps more extensively drawn upon in the western than in the eastern plains, where such woodland margin animals as deer and elk were favored. Pits clearly intended for food storage, like those commonly associated with later horticultural peoples, have not been found at the Archaic sites excavated so far, which may have been food-gathering stations for seasonal utilization.

Human populations were very likely still sparse and mobile. People who live by the hunt and by foraging, and who travel about on foot, must forego the luxury of nonessentials in the products of their crafts and industries. Small camps, brief stays, and scant litter were probably typical, though recurrent occupations year after year may have resulted in some accumulation of cultural debris. In the lower portion of the Republican basin, weapon points and other Archaic materials are remindful of cultural complexes in the eastern woodlands. In the west, the similarities and inferred relationships were probably as much, or more, with western-oriented hunting-gathering groups, such as those of the Great Basin.

Around the beginning of the Christian Era, other eastern cultural influences began to make themselves felt in the plains. To what extent these reflected the arrival of new ideas and innovations in ways of doing things, rather than actual increments of people from the Midwest, is not clear from the evidence currently available, which typically includes little skeletal material. On the Missouri River around the mouth of the Kansas River, these easterners were represented by a Hopewellian-derived cultural complex that spread in diminishing strength westward up the Kansas River drainage and left traces even up the Republican. In the Kansas City district, numerous well-marked and carefully dug storage pits imply some permanence of residence, perhaps with incipient maize, bean, and squash horticulture to supplement the intensive harvesting of wild plant seeds and other products. Some class distinctions are suggested by a few secondary and bundle burials—without many mortuary offerings—in square-cornered dry-masonry chambers of coursed stone. How deceased commoners were disposed of, if handled differently, we do not know.

Much more widespread and characteristic in the plains are simpler materials broadly categorized as Plains Woodland and chronologically equivalent to the Middle Woodland cultures farther east. Lacking here is the relatively advanced technology, social sophistication, and implied sedentary nature of the Kansas City Hopewellians. There was pottery making, but it was distinct from that of the Hopewellians and more reminiscent of ceramic traditions in Illinois and other eastern regions. Storage pits, if that is what they are, are uncommon and ill defined compared to those of the Kansas City Hopewellians. Social distinctions are absent or debatable; the dead were customarily cremated and the burned remains deposited in and under mounds or in communal ossuary pits, usually with scant offerings if the archeological evidence is not misleading us in our interpretation of findings. The occupation sites still suggest short-lived residence in a hunter-forager lifeway, probably with recurrent stays at favored locations.

Although a certain measure of sedentariness is suggested by some of the Plains Woodland manifestations, at least in the later stages in the eastern plains and perhaps on the lower Republican, a prevailingly settled way of life seems to have spread westward only in later centuries, perhaps by the eighth or ninth. Its origins are by no means clear, but it appears to have been partly based on the later Woodland cultures, with subsequent cultural and perhaps population increments from the east and southeast. If certain Plains Woodland peoples were indeed already experimenting with horticulture, which appears to have been the case, the Village Indians who followed them were unquestionably firmly committed to a settled lifeway based in substantial measure on a maize-bean-squash-sunflower tetrad, with the bison-scapula hoe as the characteristic cultivating tool. Substantial earth-covered lodges, mostly rectangular in floor plan, and well-defined storage pits were also typical, as was pottery making. On the Republican, this appears to have been essentially a "pioneer" society—small open communities, without defensive provisions, and with no indication of institutionalized trading or religious centers or of class distinctions. The appearance of this lifeway and its spread westward to or beyond the Colorado line may reflect an improved climate for maize-growing, as some climatologists have suggested, or perhaps the availability of more successful and productive crop varieties, such as the *Maiz de Ocho* or "eight-rowed maize" from the south (Galinat and Gunnerson 1963). The bison was still an important part of the subsistence economy, as were numerous other animals and plants in varying and generally lesser degrees.

In terms of material culture—arts, crafts, and industries—the Early Village Indian lifeway as it can be judged from the Upper Republican complex was more affluent than the preceding Woodland culture, with a much wider range of products in pottery, stone, bone, shell, and horn. We know almost nothing regarding their production of items from nondurable materials such as textiles, leather, or wood. Their alleged provinciality, "suggested on the basis of rare exotic items" (Wood 1969:107), may be more apparent than real and is, in any case, contradicted by archeological evidence available but not cited when that evaluation was placed in the record. Native worked copper from the east or southeast, freshwater shells from the Midwest, marine and Gulf Coast shells, and cherts from various sources all indicate contacts of one sort or another in several directions. Whether these items and materials traveled from tribe to tribe to reach the Republican valley through trade or as gifts, were handled by itinerant traders, or came in some other fashion, is impossible to say on present evidence. It should be noted that there is little or no evidence of contacts with the Pueblo Southwest in material culture at the Early Village level in the Republican valley.

Although much better represented archeologically than the earlier nonsedentary Plains people, the Early Village Indians are still inadequately sampled and their cultural variations very imperfectly known. The Upper Republican people, by whatever rubric they and their local and temporal variations come to be known by taxonomically oriented investigators, constitute the beginning stage in a Plains-directed culture type unsuspected before archeology got under way here. In the Nebraska-Kansas region, it led eventually to the development of the much more complex society and the far larger population aggregates represented by the Pawnees. But first we must consider briefly one or more peoples who replaced the villagers and hamlet dwellers, people who were resident for a much shorter period of time in the Republican River area, and who seem to have been less firmly committed to maize horticulture.

Reference here is, of course, again to the archeological entities known as the Glen Elder and the Dismal River complexes. The first, and probably the earlier of the two, is the less well known. The few sites attributed to it are usually thin, with few known subsurface features; since they tend to occur on easily eroded bluff tops and on arable creek terraces, they are quickly ravaged by agricultural development. That they were in part horticultural seems clear. So far as we know now, their material culture inventory in stone, bone, and other materials had a definite Plains flavor. Pottery, in its prevalently shell tempering and incised or trailed vessel decoration, reminds one more of Mississippi tradition wares than the earlier grit-tempered and cord-roughened Woodland and Upper Republican vessels. Although they lived relatively late and perhaps even extended slightly into the white contact period, there is at hand no archeological evidence that these people were in contact with the Euro-Americans who might have left us some record of them, their way of life, and their final fate.

Better known in the archeological record is the Dismal River complex, distributed mainly west of the 99th meridian. Representing the remains of a bison-hunting and semihorticultural people who were interacting with white men, this complex is usually seen by archeologists as a late-17th- and early-18th-century manifestation of Plains Apache culture, presumably Jicarilla. Whatever the Jicarilla may have been psychologically and culturally in the 20th century, around A.D. 1700 ± 50 years they give strong indications of being confirmed and accomplished plainsmen, at least in large part. Their communities nearer the Pueblo towns on the Rio Grande were evidently adopting maize horticulture, ditch irrigation, the manufacture of utilitarian pottery, and perhaps semipermanent dwellings in hamlet patterns. Farther out on the plains, for example in present Scott County, Kansas, their rancherias apparently provided a haven of sorts for Pueblo refugees fleeing Spanish oppression among the Rio Grande settlements, preceding and following the Pueblo Rebellion of 1680. No multiroomed puebloan structures like that in Scott County, nor irrigation ditches, milling bins, or other structures have been reported in Nebraska, but settlements of some size have been found and examined. Wherever the Dismal River complex has been studied by archeologists in the Kansas-Nebraska-Colorado area, it exhibits many more Plainslike material traits than Puebloan. In short, it looks like a Plains culture complex interacting with its neighbors on the grasslands rather than like an attenuated Pueblo culture produced by enfeebled or impoverished fugitives from the terraced towns of the Rio Grande or the Galisteo basin. What is perplexing to archeologists is the nature of the antecedents of the better-known site complexes where systematic work has been done, the character of earlier and later manifestations, and the variations in material culture at more westerly Plains sites, where environmental stringencies will almost surely be found to have produced some markedly different configurations from those we now know from the central plains. A great deal of field and laboratory investigation remains to be done before the picture slowly being developed is clarified.

Either as the florescent Lower Loup complex probably representing the *Pani* and *Panimaha* of the 18th-century French explorers or as their lineal descendants in the 19th-century, the Pawnees differed markedly from the earlier hamlet-dwelling Upper Republicans. Settlements were generally much larger, with undoubtedly more complex social, religious, and political systems, and with effective village or band chieftaincies that were able at times to combine in larger intervillage and interband enterprises and ceremonies. At the same time, people still relied heavily on bison hunting, which was customarily accomplished by communal methods that involved tribal expeditions away from the permanent villages, and a mobile lifeway in skin tents and on horseback. The stages by which the dispersed 13th-century hamlet-dwellers on the western frontier progressed to the 18th-century fortified towns, with their powerful priesthoods, formally organized and carefully oriented dwellings, the star cult, and other elaborate rituals and ceremonials, are still unclear. These matters will probably become understandable only after much more intensive and perceptive archeological work has been done at sites dating between the 12th and 14th centuries. Most of this development, I suspect, took place outside the Republican valley and quite likely in the Loup River drainage and nearby on tributaries of the Platte River.

The historical decline of the Pawnees in the 19th century, unlike earlier cultural changes in the region, took place under the observation of white men, who were indeed responsible in large part. With the Spanish and the French, the Pawnees had lived in a more or less amicable trade relationship. Neither of these European powers was seriously bent on colonization in the region, and they created no population or economic pressures on the Plains Indians. When the Louisiana Territory was transferred to the Americans, a sharply different relationship began and the Pawnees were soon launched on a new and untried course. Westward expansion brought white explorers, traders, and frontiersmen. These were followed by emigrants who traveled in ever-increasing numbers through Pawnee country, many of whom settled there and nearby. Frictions between white men and red increased, and the old freedoms enjoyed by the latter crumbled. Treaties with the Americans accomplished little for the Pawnees, except to separate them inexorably from their homeland. The war path, by which men achieved maturity and status within their group, was closed. Even for self-defense, the government never supplied the Pawnees with the promised arms and provided only temporary, short-lived, and generally inadequate troop protection. The great hunts, in which both men and women expended their energies freely along guide lines set by long experience, were increasingly curbed to prevent conflicts with other people, red and white, seeking the diminishing herds for meat, hides, and trophies. The old lifeway, in which people pitted themselves against the vicissitudes of nature through hunting and gardening, was on the verge of extinction. Replacing their former self-sufficiency was an unfolding welfare state in which, with their opportunities for self-fulfillment restricted by treaty with the Americans, the Indians were bailed out almost yearly by annuities and rations from the white men. Malnutrition, epidemic diseases such as smallpox and cholera, excessive use of illegal alcoholic liquors, and high child mortality led to a steady decline in population that was paralleled by a crumbling away of the social and religious controls by which their society had so long flourished in the Pawnee Crescent in Nebraska (Lesser 1978).

Late Village Indians, as their tenure culminated in the Pawnee experience, can be documented as residents of the Republican valley for not more than about a half century, that is, ca. 1775 to 1826 (± 5–10 years at either end). How much earlier they had been living here in permanent villages, we do not know. That they hunted here long before and also well after that span is evident, and their claims to the area by right of long usage had validity. That validity derives strong support from the archeological record, which was invoked successfully during the Indian land claims litigation for additional remuneration for the territory taken from the Pawnees by treaty and otherwise. The strength of the tribal regard for their Nebraska homeland has been manifested repeatedly by individual and group visits. These include visits to identify former village sites and sacred places by White Eagle, Skiri chief, in 1914, and by Garland Blaine, Pitahawirata-Skiri, head chief of the Pawnees from 1961 to 1973, in 1968, 1976, 1977, and 1978; in group visits to Massacre Canyon in the 1920s, 1930s, 1982, and 1983; and by visits of tribal members to museums in Kansas, Nebraska, and elsewhere in which notable Pawnee collections, records, and other memorabilia are permanently deposited. Pawnee affection for and attachment to their northern homelands on the Republican, Platte, and Loup rivers thus has long outlasted their departure from that area and has been manifested by individuals who were born and reared elsewhere.

With the removal of the Pawnees as resident villagers on the Republican, equestrian bison hunters who were better equipped with firearms, fully committed to the hunting life, and by choice predatory on the horticultural Village Indians laid claim to large portions of the Republican drainage, which became in effect a refuge for hunters and raiders. These in turn were dispossessed after the 1870s, removed to reservations, and the lands they had claimed opened to white settlement.

As Easton, Bryan, and other perceptive explorers had foreseen, white men in search of new homes in the West quickly recognized the agricultural potential of the Republican valley. Despite occasional droughts and partial crop failures, the population grew rapidly once the threat of Indian depredations was removed. As elsewhere in the Great Plains, so here the whites carried their maize agriculture westward beyond its "natural" limits, and so made themselves vulnerable to the vagaries of the climate. Irrigation from perennial spring-fed streams and seeps encouraged corn growing well beyond the 100th meridian, in what had been initially and more appropriately seen as a range and stock-raising country. The drought of the 1930s, the longest and most devastating since the coming of the white settlers, brought on sharp changes in the patterns of settlement, with most Republican valley counties suffering population losses as high as 30 to 50 percent from their levels of 1900.

In recent decades, American agriculture has further widened the gap between the natural potential of the land for crop production and the burden placed upon it by the white man to meet the burgeoning needs of growing populations and a commercial economy. Center-pivot irrigation systems have sprouted like mushrooms on the uplands, among the sandhills, and on the valley bottoms, creating miniature replicas of Iowa or eastern Nebraska landscapes. Pipes carry the life-supporting waters across valley bottoms once thought to be beyond any need for artificial distribution systems. Mostly, these function today on stored water and would be idle or at any rate much less effective if they depended on the current precipitation. The development of new high-yield hybrid maize varieties, combined with generous helpings of artificial chemical fertilizers in amounts of 200 pounds or more per acre (225 kg per ha), have produced dramatic crop yields far beyond the dreams of most farmers of six decades ago, or those of the Indians of two centuries and more ago.

Unanswered questions persist. How much longer, for example, will the underground stores of water from the Ogallala and other aquifers continue to provide the water needed to develop corn crops of a hundred plus bushels per acre? The newer methods and crop varieties are meeting present needs and will perhaps do more, but the cost is high in terms of the ground water reserves now being mined far faster than they can be replenished. The springs and seeps that once supplied the Indians and early white settlers have gone dry in many places, and they generally remain so except perhaps during wet years that briefly raise the water table. There is also a steady loss of topsoil to erosion by water and wind as a consequence of the large-scale mechanized cultivation of rolling uplands and hillside slopes that the Indian gardeners with their bone-bladed hoes and wooden digging sticks would not have disturbed.

The broad outlines of human prehistory in the Republican valley, paralleling the general picture of Plains culture history, are becoming clearer. The sequence of native cultures, their relative positions in time, the nature of their subsistence economies, and their adaptations to their local environmental settings are mostly in hand. The degree to which the successive traditions found it necessary to adjust to changing environmental conditions is yet to be determined, but leads are emerging, significant data are accumulating, and improved techniques and deepening insights can only advance our understanding.

The chronological and developmental framework we have now for Republican River prehistory has many gaps. Some of these can probably be narrowed significantly when field investigations already performed have been fully reported. The River Basin Surveys operations, as well as various projects carried out by state agencies with or without federal subvention, are a case in point. For many of these, only preliminary statements and verbal communications have been available so far. Paleo-Indian studies will benefit greatly from the publication of updated analytical and descriptive studies on such sites as Jones-Miller, Dutton, Selby, and Claypool in eastern Colorado. On a later time level, further data on the Lime Creek sites in Nebraska will add significantly to our understanding. At all of these, drastic geomorphological changes have taken place since their abandonment by the natives, and it is probable that these reflect in some measure important climatic shifts. The considerable refuse bone collections retrieved suggest that meticulous analyses are in order to determine the seasonality of the kills, the nature of the environmental setting, and the possible microevolutionary tendencies that might be identifiable. At this time level, and perhaps even more for the still perplexing interval termed variously the Atlantic or Altithermal episode, the interdisciplinary studies that are now fairly routine among western Plains archeologists should throw interesting light on, among other matters, the techniques by which prehorse people through some thousands of years of prehistory were able to mount successful and highly productive communal hunts and achieved mass kills and meat harvests that must often have rivaled quantitatively those of the historic mounted hunters performing the *cerne*.

For two decades or more, a large proportion of professional skills and fiscal resources in Plains archeology has been devoted to intensive interdisciplinary investigations into the earlier hunting and gathering cultures of several thousand years ago. This has been beneficial, clearly indicating that the bison-hunting way of life must be assumed to be the typical lifeway on the plains, and that success in the chase was not dependent on the horse. Supporting studies, such as the experimental killing of bovids with simulated Paleo-Indian points and weapons systems, and the butchering of elephants with Paleo-Indian tool types, have thrown significant new light on the thinking of western Plains archeologists.

Analogous special studies involving the sedentary and semihorticultural peoples of the prairie plains may be suggested here. Much could be learned, I am convinced, about native horticultural practices and problems by some controlled experiments with the growing of Indian crops in small valley-bottom plots, using Indian tools of bone and wood and following documented field techniques used by the Indian gardeners. Drying the harvested crops and storing them in underground pits provided with instruments for recording moisture, ground temperatures, and other possibly relevant details, as has been done in Great Britain (Coles 1973), ought to provide us with much more detailed and precise information than we now have concerning the degree and quality of protection given to crops stored under various conditions and for varying periods of time. How long, for example, can dried maize be stored in pits without spoiling and becoming either unpalatable or unviable? How long can sun-dried beef or jerky be thus stored with cereal and sun-dried vegetable crops? This is in no sense an implicit skepticism about the many historical sources or an impugnment of the veracity of the contemporary observers who described in more or less detail the procedures they witnessed. It is rather an attempt to get some precise observations through controlled tests and place some concrete measurements in the record.

Earthlodges and grass houses of Plains Village Indian types have been replicated on several occasions, both scale model and full size. In how far these have involved the use of strictly Indian tools, materials, and building techniques, eschewing metal, factory-made cordage, and other modern conveniences, is not always clear. Carefully planned and executed experiments following the Indian procedures as far as information is available are much to be desired. From these could perhaps be developed reliable figures about the relative durability of the various kinds of wood available to the natives for house posts and otherwise in direct contact with the soil. With or without house models, controlled tests in which selected kinds of wood, various post sizes, and different kinds of soil were involved, might give us useful information from which to judge length of house life and habitability, which in turn would throw some light on the intensity and longevity of settlement occupation. Helpful, too, would be precise information on the number of trees required in the construction of a small earthlodge or grass house, together with some calculations on the quantity of suitable timber growing in the marginal districts occupied by the prehistoric communities. Environmentally imposed limits on the size and amount of growing timber may well have been one of the factors controlling the size of the hamlets and homesteads in which the Upper Republican peoples disposed themselves over the landscape.

The effects of drought on native vegetation, particularly on the legumes that played so important a role in the food economy of the historic Plains Indians and inferentially in that of their predecessors, need to be studied as they apply to the concept of a scattered small town or hamlet pattern of settlement. The drastic effect of rainfall variability on modern crop yields, which involve plantings on uplands more often than valley bottoms, is well known. So far as I am aware, however, the effects of such variations on hand-tilled valley-bottom garden plots, intensively worked and perhaps even hand watered in times of severe drought, have never been explored experimentally or otherwise. From the standpoint of subsistence primarily, gardens so worked may be significantly more productive per unit of land than the acreages operated commercially by the modern agribusiness entrepreneur (cf. Brown 1978:286–287).

It is likely that prolonged and widespread droughts, in which putatively permanent springs and streams dried up as they did in the 1930s, would have sharply affected even Indian horticulture and perhaps led to population shifts. Earlier historically documented droughts such as that of 1860 did notably affect the Indians (Wedel 1941), who by that date were entangled in agriculture of the white man's kind more deeply than in their own time-tested and centuries-old method of small-scale hand tillage in bottomland plots. The Republican valley, where annual precipitation ranges from 32 to 14 inches (800–350 mm) from east to west and the summer rainfall varies from 22 to eight inches (550–200 mm) in the same direction, would seem to offer exceptional opportunities for controlled experiments on its horticultural potential using Indian techniques. Carefully done, and correlated with climatic records and their projections into the past, such observations might give us further clues to the horticultural environment of the 10th to 14th centuries in the Republican country.

The effects of maize horticulture, Indian style, on soil fertility likewise need study. Widely spaced plantings following a native system adjusted to planting only as much as the soil would bear may have slowed exhaustion. The occasional flooding of creek bottoms by heavy rains, not uncommon in the plains, may also have worked in this direction. If the Upper Republican hamlets were as short lived as some evidence seems to indicate, there may have been no significant soil depletion in this economy. But these are all conjectures. We need some facts based on direct observations.

Another highly promising field of investigation has been neglected for too long in what appears to be an unfortunate predisposition on the part of some archeologists to deal only with "hard" data that can be measured, weighed, or counted, and is thereby rated by its practitioners as "scientific." This is the still largely unstudied and unreported material in the archival records in Mexico, Spain, France, and other repositories. Not only can these be expected to broaden and deepen our understanding of activities and events already on record that involved or influenced Plains Indians, but they will undoubtedly throw useful light on other matters about which we now have little or no substantive knowledge. This is particularly true, perhaps, of happenings such as trade as they involve Spain and France, in the 16th, 17th, and 18th centuries in the plains. New details undoubtedly can be expected here that will illuminate and clarify our comprehension of events otherwise foreshadowed rather than elucidated by past and current information.[1] Reevaluation of archival studies already made would be appropriate in some instances.

More could be said about the problems that call for attention in Plains archeology as I see them after five decades of firsthand observation, but that is not my primary purpose here. Suffice it to reiterate once more that we have learned much in the past half-century about the human experience in the Great Plains as it concerns the native peoples. Today we know that people have been here for a very long time compared to the white man's sojourn, a span to be measured in millennia rather than in centuries. We recognize, too, that the natural environment, once thought to be too harsh for human welfare under prewhite conditions, instead stimulated a series of successful adaptations that varied through time and space in response, at least in part, to the vagaries of the environmental setting. Our understanding has been deepened by new and improved field and analytical techniques and viewpoints, combined with long overdue interdisciplinary programs and the preparation of better-trained and perhaps more knowledgeable workers, all of which holds promise for the future. But above all, it has become almost embarrassingly clear that with all we think we have learned, there is still so much that we do not know or understand. For one thing, will the white man who has been exploiting the Great Plains for two or three centuries leave to the generations that follow us a region as promising as the one he inherited after ten millennia or more of occupation by the Indians of the region?

Our hopes, clearly, must lie with the future. That future, following its usual pattern, will be upon us shortly. Let us be prepared for it.

Appendix A   Republican Valley Indian Populations

Concerning the appearance, physical characteristics, and biological relationships of the native Republican River valley inhabitants, we can say little. For one thing, despite the ten millennia or more of human occupation, very few burials have been found and skeletal remains are scarce. Of the earliest people, the Early Big Game Hunters, there exist cultural materials and the debris of occupation but no known skeletons. The Archaic peoples are almost as scarce, at least within the Republican valley itself, from which I know of no described and measured crania or other bones.

Burials assigned broadly to Woodland affiliations are rather more common. Often, however, they are too fragmentary to yield much useful information, or else they are found as isolated graves without clear cultural clues. Burial mounds on the lower Republican in Kansas and ossuary materials from the upper valley point to a long-headed population, perhaps more gracile in body build and musculature than were the historic hunters of the plains (Bass 1958; Cummings 1958; Bass and Grubbs 1964, 1966; Phenice 1969).

At other sites, notably the Young burials at Buzzard's Point in Scott County, Kansas, and at the Massacre Canyon Woodland site in Hitchcock County, Nebraska, single flexed burials in individual dug pits, with a few simple offerings or none at all, are thought to be associated with the Woodland culture. Here again a long-headed population seems to be indicated, with some biological resemblances to certain eastern Woodland groups on an archeological level (Stewart 1943, 1959). Farther afield, the earlier of two suggested manifestations at the Bisterfeldt potato cellar site near Scottsbluff, Nebraska, where boat-stones and other artifacts were in association (Mattes 1965; Breternitz and Wood 1965; Finnegan and Witty 1977) included primary interments, but the cranial type has not been described in detail.

On the Early Village Indian level, around A.D. 1050–1350, there are more skeletal materials, but nowhere have many individuals been described from one site that can be regarded as a single breeding community. Moreover, the practice of exposing the dead until the soft tissues decayed, then making group interment of the dissociated bones, either randomly or in orderly bundles, has provided further complications. Earlier collections are often lacking in adequate documentation and site data, and in no case are large well-controlled and statistically definitive samples extant.

Nearly 20 years ago, Bass (1964) examined a mixed Central Plains tradition series of 43 crania, only seven of which were from Upper Republican sites. In his judgment, this was a heterogeneous population, mainly brachycranic and high-headed, and without close resemblances to the later Pawnee and Arikara crania he studied (Bass 1964:117). Since then, a few more inferences have been ventured, but the prehistoric antecedents of these two principal Plains Caddoan tribes remain elusive (Jantz and Ubelaker 1981; Ubelaker and Jantz 1979). From other Upper Republican or Central Plains mound burials, scanty remains provide more puzzles and frustration than answers (Neuman 1963:300).

During the 18th and 19th centuries, the Pawnees of Nebraska were one of the most populous native tribes of the region. For much of that time, official estimates rated them variously at 10,000, 12,000, and up to 25,000 individuals, figures that were in some instances certainly too high. Yet, despite the fact that in presmallpox days they must have numbered in the thousands for some decades, and that there was for many years a flourishing activity in the excavation of graves overlooking the known Pawnee village sites, identifiable and documented Pawnee crania number today not more than a few dozen. Much of the early digging, and perhaps most of it, is perhaps best characterized as looting in a search for pipes, medals, pots, and other objects. Few record photographs or measurements were made, and descriptive notes were even scarcer. Bones, if saved, usually involved only the crania, rarely the limb bones, if they were in good condition. To most collectors, beyond the weekend and holiday gathering of grave goods, these activities were perhaps most accurately described as head hunting and a quest for trophies to be posed on the mantel or the office desk or the workshop bench.

In the most recent contribution to our problem, 189 male crania from five Plains tribes and three archeological complexes were analyzed for morphological similarities and dissimilarities. They included 12 Mandan, 134 Arikara, 9 Pawnee, 6 Ponca, and 5 Omaha. The archeological samples included 18 from St. Helena, three Central Plains, and two Lower Loup. Six of the nine Pawnee crania and two Upper Republican crania were from the Republican valley. It was concluded that the five named tribes were well separated morphologically, that only the Pawnee and Arikara showed morphological affinities, that Lower Loup was clearly affiliated with Pawnee but not with Arikara or Mandan, and that the Upper Republican sample was "nearly equidistant between Arikara and Pawnee" (Ubelaker and Jantz 1979:252). These similarities and dissimilarities help clarify certain relationships, and to some extent are more or less in line with what might have been expected on other grounds; but with respect to the older relationships, the historical tribal ancestries are still obscure and the findings leave much uncertainty among archeologists and their colleagues in working out native culture development in the central plains. Much larger series of crania from all time levels are needed, but there is growing concern that cultural practices, specifically burial methods, may impose serious obstacles on future studies. For the present it is impossible to judge the degree to which changing lifeways and subsistence bases—for example, the dietary modifications associated with changes from a primarily hunting economy to one largely semihorticultural—might have affected head form, stature, musculature, dental health, and other biological characteristics.

Some Reflections on Population Densities

The Republican River basin cuts across three Indian tribal territories as these were delineated by A. L. Kroeber (1939, map 1) in his discussion of native population densities in early white contact times, meaning roughly the period of the 16th century. Kroeber's figures were based on the earlier computations of James Mooney who, in turn, drew on a wide range of sources—explorers, government officials of various nationalities, missionaries, Indian agents, and others. At this early period there were, of course, no precise census figures for any of the native groups of this region, and the estimates for the time indicated are by extrapolation from later statements and by critical consideration of early historical information.

The lower portion of the Republican basin was assigned by Kroeber to the Kansa Indians, the middle to the Pawnees, and the upper to the Cheyenne-Arapahos. For the Cheyenne-Arapahos the earliest population estimates were by Alexander Mackenzie about 1780 (Ubelaker 1976:270). Kansa figures go back to 1702 and rest partly on French official estimates of 1,500 families and possibly 7,000 individuals. Pawnee figures vary widely, some of the early ones being improbably large because they apparently included the Wichitas and other southern "Pawnees." A census of the Nebraska Pawnees by the Reverend John Dunbar and the Indian agent John Dougherty in 1839 yielded a count of about 6,300 Indians in 270 lodges. This figure is close to the estimates of French traders residing among the Pawnees in 1843 as reported by Lt. J. H. Carleton (1943:107) of the United States dragoons. Interestingly, at the very time these figures were developed by persons in direct contact with the tribe, the annual reports of the commissioner of Indian affairs were crediting the Pawnees year after year with 12,500 souls, nearly double the Dunbar-Dougherty census count (see Wedel 1979a:88 and references cited therein).

Recognizing, then, the ambiguous nature of the Kroeber-Mooney figures, it may be of some interest to see where their use will lead us. Accepting Kroeber's allocation of the tribal territories, we should note first that the Republican valley section is but a small portion of the total land he assigned to each tribe. The total population of the three groups was calculated by Kroeber at 19,500 and their combined territories at 3,916 "metric townships" (one metric township = 100 sq km or 38.6 sq mi, which approximates one United States township of 36 sq mi). Here the density averages five persons per metric township. Adjusting these figures to the 26,000 square miles composing the Republican basin, we arrive at a total population of 3,315 persons for the entire basin of 675 metric townships, or 7.8 square miles (20 sq km) per individual.

This basinwide total is about 40 percent of the 1970 census figure for the city of McCook, Nebraska. For the Republican basin, the 1970 census shows a total population of around 175,000, roughly seven persons per square mile or 270 per "metric township." Stated in still another way, the Kroeber figures give the Republican River basin a population in aboriginal days of less than 1/50th, or 2 percent, that of the 1970 census count. If the basin at any time in prewhite days ever held a much larger population than the 3,315 estimated early historic figure, it is not demonstrable from any archeological data or methodology currently available, so far as I am aware. At the same time, it must be emphasized that no serious effort has been made to assess through a continuing and comprehensive field program the archeological potential of the Republican River basin or even of any significant portion of it.

Among the major tributaries, Medicine Creek has been the most intensively investigated to date, and even here considerable sections known to have archeological materials remain inadequately scrutinized even at the survey level. The Medicine Creek subbasin includes 1,070 square miles (2,770 sq km), about 4 percent of the total for the Republican basin as a whole. The main creek measures some 45 miles (72 km) between Cambridge at its mouth and Somerset at the head. At 4 percent, the Medicine Creek drainage might have supported in Upper Republican times 140–150 people in 15 lodges. If this seems an unacceptably small population for a creek more than 40 miles (64 km) long, we can double the figures to 300 people in 30 houses. If these dwellings were replaced or rebuilt at six- to eight-year intervals, with the population remaining constant for 100 years, there would have resulted 12 to 16 successive house units for each household and a total of 360 to 480 house units per century. In the century and a half postulated for the main occupancy at Medicine Creek judged from radiocarbon dates from the Medicine Creek reservoir (Harry Strunk Lake), from 550 to 720 house units would have been produced. Whatever the correct number, probably no more than 50 to 60 have been systematically excavated to date, and the great majority of these have occurred in a relatively limited section of the valley between Medicine Creek Dam and the town of Stockville. For various reasons having to do with the natural environment—notably topography, availability of water, wood, arable ground, and other features—this may have been the most desirable section of the creek valley, but this is admittedly a subjective judgment. In any case, given our uncertainty about the useful life of these prehistoric house units, and given further that only a fraction of all the houses ever built come to the attention of archeologists, we could still get the impression of a much larger native human population than may have been the case at any given time.

There are many uncertainties and debatable assumptions in the sort of calculating in which we have just indulged, and I regard any inferences drawn to be at best suggestive rather than indicative. For one thing, the determination of tribal territories and boundaries with any real exactitude is essentially impossible; much of the land, at least for bison-hunting purposes and in posthorse days belonged to whoever got there first and had both the will and the strength to hold it. For another, the distribution of population over the landscape was extremely uneven. Probably 80 to 90 percent of the occupants at any given period spent most of their time near the streams and waterholes, using the uplands only for hunting and gathering grounds. Again, as was the case with the white settlers, population densities tended to decline rapidly and consistently from east to west. In 1855, for example, Thomas Twiss, Indian agent at the Upper Platte agency west of the 100th meridian, reported that the population in his territory was "only about one person to 25 square miles [65 sq km], which is a sparse population even for an Indian country" (Twiss 1856).

The archeological record suggests that there was a comparable thinning out of native people in the past with increasing distance west of the Missouri River. I am mindful of the fact that a more mobile lifestyle in the west, with less household gear to pack around—much of it consisting of portable and perishable materials—may help explain the dearth of archeological remains toward the west. In the perspectives of archeology, acceptance of Pike's figure of 1,618 people inhabiting the Republican Pawnee village in 1806 implies further that this was perhaps the largest single community of humans in the Republican valley prior to American settlement following the Civil War and the final expulsion of the Indians. As I indicated earlier in this study, I regard Pike's figure as excessive and improbable unless it included many visitors from other larger Pawnee towns on the Platte and Loup rivers. I suspect, moreover, that the Kroeber-Mooney figures with which this discussion began give a high rather than a low base. Even if this is incorrect, and we double the base figure to 6,600 for the entire basin, the occupancy would still be sparse and widely scattered according to the white man's way of looking at such matters. For an extended discussion of sources and methodology of various estimates of North American Indian populations, including the northern plains, the interested reader is referred to Ubelaker (1976).

Extended consideration of the white man's experience in the Republican River basin involving population movements and demographic patterns from time to time is outside the scope of this study. Still, a few selected population figures taken from the statistical reports of the United States census bureau may be of passing interest in connection with the preceding remarks (table A.1). These figures clearly indicate the thinning out of population densities from highs in the eastern basin counties of 18 to 20 persons per square mile (8 per sq km) to lows of less than two persons per square mile (0.8 per sq km) in the western counties in Colorado. In very large part, they reflect environmental characteristics and their inhibiting influence on high population concentrations.

Of interest, too, is the variability of the figures from decade to decade, which can be in part explained by the climatic vagaries of the region. For one thing, years of favorable climate for agriculture encouraged immigration whereas the drought years that inevitably returned encouraged the departure of

Table A.1
Populations in Republican River basin counties, 1880–1970

	Area	Population				
	Sq Mi	1880	1900	1920	1940	1970
Colorado						
Kit Carson	2,171	—	1,580	8,915	7,512	7,530
Washington	2,526	—	1,241	11,208	8,336	5,550
Yuma	2,379	—	1,729	13,897	12,102	8,544
Kansas						
Cheyenne	1,027	37	2,640	5,587	6,221	4,257
Clay	635	12,320	15,833	14,365	13,281	9,890
Cloud	711	15,343	18,071	17,714	17,247	13,466
Norton	872	6,998	11,325	11,423	9,831	7,279
Phillips	897	12,014	14,442	12,505	10,435	7,888
Rawlins	1,078	1,623	5,241	6,799	6,618	4,393
Republic	718	14,913	18,248	15,855	13,124	8,498
Nebraska						
Chase	890	70	2,559	4,929	5,310	4,129
Franklin	578	5,465	9,455	10,067	7,740	4,566
Frontier	962	934	8,781	8,540	6,417	3,982
Furnas	722	6,406	12,373	11,657	10,098	6,897
Harlan	556	6,086	9,370	9,220	7,130	4,357
Red Willow	686	3,044	9,604	11,434	11,951	12,191
Webster	575	7,104	11,619	10,922	8,071	6,477

SOURCE: United States Bureau of the Census (HA201:10th, 1880; 12th, 1900; 14th, 1920; 16th, 1940; 19th, 1970).
NOTE: To convert square miles to square kilometers, multiply by 2.6.

people with limited resources or determination. For some Kansas counties, especially in the lower valley where settlement began earliest, the 1880 census count considerably exceeded that in 1970, for example, in Cloud, Clay, Jewell, and Republic counties, and farther west in Phillips. In nearly all counties, population dropped significantly between 1930 and 1940, with declines of 20 to 25 percent in some of the Colorado counties. These drops, of course, reflected the impact of the most disastrous and prolonged drought, or family of droughts, ever recorded since whites settled in the central plains region. In some measure, too, the general decline in numbers probably reflects a growing emphasis on large-scale mechanized agriculture, with diminishing need for manpower at the same time that the farmer requires more land and larger harvests to offset the greater costs involved in modern agriculture. Climate and environment, that is to say, are but part of the problem with which the white man has to deal.

Appendix B Mammal, Bird, and Molluscan Remains Identified from Upper Republican Sites.

Mammals	Weights[a]	
Bear, black (*Ursus americanus*)	200.0–500.0 lbs	90.0–225.0 kg
Raccoon (*Procyon lotor*)	12.0–35.0 lbs	5.4–16.0 kg
Mink (*Mustela vison*)	1.5–3.0 lbs	.7–1.4 kg
Wolverine (*Gulo luscus*)	35.0–60.0 lbs	16.0–27.0 kg
Badger (*Taxidea taxus*)	13.0–25.0 lbs	6.0–11.0 kg
Skunk, spotted (*Spilogale putorius*)	1.0–2.2 lbs	0.5–1.0 kg
Skunk, striped (*Mephitis mephitis*)	6.0–14.0 lbs	2.7–6.3 kg
Coyote (*Canis latrans*)	20.0–50.0 lbs	9.0–23.0 kg
Wolf (*Canis lupus*)	70.0–120.0 lbs	31.5–54.0 kg
Dog (*Canis familiaris*)		
Canid (Dog, wolf, or coyote)		
Fox, kit or swift (*Vulpes velox*)	4.0–6.0 lbs	1.8–2.7 kg
Fox, grey (*Urocyon cinereoargenteus*)	7.0–13.0 lbs	3.2–6.0 kg
Puma or cougar (*Felis concolor*)	80.0–200.0 lbs	36.0–90.0 kg
Lynx, bobcat, or wildcat (*Lynx* sp.)	15.0–30.0 lbs	6.7–13.5 kg
Woodchuck (*Marmota monax*)	5.0–10.0 lbs	2.2–5.4 kg
Prairie dog (*Cynomys* sp.)	2.0–3.0 lbs	0.9–1.4 kg
Ground squirrel, 13-lined (*Citellus tridecemlineatus*)	0.3–0.6 lbs	140.0–255.0 g
Pocket gopher, northern (*Thomomys talpoides*)	2.7–4.6 oz	76.0–130.0 g
Pocket gopher, plains (*Geomys bursarius*)	4.5–12.5 oz	128.0–350.0 g
Pocket mouse (*Perognathus* sp.)	0.2–0.3 oz	0.6–0.9 g
Kangaroo rat (*Dipodomys ordii*)	1.5–2.5 oz	42.0–70.0 g
Beaver (*Castor canadensis*)	30.0–60.0 lbs	13.5–27.0 kg
Mouse, white-footed (*Peromyscus leucopus*)	0.5–1.1 oz	14.0–28.0 g
Mouse, northern grasshopper (*Onychomys leucogaster*)	0.9–1.1 oz	24.0–31.0 g
Woodrat, eastern (*Neotoma floridana*)	7.0–13.5 oz	198.0–380.0 g
Prairie vole (*Microtus ochrogaster*)	1.0–1.5 oz	28.3–42.0 g
Muskrat (*Ondatra zibethicus*)	2.0–4.0 lbs	0.9–1.8 kg
Porcupine (*Erethizon dorsatum*)	10.0–28.0 lbs	4.5–12.6 kg
Jackrabbit, white-tailed (*Lepus townsendii*)	5.0–10.0 lbs	2.2–4.5 kg
Jackrabbit, black-tailed (*Lepus californicus*)	3.0–7.0 lbs	1.4–3.2 kg
Cottontail, eastern (*Sylvilagus floridanus*)	2.0–4.0 lbs	0.9–1.8 kg
Wapiti (*Cervus canadensis*)	700.0–1,000.0 lbs	330.0–450.0 kg
Deer, mule (*Odocoileus hemionus*)	125.0–400.0 lbs	56.0–180.0 kg
Deer, white-tailed (*Odocoileus virginianus*)	75.0–400.0 lbs	33.7–180.0 kg
Pronghorn antelope (*Antilocapra americana*)	75.0–130.0 lbs	33.7–58.5 kg
Bison (*Bison bison*)	800.0–2,000.0 lbs	360.0–900.0 kg

Birds

Goose, Canada (*Branta canadensis*)
Goose (*Chen* sp.)
Mallard (*Anas platyrhynchos*)
Pintail (*Anas acuta*)
Shoveler (*Anas clypeata*)

Teal, blue-winged (*Anas discors*)
Merganser, hooded (*Lophodytes cucullatus*)
Hawk, ferruginous ? (*Buteo regalis*)
Hawk, red-tailed (*Buteo jamaicensis*)
Turkey (*Meleagris gallopavo*)
Grouse, ruffed (*Bonasa umbellus*)
Grouse, sharp-tailed (*Pedioecetes phasianellus*)
Prairie chicken (*Tympanuchus pallidicinctus*)
Bobwhite quail (*Colinus virginianus*)
Coot (*Fulica americana*)
Owl, great horned (*Bubo virginianus*)
Woodpecker, red-bellied ? (*Centurus carolinus*)
Jay, blue (*Cyanocitta cristata*)
Raven, common (*Corvus corax*)
Crow (*Corvus brachyrhynchos*)

Mollusca
Gastropoda
   Helisoma anceps
   Helisoma trivolvis

   Physella trivolvis
   Succinea grosvenorii

Pelecypoda
   Anodonta grandis
   Anodonta grandis plana
   Lampsilis anodontoides
   Lampsilis ventricosa
   Lampsilis ventricosa occidens
   Lampsilis ovata f *ventricosa*
   Lasmigona complanata
   Leptodea fragilis

   Ligumia recta latissima
   Ligumia subrostrata
   Proptera alata megaptera
   Pleurobema coccineum
   Quadrula quadrula
   Quadrula pustulosa prasina
   Tritigonia verrucosa
   Uniomerus tetralasmus
   Sphaerium sulcatum

Exotics
Agaronia testacea
Busycon ?

   Marginella apicina
   Olivella

[a]Mammal weights are from Burt and Grossenheider (1964).

Notes

Chapter 2

1. The food potential of the prairie turnip for the white man's agricultural economy was recognized by several 19th-century Euro-American observers. In the 1840s, concurrently with the devastating potato famine (1846–1848) in Ireland, its domestication was attempted in France (Warner 1947). In 1847, a French traveler in the northern Great Plains, Lamare-Picquot, carried specimens of the plant back to Paris for analysis and experimentation. He was thereupon authorized by the French Ministry of Agriculture to return to America to collect seeds and living plants in quantity and to learn all he could about its growing requirements and its uses by the Indians. He was further instructed to gather seeds and plants of *Apios americana* (Indian potato or groundnut) and other wild plant species that also figured in the Indian economy.

In 1848, after many reverses and a meeting with the well-known missionary Rev. Stephen Riggs, Lamare-Picquot went back to France with "some kilograms of dried roots of *Psoralea* and about 350 seeds," along with the fruits, seeds, and roots of other edible plants found in the region he had traversed. Under the name of *picquotiane*, serious experimentation with the prairie turnip was begun, stimulated no doubt by a prize of ten thousand francs offered for the development of a satisfactory substitute for the potato. The effort was short lived. It was soon learned that the prairie turnip required five or six years to develop a tuber the size of a hen's egg, and that a single tuber per plant was normal. To alter these traits and compete successfully with the potato, which the prairie turnip closely resembles nutritionally (Wedel 1978a:171), would obviously require a long experimentation process with no guarantee of eventual success.

2. Captains Clark and Lewis both commented frequently on the abundance of geese, swans, and other waterfowl along the Missouri River as they ascended the stream, and on the relative ease with which they could be taken. Thus, on 4 July 1804, below present Doniphan, Kansas, Clark "saw great numbers of goslings . . . which Were nearly grown, the before mentioned Lake is Clear and contain great quantities of fish and Gees and Goslings, The great quantity of those fowl in this Lake induced me to Call it the *Gosling* Lake." On 13 July, above the mouth of the Nemaha River, Clark "killed two Goslings nearly Grown, Several others Killed and cought on Shore, also one old Goose, with pin fethers, she Could not fly." On 19 July, below Weeping Water Creek, the party "saw great numbers of young Gees." (Lewis and Clark 1904, vol. 1, pp. 66, 77, 85).

The following spring, when the party was in the general vicinity of present Canyon Ferry, Montana, Lewis observed on 21 July 1805, "We saw three swans this morning, which like the geese have not yet recovered the feathers of the wing and could not fly we killed two of them the third escaped by diving . . . we daily see great numbers of gees with their young which are perfectly feathered except the wings which are deficient in both young and old. My dog [a Newfoundland] caught several today, as he frequently dose." (Lewis and Clark 1904, vol. 2, p. 255).

3. One acre-foot is the quantity of water (43,560 cubic feet or 1,220 cubic meters) required to cover an acre (0.4 ha) to the depth of one foot (0.3 m). A second-foot is the equivalent of one cubic foot (0.028 cubic meter) per second (cfs) and is the amount of water passing each second through a channel one foot wide and one foot deep. One second-foot flowing for 24 hours delivers approximately two acre-feet.

231

Chapter 7

1. East of longitude 98°30′ west, which coincides approximately with Red Cloud, prehistoric house floors often significantly exceed these figures in the Kansas-Nebraska region. Here, and in western Iowa, floors may range upward to 1,800 square feet (162 sq m) or even more. Whether this reflects, in part, the ready availability of more luxuriant tree growth and better building materials, a more secure control of the environmental setting, growing population pressures, a changing social system and family organization, or some other factors is still undetermined. These larger and more substantially built structures could, of course, have harbored several times the number of people who could have been accommodated by the smaller lodges found on Medicine Creek and other streams on the western periphery of the Upper Republican horticultural tradition area.

2. To supply the posts, stringers, rafters, and other framing timbers required to build a house, the Upper Republican hamlet-dwellers probably cut down no fewer than twenty trees and perhaps as many as forty. Their preference may have been for smaller trees, not much exceeding eight or nine inches (20 cm), which would have been easier to fell with stone tools but which would have provided only a few posts or stringers per tree. Smaller trees and branches served for rafters and wall leaners. In a hamlet of five or six house units, this procedure would have used up 100 or more trees. If decay-resistant species were scarce, so that houses had to be rebuilt every three to five years, the rate of tree consumption would probably have exceeded the regenerative capacity of the streamside woodlands, and most of the limited timber would have been stripped from substantial segments of the creek valleys.

The pressure on available wood resources did not end with completion of the houses. In every household, a never-ending chore for the women was the collecting of firewood for cooking and for heating the living quarters in cold or inclement weather. For the prehistoric hamlet-dwellers, the principal household fuel was doubtless wood so long as the lodge or village or hamlet was within reach of trees, shrubs, and woody vines, whether these were still rooted or were deposited by floods. Deadwood, branches, sticks, and roots were all utilized. Driftwood left by spring freshets and floods was always welcome. Only in the absence or acute scarcity of wood, such as on the essentially treeless High Plains and locally during tribal hunts, were the abundant but quick-burning bison chips substituted or used as a supplement.

Data from which the daily fuel needs of a Plains Indian family or household occupying an earthlodge or a tipi could be quantified are not at hand. Outside the region, published figures from central Mexico and from California shell heaps range widely from 10 to 37 kilograms (22–83 lbs) per day (Heizer 1963:191). In the Republican valley, where subfreezing temperatures are regular wintertime occurrences and subzero (Fahrenheit) readings are not uncommon, the fuel requirements would in all probability have been greater. We do not know, of course, whether domestic fires were maintained continuously, as would appear likely, whether they were rekindled each morning, or whether there was a preferred procedure on this point (see Hallowell et al., 1973:157). The heating requirements for maintaining a comfortable or at least tolerable household ambience must have been considerably and variously affected by house size and location, the severity of the weather, the quality of construction, the furnishings, the number of occupants, and doubtless other factors.

Most prehistoric lodges in the Republican country west of the 100th meridian had a floor area of approximately 600 square feet (54 sq m) and a volume of around 6,000 cubic feet (168 cu m). At a probably very conservative twenty-five kilograms (55 lbs) of firewood per day, the family or families occupying such a structure would consume up to 20,000 pounds (9,200 kg) of wood per year, roughly the equivalent of five cords of mixed elm, cottonwood, and other hardwoods. A hamlet of three to five households occupied by 30 to 50 persons would then have burned 60,000 to 100,000 pounds or 30 to 50 tons of wood per annum. Larger houses or more hamlets or heavier daily firewood usage would have multiplied the drain on fuelwood resources proportionately.

We will probably never know what the tree stands on the creeks in the Republican country produced annually in the way of building timber and deadwood or other combustible fuel for use by the prehistoric people. Neither can we estimate how widely the supplies of these items might have varied as climatic fluctuations, prairie fires, and perhaps other circumstances increased or diminished the tree growth. From the historical record, however, it is clear that even among the much larger historic Indian villages in the eastern plains, where trees grew much more abundantly and to much greater size, the search for fuelwood was such a major problem that its collecting may have required several trips a day and occupied as much of the working time of the women as any other single workaday activity. I suspect that the inhabitants of the Republican River basin, including the Pawnees and their prehistoric antecedents who lived in earthlodges, like the Hidatsa women on the middle Missouri, were not infrequently "compelled to go a long distance, often two miles, before they [could] obtain the needed supply" of firewood (Boller 1868:193–194). If the comfort level and fireside etiquette in the Upper Republican lodges were like those reported (Abel 1939:182–183) by Pierre Antoine Tabeau, a trader among the Arikaras in 1805, the women here too may have welcomed their cooking responsibility as "their only opportunity of approaching the fire which they replenish. There is in these [earth] lodges an insupportable cold as there is in the center only a single fire of little dried sticks, always surrounded by men crowded together, who prevent heat passing beyond and reaching the women behind them."

In light of the foregoing considerations, I suggest that the consumption of live wood for house construction and the continuing drain on deadwood for fuel probably placed formidable restrictions on the westward expansion of permanent Indian communities in the Republican country in prehistoric days. Probably, too, wood shortages became more critical than the exhaustion of garden lands and eventually encouraged the abandonment of what may well have become horticulturally marginal territory. Perhaps some experimental archeology involving house construction west of the 100th meridian by Indian methods and exploring the fuelwood requirements for cooking and house warming around the year would be in order.

3. Since this description was written, another human calvarium from Nebraska that was fashioned into an artifact has been called to my attention by David Gradwohl of Iowa State University. It was collected from site 25HN36 in the Harlan County Reservoir area by a University of Nebraska field party in 1950 to 1952 and was described in an honors paper prepared by Gradwohl while he was a student at the University of Nebraska. Through the courtesy of Peter Bleed and James H. Gunnerson of the University of Nebraska, the specimen has been made available to me for examination and for photographing at the National Museum of Natural History (plate 7.6).

The calvarium consists of the lower half of the parietals, the upper third of the occipital, and a wormian at the juncture of the sagittal and lambdoidal sutures. When the piece is held in correct anatomical position, the lower dressed margin that crosses the parietals and the occipital 42 mm below *lambda* is seen to be smoothly rounded and heavily polished by use. This polish is confined to the lip, but the exterior surface of the bone generally is smoothed as if from repeated handling or use in some still unclear manner. The upper margin, 70 mm anterior to *lambda*, shows little wear but looks like a clean even fracture whose direction was not guided by prior grooving. There are four conically drilled perforations along the margins, each from 2 to 5 mm in diameter. Two are in the left parietal, one in the center of the occipital, and one in the right parietal. It is possible that a second perforation once existed here but was broken away. A few traces of red pigment reported by Gradwohl are no longer visible. Maximum breadth along the midline, i.e., along the sagittal suture extended posteriorly, is 115 mm; across the parietals the chord measures 141 mm; along the highly polished, curving occipital margin it is 220 mm; and along the parietal margin it is 260 mm.

No satisfactory explanation of the use to which this specimen was put by its prehistoric owner presents itself. The use-polish on the lip suggests contact with the skin and the drill holes were presumably for attachment of tie cords. Was the piece perhaps part of some ceremonial headdress or other ritual paraphernalia? It was found in a cultural context similar to that of the Medicine Creek specimen—an Upper Republican trash pit radiocarbon dated in the A.D. 1050–1250 time range (Neuman 1967:482). I have no knowledge of other such artifacts from the central plains region of Nebraska and Kansas at any time level.

An admittedly incomplete search of the readily available literature has turned up surprisingly few references to comparable specimens. From an apparently much earlier time level is a calvarium taken at a depth of eight feet (2.4 m) from a shell heap, CT°27, in Pickwick Basin, Tennessee (Webb and DeJarnette 1943:238; plates 278, fig. 1, and 298, fig. 1). Here "the skull cap had been removed just above the ears, the edges had been smoothed down, and two holes drilled on opposite sides [on the short axis] just below the rim of the bowl thus formed." This specimen, as it was reassembled from a number of neatly stacked fragments, does not closely resemble either of the two Republican River valley specimens herein described, but it seems to me possible that something of the same kind was attempted and bungled in the Medicine Creek piece.

A worked human skull reportedly collected by M. W. Stirling at Belle Glade, Florida, has not been relocated in the national collections, and there appears to be no photograph or other record of its nature or its whereabouts.

Several other finds of modified human crania have been called to my attention by Douglas H. Ubelaker, Douglas Owsley, and P. Willey. I have not seen these and the data at hand do not permit fruitful comparison with the Medicine Creek and Harlan County specimens described in the foregoing pages. One is an incomplete skull vault or bowl from the Utz site (23SA2) in Missouri, which has a polished edge on an occipital fragment and a cut line parallel to the polished edge. There are five wormian bones at the junction of the lambdoidal and sagittal sutures. Four fragmentary skull caps from the Crow Creek massacre bone bed (39BF11) also exhibit cut marks, cut edges, and wear polish that suggest purposeful modification. The Utz site is identified with the Oneota culture at ca. A.D. 1400–1750. Crow Creek is classified as Initial Coalescent at ca. A.D. 1325 (P. Willey to Wedel, letter 26 June 1984; D. Owsley to Wedel, letter 8 August 1984).

Chapter 9

1. Concerning the disposal of surplus crops among the historic tribes of the Nebraska region, some observations by the Indian agents involved are of interest. Thus, in 1837, John Dougherty reported from Council Bluffs (Dougherty 1838:547) that "corn is sometimes an article of trade among all the tribes of this country, but a much greater quantity is given away by those who raise it, to those who do not, than is either sold or bartered." Dougherty was referring specifically to the Pawnees, Omahas, Otos, and Missouris, for whom his agency was responsible.

From the Fort Leavenworth agency, Richard W. Cummins wrote in October 1839 (Cummins 1839:501) that the Kansa Indians "raised more corn than usual for them. I suppose they have raised a plenty to do them until the new crop comes in, if taken care of; they, however, are very generous in dividing with the Indians of other tribes that visit them for the purpose of begging; they will give anything to eat as long as they have it, and think it very strange that provisions are ever sold, but they never refuse to give; their dependence for meat is entirely on wild animals."

In 1867, the agent, Charles H. Whaley, wrote from Genoa that the Pawnees had enjoyed an excellent corn crop, from which they had given generously to the Poncas, whose crop had failed badly (Whaley 1868:234).

I have found no evidence that the Pawnees or their immediate neighbors participated in an established network of voluntary or formalized exchanges of food or other commodities (cf. Blakeslee 1975).

2. The identification of certain archeological specimens from the Hill site as possibly a cultivated *Chenopodium* (cf. *Chenopodium nutalliae*), reported in Wedel 1936:60, has since been corrected. These seeds, regarded by M. R. Gilmore and others as too large for wild chenopods, are now ascribed to the pokeberry (*Phytolacca americana*). This identification is by David L. and Nancy B. Asch, and is concurred in by Volney H. Jones (Jones to Wedel, letter of 4 December 1978). Whether the fruits from which these seeds came were eaten or used as a dye or for some other purpose is not known. By some, the fruits have been regarded as toxic to humans and animals (Bare 1979:100; Stephens 1980:25).

3. The relative importance of meat and vegetable matter in the Pawnee diet would be a matter of considerable interest, but in the present state of our knowledge it would necessarily be a highly subjective judgment. It is relevant to note Uerpmann's observation (Uerpmann 1973:319) that "an adult relying on a meat source for protein would require a minimum of 100 gm (3.5 oz) of meat per day; the calorie intake would have to

come from vegetable matter. If meat were to provide the calorific content of the diet, ca 2000 gm (4 lbs 6 oz) of lean meat would be required per adult per day. The minimum and maximum requirements are thus seen to vary by a factor of 20."

In view of the maximum meat requirement given above, it is also relevant to note the rations allowed to working employees in the 19th-century fur trade in Canada. In 1858, for example, Dr. James Hector of the Palliser expedition was given a census of the population of Fort Edmonton, which included "as a curious item the quantity of buffalo meat that is served out each day" (Palliser 1863:72, 78). For the 109 persons, including 42 men, 19 women, and 48 children, the "pounds of fresh meat for each family per diem" totaled 526 pounds or just under five pounds per person per day. Fifteen men listed as "absent in the plains" were assigned 120 pounds of meat or 8 pounds per day per man.

Hanson (1983) cites comparable figures from other Canadian posts. At Fort Pelly in 1866, "each employee received daily six pounds of fresh meat, including rabbits; if the meat was dried he received four pounds or he got three pounds of pemmican, ducks, or white fish. Women received one-half a man's ration and children one-fourth." At Fort Qu'Appelle in 1867–1868, according to Isaac Cowie, a man's ration was "twelve pounds fresh buffalo meat, or six pounds dried buffalo meat, or three pounds pemmican, or six rabbits, or six prairie chickens, or three large white fish, or three large or six small ducks beside potatoes and some milk for the children, and occasional dried berries, with a weekly allowance of tallow or fat." Rations for women and children were as at Fort Pelly.

Dietitians have been known to challenge figures of this magnitude as being beyond the physiological capabilities of the human organism's metabolism. It can be presumed, I think, that the clerks and others who recorded these ration figures exercised reasonable care in putting them down. We can also presume that the officials who set them were duly cost-conscious and would not have been likely to over-feed their employees. The figure of 3,600 calories sometimes cited as a daily requirement for a working male today may thus have been regarded as totally inadequate in the fur trade. How it would have worked out for free-roving Plains Indian big game hunters we have at present no way of knowing beyond the inferences to be drawn from the fur trade figures.

4. For Mississippi River mileages here given I am indebted to Roger Soucier, Waterways Experiment Station, United States Army Corps of Engineers, Vicksburg, Mississippi. The distance from New Orleans (French Quarter) to midcity St. Louis is calculated for the year 1800. In 1770, it may have been ten miles less. Today, owing to channel straightening, levees, and other flow-control devices, the distance is given as 1,055 river miles.

5. The Big Nemaha River empties into the Missouri River from the right (south) 3.1 miles (5 km) downstream from the U.S. Route 159 bridge and the Chicago, Burlington, and Quincy railroad bridge at Rulo, Nebraska. Prior to widespread agricultural activity and very heavy siltation, with consequent major channelization and shortening, the Nemaha was probably navigable for small craft as far upstream as the four-foot falls south of Falls City, which may have been originally perhaps 20 very sinuous miles (7.25 French or 5.8 Spanish leagues) from the Missouri River but are now approximately 12 or 13 miles distant. Whether this was the point where boat cargoes were transferred to horseback or backpack for transport to the Pawnee towns on the Republican, or whether the traders portaged around the falls and continued westward along the Big Nemaha and onto its South Fork for another 10 or 20 miles, I have not been able to determine (see also Edwards 1917:194–195).

As to the craft that might have been used in this trade, the pirogues or dugouts intended for river transport ranged widely in size, up to 40 or 50 feet (12–15 m) in length, six feet (2 m) beam, and four to four and a half feet (1.3 m) in depth. They could carry as many as 30 men and varied in freight capacity up to 45 or 50 tons. On the Missouri, they were said by Chittenden to be smaller, averaging from 15 to 20 feet (4.5–6 m) long, probably not much more than three feet (1 m) wide, and able to carry a ton (1,000 kg) or somewhat more of freight (see McDermott 1941:118). The six- to eight-oar pirogues commonly reported for the Missouri by traders bound for the Pawnees and upper river tribes were certainly significantly larger than Chittenden's average. The lower Nemaha may have been accessible only to the small one- or two-man pirogues carrying a few hundred pounds of freight and trade goods instead of the much larger quantities bound farther upriver.

6. William Clark's inventory of "Sundries for Indians Presents" (Lewis and Clark 1904–1905, vol. 6, pp. 270–277; see also Prucha 1971:16) includes the following Jefferson peace and friendship medals: first size or grand medals (105 mm), one each for the first chiefs of the Omahas, Arikaras, and Mandans; second or intermediate size (75 mm), 13 for the first chiefs of the Otos or Pawnees, and second chiefs of the Omahas, Arikaras, and Mandans; third size (55 mm), 16 for second and third chiefs of the Otos or Pawnees, third chiefs of the Omahas, Arikaras, and Mandans, and for a first chief of one of the foreign nations "beyond the mandanes [Mandans]." There were also 55 season medals of fourth size (45 mm), with various domestic scenes on obverse and "Second Presidency of Geo. Washington MDCCXCVI" on the reverse.

Lewis and Clark passed the mouth of the Platte River on their outward journey in July, at which time the Pawnees were "out in the Praries following & Hunting the buffalow" (Lewis and Clark 1904–1905, vol. 1, p. 86). There was apparently no direct or official contact between the Pawnee tribal leadership and the expedition, and so far as I am aware there is no record of the formal transmittal to that tribe of any of the medals intended for them.

7. The medal and coin diameters given in the text here may be more readily visualized in relation to the diameters of familiar United States coins of various denominations as follows:

Dollar, silver, 1921:   38 mm
Fifty-cent piece, silver: 30.5 mm
Twenty-five-cent piece, silver: 24 mm
Ten-cent piece, silver: 18 mm
Five-cent piece, nickel: 21 mm
One-cent piece, copper: 19 mm

8. The identity of this medal remains obscure. According to a news release published in the *Lincoln Journal and Star* on 14 September 1941, it was supposedly a replica of a gold medal authorized for presentation to George Washington by the Continental Congress in 1776 but not actually awarded until 1790. Thus, on 25 March 1776, it was resolved

> that the thanks of this Congress, in their own name, and in the name of the thirteen United Colonies, whom they represent, be presented to his excellency General Washington, and the officers and soldiers under his command, for their wise and spirited conduct in the siege and acquisition of Boston; and that a medal of gold be struck in commemoration of this great event, and presented to his Excellency; and that a committee of three be appointed to prepare a letter of thanks, and a proper device for the medal.
>
> *Journals of the Continental Congress* ([vol. 4, 1776] 1906:234)

The gold medal eventually awarded bears little resemblance to the Nebraska specimen. Now in the Boston Public Library, where it is displayed annually on the anniversary of the evacuation of Boston by the British, the original measures 86 millimeters in diameter and is not pierced for suspension. On the obverse is a profile of Washington, facing to the right. Around and above the profile is the following in Latin: "GEORGIO WASHINGTON SUPREMO DUCI EXERCITUM ADSERTORI LIBERTATIS," "to George Washington supreme commander of the armies defender of liberty." Below the profile are the words "COMITTA AMERICANA" or "American Committee."

On the reverse, Washington and a group of officers, mounted, are shown on a point overlooking Boston harbor, with the Continental Army in good order in the middle distance. Beyond are ships of the British fleet lined up to receive the British army under evacuation. Above is the following: "HOSTIBUS PRIMO FUGATIS," which is "the enemy's first flight" (or "the enemy at beginning of his flight"?). Below this scene are the words "BOSTONIUM RECUPERATUM" or "Boston retaken," and the date "XVII MARTI MDCCLXXVI," 17 March 1776.

The Nebraska piece is clearly not a replica of the gold original given to Washington by the Continental Congress. Rather, it appears to be one of numerous commemorative medals struck over the years in honor of the man but without official governmental sanction or sponsorship. Were the reverse available, further identification might be possible. For the present, the questions of how, by whom, and under what circumstances the General Washington medal reached the Pawnees at the Hill site remain unanswered (see also Arnold 1976).

Chapter 10

1. A more extended discussion of Pawnee sacred places or animal lodges, based on library and archival research and a field examination in August 1982, is to be found in Parks and Wedel (1985). The general location of several of these sites is indicated on the map in figure 9.2, and two are illustrated in plate 10.1.

Curaspa ko, or "Girl Hill," was described in 1914 by a Skiri chief, White Eagle, to Melvin R. Gilmore of the Nebraska State Historical Society, as "a hill on the south [right] side of the Platte River opposite the east end of [the] Grand Island . . . and shaped like an earthlodge, even to the vestibule entrance." Fitting this description rather well is a semidetached erosion remnant in the bluff line in the SW 1/4 SE 1/4 Section 25, T14N, R5W, in Hamilton County, Nebraska. Viewed from the northeast, its resemblance to an earthlodge with a vestibule entrance is strong. Other than this and its location relative to the Grand Island of the Platte and two Pawnee village sites, we have no proof that this was the *Curaspa ko* of White Eagle, and Gilmore did not precisely locate it. The feature lies about midway between the Clarks (25PK1) and Hordville (25HM1) village sites, is roughly 2.75 miles (4.5 km) from each, and rises about 70 feet (21 m) above the Platte River bottoms. Girl Hill derives its name from an episode in which the young girls of a Pawnee village group gathered on the slopes of the hill to watch a bison surround by the men on the valley bottom nearby. See M. R. Gilmore, "The Legend of Pahuk," manuscript, Nebraska State Historical Society archives, where the name is rendered *Tsuraspako*.

Pa-hur', "the hill that points the way," was described by Grinnell (1889:358) as a hard, flinty rock sticking up out of the ground, and with a great hole in its side where the miraculously endowed animals held their councils. The geology of this district today does not suggest the presence of such an outcrop, but an old photograph of 1904, generously provided by the Nebraska State Historical Society, indicates a much more striking appearance than can now be seen. Today, there is little or nothing to distinguish this spot from many other bluff points up and down the Republican River. To the best of my knowledge, there is no confirmation that there was ever a great hole in its side as reported by Grinnell, and the basis for that detail, if anything more substantial than legend, remains unknown.

Kicawi·caku, "spring on the edge of a bank," has long been known to whites as Waconda or Great Spirit Spring. It is situated in the SW 1/4 Section 25, T6S, R10W, in Mitchell County, Kansas, 3.5 miles (5.6 km) airline below the junction of the North and South forks of the Solomon River. Before its tragic submergence beneath the waters of Glen Elder Reservoir, it was a natural artesian spring supplied with highly mineralized waters from the Dakota sandstone, which rose through a fissure to the surface under hydrostatic pressure. It was situated on the top of a natural rock mound that rose 42 feet (13 m) above the Solomon River bottoms, immediately below the left (north) bluff line of the river valley. The mound consisted of hard porous limestone in the form of a truncated cone, 300 feet (91 m) across the base and 150 feet (45 m) across the top. Centered on this mound was the spring vent, approximately 54 feet (16 m) in diameter and 35 feet (11 m) deep at the center. The water rose virtually to the top of the mound, most of it escaping through openings on the flanks. The mound was formed by deposition of minerals left as the waters evaporated.

Highly charged with sodium chloride, sodium sulphate, magnesium sulphate, magnesium carbonate, calcium carbonate, and other salts, the water was believed to have valuable medicinal properties. As early as 1884, construction of a spa was begun; even earlier, beginning in the 1870s, bottled water from the spring was widely marketed under the name of "Waconda Flier."

To Plains Indian tribes, the spring was a shrine in which offerings of various kinds were deposited whenever they passed by. Grinnell (1889:358) renders the Pawnee name as *Kitz-a-witz-uk.* According to the Rev. Isaac McCoy (1840:411), the name by which this unusual feature came to be known by whites was derived from its Kansa Indian name of *Ne-Wohkon daga,* which signified "spirit water." By the same tribe, the Solomon River a few hundred yards to the south was termed *Nepaholla,* or "water on a hill" (Bailey 1902; Patrick 1906; Schoewe 1953).

For the photograph of Waconda Spring reproduced here I am indebted to Dee Messinger, Bureau of Reclamation, McCook, Nebraska (plate 10.1). For background information on its history as a health spa, I owe thanks to Dr. Carlos F. Bingesser, Cawker City, Kansas, whose family owned and operated the establishment for many years.

2. Ronald L. MacGregor, University of Kansas Herbarium, to whom I am indebted for confirmation of this identification, comments further that *Apios americana* is found

> along creeks, rivers, around seepage areas on prairie hillsides and similar sites. Livestock, particularly horses, selectively browse the plant. I have not observed this to be true for *Amphicarpa.* It is rare now that we find *Apios* in sites which are being used for pasture and I am reasonably certain *Apios* is not as common now as it was in our area before settlement. The early collectors apparently found it more frequently than we do now. I suspect, therefore, that it has largely disappeared with advent of heavy grazing. . . . In a few areas at Kanopolis Reservoir, Ellsworth County, substantial colonies of *Apios* have developed since the area around the lake was removed from grazing. . . . I recall seeing a good colony just north of Amboy, Webster County, Nebraska, which is just across the Republican River north of the Pawnee village site near Red Cloud. . . . In the Great Plains *Apios* is found over most of North Dakota; south to the Black Hills; Cherry County, Nebraska; and south to Franklin County, Nebraska. It has been collected over most of the eastern half of Kansas and with one collection from Sheridan County" (MacGregor to Wedel, letter 1 March 1979).

Chapter 11

1. A case in point is an undated, recently published manuscript map in the Paris archives, indexed as 69-20 in the Service Historique de la Marine, and without cartographer attribution. My wife, Mildred Mott Wedel, and I identified this map in September 1978 as depicting the distances and directions traveled each day by Etienne Véniard de Bourgmont on his ascent of the Missouri River in 1714. Authorship of this map remains uncertain but probably involves either Claude Delisle or his son, Guillaume. Various dates on the map can be correlated with those in notes made by Claude Delisle (AM 3JJ 277:17) from the journal or other records maintained by the Bourgmont party. These notes, it should be pointed out, were in another section of the archives, and there was no indication on either notes or map that the two documents belonged together and pertained to one and the same historical episode.

A gloss on the map, whereon the Platte River appears as the *Rivière des Panis,* locates ten villages of the *Panis* at 30 leagues (80–85 mi) up this river. In this general locality are to be found a number of protohistoric (Lower Loup) Pawnee village sites that yield definite evidence of white contact and may well date in part from the Bourgmont period. This map, or more accurately the notes on which it was based—entitled *Routt qu'il faut tenir pour monter la Rivière de Missoury*—is apparently the earliest historical record of the location of the Pawnees in terms of their distance from an identifiable landmark, in this case the confluence of the Missouri and Platte rivers (see also Wedel 1979c: 279; Véniard de Bourgmont 1714; E. R. P. Henning in Wood 1983, plate 1).

The anonymous *Exact Description of Louisiana,* attributed to Bourgmont (Giraud 1958) locates the *Panimaha* or Skiri Pawnees another 20 leagues up the Platte. Bourgmont, in common with other early-18th-century French observers, thus recognized only two major divisions of the Pawnees, corresponding to the Skiris and South Bands of later years. The Kitkahahki and Pitahawirata as band names do not appear in the historical literature until the 1770s and 1790s, respectively (see also Parks 1979:234; M. M. Wedel 1979:192).

Bibliography

Abel, Annie Heloise, ed.
1939 Tabeau's narrative of Loisel's expedition to the upper Missouri. Norman: University of Oklahoma Press.

Abel-Henderson, Annie H.
1924 Mackay's table of distances. Mississippi Valley Historical Review, vol. 10, no. 4, pp. 428–446.

Account of the Red River in Louisiana
[1806] Drawn up from the returns of Messrs. Freeman and Custis to the War Office of the United States who explored the same, in the year 1806. Peter Force Collection, Ser. 8D, Manuscript Division, Library of Congress.

Albertson, F. W., G. W. Tomanek, and Andrew Riegel
1957 Ecology of drought cycles and grazing intensity on grasslands of the central Great Plains. Ecological Monographs, vol. 27, pp. 27–44.

Albertson F. W., and J. E. Weaver
1945 Injury and death or recovery of trees in prairie climate. Ecological Monographs, vol. 15, pp. 394–433.

Aldrich, John W., and Allen J. Duvall
1955 Distribution of American gallinaceous game birds. Circular 34, Fish and Wildlife Service, Washington, D.C.

Allis, Samuel
1918 Letters from Samuel Allis, May 3, 1834, to January 16, 1849. In Letters concerning the Presbyterian Mission in the Pawnee Country, near Bellvue [sic], Nebraska. Kansas Historical Collections, vol. 14 (1915–1918), pp. 690–741.

Arnold, Howard Payson
1976 The Washington medal: in commemoration of the evacuation of Boston, 17 March 1776. Boston: Associates of the Boston Public Library.

Arthur, George W.
1975 An introduction to the ecology of early historic communal bison hunting among the northern Plains Indians. Archaeological Survey of Canada, Paper no. 37. Ottawa: National Museum of Canada.

Baerreis, David A., and Reid A. Bryson
1965 Climatic episodes and the dating of the Mississippian cultures. The Wisconsin Archeologist, vol. 46, no. 4.

1966 Dating the Panhandle Aspect cultures. Bulletin, Oklahoma Anthropological Society, vol. 14, pp. 105–116.

1967 Climatic change and the Mill Creek culture of Iowa. Archives of Archaeology 29. Society for American Archaeology.

Bailey, E. H. S.
1902 Great Spirit Spring, Waconda, Mitchell County. Mineral Waters, vol. 7, pp. 197–200. Topeka: University Geological Survey of Kansas.

Barbour, Erwin H.

1913   Nebraska green quartzite, an important future industry. Nebraska Geological Survey, vol. 4, part 19, pp. 249–252.

Bare, Janet E.

1979   Wildflowers and weeds of Kansas. Lawrence: Regents Press of Kansas.

Bark, L. Dean

1978   History of American droughts. In North American Droughts, edited by Norman J. Rosenberg, Chapter 1, pp. 9–23. AAAS Selected Symposium 15. Boulder, Colo.: Westview Press.

Barker, William T.

1969   The flora of the Kansas Flint Hills. University of Kansas Science Bulletin, vol. 48, no. 14, pp. 525–584.

Barkley, T. M., ed.

1977   Atlas of the flora of the Great Plains. Ames: Iowa State University Press.

Barrows, H. H.

1923   Geography as human ecology. Annals of the Association of American Geographers, vol. 13, no. 1, pp. 1–14.

Bartlett, Katherine

1936   The utilization of maize among the ancient Pueblos. In Symposium on Prehistoric Agriculture, edited by D. D. Brand, pp. 29–34. University of New Mexico Bulletin, Whole Number 296, Anthropological Series (formerly Archaeological Series), vol. 1, no. 5. Albuquerque.

Bass, William M.

1958   Addendum to the skeletal report of the Sweat Bee Mound, Site 14PO14 (Abstract). Bulletin 169, Bureau of American Ethnology, p. 78. River Basin Surveys Papers no. 10, Washington, D.C.

1963   Human skeletal material from the Russell Mound, 14JW207, Jewell County, Kansas. Bulletin 185, Bureau of American Ethnology. River Basin Surveys Papers no. 32, Washington, D.C.

1964   The variation in physical types of the prehistoric Plains Indians. Plains Anthropologist, vol. 9, no. 24, pp. 65–145 (Memoir 1).

Bass, William M., and Patricia A. Grubbs

1964   Human skeletal material from the Howard Hayes site, 14NT51, Norton County, Kansas: a Plains Woodland burial. Kansas Anthropological Association Newsletter, vol. 9, no. 8, pp. 1–7.

1966   Human skeletal material from a Keith focus Plains Woodland site, 14PH10, Kirwin Reservoir, Phillips County, Kansas. Plains Anthropologist, vol. 11, no. 32, pp. 135–143.

Bass, William M., and Patrick S. Willey

1966   An analysis of a human skeleton from 14RY302, Riley County, Kansas. Kansas Anthropological Association Newsletter, vol. 11, pp. 3–5.

Basso, Keith, and Morris E. Opler, eds.

1971   Apachean culture history and ethnology. Anthropological Papers of the University of Arizona no. 21. Tucson.

Bates, C. G.

1935   Climatic characteristics of the Plains region. In Possibilities of Shelterbelt Planting in the Plains region, pp. 82–110. United States Forest Service.

Bates, Craig D.

1982   A Spanish coin from the Sierra Nevada. The Masterkey, vol. 56, no. 1, pp. 13–22. Los Angeles: The Southwest Museum.

Bellrose, Frank C.

1968   Waterfowl migration corridors east of the Rocky Mountains. Biological Notes no. 61. Urbana: Illinois Natural History Survey.

Bénard, Jean-Baptiste, Sieur de la Harpe

1718–1720   Journal Du Voyage De la Louissiane fait Par Le Sr Bernard [sic] De La harpe Et Des DeCouvertes Quil a fait Dans la Party De l'ouest De Cette Colonie. [Journal of the voyage from Louisiana made by the Sieur Bénard de La Harpe and some discoveries that he made in the western part of this colony]. MSS Français 8989: fols. 1–35. Bibliothèque Nationale, Paris.

Benn, David W.

1974   Seed analysis and its implications for an Initial Middle Missouri site in South Dakota. Plains Anthropologist, vol. 19, no. 63, pp. 55–72.

Benton, Thomas Hart

1822   Annals of Congress, vol. 38, 17th sess., part 1, column 424. Washington, D.C.

Berthrong, Donald J.

1963   The Southern Cheyennes. Norman: University of Oklahoma Press.

Billon, Frederic L.

1971   Annals of St. Louis in its early days under the French and Spanish dominations, 1764–1804. St. Louis, 1886. Reprint. New York: Arno Press.

Blackman, E. E.

1903   Report of Department of Archeology. Annual Report, Nebraska State Board of Agriculture for 1902, pp. 294–326.

1905   Report of Department of Archeology for 1903 and 1904. Annual Report, Nebraska State Board of Agriculture for 1904, pp. 207–229.

1906   Archeological report for 1905. Annual Report, Nebraska State Board of Agriculture for 1905, pp. 390–400.

1907   Report of archeologist [for 1906 and 1907]. Proceedings and Collections of the Nebraska State Historical Society, vol. 15 (series 2, vol. 10), pp. 323–359.

1922   Archaeological work in 1921. American Anthropologist, n.s., vol. 24, no. 2, pp. 237–238.

1928   Archaeological work in 1927. American Anthropologist, n.s., vol. 30, no. 3, pp. 511–512.

1930   Archaeological work in 1929. American Anthropologist, n.s., vol. 32, no. 2, p. 357.

Blaine, Garland J., and Martha Royce Blaine.

1977   Pa-Re-Su A-Ri-Ra-Ke: The hunters that were massacred. Nebraska History, vol. 58, no. 3, pp. 343–358.

Blaine, Martha Royce

1980   The Pawnees: a critical bibliography. Bloomington: Indiana University Press for the Newberry Library.

Blakeslee, Donald J.

1975   The plains interband trade system: an ethnohistoric and archeological investigation. Ph.D. diss., University of Wisconsin–Milwaukee.

1978   Assessing the Central Plains Tradition in eastern Nebraska: content and outcome. In The Central Plains Tradition: Internal Development and External Relationships, edited by Donald J. Blakeslee, pp. 134–143. Report 11, Office of the State Archaeologist. Iowa City: University of Iowa.

Blakeslee, Donald J., and Warren W. Caldwell

1979   The Nebraska phase: an appraisal. Reprints in Anthropology, vol. 18. Lincoln, Nebr.: J & L Reprint Co.

Blakeslee, D. J., J. Hotopp, K. Lippincott, J. Ludwickson, and T. Witty

1982   Setting the record straight: some responses to Krause. Plains Anthropologist, vol. 27, no. 95, pp. 83–90.

Boettcher, Arnold J.

1966   Ground-water developments in the High Plains of Colorado. Contributions to the Hydrology of the United States, United States Geological Survey Water-Supply Paper 1819-I. Washington, D.C.

Boller, Henry A.

1868   Among the Indians: Eight Years in the Far West, 1858–1866. Philadelphia: T. Ellwood Zell.

Borchert, J. R.

1950   The climate of the central North American grassland. Annals of the Association of American Geographers, vol. 40, no. 1, pp. 1–39.

Bourgmont, E. V. de. See: Véniard de Bourgmont, Etienne; Villiers, Marc de; Giraud, Marcel.

Bowman, Peter W.

1927   Weather in the west central plains and its significance in archeology. Kansas Anthropological Association Newsletter, vol. 18, nos. 1 and 2, pp. 1–32.

1976   Some ecological and taxonomic aspects of the Plains Apache phenomenon. Unpublished manuscript.

Breternitz, David A., and John J. Wood

1965   Comments on the Bisterfeldt potato cellar site and flexed burials in the western Plains. Southwestern Lore, vol. 31, no. 3, pp. 62–66.

Brooks, George R.

1965   George C. Sibley's journal of a trip to the salines in 1811. Missouri Historical Society Bulletin, vol. 21, no. 3, pp. 167–207.

Brower, Jacob V.

1899   Harahey. Memoirs of Explorations in the basin of the Mississippi, vol. 2. St. Paul, Minn: H. L. Collins.

Brown, Ian W.

1980   Salt and the eastern North American Indian: an archaeological study. Lower Mississippi Survey, Bulletin no. 6. Cambridge: Peabody Museum, Harvard University.

Brown, Lester R.

1978   The Twenty Ninth Day. New York: W. W. Norton & Co.

Bruner, Lawrence

1896   Some notes on Nebraska birds. Nebraska State Horticultural Society, Report for 1896, pp. 48–178. Lincoln.

Bryan, Lt. Francis T.

1857   Explorations for road from Fort Riley to Bridger's Pass, 1856. Appendix H, Report of the Chief Topographical Engineer, Annual Report of the War Department, 1857, 35th Congr., 1st sess. Exec. Doc. no. 2, vol. 2.

Bryson Reid A., and David A. Baerreis

1968   Climatic change and the Mill Creek culture, part 1, pp. 1–34. Introduction and project summary. Journal of the Iowa Archeological Society, vol. 15, December 1968.

Bryson, Reid A., David A. Baerreis, and Wayne M. Wendland

1970   The character of late-glacial and post-glacial climatic changes. In Pleistocene and Recent Environments of the Central Great Plains, edited by W. Dort, Jr., and J. K. Jones, pp. 53–74. Special Publication no. 3. Lawrence: Department of Geology, University of Kansas.

Bryson, Reid A., and Christine Padoch

1980   On the climates of history. Journal of Interdisciplinary History, vol. 10, no. 4, pp. 583–597.

Bryson, Reid A., and Wayne M. Wendland

1967   Tentative climatic patterns for some late glacial and post-glacial episodes in central North America. In Life, Land, and Water, edited by William J. Mayer-Oakes, pp. 271–298. Winnipeg: University of Manitoba Press.

Buchner, Anthony P.

1980   Cultural responses to Altithermal (Atlantic) climate along the eastern margins of the North American grasslands 5500 to 3000 B.C. Archaeological Survey of Canada Paper no. 97, National Museum of Man Mercury Series. Ottawa: National Museums of Canada.

Burgess, William

1874   Annual report of the Pawnee agency. In Annual Report of the Commissioner of Indian Affairs for 1873, pp. 193–195. Washington, D.C.: Department of the Interior.

Burt, William H., and R. P. Grossenheider

1964   A field guide to the mammals. 2d ed. Boston: Houghton Mifflin, Riverside Press.

Carleton, Lt. J. Henry

1943   A dragoon campaign to the Pawnee villages in 1844. The Prairie Logbooks, edited by Louis Pelzer, pp. 3–152. Chicago: Caxton Club.

Carlson, Gayle F.

1971   A local sequence for Upper Republican sites in the Glen Elder reservoir locality, Kansas. Master's thesis, Department of Anthropology, University of Nebraska.

Carlson, Gayle F., and Curtis A. Peacock

1975   Lithic distribution in Nebraska. In Lithic Source Notebook, edited by Ronald A. Thomas, pp. R6. Section of Archaeology, Division of Historical and Cultural Affairs, State of Delaware, Milford, Del.

Carlson, Gayle F., and Terry L. Steinacher

[1978] A preliminary culture-historical sequence for the Plains Archaic period in Nebraska. Paper presented at symposium on Migration and Extinction in the Great Plains, 15 April, Institute for Tertiary-Quaternary Studies, Lincoln, Nebraska.

Carlson, G. G., and Volney H. Jones

1940   Some notes on uses of plants by the Comanche Indians. Papers of the Michigan Academy of Science, Arts, and Letters, vol. 25, pp. 517–542.

Castetter, Edward F.

1935   Uncultivated native plants used as sources of food. Ethnobiological Studies in the American Southwest, 1. University of New Mexico Bulletin, Whole Number 266 (Biological Series, vol. 4, no. 1). Albuquerque.

Champe, John L.

1946   Ash Hollow Cave. A study of stratigraphic sequence in the central Great Plains. University of Nebraska Studies, new series, no. 1. Lincoln.

1949   White Cat Village. American Antiquity, vol. 14, no. 4, part 1, pp. 285–292.

Champe, John L., and Franklin Fenenga

1974   Notes on the Pawnee. In Pawnee and Kansa (Kaw) Indians, pp. 23–169. New York: Garland Publishing.

Chardon, Roland

1980a   A quantitative determination of a second linear league used in New Spain. Professional Geographer, vol. 32, no. 4, pp. 462–466.

1980b   The linear league in North America. Annals of the Association of American Geographers, vol. 70, no. 2, pp. 129–153.

Cloud, W. F.

1866   Letter of General Cloud to the Superintendent, charging hostilities upon Pawnees and other tribes, and reply. Report of the Commissioner of Indian Affairs for the year 1866, pp. 222–223, Document no. 98. United States Department of the Interior.

Coker, Robert E.

1919   Fresh-water mussels and mussel industries of the United States. Bulletin of the Bureau of Fisheries, vol. 36, no. 865.

Coles, John M.

1973   Archaeology by experiment. London: Hutchinson University Library.

Colorado Department of Agriculture

1976   Colorado agricultural statistics, 1974–75, Bulletin 1–76. Colorado Crop and Livestock Reporting Service, Denver.

Condra, G. E.

1907   Geology and water resources of the Republican River valley and adjacent areas, Nebraska. United States Geological Survey Water-Supply Paper 216. Washington, D.C.

Continental Congress
1906   Journals of the Continental Congress 1774–1789, vol. 4. 1 January–4 June 1776. Edited by Worthington Chauncey Ford. Washington, D.C.: Government Printing Office.

Conybeare, A., and Gary Haynes
1984   Observations on elephant mortality and bones in water holes. Quaternary Research, vol. 22, no. 2, pp. 189–200.

Cook, Joseph W.
1882   Dakota Yankton vocabulary and sentences. MS. 1486. National Anthropological Archives, Smithsonian Institution.

Cooper, J. P.
1868   Annual report of J. P. Cooper, special agent Upper Platte agency. Papers accompanying the annual report of the Commissioner of Indian Affairs for 1868, no. 67. United States Department of the Interior.

Cooper, Paul L.
1936   Archeology of certain sites in Cedar County, Nebraska. In Chapters in Nebraska Archeology, edited by Earl H. Bell, no. 1, pp. 11–145. Lincoln: University of Nebraska.

1940   The archeological exploration of 1938. Nebraska History, vol. 20, no. 2, pp. 94–151.

Costello, David F.
1969   The prairie world. New York: Thomas Y. Crowell Co.

Coupland, Robert T.
1958   The effects of fluctuations in weather upon the grasslands of the Great Plains. Botanical Review, vol. 24, no. 5, pp. 273–317.

Cragin, F. W.
1896   On the stratigraphy of the Platte series, or Upper Cretaceous of the Plains. Colorado College Studies, vol. 6, pp. 49–52.

Culin, Stewart
1907   Games of the North American Indians. 24th Annual Report, Bureau of American Ethnology, 1902–1903. Washington, D.C.

Cummings, Robert B.
1958   Archeological investigations at the Tuttle Creek dam, Kansas. Bulletin 169, Bureau of American Ethnology, pp. 65–77. Washington, D.C.

Cummins, Richard W.
1839   Report of Richard W. Cummins, Agent at Fort Leavenworth. Report of the Commissioner of Indian Affairs, Document no. 51, pp. 500–502. War Department. Washington, D.C.

Cureau, A. L.
1915   Savage man in Central Africa. A study of primitive races in the French Congo. London: T. F. Unwin.

Cutler, Hugh C., and Leonard W. Blake
1969   Corn. In Two House Sites in the Central Plains: An Experiment in Archeology, edited by W. Raymond Wood, pp. 61–62. Plains Anthropologist, vol. 14, no. 44, part 2 (Memoir 6).

1973   Plants from archaeological sites east of the Rockies. St. Louis: Missouri Botanical Garden.

Davis, E. Mott
1953   Recent data from two Paleo-Indian sites on Medicine Creek, Nebraska. American Antiquity, vol. 18, no. 4, pp. 380–386.

1962   Archeology of the Lime Creek site in southwestern Nebraska. Special Publication no. 3. Lincoln: University of Nebraska State Museum.

Davis, E. Mott, and C. B. Schultz
1952   The archeological and paleontological salvage program at the Medicine Creek reservoir, Frontier County, Nebraska. Science, vol. 115, no. 2985, pp. 288–290.

Davis, Leslie B., and Michael Wilson, eds.

1978   Bison procurement and utilization: a symposium. Plains Anthropologist, vol. 23, no. 82, part 2 (Memoir 14).

Denman, Hampton B.

1868   Northern Superintendency [Omaha, Nebraska]. Papers accompanying the Report of the Commissioner of Indian Affairs for 1867, no. 78, pp. 260–273. U.S. Department of the Interior.

Dibble, David S., and D. Lorrain

1968   Bonfire Shelter: a stratified bison kill site, Val Verde County, Texas. Miscellaneous Papers no. 1. Austin: Texas Memorial Museum.

Dick, Herbert W., and Bert Mountain

1960   The Claypool site: a Cody complex site in northeastern Colorado. American Antiquity, vol. 26, no. 2, pp. 223–235.

Diffendal, Anne Polk

1978   A centennial history of the Nebraska State Historical Society, 1878–1978. Nebraska History, vol. 59, no. 3, pp. 311–437.

Dillehay, Tom D.

1974   Late Quaternary bison population changes on the Southern Plains. Plains Anthropologist, vol. 19, no. 65, pp. 180–196.

Diller, Aubrey

1955   A new map of the Missouri River drawn in 1795. In Imago Mundi: a Review of Early Cartography, edited by Leo Bagro, pp. 175–180. Leiden: E. J. Brill.

Dixon, Roland B.

1905   The Northern Maidu. Bulletin, American Museum of Natural History, vol. 17, pp. 119–346.

Dodge, Richard Irving

1883   Our wild Indians: thirty three years' personal experience among the red men of the Great West. Hartford: A. D. Worthington & Co.

1959   The Plains of the Great West and their Inhabitants. 1877. Reprint. New York: Archer House.

Dougherty, John

1838   Report from the agent at Council Bluffs. In Report of the Commissioner of Indian Affairs for 1837, Document no. 5, pp. 547–549. War Department. Washington, D.C.

Dunbar, John

1910   The Presbyterian mission among the Pawnee Indians in Nebraska, 1834 to 1846. Kansas Historical Collections, vol. 11 (1909–1910), pp. 323–332.

1911   Missionary life among the Pawnee. Collections of the Nebraska State Historical Society, vol. 16, pp. 268–287.

1918   Letters from Rev. John Dunbar, 6 September 1831 to 7 May 1849. In Letters concerning the Presbyterian mission in the Pawnee country, near Bellevue, Nebraska, 1831–1849. Kansas Historical Collections, vol. 14 (1915–1918), pp. 570–689.

Dunbar, John B.

1880a   The Pawnee Indians: their history and ethnology. Magazine of American History, vol. 4, no. 4, pp. 241–281.

1880b   The Pawnee Indians: their habits and customs. Magazine of American History, vol. 5, no. 5, pp. 321–345.

1882   The Pawnee Indians: their habits and customs. Magazine of American History, vol. 8, no. 10, pp. 734–756.

Dunlevy, Marion L.

1936   A comparison of the cultural manifestations of the Burkett (Nance County) and the Gray-Wolfe (Colfax County) sites. In Chapters in Nebraska Archeology, edited by Earl H. Bell, no. 2, pp. 147–247. Lincoln: University of Nebraska.

Easton, Langdon C.

1953   Report: Fort Laramie to Fort Leavenworth via Republican River in 1849 (edited by Merrill J. Mattes). Kansas Historical Quarterly, vol. 20, pp. 392–415.

Edwards, Lewis C.

1917   History of Richardson County, Nebraska. Indianapolis: B. F. Bowen & Co.

Eerde, Ellen

1980–1981   Butterflies in your stomach? R & D Mexico, vol. 1, nos. 3–4, pp. 6–8. National Council of Science and Technology, Mexico.

Ellison, L., and E. J. Woolfolk

1937   Effects of drought on vegetation near Miles City, Montana. Ecology, vol. 18, no. 3, pp. 329–336.

Emory, William H.

1848   Notes of a military reconnaissance, from Fort Leavenworth, in Missouri, to San Diego, in California. . . . Made in 1846–47. 30th Cong., 1st sess., S. Doc. no. 7., Washington, D.C.

Eyman, Charles E.

[1966]   The Schultz focus: a Plains Middle Woodland burial complex in eastern Kansas. Master's thesis, Department of Archaeology, University of Alberta, Calgary.

Fahringer, Adams M.

1877   Field notes of the survey of the subdivisional lines of township 2 south, range 43 west of the 6th principal meridian in Colorado, vol. 58, pp. 546–598. Microfiche files, Bureau of Land Management, Denver.

Fahringer, Jason S.

1878   Field notes of the survey of the subdivisional lines of township 5 south, range 43 west of the 6th principal meridian in Colorado. Microfiche files, vol. 61, Bureau of Land Management, Denver.

Feder, Norman

1978   Pawnee cradleboards. American Indian Art, vol. 3, no. 4, pp. 40–50.

Finnegan, Michael, and Tom Witty

1977   A seated burial and associated boatstone from northwestern Kansas. Plains Anthropologist, vol. 22, no. 75, pp. 23–36.

Fishel, V. C.

1948   Ground-water resources of Republic County and northern Cloud County, Kansas. Bulletin 73, State Geological Survey of Kansas.

Fitzpatrick, Thomas

1853   Report of agent Thomas Fitzpatrick. Reports . . . accompanying the annual report of the Commissioner of Indian Affairs for the year 1853, no. 44, pp. 359–371. United States Department of the Interior.

Flannery, Kent V.

1968   Archeological systems theory and early Mesoamerica. In Anthropological Archeology in the Americas, edited by Betty J. Meggers, pp. 67–87. Anthropological Society of Washington.

Fletcher, Alice C.

1904   The Hako: a Pawnee ceremony. 22d Annual Report, Bureau of American Ethnology, part 2, pp. 5–368. Washington, D.C.

Flora, S. D.

1948   Climate of Kansas. Report of the Kansas State Board of Agriculture, vol. 67, no. 285. Topeka.

Forbes, Jack

1959   The appearance of the mounted Indian in northern Mexico and the Southwest, to 1680. Southwestern Journal of Anthropology, vol. 15, no. 2, pp. 189–212.

Forbis, Richard G.

1962 The Old Women's buffalo jump, Alberta. Bulletin 180, National Museum of Canada. Contributions to Anthropology, 1960, part 1, pp. 55–123. Ottawa: Canada Department of Northern Affairs and National Resources.

Forrest, F. Wayne

1948 Field notes of the dependent survey of a portion of the west boundary and a portion of the subdivision of township 5 south, range 43 west. Pp. 738–773, vol. 479 microfiche on 6 of 7; Bureau of Land Management, Denver.

Freimuth, Glen, and Wallace LaBerge

1976 Dating and environmental reconstruction from prehistoric mud-dauber nests: some possibilities. Plains Anthropologist, vol. 21, no. 72, pp. 111–114.

Frémont, John C.

1845 Report of the exploring expedition to the Rocky Mountains in the Year 1842, and to Oregon and California in the Years 1843–44, pp. 12–693. 28th Cong., 2d sess., H. Doc. 166. Washington, D.C.

Frison, George C.

1971 The bison pound in northwestern Plains prehistory. American Antiquity, vol. 36, no. 1, pp. 77–91.

1972 The role of buffalo procurement in post-Altithermal populations on the Northwestern Plains. In Social Exchange and Interaction, edited by E. N. Wilmsen, pp. 11–19. Anthropological Papers no. 46. Ann Arbor: Museum of Anthropology, University of Michigan.

1974 The Casper site: a Hell Gap bison kill on the High Plains. New York: Academic Press.

1975 Man's interaction with Holocene environments on the Plains. Quaternary Research, vol. 5, no. 2, pp. 289–300.

1977 PaleoIndian sites and economic orientations in the Big Horn basin. Museum Journal, vol. 17, pp. 97–116.

1978 Prehistoric hunters of the High Plains. New York: Academic Press.

1982 Paleo-Indian winter subsistence strategies on the High Plains. In Plains Indian Studies, edited by Douglas H. Ubelaker and Herman J. Viola, pp. 193–201. Smithsonian Contributions to Anthropology, no. 30. Washington, D.C.

Frye, John C., and A. B. Leonard

1949 Geology and Ground-water resources of Norton County and northwestern Phillips County, Kansas. Kansas Geological Survey Bulletin 81. Topeka.

1952 Pleistocene geology of Kansas. Bulletin 99, State Geological Survey of Kansas. Lawrence.

Frye, John C., and A. Byron Leonard

1967 Buried soils, fossil mollusks, and Late Cenozoic paleoenvironments. In Essays in Paleontology and Stratigraphy: R. C. Moore Commemorative Volume, pp. 429–444. Special Publication no. 2. Lawrence: Kansas University Department of Geology.

Frye, John C., and Ada Swineford

1946 Silicified rock in the Ogallala formation. Kansas Geological Survey Bulletin 64, part 2, pp. 33–76. Topeka.

Furness, L. W.

1955 Floods in Nebraska: magnitude and frequency. Department of Roads and Irrigation, State of Nebraska, in cooperation with the United States Geological Survey.

Galinat, Walton C., and James H. Gunnerson

1963 Spread of eight-rowed maize from the prehistoric Southwest. Botanical Museum Leaflets, vol. 20, no. 5, pp. 117–160. Cambridge: Harvard University.

Garfield, Marvin H.
1932   Defense of the Kansas frontier, 1868–69. Kansas Historical Quarterly, vol. 1, no. 5, pp. 451–473.

Ghent, W. J.
1929   The road to Oregon. London and New York: Longmans, Green & Co.

Gilmore, Melvin R.
1913   A study of the ethnobotany of the Omaha Indians. Nebraska State Historical Society Collections, vol. 17, pp. 314–357.

1915   Aboriginal geography of the Nebraska country. Proceedings, Mississippi Valley Historical Association, vol. 6, pp. 1–15.

1919   Uses of plants by the Indians of the Missouri River region. 33rd Annual Report, Bureau of American Ethnology, pp. 43–154. Washington, D.C.

Giraud, Marcel, ed.
1958   Etienne Véniard de Bourgmont's "Exact Description of Louisiana." Missouri Historical Society Bulletin, vol. 15, no. 1, pp. 3–19.

Gradwohl, David M.
1969   Prehistoric villages in eastern Nebraska. Nebraska State Historical Society, Publications in Anthropology no. 4.

1982   Shelling corn in the Prairie-Plains: Archaeological evidence and ethnographic parallels beyond the pun. In Plains Indian Studies, edited by Douglas H. Ubelaker and Herman J. Viola, pp. 135–156. Smithsonian Contributions to Anthropology, no. 30. Washington, D.C.

Graham, Russell W.
1979   Paleoclimates and Late Pleistocene faunal provinces in North America. In Pre-Llano Cultures of the Americas: Paradoxes and Possibilities, edited by R. L. Humphrey and Dennis J. Stanford, pp. 49–69. Anthropological Society of Washington.

1981   Preliminary report on late Pleistocene vertebrates from the Selby and Dutton archeological/paleontological sites, Yuma County, Colorado. Contributions to Geology, vol. 20, no. 1, pp. 33–56. Laramie: University of Wyoming.

Grange, Roger T., Jr.
1968   Pawnee and Lower Loup pottery. Publications in Anthropology, no. 3. Lincoln: Nebraska State Historical Society.

1979   An archeological view of Pawnee origins. Nebraska History, vol. 60, no. 2, pp. 134–160.

1980   Archeological investigations in the Red Willow reservoir, Nebraska. Publications in Anthropology, no. 9. Lincoln: Nebraska State Historical Society.

Grayson, Donald K.
1977   Pleistocene avifauna and the overkill hypothesis. Science, vol. 195, pp. 691–693.

Grinnell, George Bird
1889   Pawnee hero stories and folk-tales. New York: Forest & Stream.

1906   Cheyenne stream names. American Anthropologist, n.s., vol. 8, pp. 15–22.

1956   The fighting Cheyennes, Charles Scribner's Sons, 1915. Reprint. Norman: University of Oklahoma Press.

1973   Two great scouts and their Pawnee battalion. Lincoln: University of Nebraska Press.

Grüger, Johanna
1973   Studies on the late quaternary vegetation history of northeastern Kansas. Geological Society of America Bulletin, vol. 84, no. 1, pp. 239–250.

Guilday, John E.
1967   Differential extinction during late Pleistocene and Recent times. In Pleistocene Extinctions: The Search for a Cause, edited by P. S. Martin and H. E. Wright, Jr., pp. 121–140. New Haven: Yale University Press.

Gunnerson, Dolores A.

1956   The Southern Athabascans: their arrival in the Southwest. El Palacio, vol. 63, pp. 346–365.

1972   Man and bison on the Plains in the protohistoric period. Plains Anthropologist, vol. 17, no. 55, pp. 1–10.

1974   The Jicarilla Apaches: a study in survival. De Kalb: Northern Illinois University Press.

Gunnerson, James H.

1960   An introduction to Plains Apache archeology: the Dismal River aspect. Bulletin 173, Bureau of American Ethnology. Anthropological Papers no. 58. Washington, D.C.

1968   Plains Apache archaeology: a review. Plains Anthropologist, vol. 13, no. 41, pp. 167–189.

1969a   Apache archaeology in northeastern New Mexico. American Antiquity, vol. 34, no. 1, pp. 23–39.

1969b   A human skeleton from an Apache baking pit. Plains Anthropologist, vol. 14, no. 43, pp. 46–56.

Gunnerson, James H., and Dolores A. Gunnerson

1971   Apachean culture: a study in unity and diversity. In Apachean Culture History and Ethnology, edited by Keith H. Basso and Morris E. Opler, pp. 7–27. Anthropological Papers of the University of Arizona, no. 21. Tucson.

Gusinde, Martin

1948   Urwaldmenschen am Ituri, anthropo-biologische Forschungsergebnisse bei Pygmäen und Negern im östlichen Belgisch-Kongo aus den Jahren 1934–35. Wien: Springer-Verlag.

Guthrie, R. Dale

1980   Bison and man in North America. Canadian Journal of Anthropology, vol. 1, no. 1, pp. 55–73.

1982   Mammals of the mammoth steppe as paleoenvironmental indicators. In Paleoecology of Beringia, edited by D. M. Hopkins, J. V. Matthews, Jr., C. E. Schweger, and S. B. Young, pp. 307–326. New York: Academic Press.

1984   The evidence for Middle-Wisconsin peopling of Beringia: an evaluation. Quaternary Research, vol. 22, no. 2, pp. 231–241.

Hafen, LeRoy R.

1961   Powder River campaigns and Sawyer's expedition of 1865. The Far West and the Rockies Historical Series, 1820–1875, vol. 12. Glendale, Calif.: Arthur H. Clark Co.

Hallowell, Benjamin, Franklin Haines, John H. Dudley, and Joseph Powell.

1973   Report of the joint delegation . . . to visit the Indians under the care of Friends, in the Northern Superintendency, State of Nebraska, 7th and 8th Mos., 1869. Baltimore 1869. Nebraska History, vol. 54, no. 2, pp. 150–211.

Hamilton, Joseph V.

1840   Report of Joseph V. Hamilton, agent at Council Bluffs. Document no. 52 in Report of the Commissioner of Indian Affairs for 1839, pp. 503–504. War Department.

Hammond, George P., and Agapito Rey

1940   Narratives of the Coronado expedition. Coronado Historical Series, vol. 2. Albuquerque: University of New Mexico Press.

1953   Don Juan de Oñate, colonizer of New Mexico, 1595–1628. Coronado Cuarto Centennial Publications, 1540–1940, vols. 5 and 6. Albuquerque: University of New Mexico Press.

Hanson, Charles E., Jr.

1969   Geminien Beauvais. In The Mountain Men and the Fur Trade of the Far West, edited by LeRoy R. Hafen, vol. 7., pp. 35–43. Glendale, Calif.: Arthur H. Clark Co.

1970   The Mexican traders. Museum of the Fur Trade Quarterly, vol. 6, no. 3, pp. 2–6.

1983   Hudson's Bay Company rations. Museum of the Fur Trade Quarterly, vol. 19, no. 1, pp. 8–10.

Harvey, Thomas H.
1848   Report of Thomas Harvey. Document no. 6 accompanying the Report of the Commissioner of Indian Affairs for 1847, pp. 832–841. United States War Department.

Haury, E. W., Ernst Antevs, and J. F. Lance
1953   Artifacts with mammoth remains, Naco, Arizona. American Antiquity, vol. 19, no. 1, pp. 1–24.

Haury, E. W., E. B. Sayles, W. W. Wasley, Ernst Antevs, and J. F. Lance
1959   The Lehner mammoth site, southeastern Arizona. American Antiquity, vol. 25, no. 1, pp. 2–39.

Havard, V.
1895   Food plants of the North American Indians. Bulletin, Torrey Botanical Club, vol. 22, pp. 98–123.

Hay, Robert
1895   Water resources of a portion of the Great Plains. 16th Annual Report, United States Geological Survey, part 2, pp. 535–588. Washington, D.C.

Hayden, Ferdinand V.
1868   Notes on Indian history. Annual Report of the Smithsonian Institution for 1867, pp. 411–412. Washington, D.C.

Haynes, C. Vance, Jr.
1964   Fluted projectile points: their age and dispersion. Science, vol. 145, no. 3639, pp. 1,408–1,413.

1965   Carbon-14 dates and early man in the New World. Interim Research Report no. 9, Geochronology Laboratories. Tucson: University of Arizona.

1969   The earliest Americans. Science, vol. 166, no. 3906, pp. 709–715.

1980   The Clovis culture. Canadian Journal of Anthropology, vol. 1, no. 1, pp. 115–121.

1982   Were Clovis progenitors in Beringia? In Paleoecology of Beringia, edited by D. M. Hopkins, J. V. Matthews, Jr., C. E. Schweger, and S. B. Young, pp. 383–398. New York: Academic Press.

Haynes, Gary
1980   Evidence of carnivore gnawing on Pleistocene and Recent mammalian bones. Paleobiology, vol. 6, no. 3, pp. 341–351.

[1984] Age distribution of elephant and mammoth assemblages. Manuscript, National Museum of Natural History, Washington, D. C.

Heizer, Robert F.
1963   Domestic fuel in primitive society. Journal of the Royal Anthropological Institute, vol. 93, part 2, pp. 186–194.

Henkel, Alice
1906   Wild medicinal plants of the United States. Bulletin no. 89, Bureau of Plant Industry, United States Department of Agriculture. Washington, D.C.

Hepner, George
1856   Document no. 29 accompanying the Report of the Commissioner of Indian Affairs for the year 1855, pp. 85–86. Washington, D.C.

Hester, James J.
1972   Blackwater Locality No. 1, a stratified Early Man site in eastern New Mexico. Dallas: Fort Burgwin Research Center, Southern Methodist University.

Hester, James J., and James Grady
1977   PaleoIndian social patterns on the Llano Estacado. Museum Journal, vol. 17, pp. 78–96.

Hill, Asa T.
1927   Mr. A. T. Hill's own story. Nebraska History, vol. 10, no. 3, pp. 162–167.

Hill, A. T., and Paul Cooper
1938 The archeological campaign of 1937. Nebraska History, vol. 18, no. 4, pp. 237–359.

Hill, A. T., and Marvin F. Kivett
1941 Woodland-like manifestations in Nebraska. Nebraska History, vol. 21, no. 3, pp. 146–243.

Hill, A. T., and George Metcalf
1942 A site of the Dismal River aspect in Chase County, Nebraska. Nebraska History, vol. 22, no. 2, pp. 158–226.

Hill, Edward E.
1974 The office of Indian Affairs, 1824–1880: historical sketches. New York: Clearwater Publishing Co.

Hind, Henry Youle
1859 Northwest Territory. Reports of progress; together with a preliminary and general report on the Assiniboine and Saskatchewan exploring expedition, made [1858] under instructions from the Provincial Secretary, Canada. Toronto.

Hoffhaus, Charles E.
1964 Fort de Cavagnial: imperial France in Kansas, 1744–1764. Kansas Historical Quarterly, vol. 30, no. 4, pp. 425–454.

Holder, Preston, and Joyce Wike
1949 The Frontier Culture complex: a preliminary report on a prehistoric hunters' camp in southwestern Nebraska. American Antiquity, vol. 14, no. 4, part 1, pp. 260–266.

Holman, Dennis
1967 Massacre of the elephants. New York: Holt, Rinehart & Winston.

Hopkins, David M., et al., eds.
1982 Paleoecology of Beringia. Edited by David M. Hopkins, John V. Matthews, Jr., Charles E. Schweger, and Steven B. Young. New York: Academic Press.

Hotopp, John
1978 Glenwood: a contemporary view. In The Central Plains Tradition: Internal Development and External Relationships, edited by Donald J. Blakeslee, pp. 109–133. Report 11, Office of the State Archaeologist. Iowa City: University of Iowa.

Houck, Louis
1909 Report of the Indian tribes who receive presents at St. Louis, November 15, 1777. The Spanish Regime in Missouri, vol. 1, pp. 141ff. Chicago: R. R. Donnelley & Sons Co.

Hough, Walter
1910 Poisons. Handbook of American Indians north of Mexico, part 2, pp. 273–274. Bulletin 30, Bureau of American Ethnology. Washington, D.C.

Humphrey, Robert L., and Dennis Stanford, eds.
1979 Pre-Llano cultures of the Americas: paradoxes and possibilities. Anthropological Society of Washington.

Hurt, Wesley R.
1966 The Altithermal and the prehistory of the northern Plains. Quaternaria, vol. 8, pp. 101–113.

Jackson, Donald
1961 A new Lewis and Clark map. Missouri Historical Society Bulletin, vol. 17, no. 2, part 1, pp. 117–132.

Jackson, Donald, ed.
1966 The journals of Zebulon Montgomery Pike. 2 vols. Norman: University of Oklahoma Press.

Jackson, Donald, and Mary Lee Spence, eds.
1970 The expeditions of John Charles Frémont. Vol. 1. Travels from 1838 to 1844. Urbana: University of Illinois Press.

James, Edwin

1823   Account of an expedition from Pittsburgh to the Rocky Mountains, performed in the years 1819 and '20 . . . under the command of Major Stephen H. Long. 2 vols. and atlas. Compiled and edited by Edwin James. Philadelphia: Carey and Lea.

Jamieson, Melvill Allan

1936   Medals awarded to North American Indian chiefs, 1714–1922. London: Spink and Son.

Jantz, Richard L., and Douglas H. Ubelaker, eds.

1981   Progress in skeletal biology of Plains populations. Plains Anthropologist, vol. 26, no. 94, part 2 (Memoir 17).

Jelinek, A. J.

1967   Man's role in the extinction of Pleistocene faunas. In Pleistocene Extinctions: The Search for a Cause, edited by P. S. Martin and H. E. Wright, Jr., pp. 193–200. New Haven: Yale University Press.

Jennings, Jesse D.

1978   Origins. In Ancient Native Americans, edited by Jesse D. Jennings, pp. 1–41. San Francisco: W. H. Freeman & Co.

Johnson, Alfred E.

1976   A model of the Kansas City Hopewell subsistence-settlement system. In Hopewellian archaeology in the lower Missouri valley, edited by A. E. Johnson, pp. 1–6. University of Kansas Publications in Anthropology no. 8. Lawrence.

1980   Archaic prehistory on the Prairie-Plains border. University of Kansas Publications in Anthropology, no. 12. Lawrence.

1981   The Kansas City Hopewell subsistence and settlement pattern. Missouri Archaeologist, vol. 42, pp. 69–76.

Johnson, D. L., P. Kawano, and E. Ekker

1980   Clovis strategies of hunting mammoth. Canadian Journal of Anthropology, vol. 1, no. 1, pp. 107–114.

Johnston, Richard F.

1960   Directory to the bird-life of Kansas. Miscellaneous Publication no. 23. Lawrence: Museum of Natural History, University of Kansas.

Kansas State Board of Agriculture

1929   Report of the Kansas State Board of Agriculture for the quarter ending September 1929. Topeka.

Kappler, Charles J.

1903   Indian affairs: laws and treaties. Vol. 2 (Treaties). 57th Cong., 1st sess., S. Doc. 452.

Kehoe, Thomas F.

1967   The Boarding School bison drive site. Plains Anthropologist, vol. 12, no. 35, pp. 1–165 (Memoir 4).

1973   The Gull Lake site: a prehistoric bison drive site in southwestern Saskatchewan. Publications in Anthropology and History, no. 1. Milwaukee: Milwaukee Public Museum.

Kehoe, Thomas F., and Alice B. Kehoe

1968   Saskatchewan. In The Northwestern Plains: a symposium, edited by W. W. Caldwell, pp. 21–35. Occasional Papers no. 1, Center for Indian Studies. Billings, Mont.: Rocky Mountain College.

Kellogg, Royal S.

1905   Forest belts of western Kansas and Nebraska. Bulletin 66, Forest Service. United States Department of Agriculture.

Kincer, J. B.

1923   The climate of the Great Plains as a factor in their utilization. Annals of the Association of American Geographers, vol. 13, no. 2.

King, James E.

1980   Post-Pleistocene vegetational changes in the midwestern United States. In Archaic Prehistory on the Prairie-Plains Border, edited by Alfred E. Johnson, pp. 3–11. University of Kansas Publications in Anthropology, no. 12. Lawrence.

King, James T.

1960a   Republican River expedition, June–July 1869. Nebraska History, vol. 41, no. 3, pp. 165–199.

1960b   The battle of Summit Springs. Nebraska History, vol. 41, no. 4, pp. 281–297.

1963   War Eagle: a life of General Eugene A. Carr. Lincoln: University of Nebraska Press.

Kingsbury, John M.

1964   Poisonous plants of the United States and Canada. Englewood Cliffs, N.J.: Prentice-Hall.

Kinnaird, Lawrence, ed.

1949   Spain in the Mississippi Valley, 1765–1794. Part 1, The Revolutionary Period, 1765–1781. Annual Report, American History Association, 1945, vol. 2.

Kivett, Marvin F.

1949   Archeological investigations in Medicine Creek reservoir, Nebraska. American Antiquity, vol. 14, no. 4, part 1, pp. 278–284.

1952   Woodland sites in Nebraska. Publications in Anthropology, no. 1. Lincoln: Nebraska State Historical Society.

1953   The Woodruff ossuary, a prehistoric burial site in Phillips County, Kansas. Bulletin 154, Bureau of American Ethnology. River Basin Surveys Papers no. 3, pp. 103–41. Washington, D.C.

1958   Notes and News: Nebraska. American Antiquity, vol. 23, p. 337.

1959   Logan Creek complex: Site 25BT3. Paper delivered at 17th Plains Conference, 17 November 1959. Lincoln, Nebr.

1970   Early ceramic environmental adaptations. In Pleistocene and Recent Environments of the Central Great Plains, edited by Wakefield Dort, Jr., and J. Knox Jones, Jr., pp. 93–102. Special Publication 3. Lawrence: Department of Geology, University of Kansas.

Krause, Richard A.

1969   Correlation of phases in Central Plains prehistory. In Two House Sites in the Central Plains: An Experiment in Archaeology, edited by W. Raymond Wood, pp. 82–96. Plains Anthropologist, vol. 14, no. 44, part 2 (Memoir 6).

1970   Aspects of adaptation among Upper Republican subsistence cultivators. In Pleistocene and Recent Environments of the Central Great Plains, edited by Wakefield Dort, Jr., and J. Knox Jones, Jr., pp. 103–115. Special Publication 3. Lawrence: Department of Geology, University of Kansas.

1982   The Central Plains phase revisited: a critical review of recent interpretations. Plains Anthropologist, vol. 27, no. 95, pp. 75–82.

Krieger, Alex D.

1950   A suggested general sequence in North American projectile points. Proceedings of the Sixth Plains Archeological Conference, 1948. University of Utah Anthropological Papers, no. 11, pp. 117–124. Salt Lake City.

Kroeber, Alfred L.

1925   Handbook of the Indians of California. Bulletin 78, Bureau of American Ethnology. Washington, D.C.: Smithsonian Institution.

1928   Native culture of the Southwest. University of California Publications in American Archaeology and Ethnology, vol. 23, no. 9, pp. 375–398.

1939   Cultural and natural areas of native North America. University of California Publications in American Archaeology and Ethnology, vol. 38. Berkeley.

1948   Anthropology. Rev. ed. New York: Harcourt, Brace & Co.

Küchler, A. W.

1964   Potential natural vegetation of the conterminous United States. Special Publication no. 36. New York: American Geographical Society.

Lappala, Eric G.

1976   Changes in the water supply in the upper Republican natural resources district, southwest Nebraska, from 1952–75. United States Geological Survey, Open-File Report 76-498. Prepared in cooperation with the Conservation and Survey Division, University of Nebraska, Lincoln.

Laws, R. M., I. S. C. Parker, and R. C. B. Johnstone

1975   Elephants and their habitats: the ecology of elephants in North Bunyoro, Uganda. London: Oxford University Press, Clarendon Press.

Lehmer, Donald J.

1970   Climate and culture in the Middle Missouri valley. In Pleistocene and Recent Environments of the Central Great Plains, edited by Wakefield Dort, Jr., and J. Knox Jones, Jr., pp. 117–129. Special Publication 3. Lawrence: Department of Geology, University of Kansas.

Leonhardy, Frank C., and Adrian D. Anderson

1966   The archaeology of the Domebo site. In Domebo: a Paleo-Indian mammoth kill in the prairie-plains, edited by Frank C. Leonhardy, pp. 14–26. Contributions of the Museum of the Great Plains, no. 1. Lawton, Okla.

Lesser, Alexander

1978   The Pawnee ghost dance hand game, Columbia University Press, 1933. Reprint. Madison: University of Wisconsin Press.

Lessig, John A.

1873   Field notes of the survey of the 1st Corr line south from the 6th guide meridian to the eastern boundary of Colorado, and the exterior lines of townships 1, 2, 3, 4, & 5 south of ranges 47 and 48, exlines townships 3, 4, & 5 south of ranges 44, 45, & 46, Ex lines townships 4 & 5 south of ranges 42 and 43 west of the 6th principal meridian in Colorado. Microfiche files, vol. 27. Bureau of Land Management, Denver.

Lewis, Meriwether, and William Clark

1904–1905   Original journals of the Lewis and Clark expedition, 1804–1806. Edited by Reuben Gold Thwaites, 8 vols. (1904, vols. 1 and 2; 1905, vols. 3–8). New York: Dodd, Mead & Co.

Libby, Willard F.

1955   Radiocarbon dating. 2d ed. Chicago: University of Chicago Press.

Lintz, Christopher

1978   The Panhandle aspect and its early relationship with Upper Republican. In The Central Plains Tradition: Internal Developments and External Relationships, edited by Donald J. Blakeslee, pp. 36–55. Report no. 11, Office of the State Archaeologist. Iowa City: University of Iowa.

1979   The southwestern periphery of the Plains Caddoan area. In Toward Plains Caddoan Origins. Nebraska History, vol. 60, no. 2, pp. 161–182.

Lippincott, Kerry

[1976]   Settlement ecology of Solomon River Upper Republican sites in north central Kansas. Ph.D. diss., Department of Anthropology, University of Missouri.

1978   Solomon River Upper Republican settlement ecology. In The Central Plains Tradition: Internal Developments and External Relationships, edited by Donald J. Blakeslee, pp. 81–93. Report no. 11, Office of the State Archaeologist. Iowa City: University of Iowa.

Logan, W. N.

1897   The upper Cretaceous of Kansas. Kansas Geological Survey, vol. 2, pp. 195–234.

Loomis, Noel M., and A. P. Nasatir

1967   Pedro Vial and the roads to Santa Fe. Norman: University of Oklahoma Press.

Ludlow, William

1875   Report of a reconnaissance of the Black Hills of Dakota, made in the summer of 1874. Engineer Department, United States Army. Washington, D.C.

Ludwickson, John

1978   Central Plains tradition settlements in the Loup River basin: the Loup River Phase. In The Central Plains Tradition: Internal Developments and External Relationships, edited by Donald J. Blakeslee, pp. 94–108. Report no. 11, Office of the State Archaeologist. Iowa City: University of Iowa.

Lushbaugh, Benjamin F.
1864   Report of B. F. Lushbaugh, agent for the Pawnees. Report of the Commissioner of Indian Affairs for the year 1863, Document no. 131, pp. 251–253. United States Department of the Interior.

McCoy, Isaac
1840   History of Baptist Indian missions. Washington, D.C.: William M. Morrison; New York: H. & S. Raynor.

McCracken, Harold, ed.
1977   Mummy Cave project in northwestern Wyoming. Cody: Buffalo Bill Historical Center.

McDermott, John F., ed.
1940   Tixier's travels on the Osage prairies. Norman: University of Oklahoma Press.

McDermott, John F.
1941   A glossary of Mississippi French, 1673–1850. Washington University Studies, New Series. Language and Literature Series no. 12. St. Louis.

McGee, W. J., and Cyrus Thomas
1905   Prehistoric North America. The History of North America, vol. 19, edited by F. N. Thorpe. Philadelphia: George Barrie & Sons.

Maglio, V. J.
1973   Origin and evolution of the Elephantidae. Transactions, American Philosophical Society, n.s., vol. 63, part 3, pp. 1–149.

Malde, Harold E.
1960   Geological age of the Claypool site, northeastern Colorado. American Antiquity, vol. 26, no. 2, pp. 236–243.

Malouf, Carling, and Stuart Conner
1962   Symposium on buffalo jumps. Montana Archaeological Society, Memoir no. 1.

Mangelsdorf, Paul C.
1974   Corn. Its origin, evolution, and improvement. Cambridge: Harvard University Press.

Margry, Pierre
1886   Exploration des affluents du Mississippi et découverte des Montagnes Rocheuses (1679–1754). Découvertes et établissements des Français dans l'ouest et dans le sud de l'Amérique Septentrional (1614–1754). Mémoires et documents originaux. Part 6. Paris: D. Jouaust et Sigaux.

Marshall, James O., and Thomas A. Witty, Jr.
[1967]   The Bogan site, 14GE1, an historic Pawnee village. An appraisal of an archeological site in the Milford reservoir, Geary County, Kansas. Unpublished manuscript. Kansas State Historical Society.

Martin, Paul S.
1967   Prehistoric overkill. In Pleistocene Extinctions: The Search for a Cause, edited by Paul S. Martin and Herbert E. Wright, Jr., pp. 75–120. New Haven: Yale University Press.

1982   The pattern and meaning of Holarctic mammoth extinction. In Paleoecology of Beringia, edited by David M. Hopkins et al., pp. 399–408. New York: Academic Press.

Martin, Paul S., and John E. Guilday
1967   A bestiary for Pleistocene biologists. In Pleistocene Extinctions: The Search for a Cause, edited by Paul S. Martin and Herbert E. Wright, Jr., pp. 1–62. New Haven: Yale University Press.

Martin, Paul S., and Richard G. Klein
1984   Quaternary extinctions: a prehistoric revolution. Tucson: University of Arizona Press.

Martin, Paul S., and Herbert E. Wright, Jr., eds.
1967   Pleistocene Extinctions: The Search for a Cause. Proceedings of the VII Congress of the International Association for Quaternary Research, vol. 6. New Haven.

Mason, Otis T.

1896   Influence of environment upon human industries or arts. Annual Report of the Smithsonian Institution for 1895, pp. 639–665. Washington, D.C.

Mathers, James, and Carolan Mathers

1844   Report of James Mathers. Document No. 71 accompanying the Report of the Commissioner of Indian Affairs for 1844, pp. 148–150. United States War Department.

Mattes, Merrill J.

1965   Archaeology of the Bisterfeldt potato cellar site. Southwestern Lore, vol. 31, no. 3, pp. 56–61.

1969   The Great Platte River Road. Publications, Nebraska State Historical Society, vol. 25.

Meko, David M.

1982   Drought history in the western Great Plains from tree rings. International Symposium on Hydrometeorology, June 1982, pp. 321–326. American Water Resources Association. Bethesda, Maryland.

Miller, R. D., R. Van Horn, E. Dobrovolny, and L. P. Buck

1964   Geology of Franklin, Webster, and Nuckolls Counties, Nebraska. Bulletin 1165, United States Geological Survey. Washington, D.C.

Minge, Ward Alan

1979   *Efectos del pais:* a history of weaving along the Rio Grande. In Spanish Textile Tradition of New Mexico and Colorado, pp. 8–28. Santa Fe: Museum of International Folk Art.

Montgomery, Mrs. Frank C.

1928   Fort Wallace and its relation to the frontier. Collections, Kansas State Historical Society, vol. 17 (1926–1928), pp. 189–283.

Moorhead, Max L.

1957   Spanish transportation in the Southwest: 1540–1846. New Mexico Historical Review, vol. 32, pp. 107–120.

1958   New Mexico's royal road: Trade and travel on the Chihuahua trail. Norman: University of Oklahoma Press.

Morgan, Dale L.

1964   The west of Wm. H. Ashley . . . recorded in the diaries and letters of Wm. H. Ashley and his contemporaries, 1822–26. Denver: Old West Publishing Co.

Morley, G. E.

1964   A floristic study of Republic County, Kansas. Transactions, Kansas Academy of Science, vol. 67, pp.716–746.

Mosiman, James E., and Paul S. Martin

1975   Simulating overkill by PaleoIndians. American Scientist, vol. 63, no. 3, pp. 304–313.

Moulton, Gary E., ed.

1983   Atlas of the Lewis and Clark expedition. Lincoln: University of Nebraska Press.

Muller, Jon

1983   The Southeast. In ancient North Americans, edited by Jesse D. Jennings, chapter 9, pp. 373–420. San Francisco: W. H. Freeman & Co.

Mulloy, William

1945   Archeological investigations in the Shoshoni Basin of Wyoming. University of Wyoming Publications, vol. 18, no. 1, pp. 1–70. Laramie.

1958   A preliminary historical outline for the Northwestern Plains. University of Wyoming Publications, vol. 22, nos. 1–2. Laramie.

Munday, Frank J.

1927   Pike-Pawnee village site. Nebraska History Magazine, vol. 10, no. 3, pp. 168–192.

Murie, James R.

1981   Ceremonies of the Pawnee. Part I: The Skiri; Part II: The South Bands. Edited by Douglas R. Parks. Smithsonian Contributions to Anthropology, no. 27. Washington, D.C.

Murray, Charles Augustus

1839   Travels in North America during the Years 1834, 1835, and 1836. 2 vols. New York: Harper & Bros.

Murray, Harold D., and A. Byron Leonard

1962   Handbook of Unionid mussels in Kansas. Lawrence: Museum of Natural History, University of Kansas.

Nasatir, Abraham P.

1929   Anglo-Spanish rivalry on the upper Missouri. Mississippi Valley Historical Review, vol. 16, pp. 359–382.

1931   John Evans, explorer and surveyor, part II. Missouri Historical Review, vol. 25, pp. 432–460.

1974   More on Pedro Vial in Upper Louisiana. In The Spanish in the Mississippi Valley, 1762–1804, edited by John Francis McDermott, pp. 100–119. Urbana: University of Illinois.

Nasatir, Abraham P, ed.

1952   Before Lewis and Clark: documents illustrating the history of the Missouri, 1785–1804, 2 vols. St. Louis: St. Louis Historical Documents Foundation.

Nebraska Department of Agriculture

1976   Nebraska agricultural statistics: annual report 1974–75. Lincoln.

Netting, Robert M.

1965   A trial mode of cultural ecology. Anthropological Quarterly, vol. 38, no. 3, pp. 81–96.

Neuman, Robert W.

1963   Archeological salvage investigations in the Lovewell reservoir area, Kansas. Bulletin 185, Bureau of American Ethnology. River Basin Surveys Papers no. 32, pp. 257–306. Washington, D.C.

1967   Radiocarbon-dated archaeological remains on the northern and central Great Plains. American Antiquity, vol. 32, no. 4, pp. 471–486.

Nickel, Robert K.

1977   The study of archaeologically derived plant remains from the middle Missouri subarea. Plains Anthropologist, vol. 22, no. 78, pp. 53–58 (Memoir 13).

Nurge, Ethel

1975   Dakota diet: traditional and contemporary. In The Modern Sioux, edited by Ethel Nurge, pp. 35–91, 1970. Reprint. Lincoln: University of Nebraska Press, Bison Books.

Obregón, Baltasár de

1928   Obregon's history of 16th century explorations in western America. Translated, edited, and annotated by George P. Hammond and Agapito Rey. Los Angeles: Wetzel Publishing Co.

Oliver, Symmes C.

1962   Ecology and cultural continuity as contributing factors in the social organization of the Plains Indians. University of California Publications in American Archaeology and Ethnology, vol. 48, no. 1, pp. 1–90. Berkeley.

Olivier, Robert C. D.

1982   Ecology and behavior of living elephants: bases for assumptions concerning the extinct woolly mammoths. In Paleoecology of Beringia, edited by D. M. Hopkins, J. V. Matthews, Jr., C. E. Schweger, and S. B. Young, pp. 291–305. New York: Academic Press.

Olson, James C.

1966   History of Nebraska. Lincoln: University of Nebraska Press.

Opler, Morris E.

1935   Apachean culture history. Anthropological Quarterly, vol. 48, no. 3, pp. 182–191.

1936   A summary of Jicarilla Apache culture. American Anthropologist, vol. 38, no. 2, pp. 202–223.

1971   Pots, Apache, and the Dismal River culture aspect. In Apachean culture history and ethnology, edited by Keith A. Basso and Morris E. Opler, pp. 29–33. Anthropological Papers of the University of Arizona, no. 21. Tucson.

1975   Problems in Apachean culture history, with special reference to the Lipan Apache. Anthropological Quarterly, vol. 48, no. 3, pp. 182–192.

1982   The Scott County pueblo site in historical, archaeological, and ethnological perspective. In Pathways to Plains Prehistory, edited by Don. G. Wyckoff and J. L. Hofman, pp. 135–144. Oklahoma Anthropological Society Memoir 3, Cross Timbers Heritage Association Contributions 1. Duncan, Okla.

Palliser, John
1863   The journals, detailed reports, and observations relative to the exploration by Capt. John Palliser of that portion of British North America which lies in latitude between the British boundary line and the height of land of the northern or frozen ocean respectively and in longitude between the western shore of Lake Superior and the Pacific Ocean, during the years 1857, 1858, 1859, and 1860. London: G. E. Eyre and W. Spottiswoode for Her Majesty's Stationery Office.

Palmer, Edward
1871   Food products of the North American Indians. Report of the Commissioner of Agriculture for the year 1870, pp. 404–428.

Parker, H. N.
1911   Quality of the water supplies of Kansas. United States Geological Survey, Water-Supply Paper 273. Washington, D.C.

Parker, J. D.
1887   Mounds in Davis County. Transactions, Kansas Academy of Sciences, vol. 10, pp. 72–73.

Parks, Douglas R.
1979   Bands and villages of the Arikara and Pawnee. Nebraska History, vol. 60, no. 2, pp. 214–239.

Parks, Douglas R., and Waldo R. Wedel
1985   Pawnee geography: historical and sacred. Great Plains Quarterly, vol. 5, no. 3, pp. 143–176.

Parmalee, Paul W.
1977   The avifauna from prehistoric Arikara sites in South Dakota. Plains Anthropologist, vol. 22, no. 77, pp. 189–222.

Parmalee, Paul W., and Walter E. Klippel
1974   Freshwater mussels as a prehistoric food resource. American Antiquity, vol. 19, no. 3, pp. 421–434.

Petter, Rodolphe
1915   English-Cheyenne dictionary. Kettle Falls, Wash.

Patrick, G. E.
1906   The Great Spirit Spring. Transactions, Kansas Academy of Science, vol. 7, pp. 22–26.

Phenice, Terrell W.
1969   An analysis of the human skeletal material from burial mounds in north central Kansas. University of Kansas Publications in Anthropology no. 1. Lawrence.

Pickering, I. O.
1906   The administrations of John P. St. John. Transactions, Kansas State Historical Society, 1905–1906, vol. 9, pp. 378–394.

Pike, Zebulon M.
1810   An account of expeditions . . . performed by order of the Government of the United States during the years 1805, 1806, and 1807. Philadelphia: C. & A. Conrad & Co.

Platt, Elvira G.
1892   Reminiscences of a teacher among the Nebraska Indians, 1843–45. Transactions and Reports of the Nebraska State Historical Society, vol. 3, pp. 125–143. Fremont.

Pool, Raymond J.

1966   Handbook of Nebraska trees. Nebraska Conservation Bulletin, no. 32. Lincoln: University of Nebraska, Conservation and Survey Division.

Powell, Father Peter John

1981   People of the sacred mountain. 2 vols. San Francisco: Harper & Row.

Prucha, Francis Paul

1971   Indian peace medals in American history. Lincoln: University of Nebraska Press.

Quaife, Milo M., ed.

1947   The western country in the 17th century: The memoirs of Lamothe Cadillac and Pierre Liette. Chicago: Lakeside Press.

Rapp, William F., Jr., J. L. C. Rapp, H. E. Baumgarten, and R. A. Moser

1958   Revised check-list of Nebraska birds. Occasional Papers no. 5. Crete: Nebraska Ornithologists' Union.

Raynolds, William Franklin

1868   Report on the exploration of the Yellowstone River. 40th Cong., 1st [2d] sess., S. Exec. Doc. 77. Washington, D.C.

Reeves, Bryan

1973   The concept of an Altithermal cultural hiatus in Northern Plains prehistory. American Anthropologist, vol. 75, no. 5, pp. 1,221–1,253.

Reher, Charles A.

1978   Buffalo population and other deterministic factors in a model of adaptive process on the shortgrass plains. In Bison Procurement and Utilization: A Symposium, edited by Leslie B. Davis and Michael Wilson, pp. 23–39. Plains Anthropologist, vol. 23, no. 82 (Memoir 14).

Riggs, Stephen R.

1852   Grammar and dictionary of the Dakota language. Smithsonian Contributions to Knowledge, vol. 4. Washington, D.C.

1890   A Dakota-English dictionary. Contributions to North American Ethnology, vol. 7. United States Geographical and Geological Survey of the Rocky Mountain Region. Department of the Interior.

Riley, Paul D.

1966   Red Willow County letters of Royal Buck, 1872–1873. Nebraska History, vol. 47, no. 4, pp. 371–397.

1973   The battle of Massacre Canyon. Nebraska History, vol. 54, no. 2, pp. 221–249.

Roberts, Ricky L.

[1978]   The archeology of the Kansas Monument site: a study in historical archeology on the Great Plains. Master's thesis, Department of Anthropology, University of Kansas.

Robinson, Sarah

1976   An analysis of charred seeds from a Middle Woodland occupation site in central Missouri. In Hopewellian Archaeology in the lower Missouri valley, edited by Alfred E. Johnson, pp. 100–109. Publications in Anthropology, no. 8. Lawrence: University of Kansas.

Rodenbough, Theophilus F., and William L. Haskins, eds.

1896   Army of the United States. New York.

Root, George A.

1934   Ferries in Kansas, Part 4: Republican River. Kansas Historical Quarterly, vol. 3, no. 3, pp. 246–288.

Royce, C. C.

1899   Indian land cessions in the United States. 18th Annual Report, Bureau of American Ethnology, part 2, pp. 521–964. Washington, D.C.

Rusco, Mary Kiehl

1960   The White Rock aspect. Note Book no. 4, Laboratory of Anthropology. Lincoln: University of Nebraska.

Rutter, N. W., and C. E. Schweger eds.

1980   The ice-free corridor and peopling of the New World. Proceedings of the Fifth Biennial Conference of the American Quaternary Association, Edmonton, 2–4 September, 1978. Edmonton: University of Alberta.

Safford, W. E.

1925   The potato of romance and of reality. Journal of Heredity, vol. 16, pp. 113–230.

Sanborn, Theo. A.

1973   The story of the Pawnee Indian village in Republic County, Kansas. Kansas Historical Quarterly, vol. 39, no. 1, pp. 1–11.

Sauer, Carl O.

1944   A geographic sketch of early man in America. Geographical Review, vol. 34, no. 4, pp. 529–573.

Saunders, Jeffrey J.

1977   Lehner Ranch revisited. The Museum Journal, vol. 17, pp. 48–64.

1980   A model for man-mammoth relationships in late Pleistocene North America. Canadian Journal of Anthropology, vol. 1, no. 1, pp. 87–98. Proceedings of the 5th Biennial Meeting of the American Quaternary Association, 2–4 September 1978. Edmonton: University of Alberta.

Schlesier, Karl H.

1972   Rethinking the Dismal River aspect and the Plains Athapaskans, A.D. 1692–1768. Plains Anthropologist, vol. 17, no. 56, pp. 101–133.

Schmits, Larry J.

1978   The Coffey site: environment and cultural adaptation at a prairie plains Archaic site. MCJA Special Paper no. 1, Mid-Continental Journal of Archaeology, vol. 3, no. 1, pp. 69–185. Kent, Ohio: Kent State University Press.

1980   Holocene fluvial history and depositional environments at the Coffey site, Kansas. In Archaic Prehistory on the Prairie-Plains Border, edited by Alfred E. Johnson, pp. 79–105. University of Kansas Publications in Anthropology no. 12, chapter 9. Lawrence.

Schoewe, Walter H.

1953   The geography of Kansas. Part 3: concluded. Hydrogeography. Transactions, Kansas Academy of Science, vol. 56, no. 2, pp. 136–138.

Scholes, France V.

1930   The supply service of the New Mexican missions in the 17th century. New Mexico Historical Review, vol. 5, pp. 93–115, 186–210, 386–404.

Schorger, A. W.

1966   The wild turkey: its history and domestication. Norman: University of Oklahoma.

Schultz, C. B., and W. D. Frankforter

1948   Preliminary report on the Lime Creek sites: new evidence of early man in southwestern Nebraska. Bulletin, University of Nebraska State Museum, vol. 3, no. 4, part 2, pp. 43–62.

Schultz, Floyd, and Albert C. Spaulding

1948   A Hopewellian burial site in the lower Republican valley, Kansas. American Antiquity, vol. 13, no. 4, pp. 306–313.

Schweinfurth, Georg

1969   The heart of Africa. Three years' travels and adventures in the unexplored regions of Central Africa, from 1868 to 1871. 2 vols. Translated by Ellen Frewer. Chicago: Afro-Am Press.

Sheldon, Addison E.

1935   The Massacre Canyon fight. Nebraska History Magazine, vol. 16, no. 3 (July–September), pp. 130–184.

Sheridan, Philip H.

1882   Record of engagements with hostile Indians within the Military Division of the Missouri, from 1868 to 1882, Lt.-Gen. P. H. Sheridan, commanding. Compiled at Headquarters Military Division of the Missouri from official records. Washington, D.C.: Government Printing Office.

Sikes, Silvia K.

1971   The natural history of the African elephant. New York: American Elsevier Publishing Co.

Smith, Carlyle S.

1950   European trade material from the Kansas Monument site. Plains Archaeological Conference News Letter, vol. 3, no. 2, pp. 2–9.

Smith, J. Russell

1925   North America. New York: Harcourt, Brace & Co.

Smith, J. Warren

1906   Relation of precipitation to yield of corn. In Report of the Kansas State Board of Agriculture for the Quarter ending December 1905, pp. 193–202. Topeka.

Stanford, Dennis J.

1974   Preliminary report of the excavation of the Jones-Miller Hell Gap site, Yuma County, Colorado. Southwestern Lore, vol. 40, nos. 3–4, pp. 29–36.

1975   The 1975 excavations at the Jones-Miller site, Yuma County, Colorado. Southwestern Lore, vol. 41, no. 4, pp. 34–38.

1979   The Selby and Dutton sites: evidence for a possible pre-Clovis occupation of the High Plains. In Pre-Llano Cultures of the Americas: Paradoxes and Possibilities, edited by Robert L. Humphrey and Dennis Stanford, pp. 101–123. Anthropological Society of Washington.

1982   A critical review of archaeological evidence relating to the antiquity of human occupation of the New World. In Plains Indian Studies, edited by Douglas H. Ubelaker and Herman J. Viola, pp. 202–218. Smithsonian Contributions in Anthropology, no. 30, Washington, D.C.

Stanford, Dennis, and John Albanese

1975   Preliminary results of the Smithsonian Institution excavation at the Claypool site, Washington County, Colorado. Southwestern Lore, vol. 41, no. 4, pp. 22–28.

Stanford, Dennis, Robson Bonnichsen, and Richard E. Morlan

1981   The Ginsberg experiment: modern and prehistoric evidence of a bone-flaking technology. Science, vol. 212, no. 4493, pp. 438–440.

Stanford, Dennis, Waldo R. Wedel, and Glenn R. Scott

1981   Archeological investigations of the Lamb Spring site. Southwestern Lore, vol. 47, no. 1, pp. 14–27.

Stephens, H. A.

1969   Trees, shrubs, and woody vines in Kansas. Lawrence: University Press of Kansas.

1973   Woody plants of the north central plains. Lawrence: University Press of Kansas.

1980   Poisonous plants of the central United States. Lawrence: Regents Press of Kansas.

Stephenson, Robert L.

1965   Quaternary human occupation of the Plains. In The Quaternary of the United States, edited by H. E. Wright, Jr., and D. G. Frey. 7th Congress of the International Association for Quaternary Research. Princeton.

Sterns, Fred H.

1918   The peopling of the American Plains by the Indians. Scientific American Supplement, vol. 85, pp. 234–235.

Stevens, J. C.

1909   Surface water supply of Nebraska. United States Geological Survey Water-Supply Paper 230. Washington, D.C.

Steward, Julian H.

1938   Basin-plateau aboriginal sociopolitical groups. Bulletin 120, Bureau of American Ethnology. Washington, D.C.

1955   Theory of culture change. Urbana: University of Illinois Press.

Stewart, T. D.

1943   Skeletal remains from Platte and Clay counties, Missouri. In Archeological Investigations in Platte and Clay counties, Missouri, by Waldo R. Wedel, pp. 245–273. Bulletin 183, United States National Museum, appendix. Washington, D. C.

1959   Description of the skeletal remains from Doniphan and Scott counties, Kansas. In An Introduction to Kansas Archeology, by Waldo R. Wedel, pp. 669–683. Bulletin 174, Bureau of American Ethnology. Washington, D.C.

Stockton, Charles W., and David M. Meko

1975   A long-term history of drought occurrence in western United States as inferred from tree rings. Weatherwise, vol. 28, no. 6, pp. 244–249.

1983   Drought recurrence in the Great Plains as reconstructed from long-term tree-ring records. Journal of Climate and Applied Meteorology, vol. 22, no. 1, pp. 17–29.

Stoddard, Amos

1973   Sketches, historical and descriptive, of Louisiana. Philadelphia: Matthew Carey, 1812. Reprint. New York: AMS Press.

Strong, William Duncan

1933   The Plains culture area in the light of archeology. American Anthropologist, vol. 35, pp. 271–287.

1935   An introduction to Nebraska archeology. Smithsonian Miscellaneous Collections, vol. 93, no. 10.

Stuiver, M. and H. E. Suess

1966   On the relationship between radiocarbon dates and true age samples. Radiocarbon, vol. 8, pp. 534–540.

Suess, Hans E.

1970   Bristlecone-pine calibration of the radiocarbon timescale 5200 B.C. to the present. In Radio-carbon Variations and Absolute Chronology, edited by Ingrid Olsson, pp. 303–311. Nobel Symposium no. 12. Stockholm.

Surrey, N. M. Miller

1968   The commerce of Louisiana during the French regime, 1699–1763. New York: Columbia University Press, 1916. Reprint. New York: AMS Press.

Talbot, Theodore

1931   The journals of Theodore Talbot, 1843 and 1849–1852, with the Frémont expedition of 1843 and with the First Military Company in Oregon Territory, 1849–1852. Edited by Charles H. Carey. Portland, Ore.: Metropolitan Press.

Taylor, D. W.

1960   Late Cenozoic molluscan faunas from the High Plains. Professional Paper 337, United States Geological Survey. Washington, D.C.

Thomas, Alfred Barnaby

1935   After Coronado. Spanish exploration northeast of New Mexico, 1696–1727. Norman: University of Oklahoma Press.

Thornthwaite, C. Warren

1941   Climate and settlement in the Great Plains. In Climate and Man, Yearbook of Agriculture 1941, pp. 177–187. Washington, D.C.

Truteau, Jean-Baptiste

1794–1796   Extract from the journals of the voyage of Jean-Baptiste Truteau on the upper Missouri, addressed to Messers the Directors of the Company at St. Louis of the Illinois, from 7 June 1794 to 4 June 1796. Archives of the Seminary of Québec: Fonds Viger Verreau, Carton 50, no. 74, Folio 52, Fonds Verreau.

Twiss, Thomas S.

1856   Report of Thomas S. Twiss, agent for the Indians of the Upper Platte. Documents accompanying the Report of the Commissioner of Indian Affairs for the year 1855, no. 2, pp. 81–85. United States Department of the Interior.

Ubelaker, Douglas H.

1976   The sources and methodology for Mooney's estimates of North American Indian populations. In The Native Population of the Americas in 1492, edited by William N. Denevan, pp. 243–288. Madison: University of Wisconsin Press.

Ubelaker, Douglas H., and Richard L. Jantz

1979   Plains Caddoan relationships: the view from craniometry and mortuary analysis. Nebraska History, vol. 60, no. 2, pp. 249–259.

Ubelaker, Douglas H., and Herman J. Viola, eds.

1982   Plains Indian studies: a collection of essays in honor of John C. Ewers and Waldo R. Wedel. Smithsonian Contributions to Anthropology, no. 30. Washington, D.C.: Smithsonian Institution.

Ubelaker, Douglas H., and Waldo R. Wedel

1975   Bird bones, burials, and bundles in Plains archaeology. American Antiquity, vol. 40, no. 4, pp. 444–452.

Uerpmann, Hans-Peter

1973   Animal bone finds and economic archaeology: a critical study of "osteo-archaeological" method. World Archaeology, vol. 4, no. 3, pp. 307–322.

United States Bureau of the Census

1883–1973   Statistics of the population of the United States. HA201: 10th, 1880; 12th, 1900; 14th, 1920; 16th, 1940; 19th, 1970. Washington, D.C.

United States Department of Agriculture

1930   Climatic summary of the United States, Weather Bureau, Bulletin 30, sections 23, 38, 39, 40, 41. Washington, D.C.

1936   Atlas of American agriculture. Physical basis including land relief, climate, soils, and natural vegetation of the United States. Washington, D.C.: Bureau of Agricultural Economics, U.S. Department of Agriculture.

1959   Food. The yearbook of agriculture 1959. Washington, D.C.

United States Department of Commerce

1952   Climatic summary of the United States. Supplement for 1931 through 1952, nos. 11–12 and 11–21. Washington, D.C.

1964   Climatic summary of the United States. Supplement for 1951 through 1960. Washington, D.C.

Utberg, Neil S.

1970   The coins of colonial Mexico, 1536–1821, and the empire of Iturbide, 1821–1823. Revised by George W. Vogt, Colonial Coins, Houston.

Valastro, S., Jr., F. J. Pearson, Jr., and E. Mott Davis

1967   University of Texas radiocarbon dates 5. Radiocarbon, vol. 9, pp. 439–453.

Véniard de Bourgmont, Etienne

1714   Routte qu'il faut tenir pour monter la Rivière de Missoury. Archives hydrographiques de la Marine, AM 3 JJ 277:17. Paris.

Vereshchagin, N. K.

1967   Primitive hunters and Pleistocene extinction in the Soviet Union. In Pleistocene extinctions: the search for a cause, edited by Paul S. Martin and Herbert E. Wright, Jr., pp. 365–398. Proceedings of the VII Congress of the International Association for Quaternary Research, vol. 6. New Haven.

Vestal, Paul A., and Richard E. Schultes

1939   The economic botany of the Kiowa Indians. Cambridge, Mass.: Botanical Museum.

Villiers, Marc de
1925   La Découverte du Missouri et l'histoire du Fort Orleans (1673–1728). Paris: Champion.

Volkmar, Lt. William J.
1869   Journal of the march of the Republican River expedition, consisting of B, C, and M Troops, 2nd Cavalry; A, B, E, F, G, L, and M Troops, 5th Cavalry, and A, B, and C Troops, Pawnee Scouts;—Brevet Brig. General Thomas Duncan commanding. Part 3, September 15–October 28, 1869. National Archives and Records Service, Record Group 393, Department of the Platte, Box 13.

Walters, Kenneth L.
1956   Geology and ground-water resources of Rawlins County, Kansas. Bulletin 117, Kansas Geological Survey. Topeka.

Ware, Eugene F.
1960   The Indian war of 1864. Lincoln: University of Nebraska Press.

Waring, A. J., Jr., and Preston Holder
1945   A prehistoric ceremonial complex in the southeastern United States. American Anthropologist, vol. 47, no. 1, pp. 1–34.

Warner, Marjorie F.
1947   Lamare-Picquot and the breadroot. Agricultural History, vol. 21, pp. 23–26.

Warren, Gouverneur K.
1856   Explorations in the Dacota Country, in the year 1855. 34th Cong. 1st sess. S. Exec. Doc. 76. Washington, D.C.

1875   Preliminary report of explorations in Nebraska and Dakota, in the years 1855–'56–'57. Annual report of Secretary of War, 1858. Reprint. Washington, D.C.: Engineer Department, United States Army.

Watt, D. K., and A. L. Merrill
1963   Composition of foods: raw, processed, prepared. Agriculture Handbook 8. Washington, D.C.: United States Department of Agriculture.

Weakly, Harry E.
1940   Tree rings as a record of precipitation in western Nebraska. Tree-Ring Bulletin, vol. 6, no. 3, pp. 18–19.

1943   A tree-ring record of precipitation in western Nebraska. Journal of Forestry, vol. 41, no. 11, pp. 816–819.

1946   A preliminary report on the Ash Hollow charcoal. In Ash Hollow Cave, by John L. Champe, pp. 105–110. University of Nebraska Studies, n.s., no. 1, appendix 1. Lincoln.

Weatherwax, Paul
1954   Indian corn in old America. New York: Macmillan Co.

Weaver, J. E.
1954   North American prairie. Lincoln: Johnsen Publishing Co.

1968   Prairie plants and their environment. Lincoln: University of Nebraska Press.

Weaver, J. E., and F. W. Albertson
1956   Grasslands of the Great Plains: their nature and use. Lincoln: Johnsen Publishing Co.

Webb, William S., and David L. DeJarnette
1942   An archeological survey of Pickwick Basin in the adjacent portions of the states of Alabama, Mississippi, and Tennessee. Bulletin 129, Bureau of American Ethnology. Washington, D.C.

Wedel, Mildred Mott
1978   La Harpe's 1719 post on Red River and nearby Caddo settlements. Bulletin 30. Austin: Texas Memorial Museum.

1979   The ethnohistoric approach to Plains Caddoan origins. Nebraska History, vol. 60, no. 2, pp. 183–196.

1982   The Wichita Indians in the Arkansas River basin. In Plains Indian Studies, edited by Douglas H. Ubelaker and Herman J. Viola, pp. 118–134. Smithsonian Contributions to Anthropology, no. 30. Washington, D.C.

Wedel, Waldo R.

1934   Preliminary notes on the archeology of Medicine valley in southwestern Nebraska. Nebraska History Magazine, vol. 14, no. 3, pp. 144–166.

1935   Contributions to the archeology of the upper Republican valley, Nebraska. Nebraska History Magazine, vol. 15, no. 3, pp. 133–209.

1936   An introduction to Pawnee archeology. Bulletin 112, Bureau of American Ethnology. Washington, D.C.

1938   The direct-historical approach in Pawnee archeology. Smithsonian Miscellaneous Collections, vol. 97, no. 7.

1941   Environment and native subsistence economies in the central Great Plains. Smithsonian Miscellaneous Collections, vol. 101, no. 3, pp. 1–29.

1943   Archeological investigations in Platte and Clay counties, Missouri. Bulletin 183, United States National Museum. Washington, D.C.

1947   Note on some potsherds from northeastern Wyoming. Journal of the Washington Academy of Sciences, vol. 37, no. 5, pp. 157–159.

1948   Prehistory and the Missouri Basin development program: Summary report on the Missouri River basin survey in 1947. Smithsonian Miscellaneous Collections, vol. 111, no. 2, pp. 1–52.

1953   Some aspects of human ecology in the central Plains. American Anthropologist, vol. 55, no. 4, pp. 499–514.

1959   An introduction to Kansas archeology. Bulletin 174, Bureau of American Ethnology. Washington, D.C.

1961   Prehistoric man on the Great Plains. Norman: University of Oklahoma Press.

1963   The High Plains and their utilization by the Indian. American Antiquity, vol. 29, no. 1, pp. 1–16.

1970a   Some observations on Two House Sites in the Central Plains: An Experiment in Archaeology, edited by W. Raymond Wood. Nebraska History, vol. 51, no. 2, pp. 225–252.

1970b   Coronado's route to Quivira, 1541. Plains Anthropologist, vol. 15, no. 49, pp. 161–168.

1978a   Notes on the prairie turnip (Psoralea esculenta) among the Plains Indians. Nebraska History, vol. 59, no. 2, pp. 154–179.

1978b   The prehistoric Plains. In Ancient Native Americans, edited by J. D. Jennings, pp. 182–219. San Francisco: W. H. Freeman & Co.

1978c   Commentary. In The Central Plains Tradition: internal development and external relationships, edited by Donald J. Blakeslee, pp. 157–162. Report 11, Office of the State Archaeologist. Iowa City: University of Iowa.

1979a   House floors and native settlement populations in the Central Plains. Plains Anthropologist, vol. 24, no. 84, part 1, pp. 85–98.

1979b   Holocene cultural adaptations in the Republican River basin. In The Great Plains: environment and culture, edited by Bryan W. Blouet and Fred C. Luebke, pp. 1–25. Lincoln: Center for Great Plains Studies, University of Nebraska.

1979c   Some reflections on Plains Caddoan origins. Nebraska History, vol. 60, no. 2, pp. 272–293.

1981   Toward a history of Plains archeology. Great Plains Quarterly, vol. 1, no. 1, pp. 16–38.

1982a   Essays in the history of Plains archeology. Reprints in Anthropology, vol. 24. Lincoln: J & L Reprint Co.

1982b   Further notes on Puebloan–Central Plains contacts in light of archaeology. In Pathways to Plains Prehistory, edited by Don G. Wyckoff and Jack L. Hofman, pp. 145–152. Oklahoma Anthropological Society, Memoir 3. Duncan, Okla.

1983a   The prehistoric Plains. In Ancient North Americans, chapter 6, edited by Jesse D. Jennings, pp. 202–241. San Francisco: W. H. Freeman & Co.

1983b   Native subsistence adaptations in the Great Plains. In Man and the changing environments in the Great Plains, edited by W. W. Caldwell, C. B. Schultz, and T. M. Stout, pp. 93–110. Transactions of the Nebraska Academy of Sciences, vol. 11, Special Issue 1983. Lincoln.

Wedel, Waldo R., and Marvin F. Kivett
1956   Additional data on the Woodruff ossuary, Kansas. American Antiquity, vol. 21, no. 4, pp. 414–416.

Weltfish, Gene
1965   The lost universe. New York: Basic Books.

Wendland, Wayne M.
1978   Holocene man in North America: the ecological setting and climatic background. Plains Anthropologist, vol. 23, no. 82, part 1, pp. 273–287.

Wendland, Wayne M., and Reid A. Bryson
1974   Dating climatic episodes of the Holocene. Cultural Sensitivity to Environmental Change IV: IES Report 21. Madison: Center for Climatic Research, Institute for Environmental Studies, University of Wisconsin.

Wendland, Wayne M., and A. Kosobud
[1980]   Evaluation of climate changes on the North American Great Plains. Paper delivered at 38th Plains Conference, Iowa City, 6 November.

Whaley, Charles H.
1868   Annual report of C. H. Whaley, agent, Pawnee agency. Papers accompanying Report of the Commissioner of Indian Affairs for 1868, no. 57, pp. 234–236. United States Department of the Interior.

Wharton, Clifton
1925   The expedition of Major Clifton Wharton in 1844. Collections, Kansas State Historical Society, 1923–1925, vol. 16, pp. 272–305.

Wheat, Carl I.
1957–1963 Mapping the Transmississippi West, 1540–1861. 5 vols. San Francisco: Institute of Historical Geography.

Wheat, Joe Ben
1971   Lifeways of early man in North America. Arctic Anthropology, vol. 8, no. 2, pp. 22–31.

1972   The Olsen-Chubbuck site, a Paleo-Indian bison kill. American Antiquity, vol. 37, no. 1, part 2, pp. 1–180 (Memoir 26).

1978   Olsen-Chubbuck and Jurgens sites: four aspects of Paleo-Indian bison economy. In Bison procurement and utilization: a symposium, edited by Leslie B. Davis and Michael Wilson, pp. 84–89. Plains Anthropologist, vol. 23, no. 82, part 2 (Memoir 14).

Wheeler, Daniel H.
1865   Annual report of Agent Wheeler, relative to Pawnee agency. Document no. 162 accompanying the Report of the Commissioner of Indian Affairs for 1865, pp. 420–423. United States Department of the Interior.

Wheeler, Olin Dunbar
1904   The trail of Lewis and Clark, 1804–1904. New York: G. P. Putnam's Sons.

Whipple, Amiel W.
1856   Report of explorations for a railway route, near the 35th parallel of north latitude, from the Mississippi river to the Pacific ocean. Explorations and surveys for a railroad route from the Mississippi river to the Pacific Ocean . . . in 1853–4. 33rd Cong., 2d sess. Exec. Doc. 78. Vol. 3. Washington, D.C.

White, Barclay

1874   Annual report of Northern Superintendency. In Annual Report of Commissioner of Indian Affairs for 1873, pp. 184–188. United States Department of the Interior.

White, Leslie A., ed.

1959   Lewis Henry Morgan: the Indian journals, 1859–62. Ann Arbor: University of Michigan Press.

Will, George F.

1924   Indian agriculture at its northern limits in the Great Plains region of North America. *Annaes do XX Congresso Internacional de Americanistas*, Rio de Janeiro, 20–30 Agosto 1922, vol. 1, pp. 203–205.

Will, George F., and George E. Hyde

1917   Corn among the Indians of the Upper Missouri. St. Louis: W. H. Miner Co.

Williston, Samuel W.

1902   An arrowhead found with bones of *Bison occidentalis* Lucas, in western Kansas. American Geologist, vol. 30, pp. 313–315.

Wilmsen, Edwin N., and Frank H. H. Roberts, Jr.

1978   Lindenmeier, 1934–1974, concluding report on investigations. Smithsonian Contributions to Anthropology, no. 24. Washington, D.C.

Wilson, Gilbert L.

1917   Agriculture of the Hidatsa Indians. Bulletin of the University of Minnesota, Studies in the Social Sciences, no. 9.

1934   The Hidatsa earthlodge. American Museum of Natural History, Anthropological Papers, vol. 33, part 5, pp. 343–420.

Wilson, Hill P.

1904   Black Kettle's last raid—1868. Kansas State Historical Collections, vol. 8, pp. 110–117.

Wilson, Michael

1974   History of the bison in Wyoming, with particular reference to early Holocene forms. Geological Survey of Wyoming, Report of Investigations no. 10, pp. 91–99.

Wishart, David J.

1979   The dispossession of the Pawnee. Annals, Association of American Geographers, vol. 69, no. 3, pp. 382–401.

Wissler, Clark

1907   Diffusion of culture in the plains of North America. International Congress of Americanists. Proceedings, 15th sess. (Quebec), vol. 2, pp. 38–52.

1914   The influence of the horse in the development of Plains culture. American Anthropologist, vol. 16, no. 1, pp. 1–25.

Witty, Thomas A., Jr.

1963   The Woods, Avery, and Streeter archeological sites, Milford reservoir, Kansas. Anthropological Series no. 2. Topeka: Kansas State Historical Society.

1968   The Pawnee Indian village museum project. Newsletter, Kansas Anthropological Association, vol. 13, no. 5, pp. 1–5.

Wood, W. Raymond

1962   A stylistic and historical analysis of shoulder patterns on Plains Indian pottery. American Antiquity, vol. 28, no. 1, pp. 25–40.

1971   Pottery sites near Limon, Colorado. Southwestern Lore, vol. 37, no. 3, pp. 53–85.

Wood, W. Raymond, ed.

1969   Two house sites in the Central Plains: an experiment in archaeology. Plains Anthropologist, vol. 14, no. 44, part 2 (Memoir 6).

Wood, W. Raymond, comp.

1983   An atlas of early maps of the American Midwest. Scientific Papers, vol. 18. Springfield: Illinois State Museum.

Wormington, H. M.

1957 Ancient man in North America. Popular Series no. 4, 4th edition. Denver: Denver Museum of Natural History.

Wright, H. E., Jr.

1970 Vegetational history of the Central Plains. In Pleistocene and recent environments of the central Great Plains, edited by Wakefield Dort, Jr., and J. Knox Jones, Jr., pp. 157–172. Special Publication 3. Lawrence: Department of Geology, University of Kansas.

Yanovsky, Elias

1936 Food plants of the North American Indians. Miscellaneous Publication no. 27. Washington, D.C.: United States Department of Agriculture.

Index

Houck, L.: 179
Hough, W.: 59
Household shrines and fetishes. *See* Altars; "Medicine birds"
House types and floor plans: 85, 96, 134; Dismal River, 140, 142, 148; historic bison hunters, 199, 211, 217; historic Pawnee, 160–161, 163, 167, 170; life expectancy of dwellings, 105–106, 226–227; Upper Republican, 102–106, 122
Hugh Butler Lake, Nebr.: 73
Humaña, A. G. de: 137
Humphrey, R. L., and D. J. Stanford: 55, 62
Hunoit, J.: 193
Hunting and hunting methods: 22, 57–58, 59, 62–63, 64; Archaic, 75; *cerne*, 167; Dismal River, 142; dog-nomads or foot hunters, 63, 136; Early Big Game Hunters, 58, 60, 65–66, 71; mounted hunters, 197, 199, 205; Pawnee, 166–170, 207; Plains Woodland, 92; Querechos, 138; Sioux, 199, 200; yields: 123–124, 168, 205
Hunts, tribal: 124, 166–168
Hurt, W. R.: 72

Idalia, Colo.: 5, 193
Illinois Indians: 124
Indian agents: 163, 164, 167, 168, 197, 202, 207, 226, 227
Indian Creek, Nebr.: 191
Indian–Euro-American contacts. *See* Euro-American–Indian contacts
Indianola burials, Redwillow County, Nebr.: 91
Indian Territory: 208
Indians, "civilized" vs "wild". *See* "Civilized" vs. "wild" Indians
Insects: archeological evidence of, 70; as potential food source, 25–27; crop hazard, 26, 121, 164, 202, 208; nutritional value, 27
InterAgency Archeological and Paleontological Salvage Program: 99
Iowa Indians: 188
Iowa State University: xv, 233 n. 3
Iron, in Indian sites: 139, 145, 161, 169, 171, 172, 173, 175, 179, 180
Iroquois Indians: 188
Irrigation: 218, 219; and crop yields, 116; effects on aquifers, 32, 219
Ish-ka-ta-pa, Republican Pawnee chief, 1825–1826: 157

Iskatappe, Republican Pawnee chief, 1806: 183

Jacal construction: 104
Jackrabbit (*Lepus*): 69, 229 App. B
Jackson, D.: 178
Jackson, D., and M. L. Spence: 191
James, E.: 17, 180
Jamestown salt marsh, Kans.: 31, 153
Jamieson, M. A.: 181
Janis (Jannis), A.: 197
Janis, N.: 197
Jantz, R. L., and D. H. Ubelaker: 224
Jaramillo, J.: 125
Jasper: see Graham jasper
Jefferson peace and friendship medals. *See* Peace medals
Jefferson, T.: 183
Jelinek, A. J.: 61
Jennings, J. D.: 55
Jerky: 168
Jerusalem artichoke (*Helianthus tuberosus*): 18, 19, 77, 121, 165, 200
Jewell County, Kans.: 111
Jicarilla Apaches: 148, 149, 216
Johnson, A. E.: xv, 74, 81
Johnson, D. L., P. Kawano, and E. Ekker: 58
Johnston, R. F.: 24
Jones-Miller site (5YM8), Colo.: 4, 55, 65, 219
Jones, V. H.: 234 n. 2
Journal of Heredity: xv
Jumanos (Wichitas): 139
Junction City, Kans.: 7, 82, 156
Juniper (*Juniperus virginiana*): 21, 93, 105

ka:kusu', "Stay Insides": 167
Kansa (Kansas) Indians: 124, 157, 177, 183
Kansas Academy of Sciences: 2
Kansas City, Mo.: 7, 81, 96
Kansas Monument site (14RP1), Kans.: 2, 36, 153, 154, 156, 157–159
Kansas-Nebraska geography, and possible population movements: 132
Kansas Pacific Railroad: 203
Kansas River: 7, 177, 189, 190; no water for boats, 157
Kansas State Board of Agriculture: 117
Kansas State Historical Society: xv, xvii, 2, 158, 159
Kaskaskia, Ill.: 173, 175
Kaw River. *See* Kansas River
Kearney, Nebr.: 33
Kehoe, T. F.: 63

Kehoe, T. F., and A. B. Kehoe: 151
Keith focus (Plains Woodland): 81, 85, 131
Kellogg, A. R.: xiv
Kellogg, R. S.: 21, 191
Kerlérec, Gov. L. B. de: 137
Kicawi'caku. See Waconda Spring
Kickapoo Indians: 188
Kidder, L. S.: 203
Kills, game: bison, 63, 64, 167–168; mammoth, 55, 58
King, J. E.: 40
King, J. T.: 204
King, N., map: 31
Kingsbury, J. M.: 59
Kinnaird, L.: 157
Kiowa Indians: 186
Kit Carson County, Colo.: 32, 228
Kitz-a-witz-uk. See Waconda Spring
Kitkahahki Pawnees: 152, 156, 173. *See also* Republican Pawnees
Kivett, M. F.: xiv, 4, 74, 81, 85, 91, 113, 131
Knife, chipped stone: Cody knife, 52; "Harahey" four-edged knife, 107, 108; Lime Creek knife, 69. *See also* Artifacts
Kofyar of Nigeria: 129
Krause, R. A.: 99, 129
Krieger, A. D.: 72
Kroeber, A. L.: 25, 211, 225, 227
Krombein, K. V.: xv
Küchler, A. W.: 21

Laird, Colo.: 4, 65
Lake Sibley, Kans.: 202
Lakin, Kans.: 188
Lamare-Picquot: 231 n. 1
Lambert, J.: 195
Lamb Spring, Colo.: 54, 55
Landsman Creek, Colo.: xv, 206
Lappala, E. G.: xv, 32
Larned's Creek, Nebr.: 196
Laws, R. M., I. S. C. Parker, and R. C. B. Johnstone: 56, 57
Legumes: 77
Lehmer, D. J.: 42
Lehner, Ariz., mammoth site: 55, 58
Leonhardy, F. C., and A. D. Anderson: 55
Lesser, A.: 156, 186, 218
Lessig, J. A.: 205
Lewis and Clark expedition: 27, 178, 190
Lewis and Clark maps: 31, 190
Lewis, Meriwether: 24, 27
Liatris (Blazing star) and maize harvest time: 167
Libby, W. F.: radiocarbon dates on Lime Creek sites, 69, 70, 71